Series in

Legal Information and

Communication Technologies

Volume 7

Law and Technology: Looking into the Future.
Selected Essays

Edited by

Meritxell Fernández-Barrera, Norberto Nuno Gomes de Andrade, Primavera De Filippi, Mario Viola de Azevedo Cunha, Giovanni Sartor, Pompeu Casanovas

EUROPEAN PRESS ACADEMIC PUBLISHING

Book cover photo by Primavera De Filippi

ISBN 978-88-8398-060-2

Copyright ©2009 by European Press Academic Publishing
Florence, Italy
www.e-p-a-p.com
www.europeanpress.it
Printed in Italy

Contents

III. ICT TOOLS FOR THE LAW

IV. THE PERSONAL SPHERE IN THE TECHNOLOGICAL MILIEU:
LIBERTY AND PRIVACY

V. BIOTECH

VI. INTELLECTUAL PROPERTY. COPYRIGHT, PATENT LAW

Dr. Giovanni Sartor

is professor of Legal informatics and Legal Theory at the European University Institute of Florence and at the University of Bologna. He obtained a PhD at the European University Institute (Florence), worked at the Court of Justice of the European Union (Luxembourg), was a researcher at the Italian National Council of Research (ITTIG, Florence), held the chair in Jurisprudence at Queen's University of Belfast (where he now is honorary professor), and was Marie-Curie professor at the European University of Florence. He is President of the International Association for Artificial Intelligence and Law. He has published widely in legal philosophy, computational logic, legislation technique, and computer law.

Dr. Pompeu Casanovas

is Professor of Philosophy of Law at the Autonomous University of Barcelona(UAB), Law School; Director of Advanced Research (ACQU), Consultant of Artificial Intelligence and Law at the Universitat Oberta de Catalunya (UOC); and Director of the UAB Institute of Law and Technology (http://idt.uab.cat). He has conducted research in several institutes and universities (UCSD, OIISL, Stanford, Bologna…). He has been principal investigator of over 35 national and international projects, and author of above 10 books and 100 scientific articles in the areas of legal philosophy, legal sociology, judicial studies, and AI and Law (the Semantic Web). He is the General Editor of the Research Series *La Razón Áurea* (Editorial Comares, Spain).

The **Infosoc Working Group**

was set up in 2006 with the support of Professor Giovanni Sartor in the Law Department of the European University Institute, Florence (http://www.eui.eu/DepartmentsAndCentres/Law/ResearchAndTeaching/WorkingGroups/WGINFOSOC.aspx), by an enthusiastic group of PhD researchers committed with the analysis of the most controversial issues emerging from the Information Society. The group has held regular meetings ever since, welcoming both the presentation of Information Society-related research undertaken in different EUI departments and external guest lectures by leading researchers in the field. Working sessions have been organised as well with the participation of European and international institutional representatives working in the area of ICTs and public sector. The organisation of *The Future of... Conference on Law and Technology* is an initiative that builds on the group's understanding of the Information Society as a complex object of study, which requires the attention not only of several research communities and scholars with different backgrounds, but as well of public institutions and, most importantly, the fruitful flow of ideas between them all.

Preface

We are very honoured to introduce this volume, which collects the proceedings of the conference "The future of law and information technology", held at EUI (European University Institute of Florence) on the 28th and 29th October 2008. The conference, as indicated by its title, had a broad scope, including any kind of prospective inquiries on future developments in law and ICT. This is reflected in the collection here presented, which provides a set of diverse analyses that are unified by the common aim of not being confined to state of the art technologies and present legal issues but extend their scrutiny to coming technologies and anticipated legal problems.

Prospective inquiries are intrinsically problematic, being apparently both impossible and necessary: impossible since, as Karl Popper argued, it is not possible to forecast technological and social developments, and necessary, since we need to anticipate such development, to be able to provide timely and reflected responses to them. The contradiction between impossibility and necessity can indeed be addressed by grounding prospective analyses in developing scenarios representing possible evolutions of the present techno-legal situation. Such scenarios are not to be understood as necessary developments but as potentialities which is up to our societies to implement or avert (within social and technical constraints), and their anticipation can indeed contribute to their realisation or to their prevention.

Prospective analyses are particularly important in the ICT-law domain, since ICTs have known the most accelerated development in the last decades (doubling their power every two years, according to the so-called Moore law) and the deepest social effects (determined the passage from the industrial society to the social formation labelled by us information, knowledge or network society), matched by pervasive legal change (from data protection, to intellectual property, to internet law). As ICT development and the ICT driven social evolution are still accelerating their step, it is necessary that the law does not remain confined to current problems and established outcomes: it needs to look into future scenarios for capturing the sense of the dynamics now underway and for preparing adequate legal responses.

We think that the present collection corresponds to the mission of prospective inquiries on ICT and law, as reflected in the six sessions of the conference, devoted respectively to "The role of the law and agency", "Public law, jurisdiction, boundaries", "ICT tools for the law", "The personal sphere in the technological milieu: Liberty and privacy", "Biotech", "Intellectual property, copyright, patent law".

The prospective nature of the conference as well as its broad scope also reflects the nature and character of its organizers, i.e., the researchers pertaining to the INFOSOC (Information society) working group at EUI. This working group, established only three years ago, collects EUI researchers having an interest on law and information technologies (both on computer law and on legal informatics), and has succeeded in providing many scientific contributions, realizing a number of workshops and conferences, developing the interest for ICT research within EUI, and establishing a network of connection with other institutions and researchers working in the ICT domain. We would like to thank the INFOSOC researchers for their excellent work in designing and organizing this conference.

The title of the Conference —*The Future of Law*— echoes the title of the well-known book by Richard Susskind (1996). Actually, the Conference took place more or less at the same time that *The End of Lawyers? Rethinking the Nature of Legal Services* (2008), where the author anticipates that recent changes into the Web challenge the lawyers' established practices and routines, urging for a more radical transformation.

In a way, the INFOSOC working group widens up this scope, claiming for a more integral knowledge of the intersections of the legal world, governance protocols and practices, the Internet, and the Web. Here you are a sample of their concerns, among many others: the Semantic Web; the link between folksonomies, taxonomies and ontologies; the emergence of multiple-agent systems regulated scenarios; the changing nature of public and private law; the emergence of markets with regulatory problems such as biotechnology out from science and technology; ubiquitous computing, ambiance and swarm intelligence. These fields of knowledge add complexity to the classical legal approach from intellectual property, copyright and patent law. Therefore, law is not regarded only from a normative (or legal) point of view, but within the broad context of other emerging specific regulatory intersecting forms. It is clear to us that the intuitions of these young researchers foster knowledge and innovation in the law and technology field.

The contributions to the volume try to shed some light to the problems and questions that arise at the crossroads. The INFOSOC researchers summarize in detail their content in the Introduction that follows. We leave the reader with them, fully convinced that he will be in good company.

Pompeu Casanovas
Giovanni Sartor

Introduction: Looking into the future...

In the future humankind will find itself in an incredibly automatic and intelligent new space, people will be surrounded by technologies that observe, monitor, analyse, interpret, simplify, anticipate and explain the world for us. Humanity will be immersed in a deep and permanent communicational status, living in a planet of machines, agents and automatic processes. A vast array of powerful interfaces, embedded in all kind of objects and gifted with some sort of intelligence, will capture, scrutinize and process data about reality and nature surrounding us, as well as about every other human being living within. Such agents will recognize, react and respond, in an intuitive manner, to the presence and to the actions of different people and electronic objects. Human action and decision-making will be increasingly delegated to artificial agents, reality visible to the human eye will be super-imposed by electronic tags, digital identifiers and virtual entities, and the current network of computers and other terminals called Internet will be a network of digital people, sharing a half-fictitious half-real space that visionaries have been for long time prophesizing as cyberspace or metaverse and that is now coming to reality under the denomination of ubiquitous computing and ambient intelligence.

The future will be dominated by interactive technologies, pervasive and ubiquitous computing, mixed realities (where the virtual and the physical realms will converge), ambient technologies, augmented reality, autonomous software agents, artificial intelligence and many other technological developments.

"The future of ..." - Conference on Law & technology

Taking a glimpse beyond the present and bearing in mind the possible and prospective technologies which will come to fruition in the future, the European University Institute (EUI), through the Law Department and in conjunction with the InfoSoc Working Group, organized "The future of ... Conference on Law & Technology," hosting the venue in Florence, on the 28th and 29th October 2008.

The conference challenged the academic community to think and foresee what challenges, problems and changes the Future will bring to Law. More than prospecting on how the future will look like, the conference aimed at collecting new ideas, concepts and theories of how

Law will accompany such future, proposing a creative exercise of upcoming world description and a prospective analysis of how law will change and evolve.

The conference intended to provide an original and ground-breaking symposium for exchanging ideas and fostering the debate about the triangle relationship between future – law – and technology, attracting quality papers dealing with prospective studies and analyses of legal developments and transformations expected in the future. Taking into account the present technological trends affecting society, the "Future of..." Conference challenged scholars to think and foresee the main problems and changes that Law will face and suffer in the upcoming future of ambient technologies, ubiquitous and pervasive computing, web 3.0, entangled realities, autonomous software agents, artificial intelligence and many other features and elements.

The conference welcomed the contribution of scholars and researchers from many different regions and cultures in the world, whose interests and research were directed towards the assessment of the evolving relationship that might develop in the future between law and technology. The numerous contributions were clustered into six different panels:

1. General issues. New dimensions in the technological environment: the role of the law and agency
2. Public law, jurisdiction, boundaries
3. ICT tools for the law
4. The personal sphere in the technological milieu: Liberty and privacy
5. Biotech
6. Intellectual property. Copyright, patent law

SESSION I:

General issues. New dimensions in the technological environment: the role of the law and agency

The first session of the Conference, entitled "General issues – New Dimensions in the technological environment: the role of law", presented two papers which analysed the interaction between law and technology, each one focussing on different aspects of such intricate relationship. The first paper, authored by Massimo Durante from the University of Turin, argued in favour of a role of mediation between the real and the virtual world assigned to law within the future evolution of information and communication technologies (ICT). The second paper, written by Sawhney, Ratnadeep and Lee, highlighted the importance of metaphors and precedents as conceptual tools to understand the development of new technologies.

Durante, through his paper "Re-designing the Role of Law in the Information Society: Mediating between the Real and the Virtual", argues that, notwithstanding the incessant technological evolution, law will keep having an autonomous and central epistemological role in representing reality. In this account, law will be assigned with the essential role of mediation between the real and the virtual world. In the words of the author, such act of mediation requires a translation of the virtual information displayed by technology (the possibility opened and made available by the application of new ICT) into real information.

In developing his main argument, Massimo Durante claims that law, assigned with the role of mediation between the virtual and the real, will ensure the conditions of reliance upon information in both directions: from the virtual reality to the real world and from the real world towards the virtual reality. Regarding the former, law is attributed with the epistemic role of appraising in what terms the effects of an action performed in the virtual reality can be judged foreseeable and thus accountable in the real world (such effects are to be appraised in terms of legal responsibility, as it is within the real world that one is responsible for [the effects of] actions displayed within virtual reality). In addition, law displays its role of mediation also in the opposite direction, i.e., from the real world to the virtual reality. In this case, law confers a real content to the real world that can be appraised within virtual reality (this is done by means of informational reliance, as it is within virtual reality that one relies on informational data in order to perform actions that are likely to produce [legal effects] within the real world). In this perspective, and as Durante asserts, law can play a fundamental role of mediation between the real and the virtual to the extent that it assures reliance upon information. Moreover, as the author concludes, the way in which law can devise an act of mediation which determines the conditions of possibility of the representation of what is refereed to as "virtual reality" within the realm of what is referred to as "physical reality" and vice versa is structured by the inter-subjective computer-mediated interaction and communication between individuals or groups.

The second paper, entitled "New Technologies and the Law: Precedents via Metaphors" and co-authored by Harmeet Sawhney, Venkata Ratnadeep Suri and Hyangsun Lee (Department of Telecommunications, Indiana University, Bloomington), provides an interesting study on the application of metaphors by courts as conceptual tools to understand and regulate new technologies. In legal terms, and as metaphors help to establish precedents, the paper explains how new communications technology have been shaped by legal precedents created by previous ones.

The article, relying upon a historical study of US case law, demonstrates how metaphors, in some cases, can be effective vehicles for the transfer of conceptual frameworks from one technology to another (as in all point-to-point networks that transport materials and information from one point to another – electric grids, highway systems, telegraph, railroad and telecommunications networks); and how, in other cases, this metaphor process breaks down (as in the case of radio and broadcasting, in which its initial conception as "wireless telegraph" or a point-to-point communication technology caused intricate juridical problems). The authors use the example of radio as a case where a metaphor based on an old technology failed to shape the new one in its image, calling such phenomenon of "metaphor vacuum", i.e., a case in which there were no readily available metaphors to think about the new broadcasting technology. Departing from the problem of "metaphor vacuum", within the example of broadcasting as a new technology for which no clear precedent had been established, the article investigates how the legal system dealt with such "stalemate." Since the case law could not proceed without a precedent, the authors observe how such tension was resolved by "stretching" a previously established metaphor. Such stretching process, moreover, is carried out until it reaches a breaking point, which creates a metaphor vacuum or a realisation that we need a radically new framework. Broadcasting technology is, therefore, used by the authors as a paradigmatic case, as the latter ended up with the standard from the world of transportation systems and public utilities, inserting a new standard of "public interest, convenience and necessity" (PICON). In other words, PICON filled the metaphor vacuum, bringing along with it a legal framework.

This article calls our attention to the fact that, in the future, metaphors used in the early stages of the development of a new technology may not prove to be appropriate over the long run, setting precedents difficult to be changed at a later stage. It is thus important to remember that "devil is in the details", i.e., to remain alert to the peculiarities of the new technology, as it is the peculiarities that eventually bring about a metaphor vacuum.

Public law, jurisdiction, boundaries

In the second session of the Conference, entitled *"Public law, jurisdiction, boundaries"*, the three papers presented deal with the need to regulate the internet, but each one with a different aim. In the first paper, Armando Cottim analyses the interaction between cybercrime (and cyberterrorism) and the boundaries of criminal law jurisdiction. As the author highlights *"the advent of cyberspace has changed the established criminal law model. Online crime happens without boundaries, as attacks can come from outside the borders of one State, thus scattering crime scenes through two or more countries, sometimes in more than one continent."*

Keeping this idea in mind, he analyses the 2001 Budapest Convention on Cybercrime, starting by giving an overview of all possible jurisdiction theories to be applied, concluding by saying that the *"Convention relies exclusively on the territoriality and nationality theories to empower parties to establish jurisdiction."* Cottim criticises the option adopted by the Convention, believing that it creates more problems than solutions.

Then, he discusses the threats that arise from the interaction between Cybercrime and Jurisdiction, where he presents the famous Yahoo Case, decided by *Tribunal de Grande Instance de Paris, "which ordered Yahoo! Inc and its subsidiary Yahoo France not only to exclude French surfers from sales of Nazi memorabilia (...), but also to destroy all the concerned files stored in their server"*, and goes also through the *Rome Labs* and *Tore Tvedt* cases.

After discussing these cases, and the issues that can arise from the impact of cybercrime and cyberterrorism on the jurisdiction of the States, Cottim concludes that *"cyberterrorism would probably not justify a convention to deal with it. The explicit inclusion of cyberterrorism in the Convention on Cybercrime by means of an additional protocol would probably suffice"*. However, *"given the path towards catastrophism and indiscriminate attack on human lives taken by modern day terrorism,"* he *"would consider possible and positive the inclusion of terrorism in the list of international crimes against humanity – in accordance with littera k of number 1 of article 7 of the Rome Statute of the International Criminal Court (ICC) – which would entitle States to have universal jurisdiction to apprehend terrorist agents, although jurisdiction to prosecute would be given to the International Criminal Court."*

The second paper *"Children Protection Online: Uneasy Steps towards a Balance between Risks and Freedoms"*, presented by Federica Casarosa, focuses on the European initiatives for the protection of Children concerning the use of internet, what is a very important issue, since *"children and young people are more and more often the first to take up and use new technologies; yet, they are not always aware of both risks and ways of dealing with them, or, whether they are, they are not always mature enough to evaluate the situations that they encounter and the possible consequences their decisions can have."*

The author recognises that sometimes the content to which children and young people have access through the internet is legal, at least for an adult, but it is "liable to harm them by impairing their physical and mental development"(COM(96) 87, par. 17).

After analysing the European framework in this area, she describes all existing risks for children in accessing the web: child abuse material; child grooming; cyber-bullying; and, unlawful privacy invasion. Then, Casarosa presents the tools developed by the European Union to fight against these risks (Hotline networks, Rating and filtering schemes, Age verification tools and Codes of Conduct).

Finally, she analyses the case of "social networks" (such as Facebook or Myspace) to conclude that "any policy aimed at protecting children, either from illegal and harmful content or from other possible online risk, due to the nature of the subject-matter, should be of a multi-faceted nature."

The last paper, by Oles Andriychuk, entitled "Concept of 'Network Neutrality" in the EU Dimension: Should Europe Trust in Antitrust?" aims at giving "a descriptive presentation of the current European regulatory framework in the areas of electronic communications and audiovisual policy".

In his paper Andriychuk analyses the evolution of the EU legislation in the field of telecommunications, highlighting that the European policy in this area *"was supposed to be governed by three major principles: liberalisation, harmonisation and competition"*.   Then, having these principles as a starting point, Andriychuk addresses the contradictions that arise from them, saying that *"The main problem is based in their ontology and methodology."*

He discusses issues concerning the "European policy of limited profitability" and the "Local Loop Unbundling", and, then, moves his focus to the European law of electronic communications, what he calls "Present-day regulatory regime". In this topic he draws a comparative analysis between EU and US concerning the "Network Neutrality", stating that in the EU this issue *"has been neither settled, nor yet properly articulated"*. Although, he believes that since public opinion plays an important role in the European decision-making process, *"the perspectives of the 'Network Neutrality' legislation appear to be quite likely"*.

Andriychuk concludes that "'Network Neutrality' is an interdisciplinary phenomenon. It can be explored from the economic, legal, societal, technical and political dimensions."

As we could observe, all the papers, in a way or another, deal with the interaction between Internet, and Law, addressing the issue on how Law can provide an up to date response to this new issue, trying to find a solution which guarantees the protection of the individuals without blocking the development of such technology.

SESSION III:

ICT Tools for the Law

Session III, entitled "ICT tools for the law", was conceived as a section to explore the characteristics and implications of the use of ICT support for legal practice. It was thus concerned with the area of study known as "Legal Informatics", "Artificial Intelligence and Law" or "Information Technology for lawyers", among other possible expressions[1]. Whereas IT Law deals mainly with the issue of analysing which are the legal problems of the new reality arising from the use of Information Technologies and how to tackle them, legal informatics is technologically oriented and explores how computer applications can be best developed to meet legal practitioners' needs. This implies a contextualised understanding of technological applications and requires, therefore, a thorough analysis of current trends and needs in the legal profession. This is precisely the main focus of Prof. Pompeu Casanovas' paper entitled "The Future of Law: Relational Justice and Next Generation of Web Services", in which he intends to bridge the evolution of web technologies (Web 2.0, Web 3.0, next generation Semantic Web) with the change of paradigm in the legal field. Prof. Casanovas carries out a detailed study of current technological trends (Web 2.0, Web 3.0, Semantic Web) and prospects of application in the legal milieu. He

---

[1] OSKAMP, A. and LODDER, A. (2006) *Law, Information Technology and Artificial Intelligence*, in A. Lodder and A. Oskamp (Eds.), "Advanced Technology in the Legal Domain. From Challenges to Daily Routine." Springer, Dordrecht, p. 3.

underlines the fact that there is a current lack of knowledge of the detailed way in which the Internet is evolving, and that some of the Semantic Web promises have not been yet fulfilled. New trends such as the next generation of web services based on personalisation and user-centred approaches are discussed. The incredible expansion of the legal market as well as the pervasive use of ICT in legal practice are presented as indicators of what is going on in the legal sphere. Some currents trends in the intersection between law and technology are highlighted, such as the obstacle that the law sometimes represents for technological evolution, and the effect the use of new technologies has in the expansion of the legal profession. In this framework a new legal paradigm is introduced, through the concepts of Relational Law and Relational Justice, based on flexibility, dialogue and autonomy, on a higher and more effective citizen participation and the increase of self-regulatory forms, all of which can be enhanced by the next generation of web services. This creates a general picture of the future of the law, underlined by the main thesis of the paper: that Semantic Web technologies should be cognitively and sociologically grounded in order to satisfy real user needs, taking thus into account " *the social situated knowledge that enables law to be created, implemented and shared in an increasingly technological social and organizational environment*".

The concept of legal informatics has indeed evolved following technological advances and requirements from the users in the legal profession. It started with the construction of the first databases of legal documents in the 60's, giving place later on to the design of large administrative databases in the 70's, to systems aimed at assisting lawyers in the task of finding legal information (legal information retrieval) and to great expectations in the field of expert systems in the decade of the 80's, which would turn out later on to be too ambitious a programme. Nowadays approaches to legal informatics have changed perspectives and regard computer applications as assistance tools to the main task accomplished by a human operator. This assistance can focus on the different information processing tasks that are part of the legal professional daily routine, one of which is legal information retrieval. This has always been central to legal reasoning, but specially nowadays when there exists a risk of information overload it becomes a pressing need to enable a more efficient access to reliable and useful legal knowledge. Indeed, legal information of different types (authoritative sources but also case law and legal doctrine[2]) is moving into the Web and therefore legal professionals and citizens as well are exposed to information overload.

Geist's paper, entitled "The Open Revolution: Using Citation Analysis to Improve Legal Text Retrieval" focuses precisely on the improvement of legal information retrieval systems, which are still based on the same technologies that were used in the 80's (mainly Boolean search) even if the systems performance presents deficiencies. The paper proposes an improvement by the introduction of citation analysis, which is an information science concept according to which citation can indicate the existence of a relationship between documents. Citation analysis was used to improve the performance of the search engine Google and the author of the paper highlights the feasibility of applying it to the search of information in the legal domain, since the network structure of the www and that of legal documents is similar. Indeed, the case study of the paper shows that the network structure of Austrian Supreme Court decisions and their headnotes is a free-scale one, just like the www network structure.

Another core issue of research in AI and Law is the representation of legal knowledge for the construction of legal computer applications. The article "Modelling European and Italian tax legislation with LKIF language", authored by Contissa, presents the Legal Knowledge Interchange Format, developed in the framework of the Estrella Project. The paper shows the results of representing the Savings Tax Directive and the Italian Savings Tax Law following the LKIF model, as part of the validation of the LKIF platform. The representation of both regulations was aimed at confronting them from a legal drafting perspective and therefore an attempt was made to make them as isomorphic as possible following the structure of the text even when there were redundancies. This exercise enables the author to appreciate some differences between both norms mainly at a formal level, that is, with regard to text structure, syntax and lexicon. However, the author highlights as well the existence of a slight content difference between both norms, that arises from the fact that the Italian legislator decided to move a norm from an article to a different one, giving place to the establishment of different obligations for the same category of subjects. The article shows, thus, on the one hand, that the LKIF model correctly represents normative content and, on the other hand, that the representation of legal content on the basis of rules can have more uses beyond the construction of expert systems, since it

---

[2] SARTOR, G., BIASIOTTI, M., FRANCESCONI, E., PALMIRANI, M., VITALI, F. 2007. *Legal Informatics and Management of Legislative Documents*. Ed. G. Sartor. Florence: EUI (European University Institute).

can be used at the moment of legal drafting for analysing the compatibility of the content of different regulations.Sometimes, however, legal informatics not only provides new tools for the assistance of traditional legal tasks, like legal information retrieval or legal drafting, but proposes the introduction of new tasks or methods for legal analysis at the same time that it provides tools to support these newly suggested tasks. This is the case of the article by Mahler, having as a title "Tool-supported Legal Risk Management: A Roadmap". Indeed the first part of the paper, presents the advantages of the introduction of a method for legal risk analysis. This implies an innovation in legal method, for even if risk management exists *de facto* in legal practice, no formal methodology has been developed by legal theory in this regard. The paper provides a definition of legal risk and illustrates through an example how a standardised method for dealing with legal risk could be applied to the assessment of the clauses of a contract. Nevertheless given that methods for legal risk assessment are still not well established, the author argues, they should be regarded as a complement to current legal methods, which are based on experience and heuristics. Furthermore, since the introduction of legal risk management methods is complex and costly, the introduction of IT support could be very valuable. In this sense, the second part of the paper suggests three ways in which IT tools could support the task of assessing legal risk: by supporting the process, helping the analyst to follow an order and to document the outcomes at every stage; by supporting the communication between different experts, which might be required to identify the risk and estimate it; by ensuring interoperability with existing legal information systems. The author claims as well that, with due care, it would be possible to include some elements of automation to support human judgement and analysis in legal risk assessment. Finally some considerations are made with regard to the limitations that legal risk analysis might have as a business model, due to its costs, but further research is encouraged due to the potential benefits it might bring about.

Beyond their application to the support of legal activity, IT, and specially Artificial Intelligence, can be regarded as possible risk sources for some rights. Calo's paper explores precisely this aspect of AI, by analysing its current developments and potential dangers for the right to privacy and how US privacy law can cope with those challenges. The approach taken in this paper is therefore different from the one taken in the previous ones: in this case, technology is analysed as a factor that alters reality and can, therefore, require a reaction from the law in order to prevent certain undesirable effects. The paper starts with an overview of the traditional concern about dangers of AI for privacy. Traditionally, AI threats to privacy have been connected to the increased capabilities of AI enhanced devices not only for surveillance, but for the organisation and the analysis of data in interesting ways making emerge from collections of data new information that might not be obvious to the human eye (data mining and knowledge discovery). The paper goes on to analyse the current trend of enhancing the social capabilities of machines, in order to make them interact more naturally with people. It highlights as well some of the effects of social machines on people, among which, the elicitation of human-directed behaviour and the increase of the sense of being observed and the corresponding feeling of uneasiness. These are controversial issues with regard to the right to privacy. Firstly, given the reaction of people to social cues present in the behaviour of machines, the collection of information by the latter will become easier, since they are endowed with an ability to persuade subtly. Secondly, the pervasiveness of social AI may hinder the possibility of being left alone in private spaces in which to be oneself with the corresponding limitations for the development of one's personality. Finally, as to the way in which US privacy law deals with the highlighted risks for the right to privacy, the author claims that the law contains already some answers, although as well education and other extra-legal solutions (like discussions around social media) are feasible specially in the short term.

SESSION IV:

The personal sphere in the technological milieu: Liberty and privacy

In the fourth session of the Conference, *"The personal sphere in the tecnological milieu: Liberty and privacy"*, all papers addressed the new challenges to privacy as a consequence of the recent development of information technologies, focusing, however, on different issues. The first paper, entitled *"Property in Personal Data: a European Perspective on Instrumentalist Theory of Propertisation"*, analyses Lessig's theory of privacy as a property right from a European perspective. Such model of data protection, which leaves to the individual the possibility to decide whether personal information can be used or not, goes in an opposite direction of the European model, which considers the right to personal data as an autonomous fundamental right, what confirms the importance of such right for the European society.

To develop such analysis, Purtova raises the question of *"whether the introduction of the property rights in personal data, whatever scope of those rights may be, is a legal option in the European Union"*.

After considering that the introduction of property rights in personal data would be *"a legal option in the EU, both on the level of the Union and individual member states"*, she concludes *"that content-wise Lessig's instrumentalist theory does not fit into the European legal context because the scope of rights in personal data it advocates for is not what is meant by property in Europe."*

Different from Purtova, in the second paper - *"The Myth of Odin's Eye: Privacy vs. Knowledge"* - Paolo Guarda discusses the risks of the access to knowledge in a digital context for individuals' privacy. He believes that individuals are not aware of the cost of our access to knowledge in a digital context, *"despite the outward gratuitousness of the provided service"*.

He analyses the cases of Digital Rights Management systems (DRM) and of "Google search engines", addressing the issues that arise from the relationship between privacy and knowledge in the digital context.

Guarda identifies *"three fundamental dimensions of the concept of privacy: "spatial", "informational", and "decisional""* linked to the consumption of intellectual works, and focuses his analysis on the last dimension, which he defines as the one that *"concerns the choice, the freedom that must be recognized to every person in order to be able to take a decision without any kind of external conditioning."*

Finally, after analysing many aspects of what he calls *"privacy vs. knowledge conflict"*, Guarda suggests that we should reconsider *"rules, technologies, and customs in the light of this new uniforming category that moves our attention to the management aspect of the exchanging flows, rather than to their inherent diversity."*

From texts described above, we can see that both authors tried to draw our attention to the challenges that new technologies pose to Law and the need to find solutions that balance all interests involved and are in line with the current digital scenario.

Session V:

Biotech

Session V of the Conference was devoted to biotechnology and to the potentialities that this scientific field promises to set off. Biotech is thus changing dramatically the world we live in, questioning our own human constitution and nature, and challenging many of our legal assumptions, principles and theories. Biotechnology is, at the present time, one of the most exciting areas for interdisciplinary research, presenting a panoply of troublesome questions and problems in the fields of agriculture, food science and medicine, among others.

One of the most interesting developments in the area of biotechnology relates to genetic engineering technology and its application to the human body, allowing namely for the genetic manipulation of the latter. Regarding this theme, Wojciech Zaluski's paper analyses the question of the admissibility of enhancing an embryo's nature through genetic engineering (calling this process genetic enhancement), tackling such question from a philosophy of law point of view, through an argument of autonomy.

The paper provides a number of important and necessary distinctions and articulations that one should bear in mind when examining the question of genetic enhancement and autonomy, such as personal and moral autonomy (and its different varieties: material and formal, weak and strong); their corresponding presuppositions; and the different types of genetic enhancement, the directed genetic enhancement and the all-purpose genetic enhancement. While arguing that personal autonomy does not have any presuppositions, Zaluski does not take a definite position concerning moral autonomy, asserting that it is not clear whether the latter has two (human agency, free will) or three presuppositions (being contingency of birth the third one).

In this account, the author distinguishes two competing conceptions of moral autonomy, one that does not presuppose contingency of birth (conception I) and the other that presupposes (conception II). Regarding such problematic presupposition, Zaluski questions Habermas claim that contingency of birth is crucial for moral autonomy, being a presupposition of human agency. According to the German philosopher, a person whose birth was not contingent cannot be expected to be able to take full responsibility for her actions, and thereby cannot be morally autonomous. Zaluski, contrarily, does not find self-evident that human agency requires that a subject's genetic constitution should not have been designed by some other person, asserting that the lack of contingency of birth does not by itself undermine human agency. In this regard, Zaluski presents arguments supporting the claim that contingency of birth is not (necessarily) a presupposition of human agency and thereby of moral autonomy. Nevertheless, the author leaves the question open, safeguarding the position of those that advocate contingency of birth as presupposition of human agency.

Finally, the fundamental question posed in the paper, the question of genetic enhancement and the violation of human autonomy, receives different answers according to the articulation established between the two conceptions of moral autonomy and the two types of genetic enhancement.

SESSION VI:

Intellectual property. Copyright, patent law

Session VI of the Conference was concerned with the future of intellectual property in the digital environment, with particular focus on the forthcoming developments of copyright law in the information society. As it is becoming an increasingly valuable asset, in fact, information has been progressively turned into a commodity, whose value can however only be exploited if appositely supported by legal and/or technological means.

In particular, the advent of digital technologies has considerably affected the production and distribution of works in the realm of intellectual property. Their impact can mostly be attributed to the increasing digitalization of content and to the growing trend towards globalization that is characteristic of the Internet network. These new technologies have made it possible for nearly anyone to produce and/or reproduce a whole variety of works and to disseminate them via the Internet, regardless of any legal or national boundaries.

Enforcing copyright law in the digital environment has therefore become a challenge that may jeopardize the traditional business models employed by the entertainment industry. While a new set of offenses has become available on the Internet, the scale and the extent of the more traditional offenses have in fact been considerably amplified. Digital technologies also have destabilized the two fundamental features of the copyright regime: the concept of artificial scarcity - originally meant to realign the properties of intangible works with that of physical goods - and the notion of exclusivity, implemented through a set of exclusive rights which are strictly and inherently national. This raises the following questions: Is the current IP regime still appropriate in the digital environment? Is it still necessary in order to protect the incentives to create and to disseminate new content? And most importantly, is it sensible to protect an intangible work in the same way as we protect a tangible one?

An initial reflection on the issue is presented by Prof. Jon Bing. In his article he shows the evolution of the trade in information through some examples and proposes the 'future' for such a trade. He starts with the Stone Age, where hunters negotiated information about good places for hunting, what in his opinion constitutes the first example of a consultancy contract. Then, he presents the 'writing' as a new way of transferring information, and the 'revolution' caused by the printing process that made the volume of books jump from 30 thousand in 1448 to 15 million in 1500, leading to the creation of 'printing rights', *"one of the origins of the modern copyright."* Prof. Bing concludes this first part of his article explaining the copyrights model and highlighting the need for a legal regime – adequate to the new technologies - for governing trade in information. Keeping this need for a new legal regime in mind, he analyses "the invisible copies", a product of the information technologies, where the trade in information is possible *"without there being"* and *"without any physical object changing hands"*. Then, he criticises the technical solutions of the Digital Rights Management (DRM) and proposes a (new) model of trade in information based on the "Lovely Rita Scenario", which he developed with Prof. Giovanni Sartor. However, he recognises that this 'new' model is incomplete or, in his words, *"the payment scheme necessary for such a scenario is not fully developed."* Finally, he concludes foreseeing that the future models of trade in information will be *"Like the 'one-click purchase' of amazon.com"*, *"models of simplicity – on the surface."*

From authors to end-users, from producers to commercial publishers, copyright law has a different impact on every party involved. While the digital environment may be regarded as a threat by certain categories of people, for others, the Internet and digital technologies constitute an exceptional tool for the production and dissemination of content.

It is commonly believed that stronger laws against the unauthorized reproduction and distribution of content (such as the DMCA in the US and the Directive on the Information Society in the EU) are necessary to provide effective remedies against copyright infringement. Yet copyright enforcement will never be successful as long as users do not consider the provisions of the copyright regime to be fair. Therefore, the need for public legitimacy should not be underestimated. If overly restrictive, copyright law will be either infringed upon or in some way circumvented, whereas an excessively lenient regime will inevitably be ignored.

Originally conceived for the purpose of encouraging cultural production, copyright law has been designed to provide authors with sufficient economic rewards through the granting of proprietary rights in the expression of any original work of authorship. It has nevertheless always been acknowledged that the protection granted by the copyright regime had to be somewhat limited, both in scope and in duration, since an optimal level of innovation could only be achieved with the establishment of a proper balance between private property and public domain.

This particular issue has been explored by Federico Morando in his paper on "The legal status of software interoperability information" where he addressed the uncertainty regarding the legal status of interoperability information by distinguishing between interface specification and interface implementation. The paper provides a throughout analysis of the actual scope and limitations of copyright protection for computer software and related interoperability information, and concludes by suggesting that certain categories of works, such as most utilitarian works, should be subject to a weaker form of protection designed to discourage free-riding without hindering the process of cumulative innovation.

Thus far, the flexibility of copyright law has allowed for the copyright regime to readjust to and/or to overcome a multitude of historically challenging circumstances, as evidenced by the increasing number of works that copyright protection has been granted to. Today, however, new solutions are being devised by the private sector who is seeking to autonomously address the challenges introduced by the digital environment, albeit from two opposite perspectives. On the one hand, insofar as it can be assimilated to a private good, information has been made excludable and artificially scarce by means of restrictive contractual agreements and technological measures of protection. On the other hand, to the extent that information is being regarded as a public good, widespread availability can be achieved through specific contractual mechanisms, such as Open Content licenses, which may encourage the widespread dissemination of works while ensuring that right holders retain a certain number of their rights.

Yet the effectiveness of private ordering depends on a variety of legal and technological factors. As highlighted by Ugo Pagallo in his paper on

"The future of P2P systems and their impact on contemporary legal networks", there exists a mutual interaction between technological progress and legislative activity. On the one hand, the development of new technologies necessarily requires traditional legal concepts to be readjusted or reformed. On the other hand, however, the legal system will determine the direction into which a particular technology may or may not develop. Accordingly, as technological advances necessarily have an impact on the legislation, the law is equally capable of affecting technological progress by either endorsing or condemning specific technological developments. Technology is, therefore, not neutral and public regulation may sometimes be required to either promote or constrain certain private mechanisms of self-help in order to allow for the deployment of new contractual and/or technological innovations.

With the introduction of an additional layer of protection for any technological means replicating the physical properties of private goods, legislative reforms have been so far endorsing private regulation only to the extent that it was intended to restore the former status quo.

However, like most areas characterized by risks and uncertainty, the digital environment may actually represent a tremendous opportunity for a variety of stakeholders. For instance, the entertainment industry once regarded the VCR as a threat, although a valuable business model has eventually grown out of this threat: the rental industry. The internet, if appropriately exploited and regulated, would definitely reap similar benefits.

Indeed, since stronger IP laws may actually hamper the potential for the creation and dissemination of works, Internet and digital technologies should perhaps be embraced as an opportunity for innovation rather than being addressed as a dangerous threat.

In her paper on "Digital Libraries and Silent Works", María J. Iglesias illustrates how the copyright regime creates a number of market failures that may result in the under-exploitation of certain categories of works. Orphan works, for instance, can be neither reproduced nor communicated to the public as long as the copyright owner has not been properly identified. Similarly, works that are no longer being produced or published because that would be inefficient from a commercial perspective may become unavailable even though they may still be valuable from a cultural point of view. Yet, according to Iglesias, the digital environment provides the opportunity to create digital libraries capable of increasing the global availability of the cultural heritage insofar as they are not restricted by the same operating rules and scarcity concerns as in the physical world.

The law nonetheless has an important role to play as far as the endorsement of a certain technology is concerned. As Ugo Pagallo demonstrated in his paper, with the advent of P2P technology, we may eventually witness the deployment of a more efficient way of producing and distributing information through the Internet. However, while the law may attempt to control its development, it is only by allowing the technology to develop independently that its corresponding benefits and drawbacks will become objectively identifiable and capable of being consequently dealt with. Instead, banning or excessively regulating a new technology at the outset would merely stifle technological progress and eventually prevent the emergence of new and more efficient business solutions.

The set of papers presented at the conference shows the richness of the debate that arises from the complex question of the future panorama of the entanglement of law and new technologies. On the one hand, the development of technologies gives place to new realities not previously foreseen by the law at the time of its creation. In this sense it is very illustrative to think of Simon's concept of an artefact and to apply it analogously to the law. An artefact is designed according to its functionality, taking into account the environment in which it is expected to work:

"An artifact can be thought of as a meeting point –an "interface" in today's terms- between an "inner" environment, the substance and organization of the artifact itself, and an "outer" environment, the surroundings in which it operates. If the inner environment is appropriate to the outer environment, or vice versa, the artifact will serve its intended purpose. Thus, if the clock is immune to buffeting, it will serve as a ship's chronometer. (And conversely, if it isn't, we may salvage it by mounting it on the mantel at home.)"[3]

If we understand the law as an artefact, designed taking into account a particular reality that it intends to regulate (outer environment), it will be natural to think of the necessity of adapting it if that reality changes. In our case, due to new technological advances and specially to their pervasiveness, reality changes and many issues arise that need a legal answer. The topics of the panels of the conference are just an example of the issues requiring further legal attention: from the right to privacy and liberty, to intellectual property debates, and issues of public law, like the boundaries of jurisdiction in the digital milieu, cybercrime and the

---

[3] SIMON, H. A. (1984 [1969]) *The Sciences of the Artificial.* The MIT Press, Cambridge, Massachusetts, London, England. p. 9.

regulation of biotechnology, among others. On the other hand, however, technologies can bring about many benefits that cannot be ignored and that have indeed received attention during the conference. In particular ICT and AI, can provide increased functionalities for computer support to the tasks that are part of legal practice, such as legal information retrieval or legal drafting. This is a sign that due to scientific and technological development not only the object of legal analysis evolves, but as well legal practice itself changes in its methods and cognitive underpinnings.

This way, even if predicting the future is not an easy task, we strongly believe the conference to at least have provided a forum of discussion for exploring open issues and current trends, in which a fruitful exchange of ideas and impressions to deal with future events in the field has taken place.

Meritxell Fernández-Barrera
Norberto Nuno Gomes de Andrade
Primavera De Filippi
Mario Viola de Azevedo Cunha
[*InfoSoc Working Group*, European University Institute, Florence, Italy]

Re-designing the Role of Law in the Information Society: Mediating between the Real and the Virtual

Massimo Durante

Department of Legal Sciences, Faculty of Law University of Turin, Italy

The aim of the paper is to envisage how the role of law will be re-designed in relation to the evolution of information and communication technologies (ICT), which progressively determines the convergence of online and offline life, as well illustrated by the recent image of computers clouding. The hypothesis proposed in this paper is that law will keep having an autonomous and central epistemological role in representing reality, namely, in providing a mediation which will enable us to bridge the physical and the virtual realms, the empirical convergence of which does not account by itself for the construction of a common epistemological ground. Mediation is the action of serving as intermediary between two terms: i.e. one term, from which the reasoning starts, and another term, to which the reasoning is leading, since the act of mediation is the condition of the representation of the second term within the epistemological realm of the first one. According to our analysis, in the information society law will be mainly meant to play the role of mediation between the virtual and the real, namely, to ensure the conditions of reliance upon information in both directions: a) from the virtual reality to the real world, by endowing the virtual reality with a real content that is able to be appraised in the real world, through assessing the normative terms of legal responsibility for the actions and the effects of actions displayed in the virtual reality; b) from the real world to the virtual reality, by providing the real world with a real content that is able to be appraised within the virtual reality, through establishing the normative conditions of reliance on the informational data processed and shared in the virtual reality, on the basis of which are performed actions likely to produce legal effects within the real world. The theoretical and nomological framework – within which we shall envisage in what sense law could devise an act of mediation that sets the conditions of possibility for the representation of what is referred to as virtual reality within the realm of what is referred to as physical reality and vice versa – is structured by the intersubjective computer-mediated communication and interaction between individuals or groups.

I. The autonomy of law: an epistemological perspective

The aim of my paper is to envisage how the role of law will be re-designed in relation to the evolution of information and communication technologies (ICT). The hypothesis proposed in this paper is that law will keep having an autonomous and central epistemological role in representing reality, namely, in providing a mediation which will enable us to bridge the physical and the virtual realms, the empirical convergence of which does not account by itself for the construction of a common epistemological ground.

This hypothesis is not intended to underestimate the change determined by the technological computer-based revolution, which tends to transform "the basic nature or the scope of the activity or institution"[1] to which technology applies. The transformation of reality resulting from technological developments is not only quantitative but also qualitative: the computer-based technological revolution not only widens the range of our own interrogations but it also changes the meaning of our questioning.[2] In more appropriate terms, this means that, even though transformation (which applies both to the world and to human beings)[3] is a crucial key in order to understand the technological evolution, a qualitative analysis does not research, in the transformed phenomenon (object, activity, institution or human being), the explication of the transformation (the technical principle). Such explication is to be researched in the transformation of the inquiry through which this phenomenon is investigated and cognitively represented.

When reflecting upon a determined activity realised by means of a technological device, we first ask ourselves how efficiently the computer performs this activity. Once the technological application has become part of the performance of such an activity, then we ask ourselves what are the nature and the value of this activity. This stratified inquiry governs how a phenomenon transformed by the technological evolution is progressively investigated and cognitively represented as being part of the technological reality. The evolution of technology not only plays a role in determining reality but also in shaping its representation and appraisal.

---

[1] J. MOOR, 'What is computer ethics?', in T. Ward Bynum (ed), *Computers & Ethics* (1985), p. 266-275.

[2] In this perspective see M. DURANTE, *Il futuro del web: etica, diritto, decentramento. Dalla sussidiarietà digitale all'economia dell'informazione in rete* (2007), p. 28-29.

[3] N. WIENER, *Cybernetics: or Control and Communication in the Animal and the Machine* (1948), and *The Human Use of Human Beings* (1954).

This is the reason why, when we reflect upon the consequences of the application of technology to the world of law, we end up wondering about the nature of law and the direction of its evolution, which is not only empirically but also conceptually absorbed within the ongoing technological revolution. This direction is necessarily connected with the direction of the technological revolution, which is mainly expressed by the ability to rapidly[4] transform the world and determine, from an epistemological perspective, a specific reality made of both an analogical and a digital dimension. This line of evolution is focused upon a representation of the world as subject to continuous transformation: the world (which is the referent of the discourse about globalisation, mondialisation[5]) is considered more and more in its own possibility, in its virtual or possible states-of-the-world, rather than in its positive reality, namely, in its fixed or stable dimension. In more philosophical terms, it is the case of a (representation of the) world in which what is held as stable (what we can rely upon either to take a decision or to behave) is no longer determined nor explained by an ontology founded upon the positive existence of a material, real object, but by a different and new ontology, founded upon the non-contradictory content of an information that is concerned with the possible states-of-the-world. This ontology cannot be simply accounted for in terms of a digital ontology as opposed to an analogical ontology. Both of them are only epistemological descriptions of the world[6], which cannot pretend to state what reality is (metaphysics) but only how reality can be experienced and conceptualised by an epistemic agent at a given level of abstraction (epistemology). In this line of research, it appears more promising, for instance, to envisage an informational ontology, according to which knowledge of the world is knowledge of its structures (intended as sets of data)[7].

II. Law as legal science: stabilization of expectations and mediation

Intended as legal science, law has always played a paramount role in

---

[4] See on this point P. VIRILIO, *La vitesse de liberation* (1995), and *Vitesse et politique* (1977). On this perspective see S. REDHEAD, P. VIRILIO, *Theorist For An Accelerated Culture* (2004).

[5] J.-L. NANCY, *La création du monde ou la mondialisation* (2002).

[6] A. LESNE, 'The Discrete versus Continuous Controversy in Physics', in *Mathematical Structures in Computer Sciences*, 17 (02), p. 185-223.

[7] L. FLORIDI, 'Against Digital Ontology', in http://www.thephilosophyofinformation.

the epistemological perspective, namely, in the representation of reality. Legal science has constructed the possibility to mediate between the real (*what is*) and the virtual (*what ought to be*) reality within the physical domain. The virtual reality of law (*what ought to be*) has never been only an infinite adjournment of the real world (*what is*) but it has always entailed a specific form of reality with its own language, consistency and categories (legal science). In addition to this, we should notice that law has not only served as a mediation between the virtual and the real world but it has also set the limits of representation of one term within the epistemological domain of the other, through the distinction between *de facto* (the phenomenon to be represented in legal terms) and *de iure* (the conditions of possibility of representation) questions.

However, this distinction belongs more to the epistemology of law than to a description of reality, that is to say that such a distinction accounts for a different and layered representation of how reality can be understood rather than for a description of how reality is: this does not mean that law produces its own reality (*constructivism*) but only the means to represent and understand it, precisely in the topological sense in which a map (that is both a mean and a piece of knowledge) represents a determined space, in order to reduce the complexity of such environment and allow people to orientate themselves within it (*ecological information*).

The evolution of law that stems from the technological computer-based revolution has, thus, to be considered primarily from a theoretical point of view, namely, from an epistemological perspective, rather than from a merely empirical one. As pointed out, we should never lose sight of the fact that law is not only concerned with the control of critical situations but is *epistematical* in itself, *i.e.* capable of producing a specific knowledge. Within the framework of the information society, where information is meant to entail an ordered series of possible states-of-the-world and therefore regularity, the evolution of law has to be thought of as the evolution of the science of what is *possible*, intended in a Kantian sense, as what possesses a *non-contradictory content* and it *conforms to the conditions of both intuition (de facto) and thought (de iure)*[8].

---

[8] See on this point, G. DICKER, *Kant's Theory of Knowledge. An Analytical Introduction* (2004), p. 79: "For Kant, to say that something is possible is not to say only that it is logically possible or free of contradiction: this is a necessary condition but not a sufficient one. Rather, to say that something is possible means that it conforms to the conditions of both intuition and thought; as Kant states it in the First Postulate: 'That which agrees with the formal conditions of experience, that is, with the conditions of intuition and of concepts, is possible'".

Contradiction has always nourished law, which has also been conceived as the attempt to overcome contradiction. The possible contradiction between the functioning of the virtual and of the real world, *i.e.* the consistency of the digital and analogical reality, is likely to undermine or at least to menace the conditions of possibility of an ordered communication within the society of information. The question is not to oppose a disposition to change (technology) to a pretension to stability (law). On the contrary, it deals with the recognition of what can be taken for *stable* in what changes, in order to make the flow of information and communication ordered and effective. In other words, law is likely to be kept charged with the role of stabilisation of expectations, but we should wonder what it means now to stabilise expectations within the networked information society.

The role to be assigned to law cannot be limited in the networked society of information to the norm's predictive power, on the basis of which the norm is expected to foresee and measure human behaviours and to govern reality. How can law govern reality, when the latter is subject to continuous transformation? Law is not to be opposed to the technological evolution (both law and technology belong to, and thus stem from, the development of human culture) but is meant to progressively become part of the informational system. In our view, law will be (kept) charged with an essential role, namely, the role of *mediation* between the real and the virtual world.

III. The concept and role of mediation

Mediation is the action of serving as intermediary between two terms: *i.e.* one term, from which the reasoning starts, and another term, to which the reasoning is leading, since the act of mediation is the condition for the representation of the second term within the epistemological realm of the first one.

The concept of mediation is based on a philosophical assumption, which is central to our analysis, namely that nothing is simply given as a stable, assured basis for something else. In epistemological terms, nothing is either immediately present in its conceptual meaning or is evident by itself in the thought process (neither the "real world" nor the "virtual reality"). This was already affirmed as the fundamental principle of Kantian epistemology: intuitions without concepts are blind, concepts without intuitions are void.[9] On the contrary, every phenomenon is to be represented and thought of by means of mediations. In this perspective, mediation is not conceived as a simple relation between two terms, since a relation compounds two already established terms. Mediation is intended as a dynamic process of thought (such as a legal reasoning) within which progressive connections represent and establish terms. Through the act of mediation, something (phenomena, terms or data) can be assumed as the stable basis for the representation and the comprehension of something else.

The concept of mediation denies abstract unrelatedness, and affirms the possibility of complex relatedness among phenomena. Therefore, mediation entails, from an epistemological perspective, a denial of a world (both real and virtual) of unrelated elements. On the contrary, it endows the world with the possibility of communication between the real and the virtual. A mediated world turns out to be more than the sum of static, empirical relations among agents of the real and the virtual world: it grows out of the communication process between epistemological stances and exists in the tension of their mutual becoming a *real* and a *virtual* world. In this perspective, the act of mediation is the condition of representation of the virtual reality within the epistemology of the real world and vice versa. This allows one term or entity of the real/virtual reality to be taken as the stable basis for the representation and comprehension of another term within the epistemology that describes how the real/virtual world can be experienced and conceptualised by an epistemic agent at a given level of abstraction.

For instance, while punishing the online steal of identity, made possible by the current informatics' technologies, we do not only judge a behaviour as being illegal, but we also endow the *virtual* identity with a *real* consistency, by delimiting to what conditions it is possible to rely upon the set of data concerning the online personal identity. In this perspective, as outlined before, we end up qualifying, at least to some extent, *what is an online personal identity*, not only in strict, legal terms,

---

[9] A significant interpretation of Kantian epistemology is offered by J. McDOWELL, *Mind and World* (1996), p. 3: "The overall I am going to consider in these lectures is the way concepts mediate the relation between minds and the world. I shall focus the discussion in terms of a familiar philosophical outlook, which Donald Davidson has described as a dualism of scheme and content. That will get us quickly to Kant. One of my main aims is to suggest that Kant should still have a central place in our discussion of the way thought bears on reality". And p. 4: "So the picture is this: the fact that thoughts are not empty, the fact that thoughts have representational content, emerges out of an interplay of concepts and intuitions".

but rather at the level of inter-subjective communication, *i.e.* of symmetrical and mutual reliance on information.

As a term can be represented and assumed as the stable basis for something else, this provides the epistemic agent with a predictive power. Such a predictive power shall be judged according to the interplay of the real and the virtual world within the information society. Since there is no prediction without representation, the conditions of possibility of representation set the structural limits of any predictive power. These conditions of possibility are to be considered within the epistemology of law, which assumes such conditions as the necessary presuppositions of the norm's predictive power.

The prediction set forth by the norm of positive law displays an informational content that enables us to stabilise our expectations. It allows us to behave in a free manner, namely, by foreseeing and measuring the predicted effects of our actions. This informational content appears to be, however, more and more static compared to the transformation of the world (this is an old argument renewed by the technological evolution) and to the flow of informational resources shared throughout the networks (this is a new argument determined by the information and communication technologies). The informational content of the norm is likely to rapidly become contradictory with the augmented reality of the infosphere, *i.e.* "the whole informational environment constituted by all informational entities (thus including informational agents as well), their properties, interactions process and mutual relations".[10]

In this perspective, law has to become part of the informational system; in contrast to a widespread opinion, this does not mean that law is either overcome or determined by technology. On the contrary, law keeps its own specificity, precisely thanks to its ability to mediate between the real and the virtual world. This act of mediation requires a translation of the *virtual* information displayed by technology, namely, the possibility opened and made available by the application of new ICT, into *real* information. The reality of information is no longer based upon the positive existence of a real, material object; actually, it is based upon the *non-contradictory* content of information, on which it is held reasonable to rely, in order to take a decision and behave.

From this consideration a basic principle should be inferred and established as a firm premise of our line of reasoning: it is possible to set

---

[10] L. FLORIDI, 'A look into the future impact of ICT on our lives', http://www.philosophyofinformation.net, p. 3.

an ordered form of communication only on the basis of reliance upon relevant information,[11] shared at an inter-subjective level.[12] The inner rationality of the multi-agent system of the networked society of information is not to be found in a set of certainties (from which the legal order ought to be deduced) but in its attitude to cope both with the flood of information deriving from the upgrading of social networks and the structural *lack of knowledge*[13] characterizing the asymmetry between environmental and systemic information.

IV. Mediating between the real and the virtual in the information society

According to our opinion, in the information society law will be thus mainly meant to play the role of mediation between the virtual and the real, namely, to ensure the conditions of reliance upon information in both directions: a) *from the virtual reality to the real world*: in this context, the concept of virtuality is endowed with a real content constituted by the idea of foreseeable consequences, whose importance and extension are progressively subject to the convergence of online and offline life. This delineates, according to many authors, the most relevant trend of the networked information society: "Nowadays, we are used to considering the space of information as something we log-in to and log-out from. Our view of the world (our metaphysics) is still modern or Newtonian: it is made of 'dead' cars, buildings, furniture, clothes, which are non-interactive, irresponsive and incapable of communicating, learning, or

---

[11] See T. MALDONALDO, *Reale e virtuale* (2007), p. 151: "Nessuno può ormai negare che la nostra percezione è satura di valori e disvalori, di giudizi e pregiudizi; sostenere però che essa non ci dica nulla di credibile sulla realtà mi sembra una conclusione abusiva. E il punto riguarda direttamente la questione del rapporto virtuale-reale. Perché, in ultima istanza, tutta la controversia sulla realtà del virtuale e sulla virtualità del reale è inseparabile dal problema dell'affidabilità (o meno) della nostra percezione del mondo reale". See also T. BERNERS-LEE, *Weaving the Web. The Original Design and Ultimate Destiny of the World Wide Web by Its Inventor* (1999).

[12] In this perspective see M. DURANTE, 'What Model of Trust for Networked Cooperation? Online Social Trust in the Production of Common Goods (Knowledge Sharing)', in T.W. Bynum, M. Calzarossa, I. De Lotto, S. Rogerson (ed.), *Living, Working and Learning Beyond Technology, Proceedings of the Tenth International Conference Ethicomp 2008*, Mantova, University Press, 2008, p. 211-223.

[13] See on this point U. PAGALLO, 'Something Beyond Technology: Some Remarks On Ignorance And Its Role In Evolution', in T.W. Bynum, M. Calzarossa, I. De Lotto, S. Rogerson (ed.), *Living, Working and Learning Beyond Technology*, above note 13, p. 623-631.

memorizing. But what we still experience as the world offline is bound to become a fully interactive and responsive environment of wireless, pervasive, distributed, *a2a* (anything to anything) information process, that works *a4a* (anywhere for anytime), in real time. This will first gently invite us to understand the world as something 'alive' (artificially live). Such *animation* of the world will, paradoxically, make our outlook closer to that of pre-technological cultures which interpreted all aspects of nature as inhabited by technological forces";[14] b) *from the real world to the virtual reality*: in this context, the concept of virtuality is endowed with a real content constituted by the idea of reliance on information. We have thus to shed light on this idea with regard to its pragmatic and gnoseological relevance. Reliance on information is a condition for a rational theory of decisions and actions. In order to decide or behave on the basis of rational criteria, I rely upon information: they are sensory data from reality (worldly ontology) or the content of knowledge (documental ontology) or instructions to behave (rules of conduct). According to Floridi, we can speak of information as reality; information on reality and information for reality.[15] Deciding and acting on the basis of reliable information has (a) the pragmatic aim of rationally guiding our decisions or actions toward a determined goal (according to a degree of probability of success) and (b) the gnoseological aim of measuring our decisions and actions by reference with an assumed parameter given by available information. Providing decisions and actions with a set of information implies giving supplementary information to the system (in terms of positive or negative feedback): this information has both descriptive (the conditions of reliance) and normative content (the degree of coherence between information and the results of decisions or actions).[16] The role of law as a mediation between the virtual and the real thus requires a more accurate analysis of the following conditions.

A. FROM THE VIRTUAL REALITY TO THE REAL WORLD

Law displays its role of mediation from the virtual reality to the real

---

[14] See L. FLORIDI, 'A look into the future impact of ICT on our lives', above note 10, p. 7.

[15] The tripartite epistemological distinction of information can be found in L. FLORIDI, 'Trends in the philosophy of information', http://www.philosophyofinformation.net, p. 8. For an analysis of such a distinction and its relevance to law see U. PAGALLO, *Teoria giuridica della complessità. Dalla 'polis primitiva' di Socrate ai 'mondi piccoli' dell'informatica. Un approccio evolutivo* (2006), p. 160-165.

[16] See on this point M. DURANTE, 'What Model of Trust for Networked Cooperation?', above note 12, p. 212.

world, by endowing the virtual reality with a real content that is able to be appraised in the physical domain. This happens by means of *terms of legal responsibility*: it is within the real world that I am responsible for (the effects of) actions displayed within the virtual reality. In other words, legal responsibility is meant to measure the friction that an action or operation performed through computers in the virtual reality generates out of the domain of its technological application.

The virtual reality is a representation (either by analogical or digital models) of reality through which some objects are substituted by some other 'objects'. In this perspective, the virtual reality is an autonomous reality since the new objects, which design a reality with an economy of means or with a novel arrangement of them, produce a new form of knowledge.[17] The relation with the virtual reality is established by means of intuition (visual, acoustic perception of the new objects), conceptualisation (appraisal of the content of the new objects) or interaction (modification of the new objects by means of interactive technological devices). These types of relation are based on a specific epistemology, which does not explain what the virtual reality is but how it can be experienced and conceptualised by an epistemic agent at a given level of abstraction. This form of knowledge is necessarily and progressively elaborated on the basis of the sets of data (the new objects), which structure the *context* of the virtual reality: this context allows us to say that we behave and act *within* the virtual reality. In this perspective, how can we say whether and when the effects of an action performed within the virtual reality encounter the real world?

Coming back to the real world is only made possible out of the forms of relation with the representation of the (virtual) reality. Coming back to the real world requires translating the acquired knowledge within the epistemological realm where the effects of the actions displayed within the virtual reality are to be appraised and judged. One of the possible situations in which the effects of an action performed within the virtual reality encounters the real world is given by the factual circumstances where one is held responsible by someone else for those consequences within the real world. For one to be held responsible, it is required that the consequences of one's actions performed within the virtual reality were to some extent *foreseeable* within the epistemology describing how the real world can be experienced and conceptualised by an epistemic agent at a given level of abstraction. In such a perspective, law is entrenched with the epistemic role of appraising in what terms the effects of an action

---

[17] See C. CADOZ, *Les réalités virtuelles* (1994), p. 93.

performed in the virtual reality can be judged foreseeable and thus accountable in the real world. This requires the legal science to establish the conditions of the representation of one term within the epistemological realm of another one. The foreseeable effects of an action are to be appraised in *terms of legal responsibility*. This does not mean that legal categories immediately apply to the technological reality nor it means that the virtual reality regulates itself by means of technological devices. On the contrary, according to the aforementioned Moor's thesis, it means that, when technology concerns the question of prediction, law is entrenched with the epistemic role of explaining how the consequences of an action can be experienced and conceptualised, in legal terms, as *foreseeable effects* both in the virtual and in the real world.

Needless to say, in our opinion the role of mediation is mainly worked out by means of legal adjudication, which not only consists in hearing and settling a case by judicial procedure but also in stabilising epistemic expectations, which mediate between the virtual and the real world. This aspect of the role of mediation of law poses both a phenomenological and a hermeneutical problem.

From a phenomenological point of view, the progressive convergence of online and offline life displaces the concept of prediction, which is no longer entrenched exclusively with the aim of inferring a future behaviour from a past one, but is also more and more concerned with the attempt of appraising the cognitive limits of the agents' representation of reality and of their rational capacity of acting,[18] which can enable us to correct our own predictions and to judge what can be held as a reasonable expectation. However, the progressive convergence of online and offline

---

[18] See G. SARTOR, 'Gli agenti software: nuovi soggetti del cyberdiritto', http://www.cirsfid.unibo.it. (2007), p. 81: "La conoscenza dei principi del funzionamento dell'agente e l'analisi del suo comportamento nel passato (l'agente può aver commesso errori) non offrono una base sufficiente per effettuare una previsione del suo comportamento futuro. Tale conoscenza può invece consentire di determinare i limiti delle capacità 'razionali' dell'agente, e quindi di individuare le ipotesi nelle quali l'agente può comportarsi in modo inadeguato. Combinando l'ipotesi della razionalità dell'agente con la conoscenza dei limiti di tale razionalità, siamo in condizione di prevedere e spiegare il comportamento dell'agente con sufficiente accuratezza. Non è diversa la strategia che adottiamo di regola nei confronti dei nostri simili: la nostra conoscenza dei limiti, delle idiosincrasie, delle attitudini di ciascuno non offre una base sufficiente per prevedere il comportamento altrui (tranne che nel caso di comportamenti dettati da riflessi automatici o da pulsioni incontrollabili). Tale conoscenza ci consente però di integrare e correggere l'ipotesi che ciascuno tenda a perseguire i propri scopi in modo razionale: possiamo spiegare e prevedere il comportamento umano combinando l'ipotesi generale della razionalità di ciascuno con la conoscenza dei limiti di tale razionalità nei singoli casi".

life does not displace the function of law, since there is still a difference between what is empirically held as a foreseeable effect and what is legitimately expected to be held, at an inter-subjective level, as a foreseeable effect.

From a hermeneutical point of view, the role of mediation of law by means of legal responsibility faces a different problem. In the ontology based on the physical reality the terms of legal responsibility are expected to be interpreted either within the context where the action took place or within the context where the action displayed its own effect (they often happen to be the same or at least to be both regulated by international law). What is the semantic context within which the actions or the effects of actions are to be legally interpreted within the networked society of information? The problem is not only concerned with legal boundaries (with the limits of both public and private international law) but also with symbolic universes: this is, in our opinion, the main problem that law has to face in its role of mediation between the real and the virtual, since data, phenomena, concepts, categories and the consequences of actions displayed within the virtual reality are likely to be culturally appraised in terms that refer to different symbolic universes.[19] The activity of mediation, by means of which one term can be represented within the epistemological realm of another one, presupposes, as we said, the possibility of a complex relatedness among data, that is to say, a unified symbolic universe. In addition to this, we should notice that the

---

[19] See in this perspective S. McROBB, Y. ORITO, K. MURATA, A. ADAMS, 'Towards an Exploration of Cross-cultural Factors in Privacy Online', in T. Ward Bynum, S. Rogerson, K. Murata (ed.), *Glocalisation: Bridging the Global Nature of Information and Communication Technology and the Local Nature of Human Beings* (vol. II, 2007), p. 380-385, at p. 381: "Most organizations and citizens in this domain share, due to their common linguistic and/or cultural heritage, assumptions that may not exist in non-Western cultures. Or, if they exist at all, they make take very different forms. By contrast, relatively little attention has yet been paid to the different meanings, values and behaviours associated with privacy in societies whose cultural compass points elsewhere than West". In the same perspective see also Y. ORITO, K. MURATA, 'Rethinking the concept of information privacy: a Japanese perspective', in T. Ward Bynum, S. Rogerson, K. Murata (ed.), *Glocalisation: Bridging the Global Nature of Information and Communication Technology and the Local Nature of Human Beings* (vol. II, 2007), p. 448-455, at p. 454: "Our proposal is made from a Japanese perspective. This may raise concerns about the effectiveness of the revised concept in the global context. However, because ICT is advancing on a global scale, the revised concept could become mandatory for a wide range of countries. Our proposal is the first step towards developing a globally acceptable concept of the right to information privacy that is appropriate for the modern information age. Societies could realise this concept through the integration of opinions about the right to such privacy based on local sociocultural and economic situations".

development of the semantic web and formal ontology is an important but only partial answer to the problem, since this development mainly aims at coping with the interpretation of (legal) texts rather than with the present delimitation of (legal) contexts. While the information and communication technology (ICT) is advancing on a global scale, the role of mediation of law appears to be, often, linguistically and/or culturally located.

B. FROM THE REAL WORLD TO THE VIRTUAL REALITY

Law displays its role of mediation, furthermore, from the real world to the virtual reality, by giving a real content to the real world that can be appraised within the virtual reality, by means of *informational reliance*. It is within the virtual reality that I rely on informational data, in order to perform actions that are likely to produce (legal) effects within the real world. In other words, if the virtual dimension of information and communication technology (ICT) is to be found in its ability to transform the world in the content of an information, the virtual dimension of law (as a mediation from the real world to the virtual reality) is to be found in its ability to set the conditions according to which it is possible to rely on the content of information processed and exchanged within the networked information society. In order to rely upon information, epistemic agents have to either explicitly or implicitly set a *norm* which should allow them to recognise intersubjectively what is reasonable to believe in and expect. In the absence of such normative dimension, the communication spread in the networked information society is radically exposed to the chance of being disordered and ineffective.

In this perspective, law can play a fundamental role of mediation between the real and the virtual to the extent that it assures reliance upon information. This does not amount at saying that the virtual reality of the networked information society should be subject to ruling: in this line of reasoning, the mediation of law is called forth only by reference to its normative function of stabilisation of expectations. This aspect of mediation poses topological problems both with respect to (1) *information and communication technologies* and with respect to (2) *networked cooperation*.

1. Information and communication technologies

In relation to information and communication technologies (ICT) the *function-of-law* consists (a) in creating *filters of relevance and reliability*, in order to select relevant and reliable information (data and channels of information), and (b) in establishing *means of moderation and meta-moderation*, in order to ensure an ordered communication, without reaffirming forms of control after decentralisation.[20]

A) *Filters of relevance and reliability.*

Communication in the networked information society has to be ordered[21] to be effective. This requires to elaborate means by which it is possible to filter information in terms of relevance and reliability. Needless to say that the creation of filters of relevance and reliability is likely to suffer from problems of agency, *i.e.* any selection is by itself significant and thus possesses the normative power of conveying (more or less perceptible) values.

However, the elaboration of these filters in the networked information society does not depend necessarily on centred and hierarchical choices (related to the ownership of channels of information). On the contrary, it has been proved[22] to depend on decentred and horizontal practices displayed by a plurality of users by means of distributed networks.[23] More precisely, there are at least two ways to create filters of relevance and reliability through the coordination of individual actions. This coordination can be either the result of the users' *cooperative will* or the outcome of their *spontaneous interaction*.

Internet users can voluntarily create means by which information is judged as relevant and reliable thanks to an assessment that has been progressively formed by the pronounces and/or the practices of a plurality of individuals, whose interaction allow them to reach a goal they would not be able to achieve by themselves. This is made possible by all technological filters of relevance and reliability created, in a distributed manner, in accordance with a *teleological hierarchy*. I define as such a hierarchy of values, the ordering of which is constructed with the scope of

---

[20] For a detailed analysis of this question, R.A. GALLOWAY, *Protocol. How Control Exists after Decentralization*, (2004). See also R.A. GALLOWAY & E. THACKER, *The Exploit: A Theory of Networks* (2007).

[21] The idea has been defended against criticism in M. DURANTE, *Il futuro del web: etica, diritto, decentramento*, above note 2, p. 259-273.

[22] See in this perspective, Y. BENKLER, *The Wealth of Networks: How Social Production Transforms Markets and Freedom* (2006), p. 215-220.

[23] For a critical account of this notion see R.A. GALLOWAY & E. THACKER, *The Exploit: A Theory of Networks*, above note 20, p. 3: "In contrast to Lovink, we maintain that in recent decades the process of globalization have mutated from a system of control housed in a relatively small number of power hubs to a system of control infused into the material fabric of distributed networks".

achieving a previously shared goal of a common concern.[24]

Internet users can, furthermore, elaborate filters of relevance and reliability as a result of a non-programmed action, that is to say in a spontaneous manner (cosmological order).[25] In this case, the coordination of individual actions is made possible by the specific configuration of networked interactions (according to topological models[26] that we cannot expound here), which tend to select information both in a relevant and ordered way. This process of selection is based on clusters of shared contents, common interests, and the presence of hubs, which filter and catalyse the informational resources distributed in the web. On the one hand, this may result, at a macroscopic level, as a *non-democratic*[27] distribution of information (*power law distribution*: very few websites have the majority of links and the majority of websites has very few links). On the other hand, this means that communication is made possible, at a regional level, since information is guided towards local communities by interests of common concern, as it is described by the topological effects of clustering, cross-linking and small worlds.[28]

B) *Means of moderation and meta-moderation.*

Communication in the networked information society implies inter-subjective interactions, which need to be moderated, in order to enable

---

[24] For such an idea see M. DURANTE, *Il futuro del web: etica, diritto, decentramento*, above note 2, p. 201: "[...] se di gerarchia si può ancora parlare, preferiamo allora qualificarla come gerarchia orientata ad un fine comune: è l'orientamento alla protezione del fine comune che designa il principio di misura e legittimità dell'atto d'autorità insito in ogni processo di revisione e accreditamento, per quanto esso sia orizzontale e decentrato".

[25] The idea of a cosmological order has been suggested by F. HAYEK, *Law, Legislation and Liberty* (1982).

[26] See on this note n. 28. See also R.A. GALLOWAY & E. THACKER, *The Exploit: A Theory of Networks*, above note 20, p. 13: "By 'thinking topologically', we mean an approach that compares the abstract spaces of different structural or architectonic systems. Pyramidal hierarchy and distributed networks, for examples, have two different topologies of organizations and control".

[27] See on this point A.L. BARABÁSI, *Linked* (2002). See also C. SHIRKY, 'Power Laws, Weblogs, and Inequality', http://www.shirky.com/writings/powerlaw_weblog.html.

[28] For an account of networked topological effects, Y. BENKLER, *The Wealth of Networks*, above note 22 , p. 300-320. On the topological configuration of small worlds paradigm see in particular, D.J. WATTS, S.H. STROGATZ, 'Collective dynamics of 'Small-World' Networks', in *Nature*, 393 (1998), p. 440-442; D.J. WATTS, *Small Worlds: The Dynamics of Networks between Order and Randomness* (1999); see also U. PAGALLO, 'Small world paradigm in social sciences: problems and perspectives', in T. Ward Bynum, S. Rogerson, K. Murata (ed.), Glocalisation: Bridging the Global Nature...", above note 19, p. 456-465.

users to equally and fruitfully participate in the community of discussion. In this perspective, the *function-of-law* consists in establishing means of moderation, *i.e.* the social norms regulating the discussion, and metamoderation, *i.e.* the social norms regulating how the norms of discussion are to be chosen and applied.

We consider a community of discussion,[29] which does not adopt a process of selection of information that makes, *ex ante*, a distinction between what can be published and what has to be prevented from publishing. The process of publishing is based on an *ex post* peer review system of selection. This means that this community endorses both a principle of freedom and a principle of responsibility: the former asserts each participant's freedom to post whatsoever information, the latter requires the participants to establish shared means of moderation and metamoderation, in order to revise information.

The process of moderation, adopted by the community of discussion, is decentred and horizontal, as it is based on the distributed power of evaluation of each moderator selected by the community. Even if distributed, this normative power has to be subject to further control by means of metamoderation, which is also a decentred and horizontal mechanism of revision. The concept of metamoderation consists in the idea that every judgement should be subject to further judgement. This does not necessarily entail an infinite regression, since metamoderation is implicitly judged by its ability to determine a fruitful and ordered discussion within the community.

The *legal constitution* of such a community deserves consideration. The community is neither constituted exclusively on inclusion nor on exclusion. Its constitution endorses both a norm including every statement in the discussion and a norm excluding some of them from there. The community does not formulate a judgement on what is included but asserts a judgement on what is excluded. This means that the community is not involved in the process of deciding what can be a priori conceived as *just*, but is indeed concerned with the process of establishing what can be a posteriori conceived as *unjust*, that is to say that cannot be accepted within the discussion.[30]

---

[29] We consider the example of moderation and metamoderation offered by the multilevel technological platform adopted by a community of discussion as Slashdot. See on this point D. TAPSCOTT – A.D. WILLIAMS, *Wikinomics: How Mass Collaboration Changes Everything* (2006), p. 144-145.

[30] See in this perspective, even tough in the context of a different line of reasoning, what has been affirmed by P. RICOEUR, *Le juste*, (1995).

2. Networked social cooperation

Networked social cooperation not only requires to rely on the information of others when deciding or behaving under the conditions of uncertainty resulting from the complexity of virtual environment, but also on someone's else behaviour (delegation). This raises a normative question as regards interpersonal interaction: must interaction be based on a previously established norm, in order to promote cooperation? Or is such a norm likely to grow out of the interpersonal interaction? Before trying to answer such a question, we should focus our attention upon the fact that the idea of establishing a norm regulating the interpersonal interaction already implies a certain degree of distrust (in the relations between agents).

The computer-mediated interaction or coordination between agents or groups may require thus different forms of normative mediation, either founded upon (a) distrust systems of mediation or upon (b) trust systems of mediation. The former is mainly concerned with technological and legal security (assured by means of rules, constraints, architectures, controls, and protocols), while the latter is mainly concerned with mental and social dispositions towards other agents.[31] Technological or legal security is necessary in regards to online commercial transactions, privacy issues, and legal contracts, but it does not suffice to assure networked social cooperation In fact, this is based on someone else's behaviour, on their willingness to cooperate with us that is never fully predictable. A trust system of mediation allows the trustier to evaluate the trustee's willingness and ability to fulfil expectations.

A) *Distrust systems of mediation.*

Internet users set norms or technological devices since they do not trust the agents to whom they delegate tasks. This system shows a negative attitude towards agents, since it applies when they do not fulfil expectations. When things are expected to go wrong, there is no particular concern for the goal to achieve. This system externalises concern for the goal, whose protection and fulfilment are attributed to a third party (normative mediation): the authority. This consists of two elements: a) the

---

[31] This perspective has been widely expounded by C. CASTELFRANCHI & R. FALCONE, 'Social Trust: Cognitive Anatomy, Social Importance, Quantification and Dynamics', *Proceedings of the first Workshop on Deception, Fraud and Trust in Agent Societies*, Minneapolis/St. Paul, 1998, p. 35-49. More recently, see also of the same authors, 'Trust Theory', 2007, http://www.istc.cnr.it/T3/trust, and 'Socio-Cognitive Model of Trust: Basic Ingredients', 2008, http://www.istc.cnr.it/T3/trust.

norm (legal rules or technological devices) set before the trustier and the trustee enter into a relation; b) the institution that administers and applies the norm established to regulate the relation between parties. The system based on distrust is ultimately based on trust, since the trustier has to trust the ability of the norm to foresee when the agents will not fulfil expectations and, above all, the ability of the authority to apply the violated norm. This normative mediation entails high transaction costs[32] in setting up an institutional authority to be trusted and feared and applying the norms regulating the interpersonal interaction.

B) *Trust systems of mediation.*

The trustier believes that the trustee will act according to predictions. This system internalises concern for the goal. A positive attitude is motivated by the Internet users' shared concern for the task to be fulfilled. This model applies when the desired outcome is produced. This system does not seem to refer to an institutional authority (normative mediation). However, it is a relationship based on a particular type of authority. This consists of two elements: a) the social norm set by the relation between agents. Trust itself sets a norm that grows out of the dynamic sphere of the communication process (interpersonal interaction): both the trustier and the trustee are aware of the fact that the latter is somehow indebted to the former, since the trustier has given the trustee some credit;[33] b) information concerning the trustee's behaviour. The act of trusting and the act of fulfilling expectations release mutual information that can be shared and processed within the web or a community (the system in relation to the virtual environment). The authority of trust lies in the possibility of tracking and sharing this information. It is a form of control by means of

---

[32] P. AIGRAIN, 'The Individual and the Collective in Open Information Communities', *Proceedings BLED Electronic Commerce Conference*, 9-11 June 2003, http://paigrain.debatpublic.net: "Transaction costs are much more than the monetary costs attached to transaction. They include cognitive costs (for instance the cost of deciding whether or not to do an action that may lead to a charge), time and information costs (for instance navigating in the transaction management layers), privacy costs, uncertainty costs (when some rights are subject to further approval), locking-in (i.e. loss of freedom due to the fact that an information service will give you access only to specific sources, or will make it difficult for you to switch to another provider). In this sense [...] control aspects are more rejected than the cost itself".

[33] See N. LUHMANN, 'Trust: a mechanism for the reduction of social complexity", in *Id., Trust and Power: Two Works by Niklas Luhmann* (1979), p. 1-103, at p. 35, who affirms that the trustor "has the possibility to set the norm according to which his reliance should not be betrayed (...). The impossibility of enchaining trust within a legal disposition does not entirely exclude trust from the domain of norms".

information feedback: negative feedback corrects an incorrect prediction; positive feedback supports the process of communication.

A trust system of mediation, built as a result of relations between agents and the stabilisation of their mutual expectations, determines a normative dimension that can reach beyond technological and legal security, since it is not affected by obsolescence (because it grounds expectations on the ongoing conditions of party relations) nor does it require full information (because it enables agents to deal with conditions of uncertainty and lack of knowledge), and thus high transaction cost, in order to be established.

V. Conclusions

The theoretical framework – within which we have analysed in what sense law can devise an act of mediation which determines the conditions of possibility of the representation of what is referred to as 'virtual reality' within the realm of what is referred to as 'physical reality' and vice versa – is thus structured by the *inter-subjective* computer-mediated interaction and communication between individuals or groups. The rationality of the interaction between agents (whether human or artificial) is not actually defined in terms of certainties or acquired knowledge but rather in terms of shared expectations and social norms, which grow out of the communication process.

The rational criteria of inter-subjective interaction have been settled thanks to the mediation of law along two directions: on the one hand, law is entrenched with the role of devising how to protect reliance on information, which assures an ordered form of communication between agents, by qualifying what is conceived as reliable information by means of legal responsibility. On the other hand, law is concerned with setting the conditions of the communication process, by means of which agents can devise what is reasonable to expect from other agents, both in terms of relevant and reliable information (filters and means of moderation and metamoderation) and in terms of trusting delegated tasks and behaviours (networked cooperation).

In both perspectives, the relation between agents can be judged as an inter-subjective interaction, since the parties are transformed by the interaction itself. To speak more properly, the communication process constitutes the parties in their own subjectivity. Whether human or artificial, subjectivity is conceived in epistemological terms as the ability to set the criteria assessing how (virtual and physical) reality can be experienced and conceptualised at a given level of abstraction. Since this ability grows out of the communication process, it is not possible to determine, as a fixed certainty, what is to be taken for stable: the shared basis of our decisions and behaviours is the result of the reduction of complexity of the environment. The act of mediation of law between the real and the virtual plays a role in the process of reduction of complexity, which is not to be underestimated, if the interplay of intuitions (the phenomenon to be represented: factual question) and concepts (the conditions of possibility of representation: legal question) deserves to be preserved.

New Technologies and the Law: Precedents via Metaphors

Harmeet Sawhney, Venkata Ratnadeep Suri, and Hyangsun Lee
Department of Telecommunications Indiana University, Bloomington

When faced with legal issues raised by new and unfamiliar technologies, courts typically rely on metaphors based on old technologies. The application of old technology metaphors tend to be quite straightforward in the initial stages, when the new technology is deployed in ways that mimick the established ones. Later, as new uses of the technology are found, the courts start stretching the old technology metaphors to accommodate the new technology within the established framework. We seek to understand how this stretching process works by examining the case of radio, which initially fit the established framework as wireless telegraph but later with the development of broadcasting disrupted it. We see the occurrence of a "metaphor vacuum," the point at which simple stretching of the old framework no longer works, as the key turning point. We discuss when metaphor vacuums occur and how they are filled.

In many ways it is futile to think about the future. There are far too many variables involved and it is almost impossible to make accurate predictions. But, in the arena of information and communications technologies (ICT), the sheer pace of technological change forces us to confront it. We have to factor in the future when we make investment, regulatory, and other decisions about ICT.[1]

The preferred device is a formal model which allows us to make predictions with a high degree of accuracy. Such a model requires a comprehensive understanding of the phenomenon and availability of accurate data. Unfortunately, the sheer complexity of the processes leading to the development of a large technical system such as the "information superhighway" does not readily lend itself to precise modelling. The processes tend to be ambiguous and ill-defined and accurate data are a rare commodity. In such situations metaphors and analogies offer a viable alternative to formal models. They help us handle situations where there is "high uncertainty, missing data, unclear goals,

---

[1] The introductory discussion excerpts from H. SAWHNEY, 'Information superhighway: Metaphors as midwives', *Media, Culture & Society*, 1996, No 18, p. 291-314.

and poorly understood parameters".[2]

We have to accept the fact that although the use of metaphors is not a particularly elegant or sophisticated technique, it is perhaps the only conceptual tool we have for understanding the development of a new technology. We should therefore direct our energies towards understanding the peculiarities of this tool: How can we leverage it to maximise the potential payoff? What are the pitfalls and how can we avoid them?

In the case of technology and law, there is an added dimension—metaphors help establish precedents. As Pool points out, "courts like to treat new phenomenon by analogy to old ones".[3] For example, in the mid-1970s when FCC removed the resale restrictions on telephone services, "the fundamental legal principle underlying the decision was a 1911 Supreme Court decision which prohibited the railroads from refusing service to freight forwarders who purchased railroad service in bulk (carload lots or greater) and resold it to smaller shippers".[4] This mode of legal reasoning has formed the basis for the development of much of the communications law. Each new communications technology has been shaped by legal precedents created by the previous ones. The problem is that the precedents are often not readily available or clear.

The Interstate Commerce Act developed for regulating the railroads has continued to influence the development of the legal framework for all the subsequent network technologies—petroleum pipelines, trucking, civil aviation, and telecommunications, among other technologies. Here metaphors were effective vehicles for the transfer of conceptual frameworks from one technology to another because they were all point-to-point networks for the movement of materials and information from one point to another. However, the process broke down in the case of radio. For example, in the beginning radio was conceptualised as "wireless telegraph" or a point-to-point communication technology. Even Marconi, the inventor of radio, saw the tendency of radio waves to scatter as a major nuisance. In fact all the institutional forces guided by the telegraph analogy were working in the 1920s towards casting radio as a point-to-point technology. The eventual emergence of broadcasting was a total surprise, and it undermined all the institutional structures set up on the wireless telegraph metaphor. The radio was clearly a case where a

---

[2] G. KLEIN, "Applications of analogical reasoning", *Metaphor and Symbolic Activity*, No 2, 3, p. 201-218 (1987), at p. 202.
[3] I.D.S. POOL, *Technologies of Freedom* (1983), p. 100.
[4] G. BROCK, *The Telecommunications Industry* (1981), p. 270.

metaphor based on an old technology failed to shape the new one in its image.

The development of broadcasting created what we call a "metaphor vacuum"—there were no readily available metaphors to think about the new technology. The term "broadcasting" was appropriated from a realm far removed from communication. The original meaning of broadcasting signified the act or process of scattering seeds.[5] Later, at the turn of the century, the women suffragists used the word broadcasting to describe the act of distributing leaflets on street corners. [6] This mode of disseminating something came closest to serving as an analog for describing the dispersive tendencies of radio.

Although "broadcasting" was an appropriate label for the new phenomenon, it was not very useful from the legal point of view, which is the focus of our paper. It described the physical phenomenon—point to multipoint communication. But it did bring with a legal framework. We are interested in understanding how the legal system dealt with the central problematic of the "metaphor vacuum." Here, on the one hand, there was a radically new technology for which no clear precedent was available. On the other hand, the case law could not proceed without a precedent. The one way this tension could be resolved was by taking an established metaphor and stretching it. We are especially interested in understanding how this stretching process works.

In this paper we first trace the legal developments from the very first case—*Marconi Wireless Telegraph vs. Northern Pacific S.S. Co.* (1918) to *Great Lakes Broadcasting vs. Federal Radio Commission* (1930), when the framework for radio regulation became a settled issue. In the subsequent section we analyse the radio case on a conceptual plane and draw lessons for the future.

I. Evolution of radio law and regulation

The initial cases dealt with minor issues. For example, the earliest court case we found, *Marconi Wireless Telegraph vs. Northern Pacific S.S. Co.* (1918), was primarily a contract dispute between two parties. At this stage, the potential for broadcasting was not well understood. Wireless was basically being used in ways that mimicked the telegraph.[7]

---

[5] E. BARNOUW, *A Tower in Babel* (1994).

[6] J. HIJIYA, *Lee de FOREST and the Fatherhood of Radio* (1992).

[7] Edison mimicked gas to get electricity, which was then a radically new technology,

Consequently, the issues it raised were relatively minor, as opposed to paradigm shifting. The ambiguity was low.

Subsequently, the cases started getting more complex. With increasing number of actors, new issues started emerging, such as copyright violations, jamming, etc. The earliest set of radio court cases— *M. Witmark & Sons v. L. Bamberger & Co. (1923), Pastime Amusement Co. vs. M. Witmark & Sons (1924),* and *Jerome H. Remick & Co. vs. American Auto Accessories Co. (1925)* —involved copyright infringement and primarily concerned broadcast of music through radio. [8] In all these cases broadcasters contested copyright infringement allegations, arguing that their broadcasts of live concerts were not "for profit" as they did not charge their audiences. Similarly, broadcasters also argued that their broadcasts were not "public" as they were received in the privacy of their audiences' homes. The courts, however, rejected these arguments in favour of the plaintiffs stating there was infringement of music copyrights because a performance by an artist for radio broadcast is "consciously addressing a great, through unseen and widely scattered audience". [9] The second set of early court cases involved re-broadcasting of radio music over closed circuit audio systems in hotels. One early case, *Buck vs. Jewell LaSalle Reality Co.* (1931) is particularly illustrative of this.[10] In this instance too, Justice Brandeis, commenting on the innovative ways in which radio broadcasting technology was being exploited, remarked that, "while this (form of exploitation) may not be possible before the development of radio broadcasting the novelty of the means used does not

---

accepted by consumers and thereby gain a toehold in the marketplace. Aware that interior lighting generated 90% of the revenue of the gas industry, Edison poured his energies into developing a small 16 candle-power electric light (equivalent to the standard gas jet of 1880s) that would be appropriate in doors. In Edison's own words, as he noted in his notebook, "Object. Edison to effect exact imitation of all done by gas so as to replace lighting by gas by lighting by electricity . . . Edison's great effort not to make a large light or a blinding light but a small light having the mildness of gas", H.C. PASSER, *The Electrical Manufacturers 1875-1900*, (1953), p.82.

For a more complete description of how Edison mimicked gas, see H. SAWHNEY and X. WANG, 'Battle of systems: Learning from erstwhile gas-electricity and telegraph-telephone battles', *Prometheus*, 2006, Vol 24, No. 3, pp. 235-256. For a discussion on how Internet phone service providers are piping in fake dial tone to make the new technology feel familiar, see D. LEONHARDT, "A voice in the calling wilderness", *New York Times*, 18th Dec. 2003, p. E1.

[8] J.C. GINSBURG, 'Copyright and control over new technologies of dissemination', *Columbia Law Review*, 2001, Vol. 101, No. 5, p. 1613-1647

[9] Ibid, p.1620

[10] Ibid

lessen the duty of the courts to give full protection to the monopoly of public performance for profit which Congress has secured to the composer". [11]

On parallel lines there was also an increasing realisation that the commerce clause alone was not adequate for regulation of radio since it gave the government ability to only issue licenses to operate but not actually regulate behaviour.

In the beginning radio was regulated on the basis of the Commerce Clause of the Radio Act of 1912. The Department of Commerce argued that since radio waves transcended state boundaries and radio broadcasting was a commercial activity, radio could be regulated on the basis of the commerce clause. Here the analogies were the telegraph and the telephone, where transmission of messages by electronic means had been construed to be interstate commerce.[12] The case of *Whitehurst vs. Grimes* (1927), presents an interesting illustration of the application of the commerce clause to the field of radio communication. The plaintiff operated a radio station in the city of Wilmore in Kentucky, under license from the Secretary of Commerce. The city of Wilmore passed an ordinance requiring all persons operating a radio station to pay a tax to the city and imposed a penalty for failure to do so. In its decision the court held that radio was inherently an interstate commercial activity and hence the ordinance by the city of Wilmore was void given that Congress had placed radio under the purview of the commerce clause. [13]

While the commerce clause became the basic framework for radio regulation, there was increasing uncertainty about its legal basis. For example, in a legal review article, C.K.U (1928) challenged the application of the commerce clause to radio broadcasting.

"Today, however, by far the larger part of radio broadcasting consists of music and other entertainment distinguishable in many respects from the conveyance of commercial messages. The act makes no distinction and its administration has included both types. It would seem that here the arguments in the telegraph and telephone cases, that those companies were "agencies in interstate commerce" or "common carriers of messages" among states, would be scarcely applicable. Indeed, such broadcasting is more like a free band concert on one side of a state line being enjoyed by the public on the other side. If the state in which the

---

[11] Ibid at 1621

[12] C.K.U, 'The radio and interstate commerce', *Michigan Law Review*, 1928, Vol. 26, No.8, p. 919-921.

[13] Ibid

*band was playing undertook to regulate its time and place of playing,
would such state be interfering with interstate commerce"...[ ] "Is a man
who places a large advertising sign on one side of a state border engaged
in interstate commerce because it can be seen across the line? Yet the act
extends its operation to pictures sent through the air by radio".[14]*

At the same time, the advancement of radio and aviation technologies
had started a debate among legal experts who stressed the increasing need
for laws regulating the usage of air space. An interesting point of view
emerged in conferences and publications that the air above an individual's
property must be treated as that individual's property and the government
must make laws that regulate the proper use of air space. With regard to
radio broadcasting, there was increasing consensus among legal experts
for the establishment of a federally controlled radio board for regulating
the radio industry's use of air space. [15]

Nevertheless, the commerce clause continued to be the basis for radio
regulation until two land mark court decisions—*Hoover (Secretary of
Commerce) vs. Intercity Radio Co.* (1923), and *Zenith Radio vs. United
States* (1926), changed it all. In both these instances the Secretary of
Commerce refused to renew broadcast licenses belonging to the plaintiffs
who in turn initiated legal action challenging the legal basis for the denial
of licenses. The courts ruled in favour of the plaintiffs arguing that the
Secretary of Commerce had no discretion to refuse licenses.[16] These
landmark court decisions "totally laid bare the absence of a legal basis"
for regulation of radio broadcasting. [17]

The Radio Act of 1912 was largely conceived to function as a registry
device for issuing licenses to all those who applied for one. However, the
subsequent policies and actions pursued by the Department of Commerce
were both allocative and regulatory in nature. The decision rendered in
these two cases completely annulled the regularly role of the Department
of Commerce by holding that "the Secretary of Commerce had no power
to make regulation and was to issue licenses". [18]

---

[14] Ibid, p. 920-921

[15] Bar Association of Tennessee, 'The Law of the Air', in *Proceedings of the 43rd annual
session of the Bar Association of Tennessee* (1998), Chattanooga, Bar Association of
Tennessee, 1924, p. 190-198.

[16] J.R. MINASIAN, 'The political economy of broadcasting in the 1920's', *Journal of Law
& Economics*, 1969, Vol. 12, No. 2, pp. 391-403.

[17] Y. BENKLER, 'Overcoming an agoraphobia: Building the commons of the digitally
networked environment (wireless telegraph regulation)", *Harvard Journal of Law &
Technology*, 1998, Vol. 11, No. 2, pp. 287-400, at p. 316.

[18] J.R. MINASIAN, above note 14, p.401.

Once the potentiality of broadcasting was fully understood—it raised a whole new set of legal issues. With the court decision in *Zenith Radio vs. United States* rendering the Radio Act of 1912 and the Department of Commerce's legal authority over radio broadcasting virtually ineffective, radio broadcasting between 1926 and early 1927 was characterised by chaos and confusion.[19] Walter S. Gifford, President of Bell Telephone Company, noted "Nobody knew…where radio was really headed. Everything about broadcasting was uncertain". [20] Recognising the fundamental deficiencies of existing regulatory tools, the then Secretary of Commerce convened four annual national radio conferences where he advocated the concept of "public interest" in radio communication. Subsequently, Congress passed the Radio Act of 1927 that led to the establishment of the Federal Radio Commission with broader powers to regulate radio broadcasting. The 1927 Radio Act employed a utility based regulation model under which broadcasters were deemed to be public trustees who were "privileged" to use a scarce public resource.[21]

After the passage of the Radio Act of 1927, a number of court decisions followed that firmly established Public Interest Convenience and Necessity (PICON) as the basis for radio broadcast regulation.[22]

In *Technical Radio Lab vs. Federal Radio Commission* (1929) the court reaffirmed Federal Radio Commission's authority to limit access to airwaves where applicants outnumbered channels available (Le Duc & McCain, 1970). In a similar case *Carrell vs. Federal Radio Commission* (1929), the court affirmed the commission's right to deny licenses to one particular class of operators in order to reduce interference.[23] *Great Lake Broadcasting Co. vs. Federal Radio Commission* (1930) was the next milestone in radio regulation. The case involved a conflict among three Chicago area broadcasters about modification of their technical facilities to minimise interference. In the process of accessing their claims, the court made nature and quality of content and its value to the community the station is serving as a basis for assessing the performance of a station under public interest standard. The Great Lakes Broadcasting decision is

---

[19] Ibid

[20] J. BROOKS, *Telephone: The First Hundred Years* (1976), p.161.

[21] E.G. KRASNOW and J.N. GOODMAN, 'The 'public interest' standard: the search for the Holy Grail', *Federal Communications Law Journal*, 1998, No. 50, No. 3, p. 606-636.

[22] Ibid

[23] D.R. Le DUC and T.A. McCAIN, 'The federal radio commission in federal court: Origins of broadcast regulatory doctrines', *Journal of Broadcasting*, 1970, Vol. 14, No. 4, p. 393-410.

considered significant in the history of radio broadcasting as it set the precedent for content as a criterion for assessing public interest.[24]

II. Lessons for the future

Most new technologies easily get beaded into the ongoing transfer of metaphors from one technology to another. The development of infrastructure networks—electric grids, highway systems, telegraph, railroad, and telecommunications networks—was marked by the transfer of frameworks from one technology to another. As noted earlier, the frameworks developed for the railroads were transferred to subsequent technologies, especially through the Interstate Commerce Act. Later, the deregulation of transportation industries in the 1970s set the stage for the deregulation of the telecommunications industry in the 1980s. [25] More recently, we have been seeing the migration of deregulatory concepts from telephone regulation to electricity regulation, especially with regard to competition in local markets. These transfers tend to occur relatively fluidly because all these infrastructures are point-to-point networks that transport materials and information from one point to another. Metaphor vacuums occur when we are confronted with a radically new technology such as radio.

In this concluding section, using the radio case as a springboard, we conceptualise the processes that lead to the creation of a metaphor vacuum and also its eventual resolution. In specific we focus on: (1) when metaphor vacuums occur, (2) how they are resolved, and (3) how the metaphors used early in the process shape the possibilities down the line.

III. The process leading to the metaphor vacuum

Even in the case of an unprecedented technology like radio, the metaphor vacuum does not occur right after the arrival of the new technology. The reason is that initially the new potentiality of the technology is not fully understood. In the early stages, the new technology is employed in ways that mimic old technologies. In our particular case, the radio was deployed as wireless telegraph. Accordingly, the cases that arise

---

[24] E.G. KRASNOW, and J.N. GOODMAN, above note 19.

[25] B. CHERRY, 'Back to the future: How transportation deregulatory policies foreshadow evolution of communications policies', *The Information Society*, 2008,Vol 24, No. 5, p. 273-291.

at this stage are of a relatively minor nature. As discussed earlier, *Marconi Wireless Telegraph vs. Northern Pacific S.S. Co.* (1918), the first case we found, dealt with a contract dispute between two parties. In general the ambiguity tends to be low in the initial cases because the new technology is used in old and familiar ways.

Later, as usage spreads, trial and error generates insights into new possibilities opened up by the new technology. These opportunities are capitalised on by various interests and the resulting cases are much more complex than the initial ones. Now, the ambiguity is significantly higher because the new usages do not simply mimic the old technologies but open up new and often unprecedented patterns of organisation and behaviour. In the case of radio, we had, on the one hand, the problem of applying old frameworks such as copyright and the commerce clause to a new mode of communication, and, on the other hand, the unprecedented problem of jamming. These complexities are dealt with by stretching the established metaphors and frameworks until a breaking point of sorts is reached which creates a metaphor vacuum or a realisation that we need a radically new framework.

IV. The filling of the metaphor vacuum

When a metaphor vacuum is generated, one would expect that a systematic process for identifying an appropriate metaphor would be in order. One such approach would be what Peirce (1931) calls abduction, wherein metaphors are treated as provisional hypothesis, which are held only as long as the facts permit. The following description of the process by which the researchers deciphered the Egyptian cuneiform descriptions illustrates abduction:

> *"In the first steps that were made toward the reading of the cuneiform inscriptions, it was necessary to take up hypotheses which nobody could have expected would turn out true,—for no hypothesis positively likely to be true could be made. But they had to be provisionally adopted,—yes, and clung to with some degree of tenacity too,—as long as the facts did not absolutely refute them. For that was the system by which in the long run such problems would quickest find their solutions".* [26]

But in reality the process is quite chaotic mainly because it unfolds amidst the cacophony of the political arena, as opposed to the

---

[26] C. PEIRCE, 'Pragmatism and Abduction', p. 112-127 in C. Hartshorne and P. Weiss (eds), *Collected Papers of Charles Sanders Peirce* (Vol. 1, 1931), at 142.

deliberateness of a seminar room discussion. When the two land mark court decisions—*Hoover (Secretary of Commerce) vs. Intercity Radio Co.* (1923), and *Zenith Radio vs. United States*—set aside the commerce clause as the basis for radio regulation, there was need for another legal framework. According to Krasnow and Goodman (1998), the legislators, while deliberating the 1927 Radio Act, were groping for a standard that would spell out the obligations of the licensees. They were looking for something that was concrete enough to provide clarity for current needs and yet flexible enough to accommodate unanticipated uses of the technology in the future. Within this context, a chance conversation between Senator Clarence Dill and a young lawyer on loan from the Interstate Commerce Commission (ICC) provided the solution. The ICC lawyer suggested "public interest, convenience and necessity" (PICON) as a standard and it caught the senator's imagination.[27] Thereby broadcasting ended up with a standard from the world of transportation systems and public utilities.[28] As Le Duc and McCain note, the public interest standard meant "a revolution in practice, at least as to broadcasting ... and with the exception of common carrier or utility matters, the idea of ... public convenience as a condition for entry into interstate commerce was unique in Federal legislation".[29] This choice had its consequences, as discussed later.

It is important to note that PICON did not fill the conceptual vacuum. It filled the metaphor vacuum. This distinction [30] is important in the case of radio because the public policy discourse had started moving towards "public interest" ever since the realisation that the spectrum is limited and that behaviour of a licensee has an impact on those of the others. In fact, as mentioned earlier, the Secretary of Commerce Herbert Hoover himself talked about the public interest in his speeches at the radio conference. Furthermore, it was not entirely a new metaphor since it also came from the railroads framework, which was already being stretched before the metaphor vacuum occurred. But there was a qualitative difference

---

[27] E.G. KRASNOW and J.N. GOODMAN, 'The 'public interest' standard: the search for the Holy Grail', *Federal Communications Law Journal*, 1998, Vol 50, No. 3, p. 606-636.

[28] This notion of trusteeship, unlike the commerce clause, allowed for the regulation of licensee's behaviour because the commission could revoke the license or deny renewal if a licensee was deemed to have violated public trust.

[29] D.R. Le DUC, and T.A. McCAIN, 'The federal radio commission in federal court: Origins of broadcast regulatory doctrines', *Journal of Broadcasting*, 1970, Vol. 14, No.4, p. 393-410, at 396.

[30] As noted, this distinction is important in the case of radio. It does not preclude the fact that a metaphor may also fill in the conceptual vacuum in other contexts.

between the stretching of the railroads framework in the pre and post metaphor vacuum phases. What we call the first order and second order stretching.

In the first-order stretching somewhat forced connections are made between technologies. For instance, radio was linked to railroads via the telegraph and telephone connections. In other words, it would have been difficult to establish a connection between railroads and radio because there is little similarity between them. The telegraph and telephone allowed for the establishment of this connection because they were similar to railroads and also to radio but in different ways. The similarities between railroads and telegraph and telephone networks are rather immediate because they all are composed of nodes and links. On the other hand, the similarities between telegraph and telephone networks and radio rest on the fact they are electronic means of communication. The telegraph and telephone served as intermediaries in linking railroads to radio. This stretched framework functioned as long the new technology was employed in ways that mimicked the old one. The stretching, which was minimal at first, kept widening as new uses of the new technology were found that had no clear analogies in older technologies. Eventually, a breaking point was reached when the old analogs did not work anymore and we had a metaphor vacuum.

In the post-metaphor vacuum phase the breakthrough came with stretching at a higher level, what we call the second-order stretching. In the pre-metaphor vacuum period, the analog at the technology level was the basis for the transfer of legal concepts. In other words, after an analog was established between railroads and radio via the telegraph and telephone connection, concepts employed for regulating railroads could now be transferred to the radio arena. In the second order stretching, there is stretching at the level of the concepts also. For instance, PICON in the realm of railroads meant something quite different from that in the realm of radio. In the realm of railroads, PICON was based on the logic that since the railroads were granted rights of ways they could be asked to undertake activities in public interests. The same logic was easily transferred to the telegraph and telephone because they also relied on rights of ways. But radio did not use rights of ways. Here the stretching occurred at the level of the rationale for PICON. In the case of radio, the basis of PICON was located in the construction that the licensees are trustees of a scarce public resource, spectrum, and their activities impact the overall culture, especially the socialisation of children. Thus the PICON in the radio context was no longer the same as PICON in its original railroad context. The former was a stretched version of the later.

In the case of radio, the metaphor vacuum was filled by the insertion of a new metaphor of sorts, which brought along with it a legal framework. The other possibility would have been a direct examination of the essential features of the new technology and the development of a brand new framework from scratch based on the first principles of law. We did not see the latter approach in the development of radio regulation. With regard to the Internet, Stephanie Gore asks a provocative question: "Why pick an analogy to begin with? ... Why shouldn't courts simply make the effort to understand the technological underpinnings of the Internet and achieve a 'metaphor-free' understanding of the technology?"[31] In fact, in the case of the Internet, where also metaphors based on old technologies have dominated the thinking, we at times see the courts recognise the inadequacies of these metaphors and search for new frameworks. For instance, consider the court's struggle with the applications of libel laws to the Internet Service Providers (ISPs).

In *Stratton Oakmont Inc vs. Prodigy Services Corporation* the plaintiffs sued Prodigy for defamatory statements made by an unidentified user on Prodigy's bulletin board service. In its decision the courts held Prodigy to the strict standards normally applied to original publishers of defamatory statements as opposed to treating them as mere distributors, as argued by Prodigy. The court reasoned that Prodigy acted more as an original publisher than as a distributor when it "advertised its practice of actively screening and editing messages posted on its bulletin boards".[32] In sharp contrast to the above judgment, in another court case, *Zeran vs. America Online,* the court rejected analogies with traditional forms of publication such as print, radio and television and refused to impose either a distributor's or a publisher's liability on an online service provider. In this case, the plaintiff Kenneth M. Zeran ("Zeran") who was the victim of a malicious hoax perpetrated via America Online's (AOL) online bulletin board services sued the company for letting these notices remain posted despite his repeated complaints.[33] Countering this accusation, AOL mounted a defence under section 47 U.S.C. § 230, which prohibits the treatment of an ISP as a "publisher" or a "speaker" and therefore the

---

[31] S. GORE, 'A rose by any other name: Judicial use of metaphors for new technologies', *University of Illinois Journal of Law, Technology, and Policy*, 2003, Vol. 403, pp. 425-431, at p.415.

[32] See Stratton Oakmont, Inc. vs. Prodigy Services Co., 1995 WL 323710 (N.Y. Sup. Ct. 1995)

[33] Zeran v. America online Inc, 129 F.3d at 327, 333 US court of Appeals 4th Cir (1997)

imposition of publisher liability in online defamation cases.[34] In order to go around these section 47 U.S.C. § 230 arguments, Zeran sued AOL as a "distributor" rather than as a publisher.[35] Thus the question before the court in this case was whether to treat AOL as a publisher or a distributor of libellous material. Ruling against the plaintiff, the court said:

> [...] "If computer service providers were subject to distributor liability, they would face potential liability each time they receive notice of a potentially defamatory statement - - from any party, concerning any message. Each notification would require a careful yet rapid investigation of the circumstances surrounding the posted information, a legal judgment concerning the information's defamatory character, and an on- the- spot editorial decision whether to risk liability by allowing the continued publication of that information. Although this might be feasible for the traditional print publisher, the sheer number of postings on interactive computer services would create an impossible burden in the Internet context [...].Thus, like strict liability, liability upon notice has a chilling effect on the freedom of Internet speech".[36]

Here we see the courts embrace the metaphors based on old technologies in one case involving libel laws and ISPs and reject the same metaphors in another case. We see similar back and forth movements in other areas of Internet law. Gore (2003) charts such movements in cases involving jurisprudence of jurisdiction. She notes that in Maritz, Inc. v. Cybergold the court concluded that "because the internet is an entirely new means of information exchange, analogies to cases involving the use of mail and telephone are less than satisfactory"[37] There is similar divergence of court opinions in cases involving the application of the Single Publication Rule to libel cases on Internet based publications.

Like the radio, much of Internet regulation is based on frameworks from old technologies. The difference is in the cases noted above where the courts rejected parallels with old technologies, something we did not see in the case of radio. Perhaps it was because the radio introduced only

---

[34] Zeran v. America online Inc, 129 F.3d at 327, 333 US court of Appeals 4th Cir (1997)

[35] This is possible because under common tort law a publisher can be held liable for defamatory statements contained in the works they distribute if they have actual knowledge of the defamatory materials. Given that Zeran had given sufficient notice to AOL about the defamatory statements, he argued that AOL must be held liable as a distributor.

[36] Zeran v. America online Inc, 129 F.3d at 327, 333 US court of Appeals 4th Cir (1997), at 333.

[37] Ibid, at p.18

one radically new configurational potentiality[38]—point to multipoint communication or broadcasting. This new configurational potentiality could be accommodated by a second-order stretch, PICON. What makes the Internet peculiarly different from radio and also other technologies is that it supports not just one radically new configurational potentiality but numerous configuration potentialities, including many that were difficult to imagine a just few years ago. Furthermore, many more radically new configurational potentialities are likely to surprise us in the future. This rapid succession of new developments creates constant strain on the existing frameworks and the courts are often frustrated enough with old metaphors to abandon them. However, they have not yet been able to generate major conceptual breakthroughs that could provide a basis for the development of new frameworks. The establishment of special courts for high-tech cases, as recommended by the Maryland Task Force, would perhaps facilitate direct examination of new technologies. The specially trained judges, with command over technical issues, would be less likely to take refuge in simplifying but inadequate metaphors and make an extra effort to understand the new technology on its own terms.[39]

The suggestion of PICON as a standard was only half the story. Its

---

[38] In H. SAWHNEY and S. LEE, 'Arenas of innovation: Understanding new configurational potentialities of communication technologies', *Media, Culture & Society*, 2005, Vol 27, No.3, p. 391-414, the authors develop this concept based on Cherry's notion of "new liberty of action." While Cherry did not explicitly define the term, he illustrated it with the example of a telephone exchange. According to him, the new liberty of action made possible by the telephone exchange was the "choice of social contacts on demand" (C. CHERRY, 'The Telephone System: Creator of Mobility and Social Change', p. 112-126 in I. POOL (ed.), *The Social Impact of the Telephone*, Cambridge, MA: The MIT Press, [1977], p. 114). In other words, for the first time in human history, the telephone exchange offered random access to subscribers dispersed across space. This new technological capability enabled the emergence of new institutional forms that changed how our society is organised. Sawhney and Lee's reasons for using "new configurational potentialities" instead of "new liberties of action" were twofold. One, the word "liberties" in "liberties of action" generated confusion because of its political overtones. The readers were prompted to see a political dimension in the concept. For example, one reader thought "new liberties" meant empowerment of disenfranchised populations via communication technology. On the contrary, the concept is limited to purely mechanical aspects of how communications channels are configured in a new communications system, point-to-multipoint communication in the case of broadcasting. The new term "new configurational potentialities" avoids this confusion. Two, Cherry's conceptualisation was limited to features intrinsic to the very nature of a technology. Internet, however, is a multi-modal platform on which myriad configurations, some quite surprising as that of Napster, can be realised. The term "new configurational potentialities" brings forth this broader understanding of the phenomenon.

[39] S. GORE, above note 31.

ready acceptance by the policy makers and the courts is the really critical part. According to Levi (1948), legal process is the application of a "system of rules," rather than a "known rule," to diverse facts. Levi notes that, "the rules are discovered in the process of determining similarity or difference. However when attention is directed towards finding of similarities and differences, other peculiarities appear. The problem for the law is: when will it be just to treat different cases as though they were the same?"[40] Therefore a working legal system should be capable of "picking out (intrinsic) similarities and to reason to the justice of applying a common classification".[41]

The reasoning process using metaphors tends to make similarity a pivotal concept in explanations. However, similarities do not always make analogical reasoning rationally compelling,[42] and legal justifications must be rationally compelling.[43] Therefore in instances where metaphors based on older technologies are invoked or when metaphors from dissimilar technologies are stretched and applied to create regulatory frameworks for new technologies or a brand new metaphor is generated, this process is likely to succeed under one important condition. That when rationally compelling arguments can be made and such reasoning relies on seemingly not obvious but intrinsically essential relatedness rather than extrinsically obvious but less essential similarities. In addition such rationally compelling arguments based on metaphors find legitimacy and validity and gain precedence over other arguments when they fit into the existing economic, legal, and regulatory frameworks that have gained legitimacy in the legal system. PICON was readily accepted because it met these conditions, especially those about legitimacy.

Wasserstrom (1961) suggests that when making legal reasoning, we should be careful about dividing reasoning into the "logic of discovery" and the "logic of justification". [44] While logic of discovery is concerned with insightfulness that can help to find logical connectedness between the two

---

[40] H. LEVI, Edward, *An introduction to legal reasoning* (1949), quoted in D. HUNTER, 'Reason is too large: Analogy and precedent in law', *Emory Law Journal*, 2001, No 50, pp. 1197-1243, at p.1252.

[41] Ibid at p. 1252-1253

[42] S. BREWER, 'Exemplary reasoning semantics, pragmatics and the rational force of legal argument by analogy', *Harvard Law Review*, 1996, Vol 109, No 5, pp. 923-1028.

[43] D. HUNTER, 'Reason is too large: Analogy and precedent in law', *Emory Law Journal*, 2001, No 50, p. 1197-1243.

[44] R.A. WASSERSTROM, 'The Judicial Decision –Towards a theory of legal justification' (1961), quoted in D. HUNTER, 'Reason is too large: Analogy and precedent in law', *Emory Law Journal*, 2001, No 50, pp. 1197-1243, at p. 1249.

cases, the logic of justification is concerned with whether the reasoning connecting the two is morally justifiable, that is, whether it can have legally compelling justification. In the process of establishing radio regulation systems based on public interest standards, we can say, what the courts did was to make serial attempts to find the logic of justification, whereas what the Congress did was to an attempt to make an insightful discovery, which can be morally justified rather easily in the judicial arena.

V. The impact of metaphors used early in the process

The radio case alerts us to the strong likelihood that the metaphors used in the early stages of the development of a new technology may not prove to be appropriate over the long run and when the new technology is more developed there may be a need for new metaphors. In the legal context, this could become a sticky problem because precedents set by initial metaphors could make change later on difficult. This problem did not occur in the case of broadcasting where initial metaphors were not an impediment for the adoption of PICON. However, the broadcasting case still demonstrates the stickiness of a metaphor once it is deployed. When Congress considered the 1927 Radio Act, the primary imagery the legislators had for broadcasting was that of airwaves as critical resources like a "public utility," such "electricity or water pipe lines". [45] Accordingly, they focused on the optimal use of a valuable public resource that could be degraded by interference absent appropriate regulation. This conception of broadcasting pushed radio into the public utilities framework, even though the legislators were aware that they were dealing with a form of speech. On the other hand, if the focus had been on speech, they would have had to treat radio as press, with all its first amendment protections, and not a public utility. Therefore, by treating radio as an electrical carrier like telegraph and telephone, they ended up regulating free speech.[46] Later, when the broadcasting aspect of radio became dominant in the 1920s, "the sensitivity of the Supreme Court to the First Amendment" arose. [47] Yet, Congress could go ahead and regulate radio speech without getting stuck in First Amendment litigation because it could point to the special characteristics of radio, especially the fact that

---

[45] C. McLAREN, 'A brief history of the public interest standard', 2005, www.stayfreemagazine.org/ml/readings/public_interest.pdf.

[46] I.D.S. POOL, *Technologies of freedom* (1983).

[47] Ibid at p. 232.

it could influence citizens' children in their own homes. Thus the use of the public utilities framework stymied the subsequent full adoption of the framework traditionally applied to the press.

The impact of the initial metaphor was much stronger in the case of a related technology—cable. It started as rural extensions of TV wherein a local entrepreneur set up an antenna on a mountain top to catch the broadcast signal from a nearby city and then channelled it via coaxial cable to subscribing homes whose direct reception was blocked by the mountain. Since cable was an appendage to broadcasting, at that stage of its development, the policy makers viewed it via the broadcasting framework. Later, after the microwave and satellites links interconnected local cable systems into national networks, cable was transformed into a competing system, as opposed to a mere appendage. Now, in its fully developed form, it seemed to many observers that cable should be regulated as a common carrier and not as a broadcaster.[48] The critical difference would be in the control of the delivery system and control of content. Under the broadcasting regime, a cable operator controlled both the wires and the content that was delivered over them. The common carrier regime would require a separation, i.e. cable operator would have no control over the cable networks (e.g. HBO, CNN, etc) the system carried. The cable operator would lease out bandwidth to other entities that would provide the programming. While the common carrier model has its merits and is worth considering, the changeover was no longer practically feasible because by now cable was deeply entrenched within the broadcasting framework. This is not an isolated case because there is a history of new technologies starting off as appendages of the established systems and in unanticipated ways developing into competing systems. [49]

In this paper we offer the above thoughts based on the analysis of a single-case—radio. Quite clearly that it is an insufficient basis for generalisation. But we do hope that we offer a useful starting point. Perhaps the insights offered here will trigger in the readers' minds

---

[48] Ibid at 32; M.O. WIRTH, 'Should cable television be regulated as a common carrier?', Paper presented at the Law and Economics Division of the Law and Society Association Annual Meeting, Denver, Colorado, 1983.

[49] For other such cases, see H. SAWHNEY, 'Public telephone network: Stages in infrastructure development', *Telecommunications Policy*, 1992, No16, pp. 538-552; H. SAWHNEY, 'Wi-Fi networks and the rerun of the cycle', *Info: The journal of policy, regulation and strategy for telecommunications, information and media*, 2003 Vol 5, No.6, pp. 25-33; H. SAWHNEY, 'Wi-Fi networks and the reorganization of wireline-wireless relationship', pp. 45-61, In R. Ling and P. Pedersen (eds.), *Mobile Communications: Re-negotiation of the Social Sphere*, London (2005).

connections with other cases and thereby get the proverbial snowball rolling. While our specific observations need further testing with other cases, we can quite confidently say that one of the reasons the process proceeds in the way described above is that the metaphors focus our attention on the similarities, a tendency that is reinforced by the legal process that seeks precedents and coherence. Conversely, the peculiarities of the new technology are overlooked. But it is in the peculiarities we get glimpses of the future possibilities opened up by the new technology. In effect, it is the peculiarities that eventually bring about a metaphor vacuum. It therefore behoves us to remain alert to the peculiarities even when we continue to employ metaphors based on old technologies because of the lack of any other device.

Cybercrime, Cyberterrorism and Jurisdiction. An Analysis of Article 22 of the COE Convention on Cybercrime

Armando A. Cottim[1]

Part I of this paper deals directly with the interpretation of article 22 of the Council of Europe's Convention on Cybercrime (2001 Budapest Convention). First, we include a brief note on the jurisdiction theories applied by courts and governments, followed by a discussion of the theories that became positive law when they were laid down in article 22. After that, we proceed with a study of the non-application clause, the aut dedere aut judicare principle, the applicability of national penal jurisdictions and positive jurisdiction conflicts, laid down in paragraphs 2 to 5 of the article sub judice.

Part II starts by discussing some cybercrime cases that present jurisdiction issues, also dealing with controlling law and international cooperation. Cases like the French court's injunction for Yahoo to ban French cybernauts from accessing Nazi memorabilia, the intrusion by two hackers in the Rome Air Development Center's network, or the conviction of Russian citizen Vasiliy Gorshkov by a court of the United States for intrusion and theft of credit card information in North American computers raise questions regarding international cooperation that are not dealt with by the Convention in a way that is totally satisfactory.

After presenting some proposals regarding a solution of these problems, the text goes on to discuss the possible threat represented by cyberterrorism and makes some remarks concerning the applicability of the Convention in cyberterrorism cases.

The concluding remarks include a brief personal statement on the inclusion of terrorism in the list of crimes against humanity and refer the inexplicable delay that major Council of Europe members are having in ratifying the Convention. The author hopes they don't do it too late.

---

[1] The author has a 5-year law degree achieved at the Lisbon University, Lisbon, Portugal, and was awarded a Master's degree in International Law, by the same University, with a dissertation on Terrorism at Sea in International Law. Being a scuba diving instructor, a musician, a computer programmer and a certified network engineer, his interests float between music, sea and cyberspace. Comments are welcome and can be sent to his email address (armando@cottim.net).

Introduction

Ever since Cain and Abel, crime is a "known known" to human kind. Modern criminal codes have dealt quite well with crime within territorial boundaries and even, sometimes, outside those boundaries, by applying themselves to crimes committed by nationals abroad. Criminal law has then been almost purely domestic, with external threats to the public order of States being dealt with by the military.

Yet, the revolution in information technologies has changed society to a point where advances in programming artificial intelligence software and in the processing capacity of desktop and/or laptop computers are leading society to a time when a cyberbot will be impossible (or at least very difficult) to distinguish from a human person.[2]

And the advent of cyberspace has changed the established criminal law model. Online crime happens without boundaries, as attacks can come from outside the borders of one State, thus scattering crime scenes through two or more countries, sometimes in more than one continent.[3]

Solutions to the problems posed must be addressed by international law, through the adoption of adequate international legal instruments.[4] The Convention on Cybercrime, opened for signature in Budapest, November 23, 2001 and entered into force in 2004,[5] aimed to meet this challenge – respecting human rights – in the new reality we now call Information Society.

However, although jurisdiction issues were addressed by the Convention on Cybercrime, some weaknesses prevent this Convention from being more effective in making international cooperation the

---

[2] Thus, J. J. STANTON, "Terror in Cyberspace. Terrorists Will Exploit and Widen the Gap between Governing Structures and the Public", in *American Behavioral Scientist*, vol. 45 (2000), p. 1022.

[3] Conveying a similar idea, S. W. BRENNER and J. J. SCHWERHA IV, "Cybercrime Havens: Challenges and Solutions", *Business Law Today*, vol. 17 (November/December, 2007), p. 49.

[4] For a thorough study of the relationship between international conventions and international customary law, with special interest in *ius cogens* rules, see E. C. BAPTISTA, *Ius Cogens em Direito Internacional*, Lisboa, Lex, 1977, pp. 491 *et passim*.

[5] In accordance with article 36, paragraph 3 of the Convention on Cybercrime, after Albania (signed: November 23, 2001, ratified: June 20, 2002), Croatia (signed: November 23, 2001, ratified: October 17, 2002), Estonia (signed: November 23,/2001, ratified: May 12, 2003), Hungary (signed: November 23,/2001, ratified: December 4, 2003), and Lithuania (signed: 23/6/2003, ratified: March 18, 2004), all members of the Council of Europe, have expressed their consent to be bound by the Convention. For a list of the States that signed and ratified the Convention, see "Convention on Cybercrime. CETS No.: 185", online at http://conventions.coe.int.

solution for cybercrime. As an additional problem, cyberterrorism also became a hazard the international community has to deal with.

Even if it seems to be a real threat,[6] cyberterrorism is a scare word that plays with the fear of two generally known unknowns – terrorism and technology[7] – and discussions rage the international *fora* dealing with terrorism, crime and cybercrime as to the reality of this threat.

Our initial concern will therefore be the analysis of article 22 of the Convention on Cybercrime, first discussing general jurisdiction theories and then the theories applied by the Convention, together with other issues dealt with in the article. Then, a discussion of several cases dealing with jurisdiction, international cooperation and cybercrime will take us to some reflection on cyberterrorism and the applicability of the jurisdiction rules of the Convention on Cybercrime in cyberterrorism cases.

I. Article 22. The Analysis

A. JURISDICTION THEORIES

No less than five different jurisdiction theories have been applied altogether by courts and governments, all leading to the ascribing of jurisdiction to one court and adversely affecting other courts' jurisdiction.

1. Territoriality theory

The theory that jurisdiction is determined by the place where the offence is committed, in whole or in part ("territoriality theory"), derives from the Westphalian[8] model of sovereignty, which is said to include

---

[6] For an examination of the use of the Internet by terrorists, extremists and activists, see K. CRILLEY, "Information warfare: new battlefields, Terrorists, propaganda and the Internet?" in Alan O'Day (ed.), *Cyberterrorism*, Aldershot, Ashgate Publishing Limited, 2004, pp. 67-74. For a discussion of the widespread use of information technology by terrorist-type organizations in recent years, for propaganda, fundraising, information dissemination and secure communications, see S. M. FURNELL and M. J. WARREN, "Computer Hacking and Cyber Terrorism: The Real Threats in the New Millennium?" in Alan O'Day (ed.), *Cyberterrorism*, pp. 113-115.

[7] See A. EMBAR-SEDDON, "Cyberterrorism: Are We Under Siege?" in Alan O'Day (ed.), *Cyberterrorism*, p. 11.

[8] On the Westphalia treaties, see C. HARDING and C. L. LIM, "The Significance of Westphalia: An Archaeology of the International Legal Order", in Christopher Harding and C. L. Lim (eds), *Renegotiating Westphalia: Essays and Commentary on the European*

three fundamental principles: ① exclusive control over the nation's territory, ② non-interference, and ③ equality between States.[9] Although discussed and opposed,[10] the model seems to have, at least, a general acceptance in what concerns these principles, even if the equality between the States is most of the times only formal.[11]

Given that the State has sovereignty over the territory, it will obviously have jurisdiction over any misconduct which occurs in that territory,[12] whether perpetrated or not by one of its nationals.[13]

A complex case of application of the territoriality theory is *Bavaria v. Somm*, tried at the *Amtsgericht* of Munich, Germany, in 1999. As Managing Director of CompuServe Information Services GmbH, Felix Bruno Somm, a citizen from Switzerland, was charged in Germany with

---

and Conceptual Foundations of Modern International Law, The Hague / Boston / London, Martinus Nijhoff Publishers, 1999, pp. 1-23.

For a vision on the centrality of the concept of sovereignty derived from Westphalia and the various international relations theories (Marxism excepted), see S. D. KRASNER, *Sovereignty: Organized Hypocrisy*, New Jersey, Princeton University Press, 1999, pp. 44-46.

[9] Thus, J. FITZPATRICK, "Sovereignty, Territoriality, and the Rule of Law", *Hastings International and Comparative Law Review*, vol. 25 (2002), pp. 304,310. S. BROWN, *International Relations in a Changing Global System: Toward a Theory of the World Polity*, Boulder, Colorado, Westview Press, 1992, p. 74, however, refers only two principles: one according to which a State is "unequivocally sovereign within its territorial jurisdiction", and the principle of non-interference.

[10] C. C. JOYNER and W. P. ROTHBAUM, "Libya and the Aerial Incident at Lockerbie: What Lessons for International Extradition Law?", *Michigan Journal of International Law*, vol. 14 (Winter, 1993), pp. 256, 257, refer that "the Westphalian concept of absolute State sovereignty is undergoing challenge from the community conception espoused by the U.N. Charter", and S. BEAULAC, *The Power of Language in the Making of International Law: The Word Sovereignty in Bodin and Vattel and the Myth of Westphalia*, Leiden / Boston, Martinus Nijhoff Publishers, 2004, pp. 71 *et passim*, considers the Westphalian system as a myth, given the centralizing relevance of the sovereignty concept in Bodin and the externalization of authority that Vattel sees in the concept.

[11] Thus, F. F. DE ALMEIDA, *Direito Internacional Público*, 2ª ed., Coimbra, Coimbra Editora, 2003, p. 15.

[12] Thus, F. ANTOLISEI, *Manuale di Diritto Penale. Parte Generale*, 15ª ed., Milano, Dott. A. Giuffrè Editore, 2000, p. 118.

[13] A comparative study of several penal codes in Europe shows that all consecrate the principle of territoriality. Thus, article 6 of the Italian *Codice Penal* states that "Chiunque commette un reato nel territorio dello Stato è punito secondo la legge italiana." Following the same path, article 113-2 of the French *Code Pénal* states: "La loi pénale française est applicable aux infractions commises sur le territoire de la République", section 3 of the German *Strafgesetzbuch* states "[d]as deutsche Strafrecht gilt für Taten, die im Inland begangen werden" and article 4 of the Portuguese *Código Penal* states that "[s]alvo tratado ou convenção internacional em contrário, a lei penal portuguesa é aplicável a factos praticados em território português, seja qual for a nacionalidade do agente."

being responsible for the access – in Germany – to violent, child, and animal pornographic representations stored on the CompuServe's server placed in the USA.[14] The court considered it had jurisdiction over Mr. Somm because, even though he was Swiss, he lived in Germany.[15]

2. Nationality theory

The "nationality theory" is also called "active personality theory" because it deals primarily with the nationality of the person who committed the offence.[16] Being widely recognised that a country has almost unlimited control over its nationals,[17] said country is considered to have the right to exercise jurisdiction over those individuals, wherever they are and whatever they do.[18] Wherever the offence is committed – at home or abroad – the offender probably has better knowledge of the laws of his own State than of the laws of the other State. Also, an act can be considered legal in the territory where it was committed, whereas it can be considered a crime in the person's homeland.[19]

The case *United States v. Galaxy Sports* seems to be a good example[20]

---

[14] *People v. Somm*, Case 8340 Ds 465 Js 173158/95 (Amtsgericht, München, Bavaria, 1999). See, also, T. STADLER, *Der Fall Somm (CompuServe)*, online in http://www.afs-rechtsanwaelte.de/urteile/artikel06-somm-compuserve1.php, last visited September 2, 2008.

[15] Mr. Somm was sentenced to an overall term of imprisonment of 2 years (paragraph II of the sentence), even if the following paragraph of the sentence suspended (*ausgesetzt*) it's execution on probation.

[16] Thus, C. L. BLAKESLEY, "Jurisdictional Issues and Conflicts of Jurisdiction", *in* M. Cherif Bassiouni (ed.), *Legal Responses to International Terrorism. U.S. Procedural Aspects*, Dordrecht, Martinus Nijhoff Publishers, 1988, p. 139.

[17] Thus, R. AUGUST, "International Cyber-Jurisdiction: A Comparative Analysis", *American Business Law Journal*, vol. 39 (Summer, 2002), p. 539.

[18] This statement is not supposed to be understood in an active, dictatorial sense (where the State controls every aspect of the citizens' life), but in a passive, securitarian sense (where the State has the responsibility to protect society against criminal behaviour).

[19] The European penal codes mentioned above considerer themselves as having jurisdiction with regard to certain actions committed abroad by nationals. Thus, article 9 of the Italian *Codice Penale*, article 113-6 of the French *Code Pénal*, section 5 of the German *Strafgesetzbuch* and article 5 of the Portuguese *Código Penal*.

[20] The sentencing of Robert Matthew Bentley, a citizen of the USA, to 41 months in prison, followed by three years supervised release, together with a restitution of $65,000, by the federal grand jury in Pensacola, Florida, USA, presided by United States District Judge Richard Smoak, in November 2007, for crimes committed in Europe through the Internet, seems to be another good example of application of the nationality theory for jurisdiction assumption. See UNITED STATES ATTORNEY'S OFFICE, NORTHERN DISTRICT OF

of the application of this theory.[21] World Sports Exchange, together with its President Jay Cohen, was one of the defendants. The company targeted customers in the United States, advertising its business all over America by radio, newspaper, and television. Its advertisements invited clientele to bet with the company either by toll-free telephone or through the Internet. [22] Because the company was Antigua-based, the court was unable to assert jurisdiction over it. It's President, however, was a citizen of the USA and could, therefore, be taken to court. Mr. Cohen was – on August 10, 2000, after a jury trial presided by Judge Thomas P. Griesa – sentenced to a term of twenty-one months' imprisonment.[23] Dealing with the appeal to this sentence, the Second Circuit Court of Appeals affirmed the judgment of the district court without even discussing the assumption of jurisdiction.[24]

3. Passive personality theory

While the "nationality theory" deals with the nationality of the offender, assigning jurisdiction to his/her homeland courts, its opposite – the "passive personality theory" – is concerned with the nationality of the victim. [25] The reasons for ascertaining jurisdiction over an offence are similar for both – the almost unlimited control over a country's nationals – but are now seen from the opposite point of view. Thus, when we follow

---

FLORIDA, "International Computer 'Hacker' Sentenced to More Than Three Years in Federal Prison", online at http://www.usdoj.gov/criminal/cybercrime/bentleySent.pdf, last visited September 2, 2008.

[21] This case was the first U.S. federal action against operators of offshore companies using Web sites to facilitate illegal gambling. The complaint names six companies, one of which is Antigua-based World Sports Exchange. For a short description of the case, see *United States v. Galaxy Sports*, Digestible Law. Perkins Coie's Internet Case Digest, online at http://www.digestiblelaw.com/gambling/logQ.aspx?entry=2305&id=16, last visited September 2, 2008.

[22] For a short description of the company's activity, see *USA v. Cohen*, Second Circuit Court of Appeals, online at http://caselaw.lp.findlaw.com/scripts/getcase.pl?court=2nd&navby=docket&no=001574, last visited September 2, 2008.

[23] Of which he seems to have served 17 months. See B. KELLEY, "Crystalball.Gov: Predicting Cyber Policy in 2008", *Journal of Internet Law*, vol. 11 (March, 2008), p. 21.

[24] See *USA v. Cohen*, Second Circuit Court of Appeals, online, quoted. For a short description of the consequences derived from Mr. Cohen's conviction, see K. B. CODD, "Betting On The Wrong Horse: The Detrimental Effect of Noncompliance in the Internet Gambling Dispute on the General Agreement on Trade in Services (GATS)", *William and Mary Law Review*, vol. 49 (December, 2007), pp. 946 *et passim*.

[25] Thus, C. L. BLAKESLEY, "Jurisdictional Issues and Conflicts of Jurisdiction", p. 139.

this theory, the courts of the State to which the victim belongs assume jurisdiction. [26,27]

Good examples of this assumption are the interception of the Egyptian plane that carried the *Achille Lauro* perpetrators by USA planes,[28] and the dispute between the USA and Italy regarding their judgment,[29] together with the several cases presented by the family of Mr. Leon Klinghoffer in North American courts against the Palestinian Liberation Organization, the Lauro company, ABC Tours, Chandris, Inc. (the company that chartered the boat) and the Port of Genoa, Italy.[30]

In the field of cybercriminology, a fine example of jurisdiction assumption by application of the passive personality theory is the sentencing, on July 25, 2003, at the federal courthouse in Hartford, Connecticut, USA, by United States District Judge Alvin W. Thompson, of the Russian citizen Alexey Ivanov, who lived in Chelyabinsk, Russia, for hacking into computers in the United States.[31,32]

4. Protective theory

The "protective theory" (also called "security principle" and "injured

---

[26] Thus, J. FITZPATRICK, "Sovereignty, Territoriality, and the Rule of Law", *Hastings International and Comparative Law Review*, vol. 25 (2002), p. 313, note 37.

[27] Article 10 of the Italian *Codice Penale*, article 113-7 of the French *Code Pénal*, Section 7 of the German *Strafgesetzbuch* and article 5 of the Portuguese *Código Penal* apply the respective national criminal law to acts against the nationals of these countries.

[28] For a careful description of the facts, see A. CASSESE, *Terrorism, Politics and Law: The Achille Lauro Affair*, Cambridge, Polity Press, 1989, pp. 31-43.

[29] For all matters dealing with the interception and subsequent reactions, see G. V. GOODING, "Fighting Terrorism in the 1980's: The Interception of the Achille Lauro Hijackers", *Yale Journal of International Law*, vol. 12 (1987), pp. 158-161.

[30] For a description of the civil suits arising out of the *Achille Lauro* incident, see D. C. ALEXANDER, "Maritime Terrorism And Legal Responses", *Transportation Law Journal*, vol. 82 (1991), pp. *467 et passim*.

[31] *U.S.A. v. Ivanov* (2003), 172 C.C.C. (3d) 551 (Nfld.C.A.). See also U.S. DEPARTMENT OF JUSTICE. UNITED STATES ATTORNEY, "Russian Man Sentenced for Hacking into Computers in the United States", online at http://www.usdoj.gov/criminal/cybercrime/ivanovSent.htm, last visited September 2, 2008.

[32] Another example is the sentencing – in the federal court of Manhattan, Southern District of New York – of the Kazakhstan citizen Oleg Zezev to 51 months in prison, for extortion and computer hacking charges, due to facts that occurred while he was still living in Almaty, Kazakhstan. See U.S. DEPARTMENT OF JUSTICE. UNITED STATES ATTORNEY, "Kazakhstan Hacker Sentenced to Four Years Prison for Breaking into Bloomberg Systems and Attempting Extortion", http://www.usdoj.gov/criminal/cybercrime/zezevSent.htm, last visited September 2, 2008.

forum theory") is probably the least used – if ever – of the theories that sanction jurisdiction. Dealing with the national or international interest injured, this theory permits the assignment of jurisdiction to the State that sees its interest – whether national or international – in jeopardy because of an offensive action.[33] In any case, there seems to be a general trend for penal laws to include this theory,[34] sometimes restricting the application to certain crimes, like counterfeiting of money and securities.

5. Universality theory

Finally, the "universality theory" is based on the international character of the offence and, contrary to the other theories, allows every State the claim of jurisdiction over offences, even if those offences have no direct effect on the asserting State, [35] therefore demanding no nexus between the State assuming jurisdiction and the offence itself.

Two requirements are necessary for assuming jurisdiction: ① the State assuming jurisdiction must have the defendant in custody,[36] and ② the crime must be especially offensive to the international community.[37] Thus, the first crime to be considered for universal jurisdiction was piracy,

---

[33] Thus, C. L. BLAKESLEY, "Jurisdictional Issues and Conflicts of Jurisdiction", p. 139.

[34] See *Codice Penale* article 7, *Code Pénal* article 113-10, *Strafgesetzbuch* section 6, and *Código Penal* article 5, number 1, *littera* a) (which specifically deals, *inter alia*, with computer crime).

[35] Thus, C. L. BLAKESLEY, "Jurisdictional Issues and Conflicts of Jurisdiction", p. 141.

[36] Questionable means (like abduction) may sometimes have been employed for this. The assumption of jurisdiction over what was (wrongly) considered as piracy led to a questionable action of the USA navy fighters over the commercial plane taking the *Achille Lauro* terrorists from Egypt, after the release of the ship. The Egyptian plane was diverted to a NATO base in Italy. What having the defendant in custody often requires is international cooperation. So, M. C. BASSIOUNI, "Policy Considerations on Inter-State Cooperation in Criminal Matters", *Pace Yearbook of International Law*, vol. 4 (1992), pp. 126-128. Thus, *v.g.* in the case of Oleg Zezev, Mr. Zezev was called for a meeting in the U.K. and the British police seized him after he recognized the facts of his crime in the presence of a disguised British police officer.

[37] Thus, M. C. BASSIOUNI, *Crimes against Humanity in International Criminal Law*, Dordrecht, Martinus Nijhoff Publishers, 1992, pp. 511-513. Mr. Bassiouni also refers that, in the Middle Ages, some cities in Northern Italy would seize and/or persecute certain types of criminals (those they called *banditi*, *vagabundi* and *assassin*) when they were under their jurisdiction, even if the crime was committed elsewhere, therefore applying the principle of universal jurisdiction for specific crime types. M. C. BASSIOUNI, *Crimes against Humanity in International Criminal Law*, p. 513.

followed by slave traffic.[38]

After WW II, war crimes, crimes against humanity, certain terrorist acts, hijacking and sabotage of planes, apartheid, torture and other violations of human rights progressively became subject to universal jurisdiction.[39]

B. JURISDICTION THEORIES APPLIED BY THE CONVENTION

An analysis of the several *litterae* of paragraph 1 of article 22 of the 2001 Budapest Convention on Cybercrime (hereafter "the Convention") shows that the Convention relies exclusively on the territoriality and nationality theories to empower parties to establish jurisdiction.

According to *litterae a* to *c*, any offence established under articles 2 through 11 of the Convention that has occurred in the territory of one Party, in a ship flying its flag or in an aircraft registered under its laws, is to be prosecuted in that State.[40] A Party is, therefore, asked by the

---

[38] Thus, *inter alia*, K. C. RANDALL, "Universal Jurisdiction under International Law", *Texas Law Review*, vol. 66 (March, 1988), p. 788.

[39] Thus, E. S. KOBRICK, "The Ex Post Facto Prohibition and the Exercise of Universal Jurisdiction over International Crimes", *Columbia Law Review*, vol. 87 (November, 1987), pp. 1523, 1524. This idea is shared by T. H. SPONSLER, "The Universality Principle of Jurisdiction and the Threatened Trials of American Airmen", *Loyola Law Review*, vol. 15 (1969), p. 49, who mentions the Nuremberg and Tokyo trials, after the end of WW II, as the concept's expansion moment.

J. D. FRY, "Terrorism as a Crime against Humanity and Genocide: The Backdoor to Universal Jurisdiction", *UCLA Journal of International Law and Foreign Affairs*, vol. 7 (2002), p. 176, refers that the UN General Assembly codified the universality principle, applied in Nuremberg, to war crimes, crimes against humanity and aggression crimes.

The Geneva Conventions of 1949 codified the universality principle in relation to war crimes. The 1948 Genocide Convention did not apply universal jurisdiction to genocide because France, the Soviet Union and the USA opposed, but many courts applied the principle to genocide, considering this should be considered customary international law. Thus, K. C. RANDALL, "Universal Jurisdiction under International Law", p. 789.

On the other hand, J. I. CHARNEY, "Progress In International Criminal Law?", *American Journal of International Law*, vol. 93 (April, 1999), p. 454, considers that the international illegality of acts such as genocide, crimes against humanity, war crimes and similar will be reinforced as a result of the statute of the International Criminal Court, showing these acts were seen as international crime before that moment.

According to J. D. FRY, "Terrorism as a Crime against Humanity and Genocide", p. 176, the principle of universality has been expanded, since de 1940s, to include torture, slave traffic and drug traffic.

[40] The fact that a Council of Europe-sponsored Convention follows this path is not surprising, given that, traditionally, the European Court of Human Rights defends an essentially territorial notion of jurisdiction. Thus, *inter alia*, *Öcalan v. Turkey* (Application no. 46221/99), Judgment, 12 March 2003, paragraph 93, and the decision of

Convention to assert territorial jurisdiction if both the person attacking a computer system and the attacked system are located within its territory. The same would be true when the attacked computer system is within a Party's territory, even if the attacker is in another country.

Litterae b and *c* specifically require each Party to establish criminal jurisdiction over offences committed on board of ships flying its flag or aircraft registered under its laws. Already implemented in the laws of many States,[41] this type of jurisdiction assumption is most useful where the ship or aircraft is not located in the Party's territory (or territorial waters/pace) at the time of the commission of the crime.

Then, according to *littera d*, when one national of one State Party commits one of the Convention-laid down offences in another State, the State of nationality of the offender also has to establish jurisdiction provided, however, the target State criminalises the said offence[42] or the offence was committed outside territorial jurisdiction, of any State, *v.g.* in the High Seas.[43]

Paragraph 4 of the Convention further allows Parties to establish jurisdiction in conformity with their domestic law, which enlarges the base for jurisdiction should a State Party so desire.[44]

---

inadmissibility of *Banković and Others v. 17 countries* (Vlastimir and Borka Banković, Živana Stojanović, Mirjana Stoimenovski, Dragana Joksimović and Dragan Suković against Belgium, the Czech Republic, Denmark, France, Germany, Greece, Hungary, Iceland, Italy, Luxembourg, the Netherlands, Norway, Poland, Portugal, Spain, Turkey and the United Kingdom), Application no. 52207/99, paragraphs 59-61.

[41] Ships are frequently considered to be an extension of the territory of the State. The same applies, *mutatis mutandi*, to aircrafts.
Based on article 91 of the UN Convention on the Law of the Sea, the applicability of the territorial principle to ships should be transparent. Because this was already expressed in 1927, in *The Case of the S.S. "Lotus"*, where the Permanent Court of International Justice assimilated a ship (the Turkish *Boz-Kourt*) to the territory of its Flag state, it would seem to be a very well established principle. Nevertheless, it wasn't so! In fact, just one year after the *Lotus* decision we find decisions in the opposite direction, held by North American courts, *v.g.* in *Lam Mow v. Nagle*, 24 F.2d 316 (9th Cir., 1928) and *Wong Ock Jee v. Weedin*, 24 F.2d 962 (9th Circ. 1928).

[42] Which means the target State might not be Party to the Convention.

[43] In this case, it is our understanding that the target of the offence could also be outside territorial jurisdiction.

[44] As an example of this enlargement of jurisdiction, the *Strafgesetzbuch* applies itself to certain acts (*v.g.* assaults against air and sea traffic – *Angriffe auf den Luft- und Seeverkehr* – or trafficking of human beings for sexual exploitation – *Menschenhandel zum Zweck der sexuellen Ausbeutung*) committed abroad regardless of the law of the place of their commission (*unabhängig vom Recht des Tatorts*). See *Strafgesetzbuch*, Section 6.

C. NON-APPLICATION CLAUSE

Paragraph 2 of article 22 of the Convention allows Parties to reserve the right to apply – or not – the jurisdiction grounds established in *litterae b* to *d*. States are thus given a great deal of liberty regarding issues related with cybercrime, even if they cannot avoid the obligation of prosecution when the offence is committed in their own territory (paragraph 1, *littera* a).

In practice, and since some offences affect several countries at the same time, this non-application clause could result in no country claiming jurisdiction over one given offence, thinking that surely other countries will have suffered more damage and will, therefore, have priority in prosecuting.[45] Therefore, this paragraph should also include an obligation for affected Parties to consult with each other, so no offence is left without appropriate punishment.

Also, to our understanding, this paragraph seems to be in absolute contradiction with the wording of paragraph 1, which transmits the idea that the adoption, by Parties, of legislative (and other) measures to establish jurisdiction is injunctive.

D. AUT DEDERE AUT JUDICARE

Paragraph 3 of article 24 establishes the international customary law[46] principle *aut dedere aut judicare*.[47] Should ① the alleged offender be found in the territory of one Party State (different from the one where the

---

[45] See S. W. BRENNER and B. KOOPS, "Approaches to Cybercrime Jurisdiction", *Journal of High Technology Law*, vol. 4 (2004), p. 3. The authors mention the fictitious example of a "script kiddie" who "concocts a new worm and, without really thinking of the potential consequences, launches it on the Internet", "causing significant damage in numerous countries around the world."

[46] There may be some discussion about this qualification. In spite of that, we believe that the continuous inclusion of the principle in various international Conventions establishes the existing feeling that the principle is customary law. Agreeing, J. J. PAUST, "Above the Law: Unlawful Executive Authorizations Regarding Detainee Treatment, Secret Renditions, Domestic Spying, and Claims to Unchecked Executive Power", *Utah Law Review*, vol. 2007, issue 2, p. 367, note 51.

[47] Established by various international Conventions, the principle *aut dedere aut judicare* began with Huig de Groot's formulation *aut dedere aut punire* (extradite or punish), and was adapted because not always the alleged offenders are actually guilty. Thus, Z. GALICKI, "The Obligation to Extradite or Prosecute ('aut dedere aut judicare') in International Law", *Report of the International Law Commission. Fiftysixth session* (3 May-4 June and 5 July-6 August 2004). Annex, p. 312, online at http://untreaty.un.org/ilc/reports/2004/2004report.htm, last visited September 2, 2008.

offence was committed), ② an extradition be required by the offended State, and ③ the Party in which territory the alleged offender (requested Party) is constrained by domestic law not to extradite,[48] the requested Party has the duty to prosecute, as well as the legal ability to undertake investigations and proceedings domestically.[49] The underlying idea is the need to ensure that no offence goes unpunished.

The fact that the obligation to prosecute or extradite allows an extension of jurisdiction to the State Party, makes us wonder whether it (the obligation) could be considered "universality by Convention" or, in other words, "a limited form of application of the universality principle". However, this is not the adequate context to discuss the philosophic idea of whether the extension of jurisdiction provided by international conventions can be interpreted this way.

The Party requesting for an extradition should do so pursuant to the requirements and conditions of article 24, paragraphs 1 to 4 of the Convention. The requested Party should comply with paragraph 6 of the said article 24.

E. POSITIVE JURISDICTION CONFLICTS

Finally, paragraph 5 of the article *sub judice* deals with positive jurisdiction conflicts. This type of conflict may occur because, sometimes, one offence (as described in the Convention) could target victims located

---

[48] Dealing with principles regarding extradition, article 24, paragraph 5, of the Convention establishes the applicability of the conditions provided by the domestic law of the requested Party.

[49] As an example, paragraph 3 of article 33 of the Portuguese Constitution allows for the extradition of Portuguese citizens only in conditions of reciprocity established by international convention, in cases of terrorism and organized crime, but on the condition the requesting State gives guarantees of a fair and equitable process. Also, according to paragraph 6 of the same article, no one is allowed to be extradited from Portugal when facing the possibility of death or irreversible harm to his/her physical integrity.

Such restrictions would not permit the extradition of a person – of any nationality – from Portugal, let's say, to China to face cybercrime charges, since China has been known to sentence hackers/cybercriminals to death (thus M. RANUM, *Face-Off: Chinese Cyberattacks: Myth or Menace?* online at http://searchsecurity.techtarget.com/magazineFeature/0,296894,sid14_gci1321716,00.html , last visited September 2, 2008). One such case happened in Canada, with Chinese hacker Fang Yong being extradited to China to face the death penalty. See "Chinese Hacker Sentenced to Death for Embezzlement", *People's Daily*, online at http://english.people.com.cn/english/200006/13/eng20000613_42866.html, last visited September 2, 2008.

in only one State;[50] whereas other times, it could target victims located in several States.[51]

This makes it quite normal that several Parties have jurisdiction over one given offence. To make proceedings efficient, the Convention establishes the possibility that the various Parties that claim jurisdiction over one offence consult with each other in order to determine the proper venue for prosecution.[52]

This would allow for an economy of means because, in some cases, it will be most effective for the States concerned to choose a single venue, whereas in others it may be best for one State to prosecute some of the alleged participants, while one or more other States prosecute another group of alleged offenders. However, since the obligation to consult is not absolute, taking place only "where appropriate", the effectiveness of this rule seems quite compromised.

II. Jurisdiction and Cyberworld threats

A. CYBERCRIME AND JURISDICTION

The fact that – as mentioned above – article 22 of the Convention establishes jurisdiction based on territoriality and nationality grounds seems to actually create more problems than it solves. This is so because of the specific type of offence dealt with in the Convention: one person

---

[50] This would be the case of Oleg Zezev, mentioned above, who – from Almaty, Kazakhstan – targeted a company (Bloomberg L.P.) in the USA.

[51] This would be the case of David L. Smith, who was sentenced to 20 months in an US Federal Prison because he was the creator of Melissa, a virulent and widespread computer virus which was found on Friday, March 26, 1999. This virus spread all over the globe within just hours of the initial discovery, apparently spreading faster than any other virus before and disrupted personal computers and computer networks in business and government, in the USA and elsewhere. Melissa was initially distributed in an Internet discussion group called alt.sex. The virus was sent in a file bearing the name "list.doc", which supposedly contained a list of passwords for websites with sexual contents. As users downloaded the file and opened it in Microsoft Word, a macro inside the document executed and e-mailed the "list.doc" file to the first 50 people listed in the user's e-mail address book. See, U.S. DEPARTMENT OF JUSTICE. NORTHERN DISTRICT OF OHIO, "Florida Man Indicted for Causing Damage and Transmitting Threat to Former Employer's Computer System (February 7, 2006)", online at http://www.usdoj.gov/criminal/cybercrime/anchetaPlea.htm, last visited September 2, 2008. (For more information on the Melissa virus, see K. TOCHEVA, M. HYPPONEN and S. RAUTIAINEN, "F-Secure Virus Descriptions: Melissa", online at http://www.f-secure.com/v-descs/melissa.shtml, last visited September 2, 2008).

[52] Thus, S. W. BRENNER and B. KOOPS, "Approaches to Cybercrime Jurisdiction", p. 41.

can send (upload) files whose contents are criminal from one computer in one country to a different computer (the server) in some other country and these files can be seen (downloaded) by viewers all over the world. In this case, where is the offence committed? In the country where the person lives and/or where the files are uploaded, in the country where the server is located or in the several countries where the criminal contents is actually seen? And, if we consider this last situation to be the correct interpretation, what if the viewer lives in a country where those particular contents are not criminal?

1. The Yahoo case

A good example of the complexity of the jurisdiction issues that arise in cyberworld is the Yahoo case. Based on the fact that the selling or exhibiting of racist objects, namely Nazi memorabilia, is illegal in France, the *Tribunal de Grande Instance de Paris*, in an *Ordonnance de Référé* of May 22, 2000, ordered Yahoo! Inc and its subsidiary Yahoo France not only to exclude French surfers from sales of Nazi memorabilia ("cesser... toute mise à disposition sur le territoire de la République à partir du site "Yahoo.com""), but also to destroy all the concerned files stored in their server ("détruire toute donnée informatique stockée directement ou indirectement sur son serveur").[53]

In this case, the files[54] were probably uploaded from an unknown source and were stored in a server in the United States. Then, one French

---

[53] For details, see the text of the sentence: TRIBUNAL DE GRANDE INSTANCE DE PARIS, *UEJF et Licra c/ Yahoo! Inc. et Yahoo France*, online at http://www.juriscom.net/txt/jurisfr/cti/tgiparis20000522.htm, last visited September 2, 2008. "UEJF" stands for *Union des Etudiants Juifs de France*; "Licra" stands for *Ligue Contre le Racisme et l'Antisémitisme*.

[54] The files to which the French court wanted no access from French citizens were digital copies of Adolph Hitler's "Mein Kampf" and of the book "Les protocoles des Sages de Sion", the supposed proceedings of a Zionist Congress supposedly held in Basel, Switzerland, in 1897. This book was thought – according to the research of Russian historian Vladimir Burtsev – to have been written by agents of the Okhrana, the secret police of Tsar Nicholas II, who himself seemed to have anti-Semitic ideas (thus, J. ALLAFORT, "Les Protocoles des Sages de Sion", online at http://www.nuitdorient.com/n138.htm, last visited September 2, 2008). Further research from Russian historian Mikhail Lépekhine, done after the opening of Soviet archives to researchers, in 1992, showed that it was, in fact, the Russian forger Mathieu Golovinski who wrote the text while living in Paris. Thus, É. CONAN, "L'origine des Protocoles des sages de Sion", *L'Express*, 16/11/1999, online at http://www.phdn.org/antisem/protocoles/origines.html, last visited September 2, 2008.

court asserted jurisdiction over them because they could be seen in France and their contents were criminalized in France.

But the case does not end here. Dissatisfied with the sentence of the French court, Yahoo decided to file a declaratory judgment action in U.S. District Court in San Francisco, hoping to obtain a ruling that the French court's order could not be enforced against Yahoo in the United States. In its lawsuit, besides discussing computer technical matters regarding the (im)possibility of excluding some users of their site from some of the Web pages (those containing Nazi memorabilia), Yahoo maintained that allowing enforcement of the foreign court's order in the United States would violate the First Amendment. U.S. District Judge Jeremy Fogel of the Northern District of California ascertained jurisdiction over LICRA and UEJF (the French anti-racism associations), agreed with Yahoo regarding the violation of the First Amendment and entered a declaratory judgment in the company's favour.[55]

It was LICRA and UEJF's turn to be dissatisfied, this time with Judge Fogel's ruling, which led them to appeal to the 9th Circuit. Eventually, the matter came up for decision before an 11-judge panel of that court and the majority of the judges concluded that the district court had jurisdiction over the defendants (LICRA and UEJF), but the judgment of the district court was reversed.[56]

Could the Convention[57] help solve complex problems like the one presented in this case? It probably could! But would it?

2. Controlling Law and International Cooperation

Immediately after establishing the jurisdiction principles mentioned above, the Convention proceeds to elaborate on international cooperation. Article 23, entitled "General principles relating to international

---

[55] *Yahoo!, Inc. v. La Ligue Contre Le Racisme et L'Antisemitisme*, N.D.Cal. 2001, Nov. 7, 2001, online at http://cyber.law.harvard.edu/is02/readings/yahoo-order.html, last visited September 2, 2008.

[56] UNITED STATES COURT OF APPEALS FOR THE NINTH CIRCUIT, *Yahoo! Inc., a Delaware corporation, v. La Ligue Contre le Racisme et l'Antisemitisme, a French association; L'Union des Etudiants Juifs de France, a French association*, No. 01-17424, D.C. No. CV-00-21275-JF, online at http://caselaw.lp.findlaw.com/data2/circs/9th/0117424p.pdf, last visited September 2, 2008.

[57] According to the Council of Europe website, the United States of America signed the Convention together with the majority of the Council of Europe members, on November 23, 2001, ratified the Convention on September 29, 2006, and it entered into force in the USA on January 1, 2007. (See online, http://conventions.coe.int.)

cooperation", creates an obligation for Parties to cooperate with each other in matters related with extradition (article 24), mutual assistance (article 25), spontaneous information (article 26) and some other details.

Good examples of international cooperation are the *Rome Labs* case and the *Tore Tvedt* case.

According to Appendix B of the Staff Statement of the US Senate's Permanent Subcommittee on Investigations, of June 5, 1996,[58] on March 28, 1994, computer systems administrators at Rome Air Development Center, Griffiss Air Force Base, New York, discovered that their network had been penetrated and compromised by an illegal wiretap computer program called a "Sniffer", which was covertly installed on computer networks by hackers to illegally collect user logons of authorized users. This program had been covertly installed on one of the systems connected to laboratory's network.

The intruders were found to be a pair of hackers calling themselves "Datastream Cowboy" and "Kuji," whose identities were unknown. "Datastream Cowboy", a 16-year old who enjoyed hacking into military networks, was located by an informant, who was able to provide a telephone number and address in the United Kingdom. US Air Force agents established a working relationship with New Scotland Yard agents and they arrested the hacker.[59] At the date of the report, "Datastream Cowboy" was pending prosecution in the UK. Three years later, Richard Pryce, *a.k.a.* "Datastream Cowboy", was fined with £1,200 for the intrusion.[60] Matthew Bevan, *a.k.a.* "Kuji", was also arrested, waited 18 months for a trial and was acquitted because it was judged not to be in the public interest to pursue the case.[61]

---

[58] STAFF STATEMENT. U.S. SENATE. PERMANENT SUBCOMMITTEE ON INVESTIGATIONS, *Security in Cyberspace*, June 5, 1996, Appendix B, online at http://fas.org/irp/congress/1996_hr/s960605b.htm, last visited September 2, 2008.

[59] STAFF STATEMENT. U.S. SENATE. PERMANENT SUBCOMMITTEE ON INVESTIGATIONS, *Security in Cyberspace*, online, quoted, p. 6. See, also, G. MOHAY, A. ANDERSON, B. COLLIE, O. DE VEL and R. D. MCKEMMISH, *Computer and Intrusion Forensics*, Norwood, MA, Artech House, Inc, 2003, pp. 308, 309, who use this as a case study for security in cyberspace.

[60] See the newspaper news published the day after the sentence was given in D. GRAVES, "'Datastream Cowboy', 19, fined £1,200 for hacking secret US computer systems", *Telegraph*, March 22, 1997, online at http://www.telegraph.co.uk/htmlContent.jhtml?html=/archive/1997/03/22/nhack22.html, last visited September 2, 2008.

[61] For a short story on Matthew Bevan, see M. WARD, "History repeats for former hacker", *BBC News*, online at http://news.bbc.co.uk/2/hi/technology/4761985.stm, last visited September 2, 2008.

The *Tore Tvedt* case dealt with the posting of racist and anti-Semitic propaganda on the Internet. Tore Tvedt, whose Web page was stored in a North American server, was the founder of the Norwegian far-right group Vigrid (an organization which professes a doctrine that mixes neo-Nazism, racial hatred and religion, claiming to worship Odin and other ancient Norse gods), and was considered responsible for the contents of the Web page – even if it was stored out of Norway's jurisdiction – and was sentenced by a Norwegian court to seventy-five days in jail with forty-five days suspended, plus two years of probation.[62]

In the *Rome Labs* case, the controlling law was that of the location where the actions in question occurred, the hacker's location. In the *Tvedt* case, however, the controlling law was that of the country in which the damage was said to have occurred. But both depended on international cooperation to be solved.

However, not all cases deal with good international cooperation. On October 10, 2001, the U.S. Department of Justice announced that Vasiliy Gorshkov, of Chelyabinsk, Russia, had been found guilty on 20 counts of conspiracy, various computer crimes and fraud, which made him face a maximum sentence of five years in prison for each count.[63]

After having discovered that some companies had suffered intrusions from hackers, the FBI created a shell company, called it Invita,[64] and eventually established contact with the hackers and lured them to the U.S. with employment opportunities. After long talks and some online testing, Vasiliy Gorshkov and Alexey Ivanov agreed to a face-to-face meeting in Seattle, where they were asked – by FBI undercover agents – about their hacking skills and assumed responsibility for various hacking incidents and activities. At the conclusion of the Invita meeting, the two men were

---

[62] See the media report with comments at "Norwegian Jailed for Web Racism", *CNN*, Apr. 23, 2002, online at http://www.con.com/2002/WORLD/europe/04/23/norway.web/index.html, last visited September 2, 2008.

[63] Thus, U.S. DEPARTMENT OF JUSTICE. UNITED STATES ATTORNEY, "Russian Computer Hacker Convicted by Jury", online at http://www.usdoj.gov/criminal/cybercrime/gorshkovconvict.htm, last visited September 2, 2008.

[64] Describing the company, "High-tech net helped FBI snag alleged hackers", *USA Today*, 02/06/2002, online at http://www.usatoday.com/tech/news/2001-05-09-fbi-tech-sting.htm, last visited September 2, 2008, stated: "Invita Security looked like a typical Internet company: it had offices, computers, employees, even a secure computer system. The only thing missing was the customers."

arrested.[65]

According to court filings,[66] the Department of Justice made several unsuccessful attempts to get Russian authorities to cooperate and seize the contents of the hackers' servers in Russia. The North American agents then accessed two servers in Russia where Gorshkov kept his data and downloaded over 1 Gigabyte of information. Subsequently, they obtained a search warrant to look at the downloaded files and got strong evidence of the men's computer hacking and fraud activities.[67]

This was one case where international cooperation did not function due to a lack of response from one of the sides. However, another case was reported where there was a will to cooperate but the law itself did not allow it.

Tens of millions of computers were affected in May, 2000, when the "Love Bug" virus swept the Internet. The virus was quickly traced back to the Philippines,[68] but then law enforcement officials ran into a problem, as the Philippines had no law against hacking.[69] Therefore, despite all the damage done,[70] nobody was ever prosecuted for the "Love Bug" virus. The United States wanted the extradition of the main suspect, [71] and there is an international extradition agreement between the United States and the Philippines. However, the lack of law against hacking in the

---

[65] U.S. DEPARTMENT OF JUSTICE. UNITED STATES ATTORNEY, "Russian Computer Hacker Convicted by Jury", online, quoted.

[66] Reported by R. LEMOS, "FBI "hack" raises global security concerns", *CNET News*, May 1, 2001, online at http://news.cnet.com/2100-1001-256811.html, last visited September 2, 2008.

[67] U.S. DEPARTMENT OF JUSTICE. UNITED STATES ATTORNEY, "Russian Computer Hacker Convicted by Jury", online, quoted.

[68] Supposedly to a Filipino computer student who wrote a thesis on stealing passwords from the Internet. "Love Bug revenge theory", *BBC News*, May 10, 2000, online at http://news.bbc.co.uk/2/hi/science/nature/743082.stm, last visited September 2, 2008.

[69] See "Philippine investigators detain man in search for 'Love Bug' creator", *CNN*, May 8, 2000, online at http://archives.cnn.com/2000/TECH/computing/05/08/ilove.you.02/index.html, last visited September 2, 2008.

[70] In the UK alone, British Telecom, Vodafone, Barclays, Scottish Power and Ford UK were among the giant firms affected, together with universities and many companies of variable size. "'Love Bug' bites UK", *BBC News*, May 4, 2000, online at http://news.bbc.co.uk/2/hi/uk_news/736080.stm, last visited September 2, 2008.

[71] See, *inter alia*, "Suspected hacker may face extradition requests", *CNN*, May 9, 2000, online at http://transcripts.cnn.com/2000/LAW/05/09/internat.hacking.law/index.html, last visited September 2, 2008.

Philippines made extradition impossible in this case.[72]

In the Invita case, the controlling law was that of the country in which the damage was said to have occurred. In the "Love Bug" case, however, the controlling law was that of the location where the actions in question occurred, the hacker's location. None of the cases depended on international cooperation to be solved. In fact, one was solved by hacking into the servers in another country, whereas the other was not solved at all due to an absence of legislation. Sometimes there is a will, but there is no way!

3. Jurisdiction Issues

Cybercrime is so broad and can be so complex that becomes very difficult to investigate. And jurisdiction adds to the complexity of investigating a technological matter. [73] This difficulty becomes more evident when dealing with international jurisdiction.

Doctrine considers jurisdiction as defining three levels of authority: ① the authority to prescribe (the capacity to establish and prescribe criminal and regulatory sanctions, normally prerogative of a government), ② the authority to judge (the competence to hear disputes, normally prerogative of courts), and ③ the authority to enforce (the capacity to compel compliance or to punish noncompliance with its laws, regulations, orders, and judgments, as well as the capacity to investigate suspect behaviours, both normally also prerogative of a government).[74]

The Convention on Cybercrime points the way toward cooperation with respect to criminalizing certain behaviours and pursuing those responsible. It does not, however, resolve the issues of international

---

[72] Thus, S. MYDANS, "Philippine Prosecutors Release 'Love Bug' Suspect", *The New York Times*,   May   10,   2000,   online   at http://partners.nytimes.com/library/tech/00/05/biztech/articles/10virus.html,   last   visited September 2. 2008.

[73] Regarding the complexity of investigation, see D. KOENIG, "Investigation of Cybercrime and Technology-related Crime", *National Executive Institute Associates*, online at http://www.neiassociates.org/cybercrime.htm, last visited September 2, 2008. Peter Stephenson, *Investigating Computer-Related Crime: A Handbook for Corporate Investigators*, Boca Raton, FL, CRC Press, 1999, p. 13, adds that most organizations are not equipped to investigate computer crime.

[74] Thus, *inter alia*, S. W. BRENNER and B. KOOPS, "Approaches to Cybercrime Jurisdiction", p. 4. According to I. BROWNLIE, *Principles of Public International Law*, 5th ed., Oxford, University Press, 2002 (1998), p. 58, law-making capabilities are one of the factors that determine the coexistence between nations.

jurisdiction. The investigation of an international crime will always have to depend on the good will of the third country, or else there is no investigation. However, even if the Convention relies heavily on international cooperation, sometimes – as we have seen – this is not enough to take the investigation to an end. We are, therefore, forced to conclude that the Convention is short on giving States the necessary weapons to fight this type of crime.

As an attempt to remedy this deficiency, we would propose three amendments to the Convention: ① that the consultations of which we have spoken above were not to take place "where appropriate", but that they would be established as an obligation;[75] ② that the Convention itself be effectively considered as an extradition convention between the Parties;[76] and ③ that the Convention be amended (or supplemented by additional protocol) to include an internal mechanism that allows police investigators from one Party to perform their work online in another Party, subject only to an informal communication to the authorities in the other Party.[77]

---

[75] Should the Convention create an obligation to consult – instead of merely allowing for this consultation, as it does with the current wording – this obligation would have the advantage of permitting the determination of the most appropriate venue for persecution, together with an economy of means that would help the international community in not leaving any crime unpunished.

[76] We are aware that paragraph 3 of article 24, allows a Party to consider the Convention as legal basis for extradition. However, the wording of the Convention is weak. The party "may consider" the Convention as legal basis for extradition, but is allowed to consider the opposite. A stronger wording would, in our view, be recommendable.

[77] The formal request to the other Party's authorities can be useful when dealing with apprehending people or computers. Nevertheless, in cybercrime, sometimes the investigator has to follow the path of the perpetrator of the offence and may find himself messing with a computer that is physically in a place where he does not have jurisdiction. A formal request would probably result in losing the evidence. However, an informal communication would allow the investigator to pursue the investigation in time.
In the Invita case, for example, if the North American agents had not entered the Russian servers without permission, there would have been no way to prove that the statements both hackers made at the Seattle interview were true, because it was expected that, as soon as the two suspects' counterparts in Russia found out about the arrests, they would have destroyed the data.
The data copied from the Russian computers had large databases of credit card information (more than 56,000 credit cards) that were stolen from Internet Service Providers. The two Russian computers also had stolen bank account and other personal financial information of customers of online banking at a couple of North American banks. Should the research have waited for a formal answer ... there would have been no proof and the information would still be usable by others. See U.S. DEPARTMENT OF JUSTICE. UNITED STATES ATTORNEY, "Russian Computer Hacker Convicted by Jury", online, quoted.

B. CYBERTERRORISM AND JURISDICTION

1. To Be or Not To Be

Cyberterrorism conjures up images of fierce terrorists unleashing catastrophic attacks against computer networks, creating chaos, and paralyzing entire nations. A frightening scenario indeed, but how likely is it to occur? From people in denial to people in distress, opinions come in all flavours.

On the denial corner, strong statements make the day. "There is no such thing as cyberterrorism – no instance of anyone ever having been killed by a terrorist (or anyone else) using a computer" says an editor of one monthly magazine from Washington, DC, USA.[78] Besides arguing that no cyberattack has ever been attempted by terrorists,[79] the main line of reasoning of those in this field is that terrorist organizations usually follow the least resistance path and, therefore, are bound to prefer a cheaper and easier alternative to cyberattacks: physical attacks.[80] Yet, are physical attacks now easier and cheaper?

On the opposite corner, statements come in no weaker form. Carnegie Mellon University computer scientist Roy Maxion is reported to have written, in 2001, to President George W. Bush warning him about the fact that the United States was at grave risk of a cyberattack that could devastate the public mind and the nation's economy more broadly than the September 11 attacks.[81] And the reasoning for this extreme position is based on the findings that al Qaeda operators spent time learning about how to disrupt critical infrastructures through the Internet and had plans to put that knowledge to use.[82] Yet, are things really this bad?

---

[78] J. GREEN, "The Myth of Cyberterrorism", *Washington Monthly*, November 2002, online at http://www.washingtonmonthly.com/features/2001/0211.green.html, last visited September 2, 2008.

[79] *Ibidem.*

[80] Referred by S. P. GORMAN, *Networks, Security and Complexity: The role of Public Policy in Critical Infrastructure Protection*, Glos, UK, Edward Elgar Publishing Limited, 2005, p. 11.

[81] See D. FITZPATRICK, "Cybersecurity expert warns of post-9/11 vulnerability", *Global Security*, September 9, 2003, online at http://www.globalsecurity.org/org/news/2003/030909-cyber01.htm, last visited September 2, 2008.

[82] See B. GELLMAN, "Cyber-Attacks by Al Qaeda Feared", *Washington Post*, June 27, 2002, page A01, online at http://www.crime-research.org/library/Barton.htm, last visited September 2, 2008.

If it is true that they are out there, what is then the measure of danger that cyberterrorists really embody? [83] The reality may have been grasped in July 2002, as the United States Naval War College, working in conjunction with Gartner Research, conducted what they called a "digital Pearl Harbour" simulation. According to the conclusions of this simulation, "a group of hackers couldn't single-handedly bring down the United States' national data infrastructure, but a terrorist team would be able to do significant localized damage to U.S. systems."[84]

The analysts concluded that it would be possible to inflict some serious harm to the US data and physical infrastructure systems, but it would require a syndicate with significant resources, including $200 million, country-level intelligence and five years of preparation time. [85]

The conclusions then show that a cyberattack on the United States is possible, but would require huge planning and a great amount of financing. Considering the above mentioned *Rome Labs* case, if one 16-year old British boy – with £ 750 worth of equipment[86] – was able to intrude a network connected to the US military, the funding requirement is probably overstated.

Cyberterrorists might not be menacing to kill people directly, as a traditional terrorist attack normally does, but one cyberattack could make life very, very difficult, maybe even destroying or severely damaging the complete economic and social system of one country. We thus conclude that cyberterrorism is definitely a real threat which, unfortunately, is here to stay. And, since the chain of terrorist events after September 11, 2001 shows terrorists to have diversified their targets, we should therefore not overlook the possibility of a cyberattack targeting some other less prepared country than the USA.

If an ounce of prevention is worth a pound of cure, we should learn at least one lesson from the catastrophic terrorism actions perpetrated in

---

[83] F. COHEN, "Cyber-Risks and Critical Infrastructures" in Alan O'Day (ed.), *Cyberterrorism*, pp. 1-8, lists several critical infrastructures and mentions nightmare scenarios for each one. He then proceeds to solve every one of those scenarios within a framework ranging from only a few hours to a few days, thus showing that a cyber attack would not create havoc for long. As he mentions the Internet, for instance, he states that there are hundreds of thousands of trained experts that could recreate a functional Internet "in a matter of days" (p. 8). He recognizes, by that, the possibility of one such attack.

[84] M. KANE, "U.S. vulnerable to data sneak attack", *CNET News*, August 13, 2002 11, online at http://news.cnet.com/2100-1017-949605.html, last visited September 2, 2008.

[85] *Ibidem.*

[86] Thus, D. GRAVES, "'Datastream Cowboy', 19, fined £1,200 for hacking secret US computer systems", online, quoted.

New York, Madrid and London: terrorists did not attack from a distance. If a cyberattack is to take place in our countries, it can be masterminded elsewhere, but will probably be executed from within our own networks.

2. Hackers, Crackers, Terrorists and Jurisdiction Issues

Hackers tend to be more of a nuisance than a danger. Most of the time, they try unauthorized access to networks for the fun of it, for the challenge, or to put networks to a test. [87] Crackers, however, are criminal hackers that also try unauthorized access to networks, but have malicious intents.[88] Cyberterrorists are people that use cyberterror to achieve political or social change. [89]

Because their motivation and goal is so much different from those of crackers and terrorists, hackers are not likely to either become terrorists or be directly employed by them. For trust reasons, it is not likely that terrorists would hire crackers. But it is not impossible for terrorists to gain hacking skills.[90]

Whatever motivation or goal leads one person (or a group) to hack into a network system, be it hacking, cracking or terrorism, the same jurisdiction problems are present to the investigator and to the judge. Obtaining proof of the action, detaining the suspects and presenting them to a court can only be achieved with quick reaction and the appropriate

---

[87] A. M. COLARIK, *Cyber Terrorism. Political and Economic Implications*, Hershey / London / Melbourne / Singapore, Idea Group Publishing, 2006, pp. 37-39, discusses the actions normally attributed to hackers, stating (p. 37) that some have even published their findings, either in academic or nonacademic venues.

[88] *Idem*, pp. 40-42.

[89] *Idem*, p. 46, states that because no legislatively defined meaning of cyberterrorism exists, "the domain is open to debate, dispute, and ultimately, ambiguity." In this text we are not trying to establish a definitive definition for cyberterrorism, for which reason we employed vague wording, as did D. E. DENNING, "Cyberterrorism", Testimony before the Special Oversight Panel on Terrorism Committee on Armed Services, U.S. House of Representatives, May 23, 2000, online at http://www.cs.georgetown.edu/~denning/infosec/cyberterror.html, last visited September 2, 2008, when she wrote: "Cyberterrorism is the convergence of terrorism and cyberspace. It is generally understood to mean unlawful attacks and threats of attack against computers, networks, and the information stored therein when done to intimidate or coerce a government or its people in furtherance of political or social objectives."

[90] Thus, A. EMBAR-SEDDON, "Cyberterrorism: Are We Under Siege?" p. 15. A. M. COLARIK, *Cyber Terrorism*, p. 51, states "Cyberterrorists exist today. The Osama bin Laden Crew is a group of self-proclaimed cyberjihadists", and proceeds to mention force multiplier tasks that cyberterrorists are supposed to be accomplishing.

international tools. This author believes that international cooperation is the way to achieve this goal; however, he also finds that existing international tools fall short on making international cooperation injunctive.

C. THE APPLICABILITY OF ARTICLE 22 TO CYBERTERRORISM CASES

As a threat, cyberterrorism would probably not justify a convention to deal with it. The explicit inclusion of cyberterrorism in the Convention on Cybercrime by means of an additional protocol would probably suffice. Whatever the choice, it is, however, this author's belief that to fight cyberterrorism there is no need for a definition. The broad acceptance of the 1988 Rome Convention for the Suppression of Unlawful Acts against the Safety of Maritime Navigation shows there is no need to use "scare words" in order to reach consensus. In fact, it was probably due to the lack of such words that the Rome Convention was so successfully adopted. Thus, given the fear of terrorism in our society, an Additional Protocol to the Convention – either detailing some offences that would be considered cyberterrorism or specifying when the offences established in the Convention should be considered more than just cybercrimes – should be enough.[91]

The effectiveness of this Protocol, as well as of the Convention itself, would however depend on the number of States that ratify them. The fact that the United States of America has ratified the Convention, in accordance with its article 36, paragraph 1, *in fine*, is a sign that major non-Council of Europe Member States will be willing to cooperate with Member States in the fight against cybercrime and, obviously, against cyberterrorism. Yet, although the Convention entered into force in July 1, 2004, key Member States of the COE – *v.g.* Germany, Russia, United Kingdom, Spain, Austria, as well as the author's own country, Portugal – have not (as of September 1, 2008) ratified the Convention, a situation that can spawn great concern.

III. Concluding Remarks

Jurisdiction, or the lack of it, seems to be the most problematic issue

---

[91] This Protocol could also include the amendments referred above (Part II, section A, subsection 3) regarding consultation between the Parties, extradition rules and the inclusion of a mechanism to allow police investigators to perform their search online, subject only to an informal communication to the local authorities.

in the fight against cybercrime and cyberterrorism. The fact that cyberattacks can come from anywhere in the world makes investigation, producing evidence and taking the offenders to court an immense task that can only be achieved through international cooperation.

The Convention on Cybercrime was designed to help accomplish the goal of reducing and/or tearing down the difficulties of the fight against cybercrime. Still, it shows itself to be insufficient because international collaboration in not injunctive and there are no rules to unload the burden of formality from the work of police specialists in charge of investigating international cybercrime/cyberterrorism cases.

Furthermore, the fact that key Member States of the Council of Europe are taking their time to ratify the Convention also leaves a bitter notion of lack of interest in cybercrime, one type of crime that is becoming increasingly important for companies all over the world. Let's hope our countries don't wake up too late. It is easy to be wise after the event!

As a final note, we would like to say that, given the path towards catastrophism and indiscriminate attack on human lives taken by modern day terrorism, we would consider possible and positive the inclusion of terrorism in the list of international crimes against humanity – in accordance with *littera k* of number 1 of article 7 of the Rome Statute of the International Criminal Court (ICC) – which would entitle States to have universal jurisdiction to apprehend terrorist agents, although jurisdiction to prosecute would be given to the International Criminal Court.

Thus, since, in the case of international conventions, the authority to prescribe still rests with the government of the State Party – because no State is forced into being a Party to a Convention and all States still have the right to sign (or not) and ratify (or not) any given Convention – the governments of the Member States concerned would only forfeit the authority to judge to the International Criminal Court. All States would keep the authority to prescribe, both domestically and by means of ratification of conventions, and the authority to enforce, should the International Criminal Court convict the agents.

Children Protection Online: Uneasy Steps towards a Balance between Risks and Freedoms

Federica Casarosa
Robert Schuman Centre of Advanced Studies, European University Institute, Florence

I. The web grows "younger"

Nowadays Internet has become a household universe. Although it was originally created as a means of communication in the scientific community, [1] it has developed into an extraordinary diffused medium used in homes, offices, schools, businesses and public administrations.

Moreover, Internet penetration and use of new technologies is still growing considerably in the European Community. This situation is not only due to qualitative improvements of technologies, but it is also related to the wider access of youngsters to this medium. As a matter of fact, a recent survey of the Eurobarometer provided evidence about the rising share of Internet usage by children up to 16 years, (for instance, in European countries, the percentage of children using Internet has reached the rate of 51% in 2006, while the first contact with new technologies lowers down to 6-8 years old). [2]

As a matter of fact, children and young people are more and more often the first to take up and use new technologies; yet, they are not always aware of both risks and ways of dealing with them, or, whether they are, they are not always mature enough to evaluate the situations that they encounter and the possible consequences their decisions can have.

At the end of the day, new technologies can improve the quality of life for children and young people, providing them better access to knowledge and widest possibilities to socialise and experiment social

---

[1] In reality, the first usage was a default communication network among military service nodes in the whole United States, and then the technical structure was devoted to the connection of Universities.

[2] See the OPTEM REPORT, *Safer Internet for Children – Qualitative Study*, May 2007, requested by the DG Information society and Media, where the rate of less than 6 years-old children using the Internet is 9%, and from 6-7 years jumps up to 34% (growing further as age increases).

skills. But, at the same time, such resources could also lead minors to decide on issues that normally they would not have to decide in real life, in particular concerning their own safety.

Recent studies shows that new risk situations arise for children with the further diffusion of new Internet enabled end-user devices, like "3G" mobile phones and new practices such as social networking[3] (where chatting includes also the possibility to use web-cams), Internet blogging[4] or file sharing.[5] Moreover, possible future technological developments and user options can increase this risky environment, also through convergent services and new modes of communication. This increase in connectivity by children will see a corresponding increase in benefits for them, but also in risks of "collateral damage". Dangers, especially for children, and abuse of the technologies continue to exist and new threats and abuses are emerging.

This paper will address, in part II, European interventions concerning children protection online distinguishing the main objectives of such interventions and the preferred tools to achieve an acceptable level of protection; part III will be then devoted to the identification of potential risks for children online, while part IV will analyse the advantages and disadvantages of the tools proposed by European institutions. In part V, a case study will be proposed, concerning social networking, in order to verify if technical and legal tools can be effective in practice. Finally, preliminary conclusions will be presented.

---

[3] A social network service focuses on building online communities of people who share interests and activities, or who are interested in exploring the interests and activities of others. Most social network services are web based and provide a variety of ways for users to interact, such as e-mail and instant messaging services. The main types of social networking services are those which contain directories of some categories (such as former classmates), means to connect with friends (usually with self-description pages), and recommender systems linked to trust.

[4] A blog (a contraction of the term "Web log") is a Web site, usually maintained by an individual, with regular entries of commentary, descriptions of events, or other material such as graphics or video. Many blogs provide commentary or news on a particular subject; others function as more personal online diaries. A typical blog combines text, images, and links to other blogs, Web pages, and other media related to its topic. Most blogs are primarily textual, although some focus on art, photographs, sketches, videos, music, audio, which are part of a wider network of social media.

[5] File sharing refers to the providing and receiving of digital files over a network, usually following the peer-to-peer (P2P) model, where the files are stored on and served by personal computers of the users. Most people who engage in file sharing on the Internet both provide (upload) files and receive files (download).

II. EU intervention

The European Union has been a forerunner in tackling children protection issues: the first steps date back to 1996, when the Green Paper on the protection of minors and human dignity in informational and audiovisual services was published. [6] It presented a three-part analysis about the existing background concerning the fight against the dissemination of content offensive to human dignity, and the protection of minors against exposure to content that is harmful to their development. Firstly, it described the evolution of audiovisual and information services from a centralised mass media model to a decentralised and individual communication model. Secondly, it analysed the current legislation and policies at national, European and international level, and finally, it pushed forward some guidelines to provide a more flexible regulatory framework capable of facing the characteristics of new services.

In particular, the Green Paper stressed the fact that:

> "The full potential of such developments [i.e. audiovisual and informational services] will depend on society as a whole striking the right balance between freedom of speech and public interest considerations, between policies designed to foster the emergence of new services and the need to ensure that the opportunities they create are not abused by the few at the expense of the many".

At the same time, the Commission published a Communication on Illegal and Harmful Content on the Internet, [7] which provided short-term measures required to deal with specific Internet related issues that go beyond the field of protection of minors and human dignity. In particular, it defined the difference between illegal and harmful content. The former may be banned for everyone, regardless of the age of the potential audience or the medium used (e.g. child pornography, extreme gratuitous violence and incitement to racial or other hatred, discrimination, and violence). The latter, on the contrary, can be defined as "content that is legal, but liable to harm minors by impairing their physical and mental development",[8] thus, access to it can be allowed only for adults.[9] The key difference between harmful and illegal content is that the former is subject

---

[6] 16 October 1996, COM (96) 483.

[7] Communication on illegal and harmful content on the Internet, COM(96) 487

[8] Ibidem, par. 17.

[9] Later, the Safer Internet Action Plan added to this taxonomy also unwanted material, like spam or undesired commercial communications. See *infra* in the Safer Internet Action Plan Plus.

to personal choice, *"based on one's beliefs, preferences and social and cultural traditions"*,[10] while the latter is a matter of state choice. This distinction is essential not to confuse the different objectives and different problems which each of them raises, and consequently the different solutions chosen in each case. With regard to illegal content, the state decides which content should be considered illegal and what consequences should be linked to this classification (for instance, prohibition of publication and distribution). [11] When tackling with harmful content, on the other hand, it is argued that the state should create an environment that enables citizens to decide for themselves (and eventually for their children) which content they consider suitable and worth accessing. Moreover, the recommendation underlined that, in this case, a balance must be struck between possible harm to minors and the preservation of the freedom of expression.

These two measures set the ground for the following community interventions that leaded to the current regulatory framework.

The following phase was the adoption of the Council Recommendation 98/560/EC, of 24th September 1998,[12] on the development of competitiveness of the European audiovisual and information services industry by promoting national frameworks aimed at achieving a comparable and effective level of protection of minors and human dignity, which defined the guidelines for the national legislation on this issue.[13]   In particular, it fostered a European and international cooperation, and it encouraged a more systematic coordination between

---

[10] J.P. MIFSUD BONNICI and C.N.J., DE VEY MESTDAGH, 'Right vision, wrong expectations: the European Union and self-regulation of harmful Internet content', *Information & Communications Technology Law*, Vol. 14, No. 2, 2005, 142.

[11] As far as *illegal content* is concerned, the point of departure is that what is illegal offline is illegal online. It should be ensured that the law is adapted so that it reflects the values of society and deals with new social phenomena. A further area of concern is the degree to which national law can be applied to activities taking place on a global network, whether under application of national rules of conflict of law or in practice. This is difficult if acts are punishable in one country and not punishable in another.

[12] Council Recommendation 98/560/EC of 24 September 1998, OJ L 270, 7.10.1998, p. 48.

[13] It is useful to note that the legal base of this recommendation was Article 130 of the EC Treaty, (actual Article 157 ECT), which requires the Community and the Member States to ensure that the conditions necessary for the competitiveness of the Community's industry exist, with action aimed, *inter alia*, at fostering better exploitation of the industrial potential of policies of innovation, research and technological development. Differently, the following interventions are based on Article 153(2) ECT, on protection of the consumer, since they are focus on the end-user – particularly parents, educators and children – and are intended to promote their safety when using the Internet and new online technologies.

government, industries, the other parties concerned in each Member State in order to enable minors to make responsible use of online audiovisual and information services, by improving the level of awareness among parents, educators, and teachers about the potential of the new services.[14]

In 1999, the aforementioned Recommendation was integrated by the first active intervention in the field: the implementation of a 'Safer Internet Action Plan' (IAP), which identified areas for concrete measures where Community resources should be focused on.[15] The Action Plan defined four specific objectives: the creation of a safer environment (through a network of hot-lines, and the adoption of codes of conduct), the development of a filtering and rating system, the encouragement of awareness-raising actions, and other supporting action (like the assessment of legal implications and the coordination with other similar international initiatives).

After the positive outcome of this four-year plan, [16] the Commission proposed a new mandate for an extended Safer Internet Action Plan (so called IAP-Plus),[17] and the Council of Ministers has recently adopted the new Safer Internet Programme proposed by the Commission for 2009-

---

[14] The recommendation was updated in 2006, (*Recommendation on the protection of minors and human dignity and on the right of reply*, 2006/952/EC) following the same objectives. One important difference, however, is the limited role given to self-regulation as a tool to provide effective protection, downgrading it to an additional measure that, alone, cannot be sufficient to protect minors from messages with harmful content; whereas, in the previous recommendation, the role of self-regulation was much more emphasised, also providing the principles on which a self-regulatory intervention should be based (involvement of all interested parties, definition of the objectives in the codes of conduct, cooperation at community level, and regular evaluation of the measures taken.

[15] European Parliament and European Council, Decision 276/1999/EC of 25 January 1999 adopting a Multi-annual Community Action Plan on promoting safer use of the Internet and new online technologies by combating illegal and harmful content primarily in the area of the protection of children and minors (OJ L 33, 6.2.1999, p.1) as amended by Decision 1151/2003/EC of the European Parliament and of the Council of 16 June 2003 (OJ L 162, 1.7.2003, p. 1).

[16] See the European Commission, Communication to the Council, the European parliament, the European economic and social committee and the Committee of the regions concerning the evaluation of the multi-annual community action plan on promoting safer use of the Internet and new online technologies by combating illegal and harmful content primarily in the area of the protection of children and minors, COM(2003) 653 final.

[17] European Parliament and European Council, Decision 854/2005/EC of 11 May 2005 establishing a multi-annual community programme on promoting safer use of the internet and new online technologies, (OJ L 149 11.6.2005, p.1).

2013.[18] This new Action plan is designed *"to be able to take into account currently unknown future developments in the online environment as the resulting threats will become increasingly important in the years ahead"*. The actions include again the promotion of a safer online environment and the public-awareness raising action, but these are framed to encompass a better 'user-empowerment' not only for parents and carers but also for children and young people, and to stimulate stakeholders to take responsibility, cooperate and exchange experiences and best practices at European and international level. Moreover, the Action plan acknowledges the need to create and build up an adequate knowledge base for addressing both existing and emerging uses, risks and consequences, and mapping both quantitative and qualitative aspects in this context; thus, it proposes the setting of a coordinated investigation activity that will be used immediately in the implementation of the programme, as well as into designing adequate actions for ensuring online safety for all users.

All the European interventions in this field have a non-binding character, moreover, they all support the development and the implementation of technical tools[19] and, among legal tools, they recommend mainly self-regulation as the best regulatory solution. This option is not only due to the fact that technical tools and self-regulation can have a higher level of flexibility and can be better fit with the needs of an ever-changing environment, but also to the general argument – clearly stated in IAPs decisions – that *"[r]eaching international agreement on legally binding rules is desirable but will be a challenge to achieve and, even then, will not be achieved rapidly. Even if such agreement is reached, it will not be enough in itself to ensure implementation of the rules or to ensure protection of those at risk"*.[20]

---

[18] European Parliament and European Council, Proposal for a Decision establishing a multi-annual Community programme on protecting children using the Internet and communicating technologies, COM(2008) 106 final, 27 February 2008, approved by the Council f Ministers on the 9th December 2008, available at http://europa.eu/rapid/pressReleasesAction.do?reference=IP/08/1899&format=HTML&aged=0&language=EN&guiLanguage=en

[19] See infra par. IV.

[20] Proposal for a Decision establishing a multi-annual Community programme on protecting children using the Internet and communicating technologies, cit., whereas (5). Previously also in Decision 854/2005/EC, whereas (6), cit.

III. The existing risks for children

Having described the current legal framework at European level, it is now necessary to provide the existing threats that children face during online surfing. This will help the analysis concerning the effectiveness of the technical and self-regulatory tools proposed by European and national actors.

A. CHILD ABUSE MATERIAL

In this category are included the cases in which children are harmed directly, as victims of sexual abuse documented through photographs, films or audio files and then transmitted online. In general child pornography refers to material depicting children being in a state of undress, engaged in erotic poses or sexual activity. Child sexual abuse occurs in the production of child pornography when sexual acts are photographed, and the effects of the abuse on the child (and continuing into maturity) are compounded by the wide distribution and lasting availability of the photographs of the abuse. For practical reasons, legal definitions of child pornography generally refer to a wider age range, including any pornography involving a minor, according to jurisdiction.

B. CHILD GROOMING

In this category are included the cases in which children are contacted by people who will befriend them in order to commit sexual abuse. Thus, the act of grooming a child sexually may include activities that are legal in and of themselves, but later lead to sexual contact. Typically, this is done to gain the child's trust as well as the trust of those responsible for the child's well-being. Sexual grooming of children also occurs on the Internet. Some abusers will pose as children online and make arrangements to meet with them in person.

C. CYBER-BULLYING

In this category are included the cases in which children are victims of bullying in the online environment.[21] Cyber-bullying involves the use of

---

[21] Despite this definition, the phenomenon is not limited to children, though is more commonly referred to as cyberstalking or cyber-harassment when perpetrated by adults toward adults. Cyber-bullying can be as simple as continuing to send e-mail to someone

information and communication technologies to support deliberate, repeated, and hostile behaviour by an individual or group that is intended to harm others. This can occur not only through text message but also through videos being uploaded on open video-sharing website (e.g. YouTube),[22] having an even more distressing effect, because the bullying in online environment has a potentially enormous audience, extending the humiliation and embarrassment of the victim.[23]

D. UNLAWFUL PRIVACY INVASION

In this category are included the cases in which children are asked to disclose personal information that can be used to profile them and send them commercial advertising. In this case, the risk is not merely the collection of personal information from children without their, or their parent's consent.[24] Rather, in wider perspective, the risk involves *"the opening up of the child's private world to the eye of the marketer, who not only watches the child but reconstructs the child's environment in order to manipulate the child's sense of self and security"*.[25] The possibility to obtain details of children's online behaviour can provide a continuous feedback to marketers, who not only can select easily which product to sell to individual children, but also can fine tune with child's online social

---

who has said they want no further contact with the sender, but it may also include threats, sexual remarks, pejorative labels (i.e., hate speech), ganging up on victims by making them the subject of ridicule in forums, and posting false statements gossip as fact aimed at humiliation.

[22] Cyber-bullies may disclose victims' personal data (e.g. real name, address, or workplace/schools) at websites or forums, or may pose as the identity of a victim for the purpose of publishing material in their name that defames or ridicules them.

[23] Home Office Task Force on Child Protection on the Internet, *Good Practice Guidance for the Providers of Social Networking and User Interactive Services 2008*, available at http://police.homeoffice.gov.uk/publications/operational-policing/social-networking-guidance?view=Binary, p. 17.

[24] Privacy concerns exist wherever personally identifiable information is collected and stored - in digital form or otherwise. Improper or non-existent disclosure control can be the root cause for privacy issues. Data privacy issues can arise in response to information from a wide range of sources, such as: healthcare records, criminal justice investigations and proceedings, financial institutions and transactions, biological traits, such as genetic material, residence and geographic records, ethnicity. The challenge in data privacy is to share data while protecting personally identifiable information.

[25] V. STEEVES, "It's Not Child's Play: The Online Invasion of Children's Privacy", *University of Ottawa law & technology journal*, 2006, 169-188, p. 186.

environment to make the child more vulnerable to advertising messages. This kind of marketing raises serious questions as it constitutes an invasion of privacy because enterprises penetrate child's private space and extract data for instrumental purposes by manipulating also their online environment.

IV. Technical and legal tools proposed by the EU

Now, we turn to the technical and legal tools proposed and implemented through the Safer Internet Action Plans, in order to analyse which are their advantages and disadvantages.

Hotline networks: hotlines are contact points where end-users can report illegal content on the Internet. All hotlines are intended to work together with police, law enforcement and awareness nodes as well as with Internet Service Providers, industry organisations and other institutions. Under the Safer Internet Action Plan a widespread system of hotlines all over Europe had been developed, coordinated by INHOPE, the International Association of Internet Hotlines.[26]

Advantages	--Better knowledge concerning the rate of illegal content available online. --Cooperation thoughout Europe in order to identify child-porn rings. --Centralised reaction in case of multiple jurisdiction issues
Disadvantages	--Difficult cooperation between hotlines and other stakeholders, in particular with police and law enforcement, (effectiveness of procedures is still low). --Lack of feedback from law enforcement authorities in order to improve the process. --Low awareness of the existence of hotlines from end-users.

Rating and filtering schemes: a rating system is a technological device that can help the user to identify in advance which are the contents of the website to be visited, usually the rating system describes the content in accordance with a generally recognised scheme (for instance, where items such as sex or violence are rated on a scale) and then filtering systems can empower the user to select the content he/she wishes to receive. Ratings

---

[26] See the website: www.inhope.org .

may be attached by the content provider or provided by a third-party rating service. There are a number of possible filtering and rating systems.[27]

Advantages	--possibility to filter in advance the content to be viewed by user --flexible tool (e.g. to be adapted to different aged children)
Disadvantages	--Low level of sophistication. --Difficult to achieve a critical mass need to provide accountable results. --Difficult to identify the appropriate labels in order to avoid that innocuous content will be blocked.

Age verification tools: obviously this kind of tool aims at ascertaining in advance the age of online user so as to keep older people away from youngsters, or vice-versa, keep young people away from website designed for adults. To accomplish either of those objectives, such tools must be able to effectively verify everyone's age by consulting reliable records about those looking to create an account on a social networking site. However, if the age verification is posed on adult's identity the proofs can be obtained from many sources,[28] while in case of children proving their age becomes more complicated, as only few can provide a similar set of proofs. Moreover, age verification can provide only a limited security effect, i.e. distinguish who can access or not to a specific website on the basis of its age; whereas no control at all is to be done on the records of the person accepted (e.g. existence of previous sex related crimes, etc.), thus, providing a false perception of security either to parents and to children.[29]

---

[27] See for instance the Platform for Internet Content Selection (PICS), which is a specification created by World Wide Web Consortium that uses metadata to label webpages to help parents and teachers control what children and students can access on the Internet. See more deeply at: http://www.w3.org/PICS/

[28] See that when government officials or even business seek to verify someone's identify or age, they can rely on birth certificates, Social Security numbers, driver's licenses, military records, home mortgages, car loans, other credit records, or credit cards.

[29] A. THIERER, "Social Networking and Age Verification: Many Hard Questions; No Easy Solutions", *Progress & Freedom Foundation Progress on Point* 14.6, 2007, available at www.pff.org/issues-pubs/pops/pop14.5ageverification.pdf

Advantages	--limitation of access to adults in children websites and vice-versa
Disadvantages	--difficult to achieve the perfect age verification --false sense of security for both parents and children --difficult coordination with freedom of speech and privacy

Codes of conduct: The Commission does not provide a specific model of self-regulation, rather it accepts the existence of multiple choices,[30] including codes of conduct; however, in any model drawn up by the relevant actors, the principles that it should respect are those of effectiveness, fairness, and transparency.[31] Furthermore, in case of codes of conduct, they should provide credible mechanisms for monitoring compliance, taking complaints and sanctions for non-compliance, together with means of making the public aware of their existence.[32]

Advantages	--quick reaction to public concerns --flexible tool --expertise of industry players
Disadvantages	--Limited level of enforceability --Risks of 'private censorship', as commercial organisations can decide what content can be considered harmful --Low awareness of the existence of codes of conduct from end-users.

---

[30] See, J-F. LEROUGE, "Internet Effective Rules: the Role of Self-regulation", in *The Edi Law Review*, 2001, 199 ff., where the Author lists the different forms of regulation: the "simple" unilateral declaration of will, the adoption of codes of conduct, the contract, the certification or labelling methods, the common practice or the emergence of a "lex electronica".

[31] See the guidelines already defined in the Recommendation 98/560/EC, cit., where the principles on which a self-regulatory intervention should be based were spelled out.

[32] According to a widely accepted definition, self-regulation norms are legal rules voluntarily created by a group of persons or their representatives from a particular sector of activities, accessible to them and therefore susceptible to be known by them and subject to sanctions in case of non-compliance, see J-F. LEROUGE, "Internet Effective Rules", cit., 197.

V. Case study: social networking

We now turn to a case study, taking an example easily available on the Internet: social networking, so as to verify the adaptability of the previously listed tools, and eventually provide the better synergy among them.

One of the most evident developments of Internet communication is its increasingly dynamic and interactive nature. Social networking is one of the new phenomena that bloomed in this evolved environment.[33] In social networks, users, once registered, can make public their personal data in order to establish a set of contacts with others who went to the same schools or universities (such as in *facebook.com*),[34] or who work in the same sector or firm (such as in *linkedin.com*),[35] or even in order to make self-promotion (such as in *myspace.com*).[36] In all these cases, users make available personal information, including sensitive data, to the entire circle of registered users. This behaviour can simplify the collection and the elaboration of users' profiles, giving leeway also to secondary use by third parties, who can take advantage of such information in different ways.[37]

Potential risks to children and young people using social networking services can include but are not limited to:
- bullying by peers and 'friends';

---

[33] These services are considered to be part of a paradigm shift in the evolution of the Internet, which is now frequently referred to as Web 2.0. Web 2.0 represents a fundamental shift away from this model, towards a more dynamic and interactive Internet where the creation of content is decentralised and more controlled by individuals or communities of users.

[34] See http://www.facebook.com. On this issue see I. BROWN, L. EDWARDS e C. MARSDEN, "Stalking 2.0: privacy protection in a leading social networking site", paper presented at the conference "GiKii returns", London University College, 19 September 2007, available at http://www.law.ed.ac.uk/ahrc/gikii/docs2/edwards.pdf, and more recently L. EDWARDS and I. BROWN, "Data control and social networking: irreconcilable ideas?", available at http://ssrn.com/abstract=1148732.

[35] See http://www.linkedin.com

[36] See http://www.myspace.com

[37] G. MACCABONI, "La profilazione dell'utente telematico fra tecniche pubblicitarie on-line e tutela della privacy", *Riv. Dir. Inf. e Informatica*, 2001, 425; C. D'AGATA, ""Self" e "strict" regulation: il trattamento dei dati personali nell'approccio "pluridisciplinare" di tutela introdotto dal codice della privacy", *Riv. Dir. Inf. e Informatica*, 2004, 883; L. EDWARDS e G. HOWELLS, "Anonimity, consumers and the Internet: where everyone knows you're a dog" in C. NICCOL, J.E.J. PRINS, M.J.M. VAN DELLEN (eds.), *Digital anonimity and the law – Tensions and dimensions*, T.M.C. Asser, The Hague, 2003, 221.

- exposure to inappropriate and/or harmful content;
- posting illegal or inappropriate content;
- posting personal information that can identify and locate a child offline;
- download viruses and *malware*;
- sexual grooming, exploitation and abuse through contact with strangers;
- exposure to information about self–harm techniques or encouraging anorexia and suicide;
- identity theft;[38]
- race hatred; etc. [39]

How can these risks be faced and overcome through the aforementioned tools?

Technical tools can help limiting the diffusion of children personal data. For instance, an 'age locking' can set profiles of users under eighteen automatically private, thus protect them from being viewed by adult users that they don't already know in the physical world.[40] This can be a useful tool that can bypass some of the aforementioned limitations of age verification *per se*, as it will only define as threshold the over/under eighteen years old.[41] This solution can be useful also to hinder grooming as children personal data (and also photographs, address, etc.) cannot be seen by over eighteen,[42] but it could not limit cyber-bulling, if the bully is

---

[38] Identify theft is defined as the case in which personal details have been stolen and are used illegally. In most cases identify theft happens through the method of *phishing* (criminally fraudulent process of attempting to acquire sensitive information such as usernames, passwords and credit card details, by masquerading as a trustworthy entity in an electronic communication) or *pharming* (a hacker's attack aiming to redirect a website's traffic to another, bogus website).

[39] Other possible threats are glorifying activities such as drug taking or excessive drinking; encouragement of violent behaviour such as 'Happy Slapping'; physical harm to young people in making video content, such as enacting and imitating stunts and risk taking activities such as playing 'Chicken' on railways; leaving and running away from home as a result of contacts made online.

[40] See for the *Joint Statement on Key Principles of Social Networking Safety*, declared by U.S. Attorneys General and MySpace on 14th January 2008, where the website agreed to implement such 'age locking' tools for new profiles so as minors will be locked into the age they provide at sign-up while 18 years old and older members will be able to make changes to their age as long as they remain above the 18 years old threshold.

[41] It must be said that any user can create a fake online profile, so as to get into the adult or children limited space, however, in such networks the evidence given by photographs and alike could clearly give information about real age or at least instil some doubts.

[42] This is also more efficiently achieved through other technical solutions, i.e. restricting 'friend requests' to only those who know email address or last name of the children,

in the same age group.[43] In the latter case, the provision of a 'report an abuse' button could be added in the site design, so as to give users the possibility to report any uneasy situation including cyber-bullying, pornography or unauthorised use. This could help in drafting a rating system based on the experience of users, (though the use of children as guinea pig would not be borne as acceptable).

However, the previous solutions are mainly on voluntary basis, as they are default settings coded in the software written for the social networking site (or they are included in clauses of the codes of conduct). In other words, these rules are applied by social networking site as long as they have incentives to do it. On the one hand, the accountability and the sensibility to acceptable children security level can enhance the usage of the website, as for instance parents will not impede to their children to access and participate to such websites. On the other hand, it must be underlined that social networking sites earn revenues through their activity, though services provided to users are (generally) free. As a matter of fact, revenues come primarily via third party advertising served to users.

For instance, a privacy policy can state that: "We do not provide contact information to third party marketers without your permission. We share your information with third parties only in limited circumstances where we believe such sharing is 1) reasonably necessary to offer the service, 2) legally required or, 3) permitted by you.";[44] however, this leaves open the question of when exactly the site "believes" that you wish to share your information.[45] In practice, the website would allow third

---

imposing 'friends only' group invite as mandatory (or as default) preference in profiles, etc.

[43] This is usually the case, as bulling starts in school, mostly among classmates.

[44] This example is taken by Facebook privacy policy, available at http://www.new.facebook.com/policy.php?ref=pf.

[45] See for a deeper analysis of privacy issues concerning social networking sites, L. EDWARDS and I. BROWN, "Data control and social networking: irreconcilable ideas?", cit., 14.

See that in the case of anonymised data this could be possible, as for instance Facebook privacy policy clearly admits: "*Facebook may use information in your profile without identifying you as an individual to third parties. We do this for purposes such as aggregating how many people in a network like a band or movie and personalizing advertisements and promotions so that we can provide you Facebook. We believe this benefits you. You can know more about the world around you and, where there are advertisements, they're more likely to be interesting to you. For example, if you put a favourite movie in your profile, we might serve you an advertisement highlighting a*

party advertisers access to its site and users, permitting them to profile users and send targeted advertising.[46]

On a completely different perspective, we should also take into account children perception of such interventions. As a matter of fact children and young people would interpret those devices as restrictions to their social networking activities. This would be self-defeating if children reaction will be to leave security-sensitive website and participate in other sites where more lax operating restrictions are available. The issue, still without easy solutions, is how to create sensible online policies without encouraging kids to operate completely surreptitiously in a "digital underground".

VI. Conclusions

A conclusion that can be drawn from the preceding case study is that any policy aimed at protecting children, either from illegal and harmful content or from other possible online risk, due to the nature of the subject-matter, should be of a multi-faceted nature.

On the one hand, in order to achieve an adequate level of effectiveness, several measures and actions should be combined in a complementary way, such as creating reporting facilities, empowerment of children as users of these technologies, self-regulatory elements and structures for cooperation between different stakeholders.

On the other hand, we should not overestimate the aforementioned solutions. For instance, technical devices will always suffer from inherent limitations and can be circumvented. A different factor that, instead, can last for a lifetime and can build a better online environment is children education.

An important and ever-increasing role should be given to teaching children how to be good cyber-citizens and how to identify and report online threats (predators, bullies, scam artists, etc.). Moreover, as children are now more savvy and sensible about online threats, it is even more important – for institutions, parents and carers – to keep being vigilant about online safety education and etiquette, providing always better and more accountable ways to give children lessons about sensible online behaviour and relations.

---

screening of a similar one in your town. But we don't tell the movie company who you are."

[46] See F. CASAROSA, "Privacy in search engines: Negotiating Control", on file by the Author.

Concept of "Network Neutrality" in the EU Dimension: Should Europe Trust in Antitrust?

Oles Andriychuk

European University Institute, Florence, Italy

The purpose of the paper is to provide the economic and legal background for the future regulatory format of the content distribution via Internet in the European Union. Based on the analysis of economic theory, case-law, existing and drafted legislation we make an attempt to evaluate the perspectives of the Internet regulation, particularly in the context of the "Network Neutrality" debates.

This paper describes the evolution of the European regulatory policy in two major content-related areas: telecommunications (electronic communications) and audiovisual industry, their fast intersection and interdependence is the consequence of unavoidable technological and commercial convergence between two previously separated spheres: management of the network infrastructure on the one hand and content production, promotion and distribution on the other.

The convergence of electronic communications, media and entertainment industries puts on the agenda the need for revisiting the existing formats of bring the content to the consumers. Technical possibility of high-speed data management impels both content-oriented and infrastructure-oriented industries for searching the new business models of advanced content delivery. Paradoxically, the higher capacity of the networks, the bigger scarcity the traffic becomes. This is the case, because Internet-users increasingly prefer "click-and-watch" over the previously dominating "click-and-wait" model of content consumption. The theoretical battle for the future format of Internet architecture constitutes the essence of the so called "Network Neutrality" debate.

I. "Network Neutrality" in the European Context

A. INTRODUCTION

"Network Neutrality" (NN) ontologically is political, not legal, term. It has been introduced by the US antitrust scholars and is established and consensually used as well in the legal literature. It constitutes the premise of original destiny of the telecommunications infrastructure as a conduit of all relevant data with (virtually) no interference of incumbent into this process. Because of its political roots it does not represent the literal meaning of neutrality. Most actors on both sides of the debate agree that not every data have to be transmitted without any prioritization (e.g. the succession of e-mail, banking and/or security services is always prioritized over other Internet-applications).

After two decades of the Community liberalization policy in the telecommunications area, the domestic European markets are becoming relatively integrated and disclosed. This gives the chance for the world-wide leaders of the electronic communications industry to enter into the regulatory homogenous, rapidly growing European telecommunications environment without the necessity to comply with 27 different administrative regimes of all the EU member states. The opening of the European telecommunications industry is a long-term process, which has to be seen in its three dimensions: "incumbents v. new entrants", "domestic telcos v. European vis-à-vis" and "European telcos v. foreign competitors". The history of interactions between these three groups of telecommunications actors shows many examples of their fierce contest in, but mostly for the markets. Every telco strives to promote its own commercial interests, often simultaneously supporting different, even controversial theoretical approaches in the different markets: from preserving strong regulation to complete de-regulation; from maintaining the monopoly position to fostering the competition; from hard protectionism to libertarian market disclosure. The position of the companies depends in what status they appear in each relevant market: as incumbents or as new entrants; domestic or European; European or foreign. However there is an area in which they reach practically unconditional consent: they are unanimous in relation to "Network Neutrality". Among the companies which represent the opposite side of this theoretical debate the situation is similar as well.

Until the moment of rapid growth of Internet-technologies, which provides high-speed traffic over the new FTTx networks (and consequently the transmission of large-sized files and applications) the discussion on "Network Neutrality" had solely theoretical dimension. With fast development of Voice over Internet Protocol (VoIP) technologies, Internet Protocol Television (IPTV), video-on-demand and movie-downloading services (otherwise large-sized files and applications) the amount of traffic over the network had been grown exponentially. Concurrently with this process there has been substantial development of the infrastructure, which inter alia now can be managed gradually by Internet Service Providers (ISP). In practice it means that ISPs, who often at the same time are owners and administrators of the networks, can range the traffic speed of different Internet applications.

Because of digital convergence and systematic elimination of the frontiers between infrastructure, platform and content of the Internet, many ISP are beginning to consider the launching for their users the provision of the different kinds of content services under different speed of traffic (i.e. two-tier Internet). Concurrently, some big Internet companies are launching their own wired and wireless networks (e.g. Google in San Francisco).

As ISP received technical possibility to range the traffic of different applications, but most importantly of different content providers, they started to consider the possibility of providing high-speed premium services for content operators, who are interested in instantaneous delivering of their services. This option is particularly important for such time-sensitive applications as broadcasting of live sports events, video conferences and some other communication services. Under such conditions Internet speed became a *killer application* for attracting new clients and gaining substantially higher revenues. There are two hypothetical models of applying this premium speed services: 1) assigning such extra-speed capacity to other content-providers for additional fee or 2) vertical integration of ISP with certain content-provider and offering content services on its own.

The merely technical capability of ISP to charge their clients (it being understood as charging on both sides of traffic: download – i.e. consumers, but also upload – i.e. content providers) brought on commercially justifiable apprehensions in the content-providing Internet industries. It might become possible that services, which have been receiving by content providers virtually for granted (i.e. by paying only for upload speed and data capacity at the upstream level), now may be obtained by these companies for additional payments at the download level (i.e. depending on the real amount of users). This scenario appears to be only hypothetical, since nobody is allowed to *degrade* the speed for particular content or application, furthermore this situation would be never possible both from the political (i.e. *freedom of speech*) and commercial (i.e. *cannibalization* of existing business model) points of view. On the other hand, however, the growing popularity of premium speed services would indirectly leave in the cold those content-providing companies who will continue to rely upon merely average "non-discriminatory" speed of data transmission.

So, does "prioritization" might mean "discrimination"? This is rather philosophical question, the answer to which definitely depends on the initial position of inquirer. As it always happened with debates in the area of competition law and regulatory policy, each party tries to obtain the *cheval de bataille* of its rectitude: benefits for consumers and improvement of general economic welfare.

This situation impelled content providers for launching wide-ranging political campaign on "Network Neutrality", intending to preserve the existing *status quo*, by means of introducing broad public discussions and implementing relevant legislative framework. The epicenter of debates initially was situated in the United States, where this topic received tremendous public coverage and scientific conceptualization. However, at the present days the "Network Neutrality" concept becomes more and more popular in other jurisdictions, particularly in the European Union and Japan, where these debates are still in their infancy.

Leaving aside such controversial issues as level of censorship, privacy, and copyrights protection of the transmitted content, apparently local Internet service providers are aware of their customers needs at least not to less extent than world-wide content providers are. Therefore they will never put in jeopardy the services of high-speed data delivery by blocking or slowing down certain applications. On the other hand, however we have to recognize that with some minor exceptions, providers of broadband Internet services are usually monopolists in the local markets and their dependence upon content-creating companies is significantly less than *vice versa*. Does this mean that their business practices need to be regulated by the sector specific instruments, such as compulsory access or neutral traffic requirement − or the traditional mechanisms of *ex post* competition law are reasonable and sufficient in the present context? What is the legal difference between the American and European approaches to the "Network Neutrality" and where exactly it is situated? These are two central questions for the present paper.

B. JURISDICTIONAL CONCERNS − *QUO WARRANTO*

Telecommunications law was not originally supposed to have the European Community dimension. "Founding Fathers" of the European integration laid down *prima facie* explicit clauses in the legal foundation of the European Community, reserving for telecommunications the national regime of regulation. That is because at that time the social and political status of telecommunications has been considered as one of the strategic domains of the internal affairs. Thus, Article 86 of the Treaty Establishing the European Community stipulates the following:

1. In the case of public undertakings and undertakings to which

Member States grant special or exclusive rights, Member States shall neither enact nor maintain in force any measure contrary to the rules contained in this Treaty, in particular to those rules provided for in Article 12 and Articles 81 to 89.

2. Undertakings entrusted with the operation of services of general economic interest or having the character of a revenue-producing monopoly shall be subject to the rules contained in this Treaty, in particular to the rules on competition, in so far as the application of such rules does not obstruct the performance, in law or in fact, of the particular tasks assigned to them. The development of trade must not be affected to such an extent as would be contrary to the interests of the Community.

3. The Commission shall ensure the application of the provisions of this Article and shall, where necessary, address appropriate directives or decisions to Member States.

Neither literal nor historical interpretation of these provisions gives us a ground for questioning the original intentions of the member states. The initial political will consisted in reserving the telecommunications policy for domestic regulation.

In the course of time, however, the pattern of reading of Article 86 has been hermeneutically moved towards substantial expansion of Community's competences in the present domain. Thus teleological and systemic interpretation provides a "clear picture of genuine mission" of the Treaty and classifies telecommunications as one of the most important *European* policy. The European Commission has been one of the most active proponents of such paradigm shift in evaluating the status of telecommunications policy in the economic constellation of the EC. This pro-European approach received its final legitimization in the judicial opinions of Community's courts, *videlicet* in the relevant case law.

Technically, the self-contradictory provisions of Article 86 might be interpreted in different ways, both in favor and against of the parties of the present dispute. Under these circumstances the decisive factor has been found in the general purpose of the European integration, which is based in striving to complete the single internal market (i.e. Articles 15, 26, 47(2), 49, 80, 93 and 95). This aim serves as common denominator for the arguments of both parties. Not surprisingly the reference to the overall value of market integration sorted all things out, manifesting the telecommunications policy as genuinely European.

C. Libéralisation! Harmonisation! Concurrence!

The European telecommunications policy was supposed to be governed by three major principles: *liberalisation, harmonisation* and *competition*. These three maxims directly correspond to three European meta-tasks: 1) completing the internal market; 2) setting out Community-wide uniform social and economic regulatory system; 3) fine-tuning the optimal competitive institutional environment.

It is noteworthy that although all three of them constitute the important elements of European economic welfare, they also quite often contradict themselves. The main problem is based in their ontology and methodology. Traditional *ex post* competition rules (i.e. antitrust law) are graduate and predictable, they provide for incumbents substantial amount of legal certainty, whereas the *ad hoc* nature of regulations, which constitute the main instrument for both the liberalisation and harmonisation conversely are rather based upon the rationale *exitus acta probat*.

There are philosophical doubts as well about the correctness of the term *liberalisation*, which in this particular context means *"liberalisation through regulation"*, but on no account *"liberalisation from regulation"*. For the definition of *negative freedom* such a formula is rather a *contradictio in terminis*. It is also true yet, that proponents of *positive freedom* consider volitional interference (i.e. *creativity*) as indispensable part of genuine freedom. In the context of the European telecommunications regulatory regime *liberalization* consequently means an aim, whereas the methods of reaching this aim are far from liberal (e.g. limitation of profitability, common carriage obligations or compulsory access).

The ontological legacy of the European telecommunications which are based upon original state ownership provides the additional – although rather rhetorical – argument for regulatory interference of the Commission. In the course of privatization of most European telecommunications giants the permanent implicit emphasis has been made, that entire network infrastructure has been built by the sweat of nation's brow, which can be euphemistically interpreted as: "the industry will continue to be regulated at least for a while".

This is particularly important, since under the current European regulatory regime, even telecommunications companies without significant market power, (as opposed to the rules, defining the dominant position in *ex post* competition legislation) may be obliged to provide in certain cases for their competitors adequate access to the infrastructure and services. The Commission recognises the exceptional character of such compulsory remedies, but proposes to preserve this practice in the new regulatory framework for telecommunications. Furthermore in order to ensure the consistent application of this condition and to avoid the imposition of inconsistent obligations without a market analysis, it is proposed to harmonise this procedure on the Community level. Supposedly this would prevent the risk of over-regulation and a fragmentation of the internal market through the imposition of inconsistent obligations. The procedure of cooperation between Commission and NRA is provided by Article 7 of the Directive on a common regulatory framework (2002/21/EC). It requires NRA to conduct a national and Community consultation on the relevant regulatory measures they intend to take. The Commission may issue comments and, under certain circumstances, block the proposed regulations.

D. European Policy of Limited Profitability

In the way to privatization of previously state-owned telecommunication companies in Europe, the most popular form of regulation was rate of investment limitation. This basically implied post-selling state's control over incumbent's tariff policy by means of requirements to restrict the scope of its returns and aggregate profitability. According to these conditions, commercial incentives of the telecommunication companies and their subsidiaries should be limited by general revenue caps. This presupposes possibility to gain solely "proportional" margin of profits, which should take into account the interests of direct, potential and maybe even hypothetical competitors.

Limitation of profitability ratios is rather objectionable and controversial instrument of telecommunications policy. From the theoretical perspective it raises substantial doubts about appropriate functioning of free market, not only restricting the genuine intention of service providers to render access to facility for highest possible price, but also confining inherent business intentions of incumbents to innovate and improve the quality of the telecommunications services.

Since the policy of limited profitability for the most part applies universally to the whole industry, often even without appropriate differentiations between various segments of telecommunications businesses, the sporadic benefits of such regulatory interventions are considerably degraded by economic damages, which are raised from the unnecessary market limitations in other allied areas of industry.

Furthermore, these restrictions are quite often applied to the markets where incumbent neither abuses nor even holds the dominant position and/or where competition is well-functioned and there is no rational necessity of regulatory intervention for public authority at all.

Per contra, because of complexity and rapid changes which occur when offering different services inside the telecommunications industry, it would be unrealistic to predict the existence of well-differentiated ranging system of regulation, which fully takes into account the specificity of various markets and submarkets, thereby providing mobile and efficient operational regime.

The limited profitability policy of telecommunication companies also does not bring any substantial benefits for consumers. Such interventional regulatory mechanisms may serve only for reaching short-term (and fairly marginal) advantages. It is the case, because in the long and middle-term perspective the lack of incumbent incentives to innovate together with their intentions to structurally optimize existing formats of business in order to adjust to regulatory pressure cannot lead either to establishing of workable competition model within internal market or to improving of services. Under the present system a large amount of incumbent efforts are re-directed to sophisticated parceling into different entities (i.e. affiliated enterprises) just to comply with the legal requirements[1], but virtually sharing gained profits "between different pockets of the same jacket".

Another important disadvantage of limited profitability rules in the telecommunications sectors is that they deform the fundamental notion of regulatory policy, impelling beliefs among dependent companies about the constant character of such well-disposed regulatory climate on the relevant market. The legacy of regulatory over-protection decreases abilities of dependent companies to compete under the conditions of workable competition. In return, it stimulates them to lobby the legislation and support the general political atmosphere in favor of conservation of the current state of affair in the industry. One can easily find persuasive arguments for regulatory protection, especially if the success or even mere existence of the dependent companies is at stake. Under this situation there is direct evidence that by definition provisional character of each *ex*

---

[1] This by no means is to argue the probability of existing of the genuine competition among companies with one and the same owner (e.g. accounting separation). On the contrary, there are sufficient evidences to believe that in some industries the ownership does not play decisive role with regard to competition (e.g. rivalry for audience among TV-channels, which legally belong to one media holding).

ante regulatory interference slowly but surely transforms into permanent state of play for a whole telecommunications industry.

By all means the regulation plays first violin in many domains of public community affairs, including those related to economy. It is indispensable *inter alia* in the relations of establishment/registration, fiscal and financial control, as well as in a range of other inspecting and administrative matters. Furthermore it is inevitable in securing performance of common carriage through provision of universal services. However, the primary task of regulatory policy in the area of market fine-tuning is to establish, improve or modify competition in the relevant market(s), but in no circumstances to substitute it by nearly command-and-control practices, such as the policy of limited profitability.

The references of the proponents of the limited profitability policy to a large extent are based on the fact that newly established competitive markets of telecommunication services are dependant upon regulatory interference, because otherwise they would undergo unbearable pressure from incumbents and will be forced to abandon the market. This presumption is increasingly gaining axiomatic features in the industry. Another reasonable argument is based upon the wide-spread (although rather deductive) experience of abusive monopolistic behavior of incumbent in the presumably unregulated environment. In the ideally-modulated world the competition in the network industries is rather temporal issue, considering that monopolization of the market is almost indispensable in the end[2]. Under such circumstances successful incumbent world be motivated to operate in the paradigm of winner-gets-all formula. It is precisely this reason why both *ex post* (competition laws) and *ex ante* (sector specific regulations) regulatory policies are called to.

As a general rule the most important instrument for public regulation of market economy appears to be the competition law. Because of its existential universality and the legal conformity, precisely this tool is considered as a commonly acceptable *raison d'être* of moderate and predictable market regulation. Competition law has its well-elaborated jurisprudence; it is based upon judicial principles and case-law. In the legal reasoning there is much more about "law" here, then about "competition". Hence competition law is an instrument, which provides substantial amount of legal certainty and refers to principles of law or at least does accept them as a value.

The *ex ante* regulatory instruments of market regulation are not characterized by the predictability and legal continuity. They are fully

---

[2] "Winner gets all".

dependant upon political context and are adopted by executive authorities as rules, but not as principles. *Ex ante* instruments are much more flexible and are easy to change. Their mission as regulators of competition lies in establishing short-term contextual tasks in accordance to everyday political necessity. The legal nature of *ex ante* regulation is *consequentialistic* with regard to results achieved in the market. Its algorithm is: "Sector specific regulations are the temporal tools for matching the market failures, which cannot be fixed by *ex post* regulation. In course of time of their legal validity they may directly contradict to competition law as *ex post* regulation, but would still apply even despite of formal discrepancy with competition law and even the plausible higher place of the latter in the formal legal hierarchy".

E. LOCAL LOOP UNBUNDLING

The European policy in the area of "Network Neutrality" has to be seen in close interconnection with the approach of the Commission to the issue of local loop unbundling. The regulatory regime of the latter may be transposed in the future to the former, since both are directly related to rules of the appropriate managing of the networks and both eventually provide very high obligations for incumbents.

Local loops constitute physical wired intermediary between telephone exchange central office and end-users telecommunications lines. The essence of local loop unbundling policy is based in allowing for incumbent competitors "fair" and "nondiscriminatory" use of the facility of monopolist. The technical characteristic of local loops does not afford their duplication under economically reasonable terms. Naturally, the opinions of the main industry players are divided, depending on the factual power in the markets of networks interconnections. Thus companies, who possess local loops (virtually, always monopolistically) are insisting upon their genuine property rights to operate with their own facilities, whereas new entrants and companies who do not have well-developed network infrastructure, refer to their right to compete and ask for permission to use local loops under the same conditions as incumbent affiliated companies do.

Another, more radical variant, of local loop unbundling constitutes *bit stream access*, which essentially is an entrance to the market of electronic communications made by a company which possesses no infrastructure equipment at all. Neither current, nor reformed European telecommunications regulatory framework does not explicitly maintain compulsory provision of bit stream access, however according to the

Directive on access and interconnection (2002/19/EC) incumbents are obliged to provide different forms of access under transparent and non-discriminatory terms and conditions. Hence, proactive interpretation of this provision may lead to compulsory access to the network by competitors, if such access has been made for at least one of them. According to the Article 1(3) of the Regulation (EC) No 2887/2000 on unbundled access to the local loop "This Regulation shall apply without prejudice to the obligations for notified operators[3] to comply with the principle of non-discrimination, when using the fixed public telephone network in order to provide high speed access and transmission services to third parties in the same manner as they provide for their own services or to their associated companies, in accordance with Community provisions".

The practice of Commission demonstrates its willingness to foster innovations in the bit stream markets, in particular outside metropolitan densely populated areas. National regulatory authorities are required to notify their market analysis with regard to several pre-defined markets to the Commission. One of these markets is the market of bit stream access[4].

One of the most appropriate solutions for this dilemma may provide the market itself, in particular, rapidly growing wireless technologies. In the predictable future wireless connection may become an appropriate platform for high-speed transmission of data. This is already the case in the most technologically developed local communities around the globe. The economic potential of wireless communications is enormous. According to the Commission, the total value of services that depend already today on use of the radio spectrum in the EU exceeds €200 billion. Wireless has been one of the strong drivers of the economic growth of Europe.[5]

Wireless technologies constitute effective substitution for traditional way of electronic communications. Their intensive usage would help to solve existing bottleneck problem in the area of local loop interoperability. There are reasonable market premises to believe that instead of strict compulsion to open the access for the local loops,

---

[3] Notified operators are the operators with significant market power.

[4] E.g. In 2006 Commission approved decision of the German regulator *Bundesnetzagentur* to open up broadband markets, including very high-speed internet access (VDSL) with regards to Deutsche Telekom.

[5] VIVIANE REDING, Member of the European Commission responsible for Information Society and Media The Review 2006 of EU Telecom rules: Strengthening Competition and Completing the Internal Market Annual Meeting of BITKOM Brussels, Bibliothèque Solvay, 27 June 2006.

regulator might re-direct its efforts to promoting wireless technologies, fostering new entrants to adopt new business strategies, which will not only establish competition in the markets, but also promote innovations for the benefits of consumers. This approach would be particularly relevant in the light of the Commission efforts to liberalize the spectrum policy and bring its regulation on the Community level.

Since the Commission proposal for review of European electronic communications framework is focused on the empowering market players and giving them the necessary legal certainty to exercise the role of innovators, it would be both effective and consistent to provide for them regulatory prerequisites for such incentives – i.e. to restrict commonly used practice of local loop unbundling and impel new entrants to look for their way to success via new wireless technologies rather then free riding on existing facilities.

II. European law of electronic communications

A. PRESENT-DAY REGULATORY REGIME

Legislative failure to include the "Network Neutrality" provisions into the Communications Opportunity, Promotion and Enhancement Act of 2006 shows at least preliminary state of affairs in the United States. This is not the case for Europe. The "Network Neutrality" issue has been neither settled, nor yet properly articulated in the European context. The debates over telecommunications in the EU take place under another methodological apparatus, with different priorities and somewhat shifted accents. What is similar to the US situation is the clear-cut definition of the European opponents and adherents of the "Network Neutrality". The group of the former consolidates most of ISPs (regardless of their legal property relation to the networks). The latter are united around the most powerful and ambitious content suppliers.

Despite the strong commitment of the main European regulatory player (i.e. the Commission) to proactive telecommunications policy, the opponents of the "Network Neutrality" are in a more advantageous position, since they have to explicate the preservation of the *status quo*, (i.e. application to presumably discriminatory conduct of ISPs *ex post* antitrust rules), whereas advocates of the "Network Neutrality" are called on to persuade the European legislator in the necessity to adopt explicit *ex ante* regulatory measures. However, taking into consideration the power of public opinion in the course of the European decision-making process, the perspectives of the "Network Neutrality" legislation appear to be quite likely. Under such circumstances the "consumer welfare" constitutes an **ultima ratio** of the future "Network Neutrality" debates in Europe.

Innovations and investments are another "golden share" in this discussion. One of the best ways to attract new investors into the telecommunications market is to demonstrate its profitability, regulatory benevolence and potential for future evolvement. Over the last years (in the case of the EU) and decades (in the case of the US) the reference to efficiency often became decisive factor during administrative scrutiny and judicial hearing. The post-Chicago approach to the analysis of monopolist economic behavior and its consequences for the market is currently applied upon an almost consensual agreement of all stakeholders. Which regulatory model – liberal or proactive – will create favorable preconditions for long term investments into the new technologies? The convincing answer to this question predetermines the attitude of regulatory authorities to the "Network Neutrality" matter.

Antitrust law is the most appropriate *ex post* regulatory "watchdog" for the European telecommunications (particularly in the area of content/application gradation) because the competition in the markets of Internet services provisions is already secured (and created) by another EU regulatory tools (i.e. European regulatory framework for electronic communications and European audiovisual policy). These instruments provide sufficient basis for opening markets and the additional "Network Neutrality" clauses will bring *de facto* regulatory duplication. If an aim of *ex ante* regulations is to establish competitive environment in the markets and not to protect competitors, "Network Neutrality" rule is unnecessary, since it does not guarantee horizontal competition between the ISPs, but only impose on them "non-discrimination" duties in regards to their vertical relations with content providers. The only *ex ante* regulatory tool which is really essential for establishing the competition between ISPs is the current European policy of local loop unbundling and/or bit stream access. We however are not pleading for these measures because of their significant infringement of essential property rights of network incumbents, but since they are already established we have to take into account their positive aspects for European economy. The legal and economic evaluations of these premises will constitute an essence of the present research.

Since at the present stage of telecommunications evolvement the networks represent the biggest "bottleneck" for content distribution, the attraction of investments into their deployment has to be seen as a major regulatory priority. Following the rationale of the liberal postulate "softer regulation is a stronger regulation", the possibility to gain vast revenue from the "gatekeeper" position is a substantial stimulus for the new investors. The widespread argument of inefficiency of the networks duplication still plays an important, but no longer decisive role in the modern telecommunications economy, in particular taking into account the vigorous potential of next generation wireless networks. In this research we will demonstrate how exactly market failures can be effectively solved by the antitrust procedures in the relevant areas.

As a result of fast technological evolution and a growing juxtaposition in a number of communication areas, a draft of the new telecommunications framework has been launched at the beginning of 2000. Because of rapid convergence among three, previously almost not interdependent, sectors (i.e. telecommunications, information technology and media), the decision has been made to cover all of them by a single regulatory regime. This new framework included regulation of both telecommunications and broadcasting aspects of communications, which previously have been regulated separately. However, the new regulatory regime of communications does not include both "content services" providing editorial control and "information society services", which do not mainly consist in transmission of signals on electronic communications networks. Besides of explicit exclusion of audiovisual services, new electronic communications proposal provided no coverage for regulation of telecommunications equipment.

On 25 July 2003 the new regulatory framework came into force. Initially this new package consisted of five directives: the Directive on a common regulatory framework (2002/21/EC), which lays out the main aims and procedures for an EU regulatory policy in the area of provision of telecommunications services and networks; the Directive on access and interconnection (2002/19/EC), which provides regulation of the access to and interconnection of networks on operators with significant market power; the Directive on the authorisation of Electronic Communications Networks and Services (2002/20/EC) – mechanism for establishing a new system of general authorisation. Under the provisions of this directive national regulatory authorities can no longer issue licenses, but only to establish a general authorization for all telecommunications services; the Directive on universal service and user rights related to electronic communications networks and services (2002/22/EC), which provides a minimum level of affordability the telecommunications services for European consumers, and the Directive on privacy and electronic communications (2002/58/EC), stipulating the rules for protection of personal data and privacy.

A main reason to propose the framework was to harmonise the communications legislation. In addition to this packages the Directive on competition in the markets for electronic communications services (2002/77/EC), the Decision on a regulatory framework for radio spectrum policy (678/2002/EC), the Decision on the minimum set of leased lines with harmonised characteristics and associated standards (2004/641/EC) the Decision establishing the European Regulators Group for Electronic Communications Networks and Services (2002/627/EC) and the Recommendation on relevant markets (C (2003) 497) have been provided latter on. It is important to note that this paper does not review all provisions of all Regulatory Framework directives; instead, we focus on specific aspects of the directives, related to "Network Neutrality" debates.

It has been acknowledged, at the current stage of the EC telecommunications development, the general political will to move towards greater application of antitrust *ex post* European principles. This gesture is still far from consensual recognition of the competition law rationale as dominant in the area of telecommunications. On the other hand, it might be interpreted as the manifest of completion of the first proactive regulatory stage in infrastructure liberalisation.

B. COMPULSORY INFRASTRUCTURE ACCESS

In accordance with the current European regulatory model, compulsory access to the network infrastructure can be justified as a means to increase competition. The Directive on access and interconnection (2002/19/EC) obliges network operators with significant market power to meet reasonable requests for access to and use of networks elements and associated facilities, stipulating that such requests should only be refused on the basis of objective criteria such as technical feasibility or the need to maintain network integrity. In cases when access is refused, the aggrieved party may submit the case to the dispute resolutions procedure referred to in Articles 20 and 21 of the Framework Directive (2002/21/EC). However national regulatory authorities are required to find a proper balance between the short-term interests of new the entrants and their incentives to invest in alternative facilities that will secure more competition in the long-term.

To one of the most important regulatory instruments of compulsory access belongs the price control. In the markets, where the competition is not well-developed incumbent are prohibited from imposing excessive prices and using price squeeze tools for eliminating competition. The Directive on access and interconnection gives to the national regulatory authorities the necessary rights for appropriate price control, such as cost accounting system and undertaking an annual audit to ensure compliance with that procedure.

It is important that compulsory access provisions may be imposed by national regulatory authorities, not exclusively upon a company with market dominance[6]. Such obligations go far beyond the *ex post* competition principles and along with liberalization bring disincentives for incumbents to innovate and expand their networks.

The new phase of telecommunications policy indicated the Commission attempt to reassess existing electronic communications regulatory framework. The main impetus for a reform came from the fast-changing nature of the telecommunications structure, from the deep convergence of various interrelated services (i.e. operation and deployment of the network infrastructure, access services, entertainment and content provision) and from the multilevel interdependence between them.

During public consultations many incumbent operators and some national authorities considered that the regulatory framework should foster more investment, and called for a major reform. Nevertheless, some have called for either withdrawal of sector-specific regulation or regulatory holidays for major investments that made significant financial injections into structural renovation of their networks.

The Proposal covers the area of common carriage services provision. Because of the fact that the fast technological progress significantly changed the conditions under which common carriage service rules operate, and keeping in mind a deep infrastructure deployment and establishment of alternative networks, in the Commission's opinion these services need substantially less regulation from the member states. Conversely, in order to apply common European standards to such services, it is proposed that common carriage services obligations of incumbents must be as much proportionate and transparent as possible. The document proposes to introduce a deadline for reviewing national common carriage rules and give a spur to liberalise the national markets and also introduce competition within newly opened segments of

---

[6] E.g. Article 3(2) of the Directive on access and interconnection stipulates as follows: "Where, as a result of ... market analysis, a national regulatory authority finds that one or more operators do not have significant market power on the relevant market, it may (sic. – O.A) amend or withdraw the conditions with respect to those operators, in accordance with the procedures referred to in Articles 6 and 7 of Directive 2002/21/EC (Framework Directive)..."

telecommunications market.

One of the most important and controversial proposals of the Commission is related to universal service provision. The current EC regulations of universal services are based on the "classic model" under which telecommunications companies may often provide both access to the network and voice communication services. In the Commission's opinion such a vertical integration model, while incumbent provides services of access to network and voice communications, may harm (or, to put it in more appropriate terms, "not foster") the competition within the internal market. That is why it offers to introduce separate obligations on providers of access infrastructure and on providers of services. One of the main reasons for such legal transformation is that the Commission foresees a rapidly growing interconnection of the different services and consequently the potential harm for the internal market if competition *for the market* will prevail over competition *in the market.*

According to Article 3 of the Directive on competition in the markets for electronic communications services (2002/77/EC) "Member States, shall ensure that vertically integrated public undertakings which provide electronic communications networks and which are in a dominant position do not discriminate in favour of their own activities". Directive on access and interconnection (2002/19/EC) stipulates that the telecommunications companies with significant market power are obliged to operate in accordance with the principle of non-discrimination, ensuring that undertakings with market power do not distort competition, in particular where there are vertically integrated undertakings that supply services to undertakings with whom they compete on downstream markets.

The attempt of the Commission to regulate the telecommunications industry in such dirigistic way may be justified by a hypothetical reaching of some efficiency gains for the European market. This policy may, however, also lead to a decrement of the general level of legal certainty in the business environment and negatively reflect on the intensions to invest into future development of infrastructure. As of today it is still hard to predict the kinds and methods of regulatory measures, which may be applied in order to impel the incumbents to give up certain part of their business. This is even less likely, if having in mind that the control over network allows them to carry on a wide range of legitimate economic leverages.

The spirit of this proposal is not consistent with the broad economic studies in the area of *ex post* competition law, because the political, industrial and academic discourses in antitrust domain reached almost unanimous consent upon economic efficiency of the vertically integrated business. The possible remedy for vertically integrated companies in the competition law may be applied solely in course of merger approval. Vertically integrated companies may undergo an additional responsibility for abuse of their dominant position, but such a responsibility may not concern compulsory separation of the incumbent, since it is the consequence of *behaviour* but not the mere *status* of the company *per se*.

C. "NETWORK NEUTRALITY" IN THE NEW REGULATORY FRAMEWORK

Another domain, which is proposed to be covered by the reformed regulatory framework, is "Network Neutrality" clause. This term has been created in US public debates by proponents of the current model of relations between telecommunications companies and providers of Internet content. The rationale of "Network Neutrality" is based upon prohibition of "double charge" for providing the Internet content to the end-users. The idea of launching "Network Neutrality" movement is based upon the eventual threat for Internet companies aroused from the intentions of Internet providers to establish the prioritised services for users or companies who are willing to pay more for substantial speed increment of data transmission.

The Commission's regulatory proposal maintains quite ambivalent statement in this regard: "In Europe the regulatory framework allows operators to offer different services to different customer groups, but does not allow those who are in a dominant position to *discriminate* between customers in similar circumstances". The distinction between the suppositions of such a formula, in all likelihood, might be established exclusively on a case-by-case basis. The Proposal contains an important clause which empowers NRA to establish "minimum quality levels" for transmission of data via networks, particularly to avoid a situation of "degradation of the quality of service to unacceptably low level". The Commission considers that any dispute, raised among parties concerning the different interpretation of "Network Neutrality" principles, should be resolved in accordance with *good faith* rules, referring to Article 5 (1) of the Access Directive: "In an open and competitive market, there should be no restrictions that prevent undertakings from negotiating access and interconnection arrangements between themselves, in particular on cross-border agreements subject to the competition rules of the Treaty".

Concerning the possibility of application of the provisions of non-discrimination in the context of "Network Neutrality" will depend on infinitude of eventual interpretations of the Article 10(2) of the Directive on access and interconnection (2002/19/EC): "Obligations of non-discrimination shall ensure, in particular, that the operator applies equivalent conditions in equivalent circumstances to other undertakings providing equivalent services, and provides services and information to others under the same conditions and of the same quality as it provides for its own services, or those of its subsidiaries or partners".

The proponents of "Network Neutrality" interpret these provisions as prohibition to prioritise the transmission of different services and applications, emphasising that in case of vertical integration of the infrastructure and content providers the conditions for premium traffic speed should be automatically (transferred to other content providers. On the other hand, however, the incumbents would reasonably refer to non-discriminatory character of premium speed services, since each company can receive access to such facility under the equivalent conditions. Hence the abovementioned provisions of the Directive on access and interconnection regulate the relationship of network operators and the new entrants, electronic communications companies, who strive to operate within the same infrastructure.

Even taking into account highly growing convergence of technologies and applications, apparently these conditions can not be directly applicable to the relations of network operators with content providers. The evolution of development of the "Network Neutrality" concept, its ontological essence and legislative regulation, both in the US and EU, will be scrutinized in particular in Section 4 of this paper.

The Commission analyses three potential scenarios for development of the telecommunications regulatory framework: 1) Removal or restriction of sector-specific regulation; 2) Adoption of an "open access" model for new network structure; and 3) No change to the regulatory framework.

The first, "free market", model is characterized by eventual advantages for current incumbents and substantial increase of the level of economic predictability and legal certainty. The removal or restricted application of *ex ante* regulation may provide an incentive for long-term investment and make European markets more attractive for transnational capital. This option envisages application in the telecommunications area *ex post* competition policy rules without considerable sector specific measures.

The biggest disadvantage of this regulatory approach lies in its disintegrational character. The removal of the uniform European regulation would authorize *status quo* in the European telecommunications, which are currently characterized by not only different levels of technical and structural development, but also by diverse approaches in regard to liberalization, often benefiting from privileged (quasi) national legal status, granted by member states.

In addition, removal of *ex ante* regulation in a market with a dominant position of incumbent operator is likely to slow down the level of effective competition and to cause consumer disadvantages. The rapid growing importance of the communications area in digitally-oriented economy demonstrates that the predictable long-term dominance does not constitute the exclusive condition for extensive investments in the new generation networks.

The second option is diametrically opposite to the removing removal or restriction of sector-specific regulation. Its essence consists in compulsory opening of the access to the incumbent networks to all potential competitors, if they correspond to certain set of established criteria. One of the versions of this option envisages the structural separation, which the Commission foresees as "could in principle be imposed under competition law instruments" (*sic.*). To the best of our knowledge, until very recently the most radical intervention of a regulatory authority in the commercial practice has been an institute of compulsory licensing of a dominant company under Article 82 EC (i.e. essential facilities doctrine).

There are many advocates and critics of this regulatory measure, both in governmental and industrial circuits. In literature there is virtually consensual agreement upon a fact, that the essential facility doctrine constitutes an utmost borderline of the regulatory interference into a domain of "societal sanctity" of private property. The most radical version of this institute provides the possibility of compulsory opening access to the piece of private property, which constitutes industrial bottleneck, but only under the principle of limited and shared access. It is almost impossible to imagine how the tools of *ex post* regulation may be used to impel the incumbents to refuse to operate on the market of communications services, leaving them merely the possibility of technical servicing the networks. The only and eventually possible way to implement this idea is via *ex ante* regulatory requirements, consisting in obliging the member states to grant the NRA the competences to provide that network operator guaranteed access to all competitors by dividing their infrastructure services from provision of Internet access. Hence, in all likelihood the Commission considers this approach as solely theoretical, using such argumentation purely in methodological purposes of comprehension of analysis. For the sake of discussion, however it is possible to simulate the situation, similar to "famous" rationale of the European courts with regard to parallel trading in intellectual property:

"the possession of property does not necessary correspond to its usage, which might have been restricted". By analogy, holding of the network does not mean unreserved right to provide electronic communications services. Hence, technically speaking, certain requirements of registration/establishing and accounting separation of incumbents might be launched by the Commission.

The Commission is absolutely right saying that the "open access" model for new infrastructure investment works well in a *tabula rasa* situation, where there is no pre-existing network or Commission initiate proactive initiatives, using structural funds. This situation may be fully justified only under free-will, but on no account under compulsory regulatory initiatives. The offered model has many advantages *per se* but because of impossibility of separation of the present-day infrastructure owners from the communications services (which often constitute the major part of their revenues) this idea remains to be hypothetical.

The third option, considered by the Commission is *no change to the regulatory framework*. The current model is characterised by high degree of predictability and harmonisation, its capability to successfully regulate the European telecommunications area has been proved in practice. For this reason it would be appropriate to concentrate the efforts on adaptation of the regulatory framework to rapid technological changes and direct them on the coverage of new-arising domains, rather than propose radical conceptual changes. The Commission considers that this model is the most appropriate option and consequently has proposed this in the associated Communication.

III. European Audiovisual policy

A. "NETWORK NEUTRALITY" CONTEXT

In regulatory terms the concept of "Network Neutrality" is in-between. Its substance is equally relating to both infrastructure and content. The fundamental essence of "Network Neutrality" is based upon the principle of fair treatment of content by network operators. Unlike traditional broadcasting, data over IP streaming has no technical borders and potentially can cover a worldwide audience. Since the issues of content management, relating to "Network Neutrality" may occur predominantly in the downstream market (i.e. content destination, places of consumption of the content by customers) in our case the attention has to be paid to European regulatory instruments of content management.

Regulation of audiovisual content represents substantial segment of European communications policy. The main legislative document in this area is Directive on the coordination of certain provisions laid down by law, regulation or administrative action in Member States concerning the pursuit of television broadcasting activities ("Television without Frontiers Directive" or TVWFD (89/552/EEC)), originally from 1989. This document has been substantially updated in 1997. After broad public debates and consultations in 2005 the Commission issued and in 2007 amended its proposal for Audiovisual Media Services Directive (AVMSD is a new title for TVWFD)[7].

The original objective of TVWFD has been the creation of appropriate conditions for free movement of television transmission within the EC. Its primary scope included all forms of public broadcasting, except electronic communications services providing information services on on-demand basis.

B. SINGLE EUROPEAN TV MARKET

In terms of *liberation-integration-competition* paradigm the main aim of this document has been definitely the second one. Unlike in the US, the broadcasting industry in its European counterparts is characterized by strong public elements. The state inheritance directly or implicitly presented both in all major European broadcasters and the whole consumer media culture in Europe. The genuine liberalisation of broadcasting industry has never been on European agenda. For this reason, apparently, TVWFD does not concentrate its efforts on liberalisation of the TV markets, but rather strives to integrate the different national regulatory environments into a single European model.

In order to pursue this important mission, the Commission tries to eliminate any regulatory borders between different member states. Hence, one of the key ideas of the TVWFD has been the prohibition for the member states to conduct any measures, which can restrict reception or retransmission of broadcast signal from other member states, apart from public safety, culture promotion and some similar to that exceptional national needs.

However, there are not enough political, economic and cultural preconditions for establishing a free market model of TV industry in

---

[7] Directive of the European Parliament and of the Council on the coordination of certain provisions laid down by law, regulation or administrative action in Member States concerning the provision of audiovisual media services (Audiovisual Media Services Directive).

Europe. As it is the case with European regulation of telecommunications infrastructure, the main efforts of the Commission are directed to the regulatory unification within the European internal market. The essence of *harmonization* of TV markets is based upon the subordination of national regulatory regimes to pan-European one. Since the meta-task of European integration is based in elimination of regulatory differences and economic borders between the member states, but by no means in erasing the obstacles for internal free market (i.e. internal market is not free market), the European audiovisual policy develops in conformity with general objectives of the European integration. These regulatory roots of the European model of TV industry play their role in the present-day situation with production and distribution of European TV content. Without unnecessary oversimplifications and fully taking into account all cultural, linguistic, behavioral and esthetic particularities of Europeans, there are enough evidences for conclusions about direct relation between strong regulatory character of the European TV industry and its poor commercial performance both in the worldwide and domestic markets.

TVWFD covers broad range of issues, related to production, transmission and reception of content in the EC. Its adoption has been originally stimulated by fast technological development in TV industry. In combination with firm intentions of establishing single European market these prerequisites became decisive for initiation of this legislative measure. Initially adopted in 1989 it has been amended in 1997 because of further development of audiovisual sector, in particular in the area of satellite TV, marketing-oriented business models, interactive technologies and future deployment of cable infrastructure.

In 2007 EU remains on the stage of revision of TVWFD. Under other circumstances and by the new title, the Audiovisual Media Services Directive is called for providing an effective regulatory tool for the area of content production and distribution in the new, digital age.

From the moment of the adoption TVWFD in 1989 and its substantial amendment in 1997 electronic technologies substantially expanded. That is the main reason of initiation by the Commission in 2002 legislative review of TVWFD. It has been officially launched by issuing the proposal for elaboration of a program for the modernization of rules of audiovisual services and a timetable of future actions. The Commission organized extensive public consultation campaign[8]. As a result of this hearing many

---

[8] The written submissions from the main European and worldwide TV companies will be analyzed in the Section 5 of this paper.

research and analytical programs and seminars have been organized by the Commission over 2003-2007 period of time. Finally in 2005 the Commission officially adopted legislative proposal for the revision of TVWFD (with the relevant amendments in 2007).

This document stresses the importance of European audiovisual environment, based on principles of pluralism, cultural diversity and consumer protection. The Commission offers in this proposal to provide the independence of national regulators in the media sector. It essentially means the striving to guarantee the tools for stronger regulatory power.

Conclusions

The aim of this research has been to give a descriptive presentation of the current European regulatory framework in the areas of electronic communications and audiovisual policy. By analyzing relevant EC directives and scholar literature we strived to put the existing model of *ex ante* regulation into the context of the "Network Neutrality" debates.

The general objective of this project was to provide a clear-cut overview of the European state of affairs in the areas related to "Network Neutrality". The purpose of the research is not to present the mono-semantic meaning of this multidimensional problem, but to show and explore the nodular issues of the academic debates over the "Network Neutrality" in the United States, to correct mistakes and afterwards to offer effective, theoretically adjusted solutions for the existing and new telecommunications operators in the European markets. The nature of argumentation will be mainly legal and (to a lesser extent) economic or societal.

Our hypothesis was rather in favor of *ex post* regulation of "Network Neutrality" and we intend to demonstrate why exactly Europe does not need its explicit mention in the *ex ante* telecommunications framework. It goes without saying that we refuse any sort of "instrumentalisation" of all explored arguments and will analyze all pros and cons without any partiality. If the evidences will contradict our hypothesis we will change the latter, not the former. The final aim of this research is the provision of alternative approach to the "Network Neutrality" dilemma in the European context. We expect to give a positive answer to the question submitted in the title of the present proposal "Should Europe Trust in Antitrust?" Because of our methodological reliance on deduction we cannot draw up the title in a more acceptable for us algorithm "Why Exactly Should Europe Trust in Antitrust?" until the end of the study. But *a priori* we believe that Europe *should* trust in antitrust.

By applying the reasoning of political philosophy we intend to prove that content *prioritization* is by far not the same as content *discrimination.* In addition, we will explore the existing US and EU case-law in telecommunications, intellectual property and antitrust areas, with the purpose to provide not only economic and societal, but foremost legal argumentation for ISPs to content/application prioritization and emphasize the relevancy of the *ex post* antitrust instruments for the companies which abuse/misuse their "natural" right to prioritize the content.

From the academic angle "Network Neutrality" is an interdisciplinary phenomenon. It can be explored from the economic, legal, societal, technical and political dimensions. This is the reason why although working primarily in the legal discourse we will not limit ourselves exclusively to positive law, but, when appropriate, will exploit the apparatus of the abovementioned sciences as well. The scope of this research does not allow us to take a comprehensive look into the technical and ethical aspects of the "Network Neutrality" concept. All implicit mentioning of the moral responsibility for the illegal peer-to-peer file sharing in the context of "Network Neutrality" issue, as well as references to problems related to fundamental freedoms, will be done optionally and as a context of analysis of relevant economic and legal theories.

The history of public debates in the United States showed a big potential of the "Network Neutrality" proponents to attract consumers. Their vivid rhetoric together with constant reference to fundamental freedoms manages to create a powerful public tool for the promotion of this idea. It is therefore important to explore and evaluate the most successful techniques, applied by the proponents of "Network Neutrality". We are *a priori* of the opinion that existence of extra-speed possibility for premium Internet services by no means degrades the other applications. The hypothesis of this research is that higher data-speed option gives to consumers an opportunity to benefit from the great variety of Internet services, particularly from those related to live-streaming.

The Future of Law: Relational Justice, Web Services and Second-generation Semantic Web

Pompeu Casanovas
Institute of Law and Technology (IDT), Autonomous University of Barcelona, Bellaterra, Barcelona, Spain

I. Introduction

This paper deals with some hopes and some concerns about the future of law, which I believe specifically related to the future of the Internet and the next generation of Semantic Web services.[1]

I will contend three theses about the integration of knowledge, regulation and semantic technology that may shed some light on how the future of law and the Internet looks like:

(1) There is a lack of scientific, reliable knowledge on how the Internet is really working and in which measurable way semantics is affecting its development; so we would need a better integration of communication, social and computer technologies to run the web.

(2) Usually, researchers in Artificial Intelligence and Law divide the field of Information Technologies (henceforth "IT") and Law into two different domains: (i) *IT Law* —data protection, copyright, security, domain names...— and (ii) *IT for Lawyers* —e-government, e-court, Online Dispute Resolution, Multi-Agent Systems...[2] Recent developments in semantic technologies, Natural Language Processing (henceforth "NLP"), legal ontologies, information retrieval technologies (henceforth "IRT") and the Web 2.0 and 3.0 may contribute to the convergence of the two approaches into a single techno-legal one. Second generation of

---

[1] Marta Poblet and I wrote two more joint papers connected to this same subject. Cf. P. CASANOVAS, M. POBLET, *Adding Semantics to the Legal Domain*. ESTC-08, Vienna, September 22th-24th 2008; P. CASANOVAS; M. POBLET, *Justice via the Internet: Hopes and Challenges of Law and the Semantic Web*. In Peruginelli and Ragona (Eds.), *Law Via de Internet*, ITTIG, Florence 30th October 2008.

[2] Cfr. M. APISTOLA AND A. LODDER, "Law Firms and IT. Towards Optimal Knowledge Management", *Journal of Information, Law and Technology*, n. 2/3, 2005, pp. 1-28; A. LODDER and A. OSKAMP "Law, Information Technology and Artificial Intelligence", in A. Lodder and A. Oskamp (Eds.), *Advanced Technology in the Legal Domain. From Challenges to Daily Routine*. Springer, Dordrecht, 2006, pp. 1-22; M. LAURITSEN , "Artificial Intelligence in the Legal Real Workplace", in A. Lodder and A. Oskamp, eds., op. cit., pp. 165-176.

Semantic Web technologies (henceforth "SW") is one of the means to facilitate this convergence.

(3) Therefore, I think that a pragmatic and cognitive approach based on a better knowledge of legal users, scenarios and contexts may be helpful to develop SW applications and legal Web Services. I will call later *Relational Justice* this hybrid, mixed-up field, as a subset of *Relational Law*.

I will rely on recent work and projects carried out by Internet scholars and by SW developers to foster a fruitful dialogue between Artificial Intelligence & Law scholars (henceforth "AI & Law") and legal theorists. I will provide definitions whenever they may be needed to follow my argumentation. Nevertheless, in this paper, more technical issues such as knowledge representation, knowledge acquisition, legal ontology building and methodology will be put aside.[3]

II. What is happening with the Internet?

Internet is growing every day. At the end of 2007, the Web had 1.3 billion users, and the growth rate in percentage for the period 2000-2007 was 920.2 % in the Middle East, and 882.7 % in Africa. Those are good news, even if we take into account the fact of the unequal distribution of resources and opportunities across the Web. However, in spite of this amazing growth, the old problem of gathering and representing content remains. How may all the generated information flow be retrieved, organized and shared in a feasible and reasonable way?

In a recent lecture on the Future of the Internet for the Semantic Technology Industries Assembly (STI), John Domingue draw a broad landscape in which a multitude of connected IT services are offered, bought, sold, used, repurposed, and composed by a worldwide network of service providers, consumers, aggregators, and brokers. This would result in a new way of offering, using, and organizing IT supported functionality, in which interoperability through Web 2.0, sensors, multimedia and what is called "The Internet of Things" (and not only

---

[3] Cfr. V.R. BENJAMINS et al. (Eds.), *Law and the Semantic Web: Legal Ontologies, Methodologies, Legal Information Retrieval, and Applications*. Lecture Notes in Computer Science 3369, Berlin, Heidelberg, Springer Verlag, 2005. See the state of the art in legal ontologies in J. BREUKER et al , "The Flood, the Channels and the Dykes: Managing Legal Information in a Globalized and Digital World", in J. Breuker et al. (Eds.) *Legal Ontologies and the Semantic Web. Channeling the Legal Information Flood*, Frontiers in Artificial Intelligence and Applications, Vol..188, Amsterdam, IOS Press, pp. 3-18.

interconnected pages) would reach a great number of end users (government, companies, businessmen, employees, scientists, employees, consumers and citizens). [4] In this vision, Semantic Technologies would be the key for the Web 3.0.

It is usually stated that the term *Web 2.0* emerged from a 2004 brainstorming session among officials of O'Reilly Media, Inc. and MediaLive International.[5] Actually it was used a bit earlier as a label or a way of speaking.[6] The term *Web 3.0* was coined by John Markoff, of the *New York Times*, in 2006. Those terms may be seen as "slippery concepts" or as shortcuts as well to refer to the interoperability and tagging allowing inputs from the users (Flikr, YouTube, Wikipedia, Facebook ...), and to adding semantics in more expressive languages to link objects and to share ontologies behind platforms and Web services. [7]

Scholars have emphasized from the beginning that the Web 2.0 is, above all, a *social network*, allowing people to connect each other and adding value through tagging to the websites that they populate with content.[8] This content should be better organized through semantic technologies. In a way, this social pragmatic approach resumes all what the SW is about.

Back to 2001, when the idea was spread out with an increasing strength, James Hendler envisaged a situation in which agents could construct ontologies to interoperate among them. An ontology-language (Hendler thought of *DARPA Agent Markup Language*, DAML + OIL) could be used to define an ontology of the terms needed to describe the invocation of services.[9] Using the example of a finite-state machine, this

---

[4] J. DOMINGUE, "Future Internet and the Role of STI International", PP Presentation, ESTC, Vienna, September 26th 2008.

[5] D.E. HARMON, "The 'New' Web: Getting a Grip on the Slippery Concept of Web 2.0", *Lawyer's PC*, vol. 23, n. 1, 2006, pp. 1-5.

[6] Cfr. E. KNORR, *2004 - The Year of Web Services, IT magazine CIO*, December 2003, p.90,athttp://books.google.com/books?id=1QwAAAAAMBAJ&printsec=frontcover&source=gbs_summary_r&cad=0_0#PPA90,M1 (accessed 12 May 2009).

[7] D.E. HARMON, op. cit. Ibid.

[8] Cfr. Among many others, E. MOTTA, "Knowledge Publishing and Access on the Semantic Web: A Sociotechnological Analysis", *IEEE Intelligent Systems*, May/June, 2006, pp. 88-90.

[9] There are at present many definitions of what an "ontology" is. I personally like the following, due to S. STAAB and R. STUDER: "Ontologies consist of concepts (also known as classes), relations (properties), instances and axioms, and hence a more succinct definition of an ontology is a 4-tuple <C, R, I, A>, where C is a set of concepts, R a set of relations; I a set of instances and A a set of axioms", P. WARREN et al. "Introduction", in

ontology would contain classes such as *State* and *Link* and have special Subclasses such *StartState* and *EndState*. Contents and properties could be described to give links a head and tail, to give states a list of the links that lead out from them, and to give a state an identifying property (Universal Resource Identifier).

Then, it would be easier to produce a domain ontology to perform social links. E.g. a "standard web sale" could be defined in some service ontology comprising a particular set of states and links.

The final result would be not only an intelligent human-interaction interface, but agent-to-agent communications that would produce social effects and perform social acts such as buying, selling and paying "between two Web agents that can use proof checking to confirm transactions".

"An agent can send an annotated proof to other agent. The annotations can be pointers to a particular fact on the Web or to an ontology where a particular rule resides. The agent receiving this proof can analyze it, check the pointers and check that the ontology is one it can read and agree with. This lets the agents recognize that a valid transaction has occurred and allows the funds to be transferred."[10]

Hendler called this perspective "service logics", and he predicted that this would be easy to achieve for the Web. However, nearly nine years later, this is still a hope, or an unfulfilled promise. *Where are all the agents?* is the title of one of his challenging *Letters from the Editor* for IEEE Intelligent Systems.[11] After being involved in the creation of Darpa Agent Markup Language (DAML) and the Ontology Web Language (OWL), a standard since February 2004, Hendler recognizes that although there are enough ontologies, interoperability at the data level is being solved and the existence of open source toolkits, still, there are no intelligent-agent based systems operating in the web and no venture-capital really available (no business plan)[12]. So, "what happened"?

This is a difficult question. Very likely, there is no unique answer. Developing and implementing technology involve complex processes. However, putting aside the technical aspects, some reasons may be related

---

J. Davies et al., *Semantic Web Technologies, Trends and Research in Ontology-based Systems*, Chichester, John Wiley & Sons, Ltd., 2006, p. 4.

[10] J. HENDLER, 2001, op.cit. pp. 34-35.

[11] Cfr. J. HENDLER, "Where Are All the Intelligent Agents?" *IEEE Intelligent Systems*, May/June, 2007, p.p. 1-3.

[12] In the same sense, V.R. BENJAMINS et al., *Near-term Prospects for Semantic Technologies*, IEEE Intelligent Systems, January/February, 2008, p. 76: most SW applications deal with search, and only a few of them are deployed with corporate budgets.

to the obstacles the Internet is facing today which are hindering a real science of the Web and getting a clear landscape of scenarios and possibilities. It is again a matter of lack of knowledge, but it is a battle over corporate, political and economic interests as well.

This may be a bit surprising, but the same social and economic networks that are fostering the growing of the Internet are actively becoming obstacles to the development of its full potential, and lawyers may have some responsibility on that. This was anticipated, e.g. by Dan Hunter in 2003 when he warned IT lawyers about "the anti-commons paradox": "We are enclosing cyberspace, and imposing private property conceptions upon it. As a result, we are creating digital anti-commons where sub-optimal uses of Internet resources are going to be the norm."[13]

But let's start with the explanations on social links among pages which constitute the kernel of the *Web 2.0* before going into it. The power of the Web emerges through the link space realized between Web pages. This is known as "the network effect". From the physical point of view (the first layer of the Internet), this is a "scale-free network".

The difference between a random and a scale-free network is the following: (a) The random network is homogeneous: most nodes have approximately the same number of links; (b) The scale-free network is inhomogeneous: the majority of the nodes have one or two links, but a few nodes have a large number of links, guaranteeing that the system is fully connected.[14]

In the connectivity distribution P (k), k is the number of links connecting to a node. Scale-free networks are characterized by a power law decay of the cumulative distribution $P(k) \sim k^{-\tau}$, meaning that the probability of attaining a certain size t is proportional to $k^{-\tau}$. When τ is greater than or equal to 1 we are under a Zipf law.[15]

At a large scale, many social phenomena show this kind of decreasing connectivity: fast development of diseases and epidemics, gossiping, city sizes or, even, the distribution of the human sexual contacts for males and females.[16] For the Web, scale-free networks may be formed due to

---

[13] Cfr. D. HUNTER, "Cyberspace as a Place and the Tragedy of Digital Anti-commons Paradox", *California Law Review*, Vol. 91, 2003, 439.

[14] Cfr.A.L. BARABÁSI et al., "Mean-field theory for scale-free random networks", *Physica A*, n. 272, pp. 173-187; H. JEONG, "Complex scale-free networks", *Physica A* n. 272, 2003, pp. 226-237.

[15] Cfr. L.A. ADAMIĆ, B.A. HUBERMAN, "Zipf's law and the Internet", *Glottometrica* V. 3, 2003, pp. 143-150.

[16] Cfr. F. LIJEROS et al., "The Web of Human Sexual Contacts", *Nature* n. 411, 2001, pp. 907-908.

preferential attachment, *i.e.* new links are established preferentially between nodes with high connectivity. Therefore, "the rich do get richer".[17]

The "network effect" has also come to be known as Metcalfe's law. In the early 1980s Bob Metcalfe explained to his customers why they needed more Ethernet boards than they were buying, because while the cost of the network grew linearly with the number of connections, the value was proportional to the square of the number of users.[18]

However, it is worthwhile to keep in mind that all those reckonings, in a way, are hypothesis, *Gedanken, thought experiments*. If we think of the upper layers and the annotation languages, researchers have come slowly to realize that we don't know many things about the real size and functioning of the Internet, including the effects of adding semantics to the Web. James Hendler and Tim Berners-Lee have put it crudely:

"Google receives more than 100 million queries per day, and if 20% of them are unique, then more than 20 million links, represented as new URIs that encode the search term(s), should show up in the Web graph every day, or around 200 per second. Do these links follow the same power laws? Do the same growth models explain these behaviors? *We simply don't know.*" [19]

III. Legal markets, ITC law and ITC for lawyers

So, "what happened"? The though criticism that Kimberly Claffy, from the CAIDA San Diego Supercomputation Center, hold recently before the Stanford lawyers is entitled *Ten Things Lawyers should Know about the Internet* (2008). Many obstacles prevent good measurements both of the Internet and of the Web. Claffy summarizes in four points the main problems she encounters in mapping the web: (i) *security*: "the fundamentally insecure software ecosystem"; (ii) *scalability*: "the fundamentally unscalable routing and addressing architecture"; (iii) *sustainability*: "the fundamental unsustainable economic architecture"; (iv) *stewardship*: "a stewardship model broken along so many dimensions, that solving or even studying the first three points is no one

---

[17] Ibid. p. 908.
[18] Cfr. J. HENDLER and J. GOLBECK, "Metcalfe's Law, Web 2.0 and the Semantic Web" ,*Web Semantics: Science, Services and Agents on the World Wide Web*, Vol. 6, n.1, February, 2008, pp. 14-20.
[19] J. HENDLER et al. "Web science: An Interdisciplinary Approach to Understanding the Web". *Communications of the ACM*, July, vol. 61 n. 7, 2008, pp. 60-69.

responsibility."[20]

The situation is this one.[21] National legislation sometimes does not help either, like in the case of the European ID cards.[22] However, I believe that professional behavior under economic, political and cultural corporate constraints has much more to do with all of this. As we will see, *Law & Society* scholars keep studying lawyers and lawyering since the seventies, and there is already a bulk of available research on what happened in between.

In *Urban Lawyers* (2005) [23], *e.g.*, Heinz and Nelson revisit their precedent study of 1975 on *Chicago Lawyers*[24]. Their insights are derived from a comparison of two surveys of the Chicago bar. The first was conducted with 777 lawyers in 1975 (when the profession was still numerically stable). The second was conducted on 787 Chicago lawyers in 1994 and early 1995. The authors show that the profession has experienced a dramatic change. For the first time, women, African Americans and Latinos have been involved in the profession, but in marginal roles in law firms and in lower-status practice settings. There is a growing divide between prestigious (corporate and tax law) and less-

---

[20] K.C. CLAFFY, *Ten Things Lawyers should Know about the Internet*, 2008, http://www.caida.org/publications/papers/2008/lawyers_top_ten/ .

[21] See K.C. CLAFFY et al. "The (un)Economic Internet?" *IEEE Intelligent Systems*, May, June, 2007, pp. 53-58. "Because no systemic measurements activities exist for collecting rigorous empirical Internet data, in many ways, we don't really know what the Internet actually is. Thus, we don't know the total amounts and patterns of data traffic, the Internet's growth rate, the extent and locations of congestion, patterns and distribution of ISP interconnectivity, and many other things that are critical if we're to understand what actually works in the Internet. These data are hidden because ISPs consider such information proprietary and worry that competitors could use it to steal customers or otherwise harm their business. The information might not even be collected because no economic incentive exists to do so, nor do any regulations require this collection" .

[22] F. LJUNGGREN, "Complexity is the Achilles Heel of eID. The Swedish eID system.", *ENISA Quarterly Review. Security and Interoperability of eID*. Vol. 4 No. 3, Jul-Sept, 2008, p. 16: "The result of legislation is that it has prevented the adoption of electronic identification instead of promoting it. The failure is evident by looking at what has been achieved so far. After 10 years of intense bureaucracy and tens of millions of Euros, we have not been able to implement a national eID scheme in Sweden. Even though there is a Swedish national ID card (INIDEL) capable of holding an electronic ID, it is empty. The card is essentially a brick! Essentially we are at the same point now as we were a decade ago. It is clear that something is fundamentally wrong."

[23] J.P. HEINZ, R. L. NELSON, R. L. SANDEFUR, and E.O. LAUMANN, *Urban Lawyers. The New Social Structure of the Bar.* The University of Chicago Press, 2005.

[24] J.P. HEINZ,R.L. NELSON,   Chicago Lawyers Survey , 1975 (ICPSR 8218), http://www.icpsr.umich.edu/cocoon/NACJD/STUDY/08218.xml

prestigious fields of law.[25] A greater proportion of Chicago lawyers focus their work on corporate clients, get much more money and their economic values have become close to the business interests. Therefore, the profession has become more segmented and more conservative.[26]

Brian Tamanaha conceptualizes the emergent situation as a new "legal instrumentalism" opposed to a principled and more integer conception of the law that American lawyers had in the seventies and eighties.[27] The relentless competition of lawyers, the system of billable hours, and the pressures to the partners to bring in clients have shaped new legal professional practices contrary to a vision of law as a matter of principle and reason. I am afraid he is right.

Some recent data may give some support to this statement. According to the *The American Lawyer 100 Report* —the top-grossing law firms in the United States— total revenues reached $ 64.6 billion and increased 13.6 % in 2007. At the top rank, two big firms, Skadden Arps Slate Meagher & Flom and Lathan & Watkins, reached more than $ 2 (American) billion (gross revenue) and $ 1.17 and 1.05 million per lawyer. We may wonder whether such numbers are sustainable in the new economic landscape after the crisis of the Wall Street financial model. Lawyers themselves are starting to wonder whether such numbers are sustainable.[28] Some prudence is required before answering such a question.

However, as stated earlier, those are not surprising news. Describing increasing legal revenues related to the so-called *big bang* of lawyers since the seventies is a well-trodden path by economists, legal theorists and *Law & Society* researchers. Table 1 shows the reckoning of expected value from 2003 to 2008.

---

[25] However, the self perception of the profession is not problematic in itself: "the most striking findings in the Chicago study, however, are the generally high levels of satisfaction reported by all categories of lawyers. Even among black lawyers, 71.4% of the respondents were satisfied or very satisfied." J.P. HEINZ et al. "Lawyers and Their Discontents: Findings from a Survey of the Chicago Bar", *Indiana Law Journal*, vol . 75, p. 758.

[26] J.P. HEINZ et al., *Urban Lawyers: The New Social Structure of the Bar*, Chicago, University of Chicago Press, 2005.

[27] B.Z. TAMANAHA, *Law as a Means to an End: Threat to the Rule of Law*, New York, Cambridge University Press, 2006.

[28] A. PRESS; J. O'CONNOR, "Lessons of the Am Law 100: Is the Golden Age Over?", *The American Lawyer*, 05/01/2008.

Country	Value in 2003	Growth 2002-03	Expected value in 2008
USA	140.3 billion $	5.6 percent	174.1 billion $
UK	28	3.6	31.6
France	14.7	14	16.7
Australia	5.9	11.6	9.4
South Korea	1.35	-3.3	1.9
China	1.34	7	1.9
Japan	0.9	8	1.6

Table 1. Legal markets size. Source: Data Euromonitor, elaborated by
M. POBLET et. al. 2007)

What is new is the convergence between lawyering and technical knowledge either of the Internet or the *World Wide Web* (WWW). [29] Practicing law becomes easier as long as legal operators use electronic devices to perform their jobs.[30] Of course, we may take into account that size makes a big difference between soloists and corporate lawyers. But, still, *ITC for lawyers* is an emerging flourishing field both for small and big companies. Law firms may diverge in the toolkits they use and seek for, but not in the fact that their daily work relies increasingly on the use

---

[29] Cfr. M. POBLET et al. *Exploitation strategies for the Spanish legal market*, SEKT D12.5.5. EU-IST Project 506826, 2007, pp. 1-54; M. POBLET et al. "Technology and Law: The Not So Odd Couple", in P. Warren et al. (Eds.), *ICT Futures. Delivering Pervasive, Real-time and Secure Services,* John Wiley & Sons Ltd, Chichester, 2008, pp. 201-211. J. BREUKER et al. , "The Flood, the Channels and the Dykes: Managing Legal Information in a Globalized and Digital World", in J. Breuker et al. (Eds.), op. cit. 2009, pp. 3-18.

[30] The expansion of lawyering is related to an increasing use of ITC tools, as shown by the *American Bar Association (ABA) surveys*. In 2008, e.g., over 40% of the USA firms indicated an average $ 8.000-$ 7.000 spending per attorney. 72% of respondents report that the firm files court documents electronically, up from 55% in the 2007 survey (ABA, 2008). Respondents are asked how they collaborate on documents. The methods reported most often are e-mail attachments (92%, up from 80% in the 2007 survey), fax (65%), Microsoft Word track changes or equivalent (64%), and in person (58%). Nearly all respondents report the ability to check work e-mail while away from the office (98%). The method reported most often by respondents as used to check e-mail while away from the office is via Smartphone/BlackBerry (59%). AMERICAN BAR ASSCIATION TECHNOLOGY RESOURCE CENTER *2008 ABA Legal Technology Survey Report: Online Research* http://meetings.abanet.org/ltrc/index.cfm?data=20080909.

of technology. Semantic technology is being developed in the law field according to these needs.

Collaborative tools (extranets, *blawgs*, wikis..) and meta-data use (watermarking documents, digital times stamping, *clickwrap* agreements…) are being commonly adopted, especially by young lawyers. Less attention is paid for the moment to XML technologies and legal multimedia trends (beyond videoconferences).[31]

But perhaps the best example of how *ICT Law* and *ICT for Lawyers* are related and will be even more related in the next future is the e-Discovery development.

E-Discovery is experiencing a spectacular growth because of the nature of the legal process itself. *Electronic Data Discovery* (EDD, or *e-Discovery*) may be defined as "a process (or series of processes) in which electronic data is sought, located, secured, and searched with the intent of using it as evidence in a civil or criminal legal case, or as part of a court-ordered or government sanctioned inspection."[32] *Electronic Stored Information* (ESI) is difficult to recover and retrieve because of its massive character. It is usually saved on back up tapes that are not labeled, catalogued or organized properly. Indexing and tagging requires both legal knowledge and computer expertise.

Moreover, as Will Uppington has pointed out, EDD is a field in which it becomes necessary to combine concept and keyword search with content categorization technologies.[33] Therefore, there is room enough for

---

[31] A broader landscape is offered in P. CASANOVAS, M. POBLET, *Adding Semantics to the Legal Domain*. ESTC-08, Vienna, September 22th-24th 2008. See also G. SARTOR et al. "Computable Models of the Law and ICT: State of the Art and Trends in European Research", in P. Casanovas et al. , *Computable Models of the Law. Language, Dialogues, Games, Ontologies*., LNAI n. 4884, Heidelberg, Berlin, Springer Verlag, 2008, pp. 1-20; BIAGIOLI, C. et al. (Eds.), *Proceedings of the V Legislative XML Workshop*, European Publishing Academic Press, Florence, 2006; E. FRANCESCONI ,*Technologies for European Integration. Standards-based Interoperability of Legal Information Systems*, European Publishing Academic Press, Florence, 2007.

[32] S. ATTFIELD; A. BLANFORD. *E-discovery viewed as integrated human-computer sensemaking: The challenge of 'frames'*, 2008, http://eprints.ucl.ac.uk/9135/1/9135.pdf, , p.1.

[33] W. UPPINGTON *Concept Search Versus Keyword Search in Electronic Discovery*.   http://www.clearwellsystems.com/e-discovery-blog/2008/11/12/concept-search-versus-keyword-search-in-electronic-discovery/: "Surely, concept search technology is better than old, boring keyword search. Well, actually it's not that clear-cut. The problem with concept search technology is that while it might find more relevant documents than plain keyword search, it will also likely find more false positives. Imagine searching for documents containing "terminate" in an employment matter and your concept search

a plurality of approaches, which lie on the different purposes and aims of users.

End users —customers, citizens, rulers, administrators...— and not only law firms or tech companies are real players in the field as well, because eventually someone has to pay the high costs of e-Discovery programs, as the main players have become to understand.[34]

IV. Web Services and Second Semantic Web generation

The main objectives of next generation of the SW are related to this plural and hybrid approach. What conception of law may be figured out to comply with them? I will link the two issues in my answer in the next two sections.

Comparing first and second generation of Semantic Web applications, Enrico Motta and Marta Sabou (2006) identify several features of the new orientations: (i) reuse (vs. semantic data generation); (ii) multi-ontology systems (vs. single-ontology systems); (iii) openness with respect to semantic resources, (iv) scale as important as data quality, (v) openness with respect to Web (non-semantic resources), (vi) compliance with the Web 2.0 paradigm, (vi) openness to services.[35]

Personalization, user-centered approaches, semantic wikis, hybrid ontological solutions, synergies between folksonomies and ontologies, scalability and meta tagging of great amount of web-stored available data,

---

technology automatically searching for "fire", "dismiss", etc. as well. You'll find more documents related to the termination of employees, but you'll also find a lot more non-relevant documents concerning house fires, the fire department, etc. So concept search can help address the under-inclusive problem with keyword search, (though it won't solve it) and can be helpful during analysis. But it can often increase the over-inclusive problem."

[34] Cfr. J. SCHECK, "Tech Firms Pitch Tools for Sifting Legal Records", *Wall Street Journal*, 22 August 2008.: "Hewitt Packard says using lawyers to search through 100 gigabytes of data would cost about $ 180.000. But since its software automatically culls irrelevant documents, attorneys in such a case would have to go through only a small portion of that data —for a cost of about $ 25.000. [...] Recently, tech companies and lawyers have taken steps to solve their conflict. Some law firms that handle big business cases —such as Fenwickand San Francisco's Howard, Rice, Nemerowski, Canady, Falk & Rabkin, among others— now consult with clients on which e-Discovery software to choose and how to use it."

[35] E. MOTTA AND M. SABOU, "Next Generation Semantic Web Applications", in R. Mizoguchi et al. (Eds.) [ASWC 2006], *The Semantic Web*, LNCS 4185, Springer, Heidelberg, Berlin, pp. 24-29.

and web-services orientation seem to be the next step.[36] Dieter Fensel envisages the future of the SW as a "Web of services" in which "scalable interoperability not only requires semantics, but it cannot even be imagined without the usage of semantics". [37]

In 2002, Fensel and Bussler provided a fully-fledged framework —*Web Modeling Service Framework* (WMSF)— , a conceptual model to develop services according to the principle of maximal decoupling complemented by a scalable mediation service: (i) strong decoupling of the various components that realize an e-commerce application; (ii) strong mediation service enabling anybody to speak with everybody in a scalable manner. [38]

Web Services connect computers and devices with each other using the Internet to exchange data and combine data in new ways. They may be defined as software objects that can be assembled over the Internet using standard protocols to perform functions or execute business processes. It seems to me that Fensel and Bussler's dynamic framework does not translate Hendler's original idea of "services logic", but goes in the same direction.

In contrast, some researchers —from Yahoo! Research, *e.g.*— recall that information retrieval is still one of the main functionalities of the Web. Bridging SW and information retrieval technologies faces scientific problems on knowledge representation and natural language understanding that remain still unsolved. The SW would fail to achieve the impact envisioned a decade ago on search on the WWW. The question is this one: Why has the SW had so little effect on search services?

"We put forward three possible reasons. First, this integration is an extremely hard scientific problem. Second, the Web imposes hard scalability and performance restrictions. Third, there's a cultural divide between the Semantic Web and Information Retrieval disciplines."[39]

---

[36] Cfr. V..R. BENJAMINS et al. *Near-term Prospects for Semantic Technologies*, IEEE Intelligent Systems, January/February, 2008, pp.76-88; D. FENSEL *STI Technical Report* 2008-01-10,   STI   Innsbruck,   http://www.sti-innsbruck.at/fileadmin/documents/SemanticTechnology.pdf; P.WARREN, J. DAVIES, D. BROWN, (Eds.), *ICT Futures. Delivering Pervasive, Real-time and Secure Services*, John Wiley, Chichester, 2008.

[37] Cfr. D. FENSEL, *STI Technical Report* 2008-01-10, STI Innsbruck, http://www.sti-innsbruck.at/fileadmin/documents/SemanticTechnology.pdf .

[38] Cfr. D. FENSEL; C. BUSSLER, "The Web services Modeling Framework (WSMF)", *Electronic Commerce: Research and Applications*, vol. n.2, 2002, pp. 113-137.

[39] R. BAEZA-YATES et al. "Search, Web 2.0, and the Semantic Web", in Benjamins, V.R. (Ed.) *Near-term Prospects for Semantic Technologies, IEEE Intelligent Systems,*

This is true, and it is out of discussion. But *hybrid* theoretical approaches and more pragmatic perspectives are possible as well. In other words, it is not necessary to carry out first a complete fundamental research on the web to develop toolkits and strategies. Knowledge and the Internet in a whole are growing faster than that, stemming from practice and competition among technology companies and research institutes. We learn and we develop and test new languages, applications and theories with the same blow. Relying on this experience, a sharp distinction between fundamental and applied research does not make a lot of sense in this domain. The science of the Internet may combine many different approaches at the same time.

This has been noticed, again, by James Hendler when describing how Web 2.0 and web 3.0 are technically related. Table 2 shows the way Web 3.0 extends current Web 2.0 applications using Semantic Web technologies and graph-based, open data.[40]

Web 3.0	
Web 2.0	Semantic Web (RDFS, OWL)
	Linked Data (RDF, SPARQL)

Fig. 2 Source: James Hendler (2009)

January/February, 2008, p. 81; R. BAEZA-YATES, "From Capturing Semantics to Semantic Search: A Virtuous Cycle", in S. Bechhofer et al. (Eds.), *ESWC 2008*, LNCS 5021, Springer verlag, Berlin, Heidelberg, 2008, p. 2: "In fact, explicit and implicit folksonomies can be used to do supervised machine learning without the need of manual intervention (or at least drastically reduce it) to improve semantic tagging. After, we can feedback the results on itself, and repeat the process. Using the right conditions, every iteration should improve the output, obtaining a virtuous cycle. As a side effect, in each iteration, we can also improve Web search, our main goal."

[40] J. HENDLER "Web 3.0 emerging", *IEEE Intelligent Systems*, January 2009, p.89 : "RDF Schema (RDFS) and the Web Ontology Language (OWL) provide the ability to infer relationships between data in different applications or in different parts of the same application. These Semantic Web languages allow for the assertion of relationships between data elements, which developers can use, via custom code or an emerging toolset, to enhance the URI-based direct merging of data into a single RDF store".

We may bear in mind, as shown by the *Gartner Hype Cycle for Legal and Regulatory Information Governance* (July 16th 2007, November 12th 2008) that SW is not a completely mature technology, at least not yet. [41]

A Hype Cycle is a "graphic representation of the maturity, adoption and business application of specific technologies".[42] Gartner uses Hype Cycles to characterize the over-enthusiasm (or *hype*) and disappointment stages that typically happens with the introduction of new technologies. Hype Cycles also show how and when technologies overcome the hype, achieve practical benefits, and become eventually accepted. This may happen now with Semantic Technologies.

However, there are more reasons of theoretical nature to explain the actual development of the SW towards a combination of top-down, bottom-up and middle-out strategies. It has been repeated many times in the literature that the SW should not be confused with Artificial Intelligence techniques. AI is about engineering. On the other side, the SW is a "web of data": "a technological infrastructure to enable large scale data interoperability".[43] In this sense, the SW has to be combined with other artificial devices to be effective. Adding semantics to the web, alone, does not solve either classical AI problems or satisfy users' needs and demands.

This is especially true in the law field, because in spite of the already many available ontologies, very few applications have been built up following SW specifications. Law is not one of the main domains in which SW developments have been applied.[44] Ontologies are hard to build and especially to maintain. Martin Hepp talks about the *expressivity-community size frontier*: "the more detailed and expressive the ontology, the smaller the actual user community will be because it increases the resources necessary for reviewing and understanding the specification and associated documentation, which makes committing to the ontology

---

[41]Cfr.   http://www.gartner.com/DisplayDocument?id=509672&ref=%27g_fromdoc%27
http://www.gartner.com/DisplayDocument?doc_cd=162673

[42] Cfr. http://www.gartner.com/pages/story.php.id.8795.s.8.jsp

[43] M. D'AQUIN et al., "Toward a New Generation of Semantic Web Applications", *IEEE Intelligent Systems*, May/June, 2008, pp. 20-28.

[44] Law is not even mentioned in the JORGE CARDOSO survey on the subject. According to him, education, computer software, government, business services and life sciences are the main domains of SW applications. See J. CARDOSO, "The Semantic Web Vision: Where We Are?", *IEEE Intelligent Systems*, September/October, 2007, p.p. 84-88.

reasonable only for a smaller number of individuals".[45]

If SW is not only a web of information, but a web of knowledge, then the *nature* of knowledge to be modeled does matter as well. In the SEKT project[46], we defined legal knowledge as being practical, dynamic and changing according to the community that is producing and using it. There is a lay knowledge of law, and a *professional legal knowledge* (PLK) which is shared across members of a legal social group (lawyers, attorneys, judges, prosecutors...) having in common their experience and practical knowledge of the law.[47] These features facilitate the building of *ontologies of professional legal knowledge* (OPLK) and the *ontology of professional judicial knowledge* (OPJK).[48]

However, this leads to a kind of paradox, because assembling, classifying, sharing and reusing experiences are different and not necessarily coordinated and consistent tasks. Consistency between sharing and reusing cannot be taken into account. Some strategy is explicitly required if the object to be modeled is *experience* or *practical knowledge*, as Enric Plaza is pointing out in the so-called EDIR cycle (Express, Discovery, Interpret, Reuse).[49] This is still an open discussion.

V. Relational Law and Relational Justice

Let's go into the *experiences of law* now. Law, and not only the web, is changing fast too. Traditional fields of legal drafting, private contracting, judicial sentencing and administrative management have been enlarged with all the Online Dispute Resolution (ODR) initiatives and new forms of self-regulation and access to justice. In sharp contrast to corporate law practices, the web fosters new *personal* strategies. Citizens —as individual persons as much as citizens belonging to a political

---

[45] M. HEPP, "Possible Ontologies. How Reality Constraints the Development of Relevant Ontologies". *IEEE Intelligent Systems*, January/February, 2007, pp. 90-96.

[46] http://www.sekt-project.com/ [Semantically Enriched Knowledge Technologies]

[47] P. CASANOVAS et al., "Supporting newly-appointed judges: a legal knowledge management case study". *Journal of Knowledge Management* (Special issue on SEKT Technologies), Vol. 9 No. 5, 2005, pp. 7-27; P. CASANOVAS et al. "An Ontology-based Decision Support System for Judges", in J. Breuker el al., *Legal Ontologies and the Semantic Web. Op. cit.*2009, pp. 165-175.

[48] Cfr. N. CASELLAS, *Modelling Legal Knowledge through Ontologies. OPJK: the Ontology of Professional Judicial Knowledge.* PhD Dissertation. AKA/IOS Press, Heidelberg, 2009 (forthcoming).

[49] E. PLAZA. "Semantics and Experience in the Future Web". In K.D. Althof et al. (Eds.) *ECCBR 2008, LNAI*, Springer Verlag, Berlin, Heidelberg, 2008, pp. 44-58.

body— require a greater participation and faster and more effective ways of facing their legal activities. Dialogue, flexibility and autonomy seem to be the aim of new legal forms of *relational justice*.

Originally, we coined this concept for the sake of Restorative Justice, in a broad sense. *Relational Justice* (RJ) was defined as a bottom-up justice, the justice produced through cooperative behavior, agreement, negotiation, or dialogue among actors in a post-conflict situation (the aftermath of private or public, tacit or explicit, peaceful or violent conflicts).[50] The RJ field included ADR and ODR, mediation, commercial, labor and economic mediation, victim-offender mediation (VOM), restorative justice (dialogue justice in criminal issues, for juvenile or adults), transitional justice (negotiated justice in the aftermath of violent conflicts in fragile, collapsed or failed states), community justice, family conferencing, and peace processes.[51]

However, recent developments of the Internet and recent trends in the SW area have convinced us to expand and change this definition in a more framed and regulatory way. *Relational Justice* may be defined as the substantive and formal structure that allows end users, in the broader sense (as citizens, consumers, customers, clients, managers, officials...), to participate in the making of their own regulation and legal outcomes through all the mixed and plural strategies that the SW framework allows. This implies the coexistence of legal and social norms, rights and duties to be shared by subjects (artificial or natural agents) in a structured environment. Therefore, user centered strategies of the next SW generation fit into a middle-out legal approach in which there are rights to be protected and duties to be put in place. The expressive content of Web 2.0 may be shaped as well by the service-oriented motivation of the Web 3.0.

From a more traditional point of view, Relational Justice may be described as a subset of *Relational Law*. This is not a new concept, either in public or private law. The use of the term *relational* applied to law goes back to Roscoe Pound and the Common Law tradition.[52]

---

[50] Cfr. P. CASANOVAS and M. POBLET, "Micro-foundations of Restorative Justice". In: *Images of Restorative Justice Theory*, R. Mackay et al. (Eds), Ed. Polizei und Wissenschaft. Frankfurt, 2007, pp. 235-256.

[51] Cfr. P. CASANOVAS and M. POBLET, "Concepts and Fields of Relational Justice", in P. Casanovas et al. (Eds.) *Computable Models of the Law: Languages, Dialogue, Games, Ontologies*, LNAI 4884, Springer Verlag, Berlin, Heidelberg, pp. 323-324.

[52] R. POUND, *The Spirit of the Common Law*, Marshall Jones, Francestown, NH, 1921, p.2: "For the strength of the common law is in its treatment of concrete controversies, as

Regulatory bonds through the emergence of a shared context are the base of several sociological descriptions[53], some distinctions in international law doctrine[54], and well-known classifications of contracts under new corporate global conditions —e.g. the notions of *relational contract*[55] and *relational exchange norms.*[56]

On the other side, global justice and governance have been described many times as *relational*, to emphasize the contrast with public law theories based on the abstraction of a social contract to found some kind of sovereignty. For some criminologists, relational justice is a perspective to bear upon the problems raised by the criminal justice system: "to regard crime primarily as a breakdown in relationships; even in those cases where the offender does not know the victim, a relationship can be said to exist by virtue of their being citizens together, bound together by rules governing social behavior"[57].

Legal theorists with a high degree of commitment with the Restorative Justice movement use to emphasize the role of privileged actors to counter-balance power in the political arena. For instance, in their thorough and well-known book *Global Business Regulation* (2000), John Braithwaite and Peter Drakos state at the end: "Our conclusion is

---

the strength of its rival, the modern Roman law, is in its logical development of abstract conceptions".

[53] S. MACAULAY, "Non-contractual relations in business: a preliminary study", *American Sociological Review* vol. 28, 1963, pp. 55-67.

[54] Vid. The distinction between *droit institutionnel* and *droit relationnel*, R.J. DUPUY, *Communauté internationale et développement* , Economica, UNESCO, Paris, 1986.

[55] Cfr. I.R. MACNEIL, "Relational Contract: What We Do and Do Not Know", *Wisconsin Law Review*, 1985, n. 3, pp. 483-525; P.I. BLUMBERG, "The Increasing Recognition of Enterprise Principles in Determining Parent and Subsidiary Corporation Liabilities", *Connecticut Law Review*, vol. 28, 1996, pp. 295-346; P.I. BLUMBERG, "The Transformation of Modern Corporation Law: The Law of Corporate Groups", *Connecticut Law Review*, 1995, vol. 37, pp. 605-615.

[56] Cfr. I.R. MACNEIL, *The New Social Contract*, Yale University Press, New Haven, 1998. Some empirical support has been found for two of MacNeil's exchange norms (solidarity and role integrity). Cfr. P. J. KAUFMANN and L.W. STERN, "Relational Exchange Norms, Perceptions of Unfairness, and retained Hostility in Commercial Litigation", *The Journal of Conflict Resolution*, 1988, Vol. 32, n.3, pp. 534-552.

[57] M. SCHLUTER, "What is Relational Justice?", in J. Burnside and N. Baker (Eds.) *Relational Justice: Repairing the Breach*, Waterside Press, Winchester, 1994, pp. 17-27, reprinted in G. Johnstone (Ed.) *A Restorative Justice reader. Texts, sources, context.* Willan Publishing, Cullompton, Devon, 2003, p. 309.

that NGOs are the key to invigorating global good governance".[58]

Nevertheless, I think that Web 2.0 and Web 3.0 are beyond political activism, and this perspective may not be easily captured under private or public law either. The magnitude of relational bonds and trends becomes evident once we show the numbers. It is worthwhile to quote here explicitly a forthcoming paper by Colin Rule, from e-Bay:

> *"If you have any doubt that consumers are moving to online commerce, take a look at eBay, the online auction company. In the 13 years since it was founded, eBay has grown into the largest marketplace in the world. In the first half of 2008, there were more than one billion product listings added to eBay worldwide. At any given moment, there are more than 100 million listings around the world, and approximately 7.1 million listings are added each day. eBay users trade almost every kind of item imaginable, in more than 50,000 categories. On eBay, a pair of shoes sells every 7 seconds, a cell phone sells every 7 seconds, and a car sells every 56 seconds. The daily volume of trade on eBay is greater than the daily volume of the NASDAQ."*

Unsurprisingly, all of these transactions generate a lot of consumer disputes. Even though less than 1 percent of purchases generate a problem, the incredible volume on the site means eBay handles more than 40 million disputes a year, in more than 16 different languages".[59]

It has been highlighted the *democratic* model that the Web 2.0 implies. People can cooperate and build up in common their ideas.[60] Enriching this process seems a quite natural move from the SW perspective. But this is not an easy task.

Web services, collective work[61] and, lately, service parks[62] constitute the natural path leading from Web 2.0 to Web 3.0 too. However, this means accepting that what Petrie and Bussler call *the Academic Web Services Dream*, "a dream of an open and free Internet that could offer

---

[58] JOHN BRAITHWAITE and PETER DRAKOS, *Global Business Regulation*, Cambridge University Press, 2000, p. 36.

[59] C. RULE , "Making Peace on eBay: Resolving Disputes in the World's Largest Marketplace", *ACResolution Magazine* (forthcoming), 2009. I thank Colin Rule for allowing me to quote his still unpublished paper. See also C. RULE, "Rethinking the legal profession", posted on April 4, 2009 - 12:31am, available at http://cyberlaw.stanford.edu/node/6150.

[60] E. MOTTA, "Knowledge Publishing and Access on the Semantic Web: A Sociotechnological Analysis", 2006, op. cit., pp. 88-90.

[61] C. J. PETRIE, "Collective Work", *IEEE Internet Computing*, March/April 2008, pp. 80-82.

[62] C. J. PETRIE, C. BUSSLER, "The Myth of Open Web Services: The Rise of the Service Parks", May/June, *IEEE Internet Computing*, pp. 80-82.

everyone a nearly infinite choice of services and ways to combine them" is changing as well.[63] Big players count and are able to offer more flexible and friendly user services to a kind of customer seeking for brand and simplicity. Sets of services come with their own set of rules, adding complexity to the managing of the service and the interface with users. From a legal point of view, managing conflicts are as important as managing transactions, and copyright and copyleft are coexisting and overlapping in the web.

Those are some of the reasons why we chose as a research strategy building up legal platforms, easily accessible, and cooperating into the development of electronic agents able to negotiate, to reach agreements and help in regulatory tasks.

As Kalfaglou et al. noticed at the beginning of this process, "the increasing use of Web services to express computation on the SW points to a purely procedural notion of agency, while the kinds of reasoning which are envisaged in the description of the SW appear to require something more complex, e.g. proactive behavior".[64]

Agency, trust, dialogue protocols, dialogue games and social policy require a cooperative effort coming from lawyers, legal theorists and computer scientists. Some of the new trends have to concentrate on well-known areas with unsolved problems (such as information retrieval); some of them point to the same direction as SW developments (as Web services do); some of them face genuinely new challenges that anticipate the cognitive behavior of users in the web (as legal multimedia, imaging and the building of multimedia ontologies introduce). But *all of them* require a fast change of perspective in favor of interdisciplinary knowledge and cooperative work at theoretical level.

Moreover, computation is increasingly applied to solve or at least to manage social and regulatory problems than in the past where led to the only application or enforcement of law. Security and immigration are privileged fields in EU and USA. Business and corporate governance is another organizational field in which regulation is reached through a combination of principles, protocols, legal rules, ontologies and automatic (or semiautomatic) computation of internal logs. Thus, not only law, legal concepts, and reasoning[65] but also the social situated knowledge that

---

[63] Ibid. p. 81.

[64] Y. KALFAGLOU et al. "On the Emergent Semantic Web and Overlooked Issues", in A. Mciraith et al. (Eds.), *ISWC 2004*, LNCS 3298, 2004, p. 579.

[65] G. SARTOR, Legal Reasoning: A Cognitive Approach to the Law. Vol. 5. Treatise on Legal Philosophy and General Jurisprudence. Springer, Berlin, Heidelberg, 2005.

enables law to be created, implemented and shared in an increasingly technological social and organizational environment, may be conceived and explained as a *cognitive technology* .

Acknowledgements

NEURONA TSI-020100-2008-134; ONTOMEDIA CSO2008-05536/ SOCI, TSI-020501-2008-131; INTEGRA (CENIT 2008).

The Open Revolution: Using Citation Analysis to Improve Legal Text Retrieval

Anton Geist

Centre for Computers and Law, University of Vienna

I. Introduction

The legal discipline is an unusually information-rich one. Contrary to other disciplines, there is not only an enormous mass of texts about the law, but also the law itself is textual in nature.[1]

Consequently, being able to automatically retrieve texts from large document collections was one of the first applications of computer science in the field of law.[2]

Today, when legal professionals log onto online databases of legal service providers in order to retrieve the text of court cases, statutory material or other legal documents, the process of obtaining those documents is called legal text retrieval. Put simply, legal text retrieval systems like Westlaw (United States, United Kingdom), LexisNexis (United States, United Kingdom and other countries), Beck-Online (Germany) and RDB (Austria) provide electronic access to legal documents and enable users to search within their text collections.

Citation analysis looks at citations to and from documents. The theoretical foundation on which the indexing of citations is built upon, is as follows: if there is a citation between two documents, there is some kind of relationship between these texts.[3] This relationship can be further explored and used to learn more about the characteristics of the connected documents.

Citation analysis of World Wide Web documents enabled the Internet search engine Google to outperform all other Web search engines that did not yet make use of the citation structure of the Web. Google decides on the relevance of Web pages to users' queries not only because of the text

---

[1] R. WIDDISON, "New Perspectives in Legal Information Retrieval", *Int J Law Info Tech, 10*(1), 2002, pp. 41–70, at p. 4.

[2] M.-F. MOENS, "Innovative techniques for legal text retrieval", *Artificial Intelligence and Law, 9*(1), 2001, pp. 29–57, at p. 29.

[3] J. FEATHER & R.P. STURGES, *International encyclopedia of information and library science* (2. ed), London: Routledge, 2003, at p. 76.

of those Web pages, but also because of their link structure. So far, no similar technological change has occurred in the area of legal text retrieval.

II. Legal Text Retrieval Systems Today

When we take a closer look at the legal text retrieval systems just mentioned, it is worth trying to put their use in a wider perspective.

The global market for legal text retrieval is big, with revenues of about EUR 3 billion per year to a vast number of online services around the world.[4]

After some experimental work, both in the USA and in Europe, the first legal text retrieval systems were implemented in the 1970s. Today it would be difficult to imagine the practise of law without the use of online legal databases, be it to retrieve legislative texts, court cases or legal literature. Distributed computing made it possible for lawyers to perform so-called computer-assisted legal research tasks from their own desks, rather than from a shared terminal.[5]

When commercial legal search engines were introduced, they were custom-built, often proprietary, software. Professional legal users have been expected to undergo some kind of special training in order to effectively use the specific legal databases.[6]

Technologically speaking, legal database providers around the world generally still use the same search technologies that they did when the databases were built. Those technologies, that belong to the "extended Boolean model", require the users to formulate strict queries, using so called Boolean operators (AND, NOT, OR, and others) to tie together individual words or phrases that form the search query.[7]

A characteristic of Boolean retrieval models is their "exact match" nature. They do not take into account any partial matches of queries. The

---

[4] L. KLASÉN, "Legal IR services - from past to present", In C. Magnusson Sjöberg (Ed.), *Legal Management of Information Systems - incorporating law in e-solutions,* Lund: Studentlitteratur, 2005, pp. 337–358, at p. 338.

[5] C. TAPPER, "Out of the box", *International Review of Law, Computers & Technology, 19*(1), 2005, pp. 5–11, at p. 8.

[6] P. JACKSON & I. MOULINIER, *Natural language processing for online applications: Text retrieval, extraction and categorization* (2nd rev. ed., Vol. 5), Amsterdam Philadelphia: John Benjamins Pub, 2007, at pp. 64-65.

[7] C.D. MANNING, P. RAGHAVAN & H. SCHÜTZE, *Introduction to information retrieval.* New York: Cambridge University Press, 2008, at pp. 14-15.

search engine will return results that fulfil all the criteria defined by the query, and only those. If a document fulfills all but one requirement, it will still not be returned as a result. Besides that, (extended) Boolean retrieval models do not employ any sophisticated technologies to rank the listed results.

Consequently, legal database providers still (have to) provide special training for their users outlining the peculiarities of Boolean syntax, proximity operators and field searching.

The main legal database providers have not ignored all technological advances in search technology in the past decades. It appears, however, as if both providers and customers have somehow agreed on settling for search technology that would be considered to be dated in most other disciplines.

Let us look at the example of Westlaw: The database provider is the largest commercial legal search service in terms of the number of paying subscribers. Over half a million subscribers perform millions of searches a day over tens of terabytes of text data.[8]

Today, Boolean search (called "Terms and Connectors" by Westlaw) is still the default search mode on Westlaw, and used by a large percentage of users. A technologically more advanced ranked retrieval search mode (called "Natural Language" by Westlaw) is available, but most users prefer the Boolean search.[9]

One is tempted to think that the legal material is simply not suited for more advanced search technologies. If the described Boolean legal text retrieval systems were performing well as legal research tools, there would really be nothing wrong with legal text retrieval using long established search methods. Ironically, however, the deficiencies of Boolean legal text retrieval have been known for decades.

The so-called STAIRS study conducted by Blair and Maron in the mid-1980s was the first legal retrieval experiment in a realistic operational environment. The searchers had a predefined goal to work on their queries until they were confident that the search had retrieved at least 75 percent of the total number of relevant documents. Further investigation, however, proved that while the result lists did not include a lot of off-topic results ("precision" was 79 percent), the average "recall" achieved by the Boolean system was no better than 20 percent. In other words: When the

---

[8] C.D. MANNING, P. RAGHAVAN & H. SCHÜTZE, *Introduction to information retrieval*, at pp. 14-15.
[9] P. JACKSON & I. MOULINIER, *Natural language processing for online applications*, at p. 28.

searchers thought that they had built a query that would give them 75 percent of all the relevant documents, the text retrieval system was only able to locate as little as 20 percent of those relevant documents.[10]

Although the Blair and Maron study has been triggering a passionate debate on the effectiveness of Boolean information retrieval systems in large full-text databases, legal text retrieval systems still build upon the same search technology that they did in the mid-1980s.

III. The Need for Better Legal Text Retrieval

A thorough discussion of why both providers and customers of legal text retrieval systems have (implicitly) accepted using dated search technologies is far too complex to be dealt with within this paper. A mix of several characteristics seems to be responsible for this. Let me just mention one of the major reasons for this fact. It not only explains why people do not use more up-to-date technology in the legal domain, but also shows very clearly why this situation must be changed.

Attorneys have the legal obligation to provide competent representation to their clients. In the U.S., but also in Europe, it has long been decided that the ability to perform adequate legal research is a component of this legal obligation. If an attorney fails to perform competent research, this constitutes a violation of their ethical duty and has led to malpractice suits against negligent lawyers.

As new computerised research tools have become available to lawyers, the standard of competence for attorneys concerning what "adequate legal research" means has arguably been increased.[11]

This puts the providers of legal text retrieval systems in a difficult situation: They want to provide their customers with electronic research tools, but at the same time they are eager to make sure that (sued) attorneys cannot argue that it was not them, but the search engine that failed to do "adequate legal research". The situation of the systems' users, on the other hand, is quite special too: They are certainly interested in tools that facilitate their legal research, but at the same time they want to avoid any increase in their standard of competence. A silent agreement that old search technology is "good enough" seems to be a plausible

---

[10] D.C. BLAIR & M.E. MARON, "An evaluation of retrieval effectiveness for a full-text document-retrieval system", *Commun. ACM, 28*(3), 1985, pp. 289–299.

[11] M. WHITEMAN, "The Impact of the Internet and Other Electronic Sources on an Attorney's Duty of Competence Under the Rules of Professional Conduct", *Albany Law Journal of Science and Technology, 11*, 2000-2001, pp. 89–103, at p. 90.

solution for both parties.

As soon as we remind ourselves that it is really not only the two mentioned parties who have to deal with the effects of more or less advanced search technology, it becomes obvious why it is in fact a necessity to use the most sophisticated search tools available. Legal documents build the foundation of every legal system. Better retrieval of legal texts effectively improves the work of all legal professionals, be it the judiciary, lawyers or legal researchers. This improvement, in turn, is useful for everyone who is affected by the legal system, which is society as a whole.

IV. Importance of Citations for Legal Research

For a long time lawyers have consequently developed very sophisticated forms of citation handling. One just has to think of the various manuals of legal citations that are published, contrary to other disciplines. Part of the reason for the great importance of citations in legal texts lies in the nature of legal texts themselves. There is no physical "legal object" that is described in texts, the texts themselves constitute the law.[12]

When judges write opinions, they perpetually cite cases and other authorities. Legal scholars write articles and treatises that cite cases and other authorities, and which in turn are, at least sometimes, cited by cases and other authorities. These citations hold a great amount of information in them. Judges cite those cases that they think are the most relevant ones to the case they are deciding. Therefore, when two judges who are deciding different cases, cite some of the same authorities, this does mean that those cases are, at least somehow, relevant to each other.[13]

In common law countries, because of the eminent importance that citations play in those legal systems, there are specific tools and services that aim to assist attorneys in citation research. So-called Citator services allow users to see all citations that directly refer to a given case. Globally, the two biggest Citator services are LexisNexis's Shepard's, and WestLaw's KeyCite.[14]

---

[12] C. TAPPER, "Citation Patterns in Legal Information Retrieval", at p. 258.

[13] T.A. SMITH, "The Web of Law", *The San Diego Law Review, 44,* 2007, pp. 309–354,at p. 341.

[14] P. ZHANG & L. KOPPAKA, "Semantics-based legal citation network", In *Proceedings of the 11th international conference on Artificial intelligence and law,* Stanford, California: ACM, 2007, pp. 123–130, at p. 123.

But citators not only allow researchers to verify the authority of a precedent by listing subsequent sources that have cited a source. They are also used by legal professionals to find additional sources relating to a given subject, by using the compiled citations as references to (somehow) related material.

Online legal databases certainly do provide access to citator services online, but given the enormous practical use of citators, it seems strange that they do not make use of legal citations to improve their (keyword) search results. So far, the result lists of legal text retrieval systems like Westlaw or LexisNexis are based solely on word occurrences, not on citations between legal documents.

V. Using Citations for Legal Text Retrieval

Taking into account the importance of citations in legal research and the deficiencies of current legal text retrieval systems, it appears to be just a question of time that legal databases will have to make use of citation analysis of their document collection to improve their search results. A few observations further underline this claim.

Citation analysis is part of the academic science of bibliometrics, which is a set of methods used to study or measure texts and patterns of publication.[15]

In his 1955 paper, Eugene Garfield, one of the founders of bibliometrics, actually used the already existent legal citation research tool, Shepard's Citations, to explain his then futuristic ideas of citation indexes for science.[16]

Today, those citation indexes have long become reality in many research areas and their use has been expanded to improving text retrieval systems in various areas. In the legal domain, however, the use of Shepard's citations as a mere reference collection has stayed the same, except for the possibility to use Shepard's online. The use of Shepard's has therefore remained limited, while the tools that it inspired have been used, among other areas, to improve the performance of text retrieval in their respective areas.

Thus, it seems strange that legal citations are not used for indexing.

---

[15] . FEATHER & R.P. STURGES, *International encyclopedia of information and library science* (2. ed), at p. 38.

[16] E. GARFIELD, "Citation indexes for science; a new dimension in documentation through association of ideas", *Science, 122*(3159), 1955, pp. 108–111, at p. 108.

Every single citation that an author includes in their texts can also be seen as an act of indexing. When authors put references in their work, they include terminological interpretations in their texts.[17]

Also, returning to the comparison of modern Web search and legal text retrieval, I want to highlight one more aspect of legal citations. Google has shown us that link analysis in Web search has the potential to greatly improve search results.

As already shown, however, connections between documents are more central to the discipline of law than they are to any other field. Lawyers, legal scholars, and judges all pepper their writings with links to earlier sources, the only difference being that these links are called "citations" or "quotations."[18]

In fact, one might even argue that tightly linked court cases have to be even more closely related than equally linked Web pages: citations within court decisions are nothing but arguments themselves. Citations have to persuade higher courts that the decision the judges made was correct. Therefore, judges have strong motivations to include citations thoughtfully.[19]

VI. Case Study: Austrian Supreme Court Decisions

In order to show that there is a direct correlation between the number of citations to legal documents and their legal impact, I have started to conduct a study with Austrian Supreme Court cases.

At www.ris.bka.gv.at, the Austrian Federal Chancellery operates the Legal Information System of the Republic of Austria ("Rechtsinformationssystem", abbreviated "RIS").

The objectives of RIS have been to provide up-to-date and exhaustive legal information in an electronic format to both state organs and the general public.[20]

Another objective of providing "cost effective legal information"[21] has become obsolete because since 1997 the respective content of RIS has

[17] E. GARFIELD, "Citation indexes for science; at p. 110.

[18] F.R.. SHAPIRO, *Collected papers on legal citation analysis*, Littleton Colo.: F.B. Rothman., 2001, at p. 161.

[19] T.A. SMITH, "The Web of Law", at p. 345.

[20] BUNDESKANZLERAMT, *Rechtsinformationssystem des Bundes: RIS ; eine kurze Einführung*, Wien: Bundeskanzkeramt-Verfassungsdienst, 1994, at p. 1.

[21] BUNDESKANZLERAMT, *Rechtsinformationssystem des Bundes: RIS ; eine kurze Einführung*, at p. 1.

been accessible for everyone free of charge via the Internet.

The RIS application "Case Law" ("Judikatur", http://www.ris2.bka.gv.at/Judikatur/) contains - among other documents - the full texts of the Austrian Supreme Court decisions. The RIS system is, however, able to provide not only the full texts of the decisions, but also headnote documents created by the Publication Office of the Supreme Court. Each decision document is intellectually processed by a legal specialist at the court, and if a decision has introduced a new interpretation of Austrian legal statutes, special headnotes called "Rechtssatzdokumente" are created and cite to the respective court decisions.

Using a document collection that consists of more than 100,000 full-text decision and headnote documents, I have constructed a network of all Austrian Supreme Court cases since 1985. Although various practical problems did arise, my methodology has been quite simple so far: the computer code I developed counts the number of citations from within headnote documents to Supreme Court decisions, and ranks the court decisions according to their citation totals. By doing that, I was already able to show - for the first time - that this network is a scale-free one, which means that a few court decisions have many headnotes attached to them, while most decisions have only a few headnotes, or none at all. This observation by itself already suggests further looking into the possibility of using Web search ranking algorithms in legal information retrieval systems, because the network structure of the World Wide Web is a scale-free one as well.

I am now turning to traditional indications of impact concerning Supreme Court cases, including the publication in an official legal reporter or high citation counts in annotated codes. By examining the cases returned by those means of traditional legal research with respect to their position in the "Web of Supreme Court Cases", I will be able to further explore the exact nature of the correlation between the number of headnote citations to Supreme Court decisions and their legal impact.

VII. Conclusions

Court cases, statutes and other legal authorities are linked together by citations. This legal citation network is in fact not only extremely large, but also one of the best-documented existing human-created networks.[22]

---

[22] T.A. SMITH, "The Web of Law", at pp. 310-311.

Legal text retrieval systems have not made any major changes to their search technologies within decades, although the shortcomings of current legal text retrieval have been well-documented.

This paper has set out that possible improvements for legal text retrieval constitute a necessary area for research, and that legal citation analysis can serve as a means to improve current systems.

Using only freely available data from the Legal Information System of the Republic of Austria, I have been able to show that the network structure of Austrian Supreme Court decisions and their headnotes is similar to the one of the World Wide Web. This already suggests the general feasibility of using Web ranking algorithms in legal information retrieval systems. The next step will be the computation of a more sophisticated automated ranking of Austrian Supreme Court cases that is fully in line with methods of traditional legal research.

Modelling European and Italian tax legislation with LKIF language

Giuseppe Contissa
CIRSFID – University of Bologna, Italy

I. Introduction

The present work is based on a part of the research carried out in the EU project Estrella.[1] One of the main technical objectives of the Estrella project is to develop a Legal Knowledge Interchange Format (LKIF), allowing for different kinds of legal knowledge to be modelled, including: meta-level rules for reasoning about rule priorities and exceptions, legal arguments, cases and case factors, values and principles, and legal procedures.[2]

LKIF has been developed primarily to model legal rules of the kind found in legislation and regulations: for this reason, in LKIF the rules are modelled as defeasible inference rules.[3] To demonstrate and validate the Estrella platform, European tax related legislation and national tax legislation of two European countries (Italy and Hungary) have been modelled with LKIF and used in pilot applications.

The Italian Pilot, in particular, was based upon the representation of the norms relating to the taxations of savings income in the form of interest payments, both at the level of the original EU Directive[4] and of the consequent Italian national law.[5]

The aim of the savings directive (and also of the Italian transposition law) is to determine when and how a "paying agent" is bound to collect some information regarding an "interest payment", made in favour of a

---

[1] The European project for Standardized Transparent Representations in order to Extend Legal Accessibility (Estrella, IST-2004-027655)

[2] Estrella Deliverable 1.1 - "Specification of the Legal Knowledge Interchange Format", available at: http://www.estrellaproject.org/doc/D1.1-LKIF-Specification.pdf

[3] Estrella Deliverable 4.1 - " The Legal Knowledge Interchange Format (LKIF) ", available at: http://www.estrellaproject.org/doc/Estrella-D4.1.pdf

[4] EC Council, *Directive on Taxation of Savings Income in the Form of Interest Payments*, No 2003/48/EC, 3 June 2003, *Official Journal*, 26 June 2003, L157.

[5] Italian Legislative Decree 18 april 2005 relative to the Implementation of Directive 2003/48/CE on Taxation of Savings Income in the Form of Interest Payments, *Gazzetta Ufficiale*, No 118, 23 may 2005.

"beneficial owner", then what is the minimum amount of information to be transmitted and which "competent authority" is competent to receive the information. The directive and the national law have slight different perspectives: the first one is directed to member states as recipients, while the second one addresses all entities and activities subject to the Italian law. This different perspective has caused a different approach in legal drafting, and resulted also in a different kind of issues in the phase of representation of the normative content.

Since the representations were aimed at confronting EU and Italian norms in a legal drafting perspective, a high degree of granularity was requested and they were developed to be isomorphic to the maximum possible extent, as described by Bench-Capon[6] and Karpf[7]: each norm from the legal source text was represented in a correspondent rule (or set of rules). No deviations were made, as long it was possible, from the original structure of the text, even when it was redundant or confusing.

The representation was carried using the LKIF rules s-expression syntax,[8] using the IDE provided with the Dr-Scheme system distribution. The representations were tested trough the Carneades reference inference engine implemented in PLT-Scheme.[9]

II. Representation of the Savings Tax Directive

The text of the Directive is divided in four chapters: "introductory provisions" (I), "exchange of information" (II), "transitional provisions" (III) and "miscellaneous and final provision". The core part of the directive, to be represented in LKIF rulebases, has been identified with in chapter I and II, correspondent to articles 1-9: article 1 statues the aim of the directive, then articles 2-3 are focused on the definition of "beneficial owner" (the final recipient of the interest payment), and on the procedures to correctly identify beneficial owners and their residence. Articles 4 to 6 define respectively the concepts of "paying agent", "competent authority", and "interest payment", article 7 defines the territorial scope of the directive, while articles 8 and 9 list the minimum amount of information

---

[6] T.J.M. BENCH-CAPON, F. COENEN, "Isomorphism and legal knowledge based systems", *Artificial Intelligence and Law*, 1992, No 1, pp. 65–86.

[7] J. KARPF, "Quality assurance of Legal Expert Systems", *Jurimatics*, 1989, No 8.

[8] While the Lisp s-expression syntax for rules is still supported by the LKIF reference inference engine, the final version of LKIF is available as an XML Schema presented in Relax NG syntax.

[9] Carneades is available at the following address: http://carneades.berlios.de/

to be transmitted by the paying agent to the competent authority.

The LKIF model, roughly composed of 80 rules, represents almost all the norms of the core part of the directive.

III. Representation of the Italian Savings Tax Law

The Italian Savings Tax Law is the transposition in the Italian Legal Domain of the norms contained in the EU Directive. The Italian Law partially differs both in structure and in content from the source European Legislation, undertaking a reorganization of the core content of norms coming from the directive, expanding the latter in order to make them consistent with the pre-existent Italian regulation. Several deviations were made by the national lawmaker in respect to the text of EU Directive, partly justified by the change of perspective between a Directive (directed to Member States) and a national law (directed to all individuals and entities subject to the Italian law), and partly dependent on different choices in legal drafting.

The representation of the Italian Savings Tax Law was carried out with the same approach used in the EU Savings Tax Directive: the law was analyzed to find the core part to be modelled, keeping a correspondence with the modelled part of the Directive. In particular, the modelled part corresponds to articles 1 to 7: subjects bound to communications (art. 1), interest payments (art. 2), obligations of subjects making communications (artt. 3 and 4), object of the communication (art. 5), transmission of the information (artt. 6 and 7).

This representation is different in structure and content from the work done on the directive. This variation was due, firstly, to the use of a newer version of the language, which was developed taking into account the outcomes from the work previously done on the EU directive. Secondly, other differences derived from the "physiological" difference between a Directive (which is directed to Member States) and a national law (which is directed to a community of subjects pertaining to of a National State). Finally, some discrepancies are the result of different choices in terms of legal drafting, a number of which seem to be somewhat questionable. An example of this can be seen by looking at the two respective definitions of "Paying agents": while the directive chose to list the requisites for any subject to be considered as a paying agent ("elastic" definition), the Italian Law instead opted, in art.1, for an analytical enumeration of all the subjects that, under the Italian Law, shall be considered as paying agent ("rigid definition"). After this definition, even if the title of article is just "subject held to communication", also the procedure of communication itself is defined. Then, still in the same article, a totally different concept, the "beneficial owner", is also introduced, while the last sentence goes back to the concept of paying agent, and a second definition is added, this time more similar to the one given in the Directive.

Since the approach of the pilot was to keep an isomorphic representation of the source material, this resulted in a higher complexity of rules, in modelling this and other similar articles of the Italian transposition law.

IV. Comparative tests on representations

The rulebase has been tested under Carneades, along with sets of cases provided by experts pertaining to the Italian Ministry of Finance. Given several starting facts and relative final goals, the reference inference engine was able to generate answers consistent with the source norms. In order to illustrate the inference process, some diagrams will be shown at the end of this paper.

The Italian representation was tested against the same facts used for the EU representation and the results were confronted. In general, the results of the work were satisfactory, with all the rulebases having similar expressivity, except for a discrepancy referable to a very slight normative difference between the two laws. Such discrepancy was caused by the choice of the Italian legislator to shift a norm from an article to another, modifying the logical connection between the norms, as expressed in the source EU Directive. This issue, moreover, constitutes the focus of the second part of the work, which is introduced in the following section.

V. LKIF arguments: representation of a discrepancy between the EU directive and the Italian National Law

The second part of the work was targeted to a deeper analysis of a particular case whose solution would require the system to reason by combining norms of high complexity, which were – furthermore - rather different in the way they are textually expressed in the European Directive and in the Italian Law. The norms coming from both laws were firstly manually represented using LKIF argument syntax. Besides, using

Carneades functionalities, the respective argument graphs[10] of the two representations were produced.

The research was focused on a particular case of tax saving regulation, in which a first subject, the paying agent, pays an interest to a second subject, a beneficial who is not the final recipient of the interest, but in turn transfers the interest to a third subject, who is the final recipient and therefore is considered as the beneficial owner according to the law. When the first subject has the information suggesting that the second subject is not the final recipient, the former is required to report this information (as well as the information required to identify the second subject) to the competent authority. Besides, the second subject, being in turn a paying agent in relation to the payment made to the third subject, is required to report to the competent authority all the information necessary for identifying the third subject. Therefore, the "intermediate" subject is generally considered as a paying agent.

The Savings Tax Directive introduces a number of exceptions to this general rule: one of those is the fact that the first subject has information suggesting that the second subject is a legal person, and therefore should not to be considered as a paying agent (article 4(2)). But this exception has also in turn an exception, the fact that the second subject is one of the legal persons listed in a different section of the law (article 4(5)).

This "exception of the exception" is differently expressed in the EU directive and the Italian Law: briefly, the EU directive norm introduces "the exception of the exception" as part of the norms that define the second subject as a paying agent, while the Italian Law expresses the same norm only when defining the second subject as possible object of communication from the first subject (art. 4(4)(a) of the Legislative Decree 84/2005).

The discrepancy is evident when confronting the argument graphs generated from the two different models of EU and Italian law: according to the EU directive (fig. 1), when the "exception of the exception" occurs, the second subject is considered a paying agent, and therefore: (i) the second subject is required to transmit the information on the third subject; (ii) the first subject is required to transmit information on the second subject.

---

[10] Argument graphs, also called `inference graphs', are a generalization of `and/or' graphs useful for representing proofs and providing a basis for generating explanations. For details, see Estrella Deliverable 4.1 - " The Legal Knowledge Interchange Format (LKIF) ", available at: http://www.estrellaproject.org/doc/Estrella-D4.1.pdf

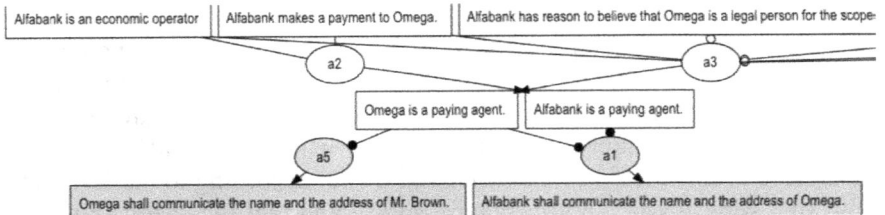

Fig. 1 Extract from EU Directive argument graphs.

According to the Italian law (fig. 2) when the "exception of the exception" occurs, the second subject is not considered a paying agent, and therefore: (i) the second subject is not required to transmit information on the third subject; (ii) the first subject is however required to transmit information on the second subject.

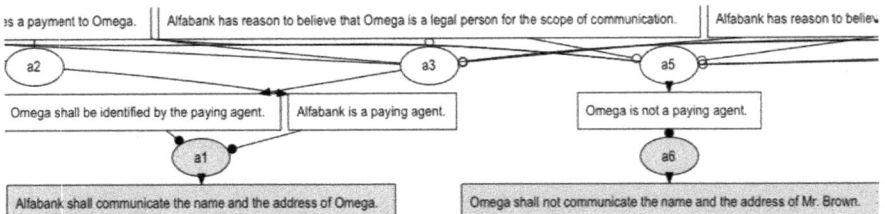

Fig. 2 Extract from Italian Law Argument Graphs.

VI. Conclusions

The first part of the work was able to show several differences between the EU Savings Tax Directive and its transposition into the Italian Legislative Decree 48/2005, in particular regarding the structure of articles, the syntax and lexicon. Nevertheless, these differences have not influenced the inner normative content, except for a very slight normative difference between the two laws (which was the focus of the second part of the work).

The LKIF rule language, tested against a rather complex set of norms, proved to correctly capture the normative content of the source legislation. Besides, the present work has been also useful in providing further suggestions for the improvement and refinement of the language. The last test, on the contrary, highlighted a normative difference between the two laws, caused by the choice of the Italian legislator to shift a norm from an article to another, modifying the logical connection between norms, as expressed in the source EU Directive.

In conclusion, this work has showed that developing rule-based representation of the law, can be not only oriented to the development of expert-system that apply the law, but can also directly support the task of legal drafting, helping to confront different sets of norms, in order to understand whether they are coherent between them or not, and where and why they can potentially lead to different results.

VII. References

T.J.M. Bench-Capon, F. Coenen, "Isomorphism and legal knowledge based systems", *Artificial Intelligence and Law*, 1992, No 1, pp. 65–86.

J. Karpf, "Quality assurance of Legal Expert Systems", *Jurimatics*, 1989, No 8.

T.F. Gordon, "Visualizing Carneades argument graphs", *Law, Probability and Risk,* 2007, No 6, pp. 109-117.

T.F. Gordon, "Constructing arguments with a computational model of an argumentation scheme for legal rules*"*, in *Proceedings of the Eleventh International Conference on Artificial Intelligence and Law*, 2007, pp. 117-121.

T.F. Gordon, "Constructing legal arguments with rules in the Legal Knowledge Interchange Format (LKIF)", in P. Casanovas, N. Casellas, R. Rubino, and G. Sartor, Lecture Notes in Computer Science: Computable Models of the Law, 2008, No 4884, pp. 162–184.

T. F. Gordon, H. Prakken, D. Walton, "The Carneades model of argument and burden of proof", *Artificial Intelligence*, 2007, No 171, pp. 875–896.

EC Council, *Directive on Taxation of Savings Income in the Form of Interest Payments*, No 2003/48/EC, 3 June 2003, *Official Journal*, 26 June 2003, L157.

Italian Legislative Decree 18 april 2005 relative to the Implementation of Directive 2003/48/CE on Taxation of Savings Income in the Form of Interest Payments, *Gazzetta Ufficiale*, No 118, 23 may 2005.

Tool-supported Legal Risk Management: A Roadmap

Tobias Mahler

Norwegian Research Center for Computers and Law, University of Oslo, Norway

This paper discusses possible methods and tools for legal risk management. Risk management refers to coordinated activities used to direct and control an organization with regard to risk. Risk management involves applying logical and systematic *methods* for identifying, analyzing and treating risk within any activity, process or project. *Legal risk management* focuses on the systematic identification, analysis and treatment of *legal risk*. The first part of the paper discusses how a legal analysis, for example of a contract's terms and conditions, can be carried out based on a *method* that is compliant with key international risk management standards. The second part of the paper examines how IT *tools* could be used to (1) carry out a systematic risk management process and document its results, (2) support a legal risk analysis through the use of graphical models and (3) provide an integration between existing legal information systems and any risk analysis tools, (4) possibly using some elements of automation. The present roadmap is intended to facilitate a discussion about the goal of legal risk management and an analysis of possible ways to reach this goal. The paper's central thesis is that structured risk management methods could be a supplement to existing legal methods. Any potential benefit of introducing such methods depends partly on the availability of adequate and usable IT tools.

I.Introduction

In *The Future of Law*,[1] Richard Susskind predicts a paradigm shift in the approach to legal problems from *problem solving* to *problem prevention*:

> *"While legal problem solving will not be eliminated in tomorrow's legal paradigm, it will nonetheless diminish markedly in significance. The emphasis will shift towards legal risk management supported by proactive facilities, which will be available in the form of legal information services*

---

[1] R. SUSSKIND, *The Future of Law* (1998), p. 290.

and procedures. As citizens learn to seek legal guidance more regularly and far earlier than in the past, many potential legal difficulties will be dissolved before needing to be resolved. Where legal problems of today are often symptomatic of delayed legal input, earlier consultation should result in users understanding and identifying their risks and controlling them before any questions of escalation."

This paper presents a roadmap towards a tool-supported legal risk management. Imagine a future in which some lawyers are also seen as *legal risk managers* by their clients or employers. Susskind considers the legal risk manager as one of the five main future roles for lawyers.[2] Such lawyers will specialize in the identification of legal risk and will be experts in the structured assessment and treatment of risk in the legal context. Those lawyers focusing on legal risk management will use specialized methods and software tools in their risk assessments. Again we can refer to Susskind:[3]

"This category of lawyer is sorely needed and is long overdue. Senior in-house lawyers around the world insist that they are in the business of legal risk management – clients prefer avoiding legal problems rather than resolving them. And yet [...] hardly a lawyer or law firm on the planet has chosen to develop methods, tools, techniques or systems to help their clients review, identify, quantify and control the legal risks that they face. I expect this to change. [...] This could fundamentally change the way in which the law is practised and administered."

The topic of the present paper is a set of potential future developments; however, I will seek to avoid making predictions. Of course, it is necessary to develop some assumptions about the future, but these are only extensions of current developments, without the addition of anything substantially new. Really new developments, particularly discoveries, are unforeseeable for epistemic reasons.[4] The present roadmap[5] for legal risk management is by no means a deterministic prediction, but should rather be read as a discussion of goals and ways to attain these goals. This roadmap should be seen as a contribution to a discussion about future *directions*, rather than as a literal map indicating

---

[2] See R. E. SUSSKIND, *The end of lawyers? Rethinking the nature of legal services* (2008) p. 272.

[3] Ibid, p. 272.

[4] See N. N. TALEB, *The Black Swan: The Impact of the Highly Improbable* (2008).

[5] See in general about technology roadmapping R. PHAAL, C. J. P. FARRUKH and D. R. PROBERT, 'Technology roadmapping: A planning framework for evolution and revolution' *Technological Forecasting & Social Change* 71 (1-2) 5-26.

the path itself. As Winston Churchill put it, plans are of little importance, but planning is essential. Planning views the future in a non-deterministic way, where we can influence central elements of future developments, despite the likely prospect that the plan itself may need to be adapted along the way.

II.Legal risk management

This section introduces legal risk management as the proposed goal for this roadmap. Risk management is today used in many different disciplines as a structured approach for dealing with risk. Enterprise risk management focuses on risks to an enterprise, while financial risk management deals with risks, for example, in an investment portfolio. Engineers use risk analysis, such as to analyze the risk of technical failure of a system. The characteristic element in *legal risk management* is the focus on legal issues in the context of risk. This legal perspective on risk becomes visible in the management of *legal risk*[6], a perspective which in itself is not new: practicing lawyers already deal with risks on a daily basis. The only proposed new elements are (1) the *conceptualization* of these activities as a type of risk management, (2) the search for more *structured methods* to carry out legal risk management tasks and (3) the possible development of *software-based tools* to support legal risk management.

The *conceptual question* is a contemporary rather than a future issue. As Wahlgren[7] has indicated, some of the risk-related work tasks of practicing lawyers can be seen as a type of risk management. According to the ISO, the term "risk management" refers to "coordinated activities to direct and control an organization with regard to risk".[8] By relating legal risk management to other risk management approaches, we may contribute to the development of a practical theory of proactive legal practice, which today is rather immature. There is an abundance of theory about how to interpret the law, once a problem arises. But legal theory has relatively little focus on how to avoid problems. Understanding and denoting some of lawyers' tasks as risk management tasks provides us with a set of risk-related concepts and analyses, which may turn out to be

---

[6] T. MAHLER, 'Defining Legal Risk' in S Nystén-Haarala (ed) *Corporate Contracting Capabilities: Conference proceedings and other writings* (2008), pp 51-76.

[7] P. WAHLGREN, *Juridisk riskanalys: mot en säkrare juridisk metod* (2003).

[8] ISO, *Committee Draft 2 for Risk management - vocabulary* (Guide 73, 2008).

helpful also for the analysis of legal risks.[9]

In my opinion, there are few alternatives to the conceptualization of lawyers' risk-related tasks as legal risk management. When a lawyer analyzes potential risks (e.g., when drafting a contract) and how to avoid a negative outcome (e.g., when choosing the best wording for a contract), this may *also* be seen as *risk management.* However, the interesting question is not the conceptual or terminological issue of *whether* lawyers do risk management, but *how lawyers should manage risk.* The answer to this second question will be discussed in the remainder of this section. An analysis of legal risk management *methods* is a necessary basis for a discussion of possible legal risk management *tools,* which will follow in Section III.

A.LEGAL RISK MANAGEMENT METHODS

Susskind's future of law predicts that "legal risk management, supported by proactive facilities ... will be available in the form of legal information services and procedures". Could such *procedures* and *proactive facilities* for legal risk management be based on established risk management methods?

There have been some suggestions in legal literature to use formalized risk management approaches in law[10], but so far, legal risk management is, if anything, still emerging as a methodological approach. The goal for legal risk management is to facilitate the management of legal risk. While risk management also may be carried out informally, there may be some situations and contexts in which a more formalized risk management process and established methods may be advisable. The term *method* is here used as a *codified set of recommended practices.* Interestingly, discussions of explicit practical proactive methods do not have a strong academic tradition in law. However, this does not necessarily indicate that a structured methodological approach is entirely irrelevant for, or

---

[9] See further T. MAHLER and J. BING, 'Contractual Risk Management in an ICT Context -- Searching for a Possible Interface between Legal Methods and Risk Analysis' *Scandinavian Studies in Law* 49 339-358.

[10] See K. REID, *Risk-e-business: A framework for legal risk management developed through an analysis of selected legal risks in Internet Commerce* (University of New South Wales 2000); WAHLGREN, *Juridisk riskanalys: mot en säkrare juridisk metod* above note 7; P. KESKITALO, *From assumptions to risk management: an analysis of risk management for changing circumstances in commercial contracts, especially in the Nordic countries: the theory of contractual risk management and the default norms of risk allocation* (2000); P. KESKITALO, 'Contracts + Risks +Management = Contractual Riskmanagement?' *Nordic Journal of Commercial Law* [2006] (2) .

inapplicable to, complex tasks typically carried out by lawyers. Rather, the lack of academic studies on practical methods seems to reflect the tradition of leaving the practical methods to the legal practitioners. However, given the increased complexity of legal practice in a diversified international context, it may nevertheless be useful to devote some research efforts to developing practical methods with clear interfaces to methods used in other disciplines.

1. Risk management

In general, risk management consists of one or more *risk assessments.* Typically, a risk assessment involves risk identification, risk estimation, risk evaluation and risk treatment. For example, a strongly simplified version of an engineering risk assessment may (1) identify the risk of a bridge collapse because it cannot withstand an earthquake (risk identification). Then, (2) the engineer would analyze the uncertainty and assess the likelihood and the consequences of a bridge collapse due to an earthquake (risk estimation). The next step (3) would be to assess whether this risk is acceptable (risk evaluation). Depending on the evaluation results, the engineer would then (4) proceed to discuss the effect and cost of possible technical or other measures to manage the risk (risk treatment).

Could a similar approach be used to assess legal risk? This would require a risk assessment that not only focuses on factual events, but also on the application of legal norms to these facts. A legal risk assessment should assess how the application of legal norms may have an effect on the stakeholder.

I suggest as a starting point that a legal risk assessment should concentrate on the identification, estimation and treatment of legal risk. Thus, we need to clarify the meaning of the term "legal risk".

2. Legal risk

There does not seem to be any agreement about the definition of legal risk in literature and in practice.[11] In particular, it is not clear (1) whether legal risk implies that there must be uncertainty about the outcome and (2) whether this uncertainty must necessarily be legal uncertainty, or if uncertainty about facts is sufficient. For the purposes of this paper, I suggest the following working definition of legal risk: legal risk refers to

---

[11] MAHLER, 'Defining Legal Risk' above note 6.

the risk related to a decision in a legal case.

Two observations should be made with respect to this working definition. First, this definition does not focus on how legal risk is caused, but rather on how legal risk materialises (in a legal case). Second, the definition depends on two other terms, namely "risk" and "legal case", which both need to be clarified. There is no need to define risk differently than in other contexts, so I suggest we use the definition contained in the draft revision of the risk management vocabulary, issued by the International Organisation for Standardisation (ISO).[12] There, risk is defined as the "effect of uncertainty on objectives." The use of this definition in the context of legal risk thus implies that also legal risk must be an effect of uncertainty. Uncertainty is defined by the ISO as the "state, even partial, of deficiency of information related to or understanding or knowledge of an event, its consequence or likelihood". An *event* is, according to the ISO, the occurrence or change of a particular set of circumstances. Thus, in the context of legal risk, uncertainty could be the deficiency of information, understanding or knowledge of a legal decision, its consequences or likelihood. Now we need to introduce at least a preliminary definition of the term "legal decision". For the purposes of this article, the term "legal case" refers to any type of decision about facts (circumstances), which is taken based on one or several legal norms.

The term "legal case", as it is introduced here, is meant to include at least two types of rather distinct legal decisions. The *first* type of legal decision is the *legally binding decision* by an actor who holds a particular legal power. The ideal type of the binding legal decision is of course a judge's judicial decision in a court case. However, other relevant decision makers could be authorities or even a third party, like a contract partner, who holds a particular legal power.

The second type of legal decision of relevance for legal risk is the decision which is taken by any actor *in light of the legal norms that apply to the decision*. This type of decision is much less formal and visible than the first type. The decision may not have to be conscious, and it may or may not even be easily discernible in the actor's behaviour.[13] This type of decision is not characterized by its bindingness (even though it is possible

---

[12] ISO, *Committee Draft 2 for Risk management - vocabulary* above note 8.

[13] The actor may (unconsciously) decide to do nothing. For example, an actor faced with an economic loss decides not to make any claim, because no claim would have sufficient support in the law. It would be possible that the actor does not even think about the potential option of making a claim.

that the decision has certain binding effects on others), but rather through the direct effect the decision has on the actor's behaviour. One example of this type of decision is a *compliance decision*.[14] The compliance decision is taken by the complying actor, based on the identified set of norms that apply to the decision. An example is my decision to pay a certain sum of money to someone else, *because* I am obligated to do so. Another example of this type of legal decision is the decision to *bear a negative outcome*, without making any legal claim (e.g. for compensation). In both examples, the actor acknowledges the binding force of the legal norms. For lack of a better name, such decisions will subsequently be referred to as an *actor's acceptance of consequences*.

We may ask why it is necessary to include this second type of legal decision when identifying legal risk. Isn't it sufficient to focus on the binding decisions of judges, authorities and others? Doesn't the bindingness of these decisions represent the core element of the law, as a set of binding rules? The answer is a rather simple combination of empirical facts and pragmatic judgment. *First*, very few legal problems are ever brought to court. In most cases we either comply immediately, or after some negotiations, or simply do not comply with the law at all. This needs to be taken into account when we identify how the law may have an effect on us in the future. *Second*, the actor's acceptance of consequences is included because its economic and other effects on the actor are to a certain degree comparable to binding legal decisions. From a practical perspective, I am affected both by a judicial decision which states that I have to pay a sum of money, and by my own decision to comply with my payment obligations. Of course, there are differences between the two types of decisions, and these should not be neglected. In particular, my own decision surely has an immediate effect on me, while a future judicial decision may be uncertain both in terms of whether I have to pay and how much I will have to pay. However, these differences do not justify omitting the second type of decision from the analysis of legal risk.

Instead, we should rather highlight how the two types of legal decisions are connected. In the case of a binding decision, the actor is forced to consider the effects of that binding decision, particularly in light of a possible enforcement. If the binding decision does not directly initiate enforcement actions, then the actor is again faced with a decision about

---

[14] A relevant question is how we should deal with non-compliance. Most likely, non-compliance has a different place in the context of legal risk. Non-compliance may be one of the causes of a legal risk, but not of the consequences. However, this aspect must be left open for the time being.

accepting the consequences of the decision. Thus, the actor's assessment of its options (including in particular to appeal, to do nothing, to await enforcement, or to comply) can again be characterized as the acceptance of consequences. The important point is that both types of decisions may have an effect on the actor's objectives. This potential future effect is the main reason why legal decisions are of key relevance to legal risk assessment.

3.Risk assessment method

One key difference between the example of engineering risk assessment and a lawyer's risk assessment is that lawyers typically do not follow a standardized method. However, the following *typical practice* may be discerned by comparing the above procedure to the steps that arguably will be followed by many lawyers when analyzing a future situation. Generally speaking, a lawyer might typically (1) identify risks, then (2) *analyse* how the relevant law (or contract) regulates the issue at stake (*hypothetical application of the law*), and then (3) evaluate whether the legal outcome serves the interests of the client, concluding by (4) proposing to *treat* the risk with adequate measures. These measures could then be implemented by the lawyer's client, based on an informal cost-benefit assessment, which also takes the legal validity of the measures into account. The key difference between the lawyer's assessment and the engineer's risk assessment lies in the fact that the lawyer typically does *not estimate the risk value*, that is, the likelihood and consequences of the risk. At most, the hypothetical application of the law will include an *estimation of a likely legal output*, which depends on legal uncertainty. However, this output is often not quantified in terms of consequences (e.g., financial) and a likelihood value.

Nevertheless, the above legal practice could be understood as a purely qualitative legal risk assessment method, which may be supported by some of the tools described in Section III. In addition, it might in some situations even be useful and cost efficient to go a step further and *estimate risk values*, as it is practised in other disciplines' risk management methods. In the following, I will exemplify how a full-scale semi-quantitative risk assessment method could be used to assess the clauses of a contract.[15]

---

[15] This section is based T. MAHLER, 'How can we manage contractual risk?' *Contracting Excellence* [2008] 1 (5) 15-16.

B.EXAMPLE: CONTRACT RISK ASSESSMENT

The method discussed below is based on an adaptation of existing international standards for risk management to the requirements of a contract analysis. The relevant standards include the Australian Standard AS 4360/2004 and the currently available draft version of the upcoming ISO standard 31000, "Risk management – Principles and guidelines on implementation". The process of risk management is a continuous one, which is carried out through *risk assessments*. If we want to examine a contract in a formalized risk assessment, then some of the steps specified in the above-mentioned standards need to be adapted. This article may be complemented with literature on the use of the Australian Standard, which explains the details of the general process that cannot be sufficiently covered here.[16]

A contractual risk assessment can consist of the following steps:

- Specify the context, target and scope of the risk assessment. What exactly do you want to analyze?
- Identify risk, that is, describe possible events and legal decisions (legal cases), based on the contract clauses as applied to the contractual relation. Based on the contract clauses and the business context, what legal decisions may have an effect on the stakeholder?
- Estimate the likelihood and consequences (for example, monetary) of each identified risk. The estimation of likelihood should consider both the likelihood of facts and a relevant interpretation of the contract clauses.
- Evaluate the risks, distinguishing between acceptable risks and those risks that should be considered for treatment. This evaluation should be based on both the risk values (that is, high or low risk) and a suitable set of decision criteria.
- Consider how risks can be treated through practical measures or a suitable contract amendment.
- The decision about treatment implementation depends on a cost-benefit analysis.

Consider the following scenario. The management at an automotive supplier requests that a lawyer assess the general purchasing terms and

---

[16] STANDARDS AUSTRALIA and STANDARDS NEW ZEALAND, *Risk Management Guidelines Companion to Australian/New Zealand Standard AN/NZS 4360: 2004 (HB 436:2004)* (2004). See also STANDARDS AUSTRALIA and STANDARDS NEW ZEALAND, *Legal risk management* (2007).

conditions of a car manufacturer. Let us assume that the supplier's management has had positive experiences with risk management in other contexts, and suggests that the lawyer use a standard risk management method. The overall objective is to negotiate a side letter, containing more beneficial terms and conditions regarding those contract clauses that imply too much risk. As a preliminary step in preparing and negotiating this side letter, the lawyer has to clarify *how risk management can be applied to contract drafting.*

The idea of relating contracting with risk management is in itself not new, but there is relatively little literature on how contractual risk management should be carried out in practice.[17] In the following, we will take a closer look at the steps introduced above as they relate to contractual risk assessments. The method has been applied in practical case studies, including the above-mentioned scenario, and is currently under evaluation.

1. Context, target and scope

Every risk assessment should start with specifying its exact scope and target, which in our context needs to be related to the rules in a contract. Depending on the time available and the importance of certain issues, the risk assessment could *target* either the whole contract or selected parts of it. Of course, if parts of the contract are excluded from the formal risk assessment, they should still be assessed less formally outside the risk assessment. The *scope* of the assessment depends on the client's requirements to cover, for example, certain types of risks or to analyze a particular set of documents. It may be necessary to spend some time on establishing the *context* and describing what the contract aims to regulate. Preferably, this background information should be well-documented and available for review during the remaining assessment steps.

The quality of the risk assessment results depends to a large extent on the available experience about, and knowledge of, the domain in question. Typically, few individuals have a comprehensive understanding of all relevant aspects of a complex business contract. A lawyer is competent to analyze the contract clauses, but often lacks detailed operational knowledge. Similarly, technical experts may lack detailed information

---

[17] See in detail, T. MAHLER, 'The State of the Art of Contractual Risk Management Methodologies' in H Haapio (ed) *A Proactive Approach to Contracting and Law* (2008), p. 58-72.

about the financial and legal consequences of technical problems. For complex commercial contracts it may therefore be advisable to carry out a contractual risk assessment with a suitable *inter-disciplinary team* of *experts*, covering, for example, legal, financial, technical, market and other perspectives.[18] A lawyer with experience in risk management could lead the assessment if the main focus is on legal aspects.

Every risk analysis focuses on identifying events (including legal decisions) that may impact the client's objectives or key assets. Therefore, the assessment should specify what the client wishes to protect, by listing relevant *objectives* (including the protection of its *assets*). It is also useful to initially set out how risk will be documented and measured (for example, quantitative or qualitative *risk values*) and what *criteria* for risk evaluation the client wishes to use. Guidance on the latter questions is available, for instance, in literature on the use of the Australian Standard for risk management.[19]

2. Risk identification

The second step consists of identifying the risks. In general, this involves identifying what, why, where, when and how *events* could impact the achievement of the organization's objectives or the value of its assets. In the context of a contract draft, we are particularly interested in legal decisions that are based on the contract text. Therefore, one possibility for risk identification is to analyze one clause at a time, seeking to find out *how each clause could lead to a legal decision that impacts the organization's objectives or assets*. In practice, this involves brainstorming about likely facts and subsequent decisions that could negatively impact the client's objectives. In this context, the risk identification also needs to consider the *interplay between different contract rules,* which may be relevant to a legal decision. For many decisions, several clauses need to be read in a suitable combination. For example, the contract may include a clause that obligates the supplier to pay consequential damages in case of delay. In order to assess the risk, the analysis of course also needs to assess what impact the applicable law and other relevant material may have on the rights and duties of the contract

---

[18] However, the costs of such a comprehensive analysis will only be justified for exceptionally high-value or high-risk contracts.

[19] See e.g. STANDARDS AUSTRALIA and STANDARDS NEW ZEALAND, *Risk Management Guidelines Companion to Australian/New Zealand Standard AN/NZS 4360: 2004 (HB 436:2004)* .

parties. The outcome of this step is a list and a description of possible future legal "cases", which should include a description of both the anticipated facts and the likely legal assessment thereof. Such "cases" may be either binding decisions by courts or other authorities, or the actor's acceptance of consequences, in recognition of the legal norms included in the contract or in the background law.

3. Risk estimation and evaluation

The analysis could subsequently make an effort to estimate the likelihood and consequence values for all identified legal decisions. The *consequence* value is an estimation, for example, of the monetary consequence of the legal decision. The *likelihood* value is an estimation of the frequency or probability of the decision. The likelihood of the decision may directly depend on the rules contained in the contract. Because the interpretation of the rules is not always certain, this uncertainty should be directly included in the analysis. The likelihood of the legal decision may thus depend on *likely facts* and a *likely interpretation of the contract*. For example, the analysis can combine the assessment of the *factual* likelihood of a delay with an estimation of the *legal* likelihood of a particular contract interpretation that implies a payment obligation in case of delay. For example, the legal likelihood may be that it is unlikely that the contract can be interpreted to the effect that the client has to pay damages for delay. Likelihood values can be combined based on the basic rules of probability, which can not be covered in any detail here.[20]

The combination of *likelihood* and *consequence* values renders the risk value, according to which the analyst can prioritize the risks. Subsequently, the team should *evaluate* which risks can be accepted, for example based on their low risk value, and which need be considered for treatment. This evaluation should be based on the client's risk appetite, the balance of risks and benefits in the contract and other criteria, for example, the degree of influence the client has on the manifestation of the event. However, great care has to be exercised with the use of risk values. If the empirical basis for the risk estimation is shaky, as will often be the case in the early phases of a contractual relation, then one should be even more cautious about understanding risk values as reliable and exact predictions of the future. Rather, the risk values should be used as one out of several relevant inputs in a discussion about adequate risk treatment

---

[20] For details see I. HACKING, *An introduction to probability and inductive logic* (2001).

measures.

4. Risk treatment and cost-benefit

The final phase focuses on how the identified risks can be treated. There are two key types of treatment of particular relevance to contracts. First, the risk may be treated by *practical measures* that ensure that a particular legal decision is less likely to happen, or will be less costly. Second, it may be possible to *amend certain contract clauses during contract negotiation.* For example, if the contract includes a clause about consequential damages in case of delay, and the risk analysis team considers that there is a risk that the supplier will have to pay a substantial sum in damages for delay, then the treatment options include both contract amendment (e.g. liability limitation or liability exclusion, the details of which depend on the applicable law) and practical measures to reduce the likelihood of delays. The choice among the treatment options depends on a *cost-benefit analysis.* The benefit corresponds to the anticipated effect of the treatment on the risk level. This benefit needs to be related to the estimated cost of implementing the treatment. The cost-benefit analysis thus results in a recommendation of actions to manage the identified risks, which can be presented to the decision maker.

C. A METHODOLOGICAL SUPPLEMENT

It is difficult to anticipate the potential role of the above introduced approach within the portfolio of proactive legal methods available to lawyers. Today, there is no standard way of analyzing risk in a legal context.[21] While engineers, IT security experts and enterprise risk managers are increasingly using standardized assessment methods, we lawyers seem to use experience-based heuristics to manage complexity and risk. This established approach has worked well in the past, and we should be very cautious about replacing it. In fact, given the immaturity of methods for legal risk management, it is so far an unrealistic alternative for the daily practice of most practising lawyers. Structured legal risk management should *not replace* existing legal methods, but it could support and accompany existing approaches as a supplementary method. The above described semi-quantitative method for contract risk assessment could be used in a situation where:

---

[21] MAHLER, 'The State of the Art of Contractual Risk Management Methodologies', p. 58-72.

- there is a need or desire to obtain a more comprehensive and detailed understanding of the risks inherent in a contract compared to a traditional non-formalized analysis;
- the contract text is stable during a sufficient time to carry out the analysis; and
- sufficient time is available for a detailed assessment — the necessary time depends on how selectively the assessment scope is chosen, but the required time for a detailed risk assessment could easily be several times the duration of a traditional contract analysis.

Legal risk management methods may be used for other purposes besides contract analysis. There are several incentives for adopting a structured approach to legal risk management. For example, in an enterprise risk management (ERM) assessment, the general counsel of a company may be asked to identify and estimate risks within his or her field of responsibility. In this case, the general counsel would need to follow the established ERM method to identify and estimate risk. The need for sufficient overall risk management in a company may subsequently require the law department to identify and estimate risk in their daily practice in order to be able to report consistently. The dynamics of the largely soft-law based trend towards ERM and its implications for legal practice are difficult to anticipate. In some countries, including Germany, some companies are already required by law to have consistent ERM systems. Such requirements could be extended in the future.

Similarly, a systematic approach to risk management may be requested by customers of legal services. For example, the handbook for legal risk management, issued by Standards Australia and Standards New Zealand, encourages its readers to request that their legal advisors follow a systematic risk management approach.[22] However, a key problem with risk management is that it is rather time-consuming, costly and complex. Therefore, any success of the methodological approach may partly depend on adequate and efficient tools.

III. Tools for legal risk management

Risk management is cognitively challenging because the analyst and any other involved experts typically need to handle and take into account

---

[22] STANDARDS AUSTRALIA and STANDARDS NEW ZEALAND, *Legal risk management* .

a rather complex set of statements about what may happen in the future, in addition to estimations of possibly dependent values of likelihood and consequences. Therefore, risk managers often use targeted software tools, which simplify risk identification, estimation, evaluation, treatment and, not least, communication. Of course, because enterprise risk management and financial risk management are carried out differently, they are supported by specialized tools — the same would have to be true for legal risk management.

How could the above introduced method for risk management be supported by tools? I will propose three complementary approaches, which could be implemented in combination or separately. The three approaches follow naturally from the risk management method. The keywords are (1) legal risk management *procedures and processes*, (2) support for the difficult tasks of risk identification and estimation, which may involve communication between lawyers and non-lawyers, and (3) the implementation within, or interoperability with, existing legal information systems. Moreover, all three types of tools or systems may cautiously introduce selected elements of automation.

A. LEGAL RISK MANAGEMENT PROCESS AND ADMINISTRATION

Tools that structure, simplify and facilitate a coherent analysis are often used to support risk management in other fields. Typically, risk managers need to capture and document the identified risks, their values and potential treatments. These administrative functions are already available in existing risk assessment tools. A good risk assessment tool assists the risk analyst in carrying out the relevant analysis steps in a suitable order, and helps to document all results in a consistent way, ideally in a reusable fashion. However, existing tools are insufficient in a legal context, because legal aspects are typically not adequately integrated into these analyses. Moreover, most risk assessment tools are discipline specific and focus on financial, technical or other issues. Nevertheless, tools from other disciplines, in particular enterprise risk management, might be adapted or extended to support legal risk assessments.

B. GRAPHICAL TOOLS TO SUPPORT RISK IDENTIFICATION AND ASSESSMENT

The second type of tools is likely to be more challenging than the above process and administration tools. Risk analyses often involve brain-storming activities in interdisciplinary groups of experts. This part of risk analyses is often rather difficult, because it requires (1) discussions and agreement about what may happen in the future, (2) the intellectually challenging estimation of probabilities and (3) the estimation of financial or other consequences of events. Different experts will often have diverging views about all of these aspects. This is arguably even more difficult if the risk estimation is not limited to the likelihood of "facts" but also includes the likelihood of "legal outcomes".

For example, imagine a company that wishes to assess the risk of a particular technical failure leading to liability according to the clauses of a major contract, in the context of the applicable background law. In this example, an engineer would be able to estimate the likelihood of the technical failure, and a lawyer may need to be consulted when the legal consequences are assessed. In the same example, the risk analysis might also need to assess the legal and contractual consequences of market changes, e.g. major raw material price increases. In this case, it would be useful to convene lawyers, engineers and managers together, in order to discuss and estimate the risk consistently. This clearly requires communication and mutual understanding of the others' disciplinary perspectives. Of course, such communication already happens, and is often successful. However, sometimes such communication may be challenging due to the different methods and concepts used by the different disciplines. Just imagine a meeting where the lawyer brings the customer's general terms and conditions of purchase, under which the product will be supplied (45 pages), together with a book about the applicable law. The manager or the chief risk officer presents a set of spreadsheets that include financial information and risk estimates. The engineer contributes a set of technical drawings and the results of the engineering risk analysis (e.g. a failure modes and effects analysis, FMEA). Such an imaginary, but not unrealistic, meeting illustrates the clash of intellectual concepts behind the different disciplines which need to participate in the risk assessment.

My (unverified) impression from talking to managers and engineers in several companies is that *such meetings often do not happen* at all. Instead, the manager would at best send an e-mail to the lawyer, who then assesses the contract separately, with limited or no regard to the business and technical issues at stake.[23] At worst, the lawyer will not at all be consulted by the decision maker, perhaps to avoid a delay in the contracting process or in anticipation of an incomprehensible and lengthy

---

[23] Such an assessment is likely to follow the traditional method as introduced above, in the introduction to section II.A. This may, of course, be sufficient for standard cases. However, if the issues are complicated and the law department or law firm has little experience with this type of business, more communication may be necessary.

legalese statement, which is not related to the technical and business issues at stake.

This *communications problem* may be amongst the *causes* for Susskind's observation[24] that "legal problems of today are often symptomatic of delayed legal input". Susskind assumes that "earlier consultation should result in users understanding and identifying their risk and controlling them before any question of escalation." However, if communications problems are amongst the causes for *delaying* legal input, then these communication problems may need to be addressed by lawyers and their customers or colleagues. The difficult communication regarding identified risks, their estimation and treatment needs to be supported by a number of complementary approaches, including education, improved internal culture in an enterprise and, possibly, IT tools.

Tools for communication support should of course be inspired by solutions that have proved successful in other disciplines. In computer science, graphical models are often used in systems design and analysis to illustrate the intended functions of the IT system. The Unified Modelling Language (UML) is a graphical language used for visualizing, specifying, constructing and documenting the artefacts of a software-intensive system. The UML offers a standard way to write a system's blueprints, including conceptual aspects such as business processes and system functions as well as concrete features such as programming language statements, database schemas and reusable software components.[25]

Visualization is an interesting approach in the legal context because some of the problems outlined above are not that different from the underlying analytical challenges of IT systems development, despite the obvious differences. IT systems development needs to deal with complex technical issues related to hardware and software, and the end product is essentially code, which may be unreadable by humans. This code has a mathematical and logical basis, but what counts is ultimately whether the IT system fulfils the users' requirements, i.e. whether the system works for and with human beings. The latter aspect is captured best in graphical models, which can be understood by non-experts who participate in the specification of the system requirements. Because the code may be illegible, one uses simple graphics to facilitate informed decision making

---

[24] See above, note 1.

[25] For an introduction to the UML, see www.wikipedia.org. For more details, see M. FOWLER, *UML distilled a brief guide to the standard object modeling language* (3rd ed edn, 2004). A comprehensive work is J. RUMBAUGH, G. BOOCH and I. JACOBSON, *The unified modeling language reference manual* (2nd edn, 2004).

during systems development.

Code is not an unknown concept for lawyers, as observed by Lawrence Lessig,[26] who refers to laws as "east coast code" and to technology as "west coast code". However, problems with the readability and understandability of code are treated rather differently in computer science and in law. This is obviously partly related to the fact that source code is not written in natural language and thus may be both *highly complex* and *very difficult to read*, while legal texts do use natural language. Legal texts may be *difficult* to understand for the inexperienced, but they should normally not be completely incomprehensible (even though there are sufficient examples of incomprehensible legalese nonsense).[27] Moreover, it cannot be neglected that understandability problems arise for completely different reasons. In most cases, "legalese" is used as a matter of tradition, and legal terms are used because of their specific legal meaning in the relevant legal community (as a *terminus technicus*). However, in some cases, the use of excessive legalese may even be employed as a strategy to inhibit the other party from understanding and appreciating its risks.[28] In any case, legal work also has to face the problem of code which is difficult to read, understand and evaluate from the perspective of risk. Nevertheless, lawyers have traditionally been reluctant to introduce (standardized) graphical models to understand, analyze and manage complex legal issues. There may be many reasons for this, not least the lack of availability of such graphical models. However, in addition there may be some underlying problems that could inhibit a modelling approach. Again, the *qualitative perspective* in legal reasoning may make it difficult to press law and justice into formalized and partly quantitative models. Even so, we cannot assess the potentials and limitations of graphical modelling for legal risk management before we have developed and tested such systems.

In risk management there is also an extensive use of graphical visualization methods to support risk assessments. For example, fault trees or Bayesian networks can be used to estimate the likelihood of a risk event. In the following I will sketch a possible approach for the visualization of legal risk. This is illustrated in Fig. 1. The graphical

---

[26] L. LESSIG, *Code version 2.0* (2006).

[27] An example can be found in C. KESSEL and V. PASSAUER, 'Einkaufsbedingungen in der Automobilindustrie' *Betriebsberater* (Heft 37) 1974.

[28] However, e.g. under German law, the issuer of general terms and conditions "bears the risk" of including an unclear clause, since the courts are reluctant to reduce such a clause to a valid and clearer one, see BGH ZIP 2007, p. 31 = Betriebsberater 2007, p. 177.

models used here are based on the above introduced concepts of legal risk management, which are an extension of the ISO vocabulary for risk management.[29]

The lower part of the figure is essentially a simplification and adaptation of the CORAS language for security risk assessment, developed by computer scientists and inspired by the UML.[30] This part of the figure reads as follows. The event e (described in the leftmost vertex), which has the estimated likelihood l_1, leads to the effect f on objective o (described in the rightmost vertex). This effect on the objective can be quantified by the estimated values for likelihood l_3, consequence c and their combination, v.

The upper part of the figure illustrates how the effect is achieved *because* a legal norm n is applied to the circumstances of the case, i.e. the event.[31] The legal norm is derived from a legal source s, which may be any source of law or a contract. If there is uncertainty about the norm, then this uncertainty may also be expressed by adding likelihood value to the norm. This likelihood is in Fig. 1 referred to as likelihood l_2.

---

[29] This paper is based on draft risk management vocabulary, see ISO, *Committee Draft 2 for Risk management - vocabulary* footnote 8. The latter was chosen, rather than the currently valid version (ISO 2002), because it is likely that this draft will be adopted in the near future. Implicitly, I accept the risk that the ISO may deliberate differently.

[30] F. VRAALSEN, T. MAHLER, et al., 'Assessing Enterprise Risk Level: The CORAS Approach' in D Khadraoui and F Herrmann (eds) *Advances in Enterprise Information Technology Security* (2007).

[31] This part of the model is inspired by Toulmin's model of legal arguments, see S. E. TOULMIN, *The Uses of Argument* (2003). For a critique of Toulmin's argument model, see J. B. FREEMAN, *Dialectics and the macrostructure of arguments a theory of argument structure* (1991). The Toulmin scheme exists also in other variants, see G. KREUZBAUER, 'Visualisierung juristischer Argumentation' in E Hilgendorf (ed) *Beiträge zur Rechtsvisualisierung* (2005). The Toulmin approach has even been suggested as a basis for risk-based negotiation and decision support systems, see J. ZELEZNIKOW, 'Risk, negotiation and argumentation--a decision support system based approach' *Law, Probability and Risk* 1 (1) 37.

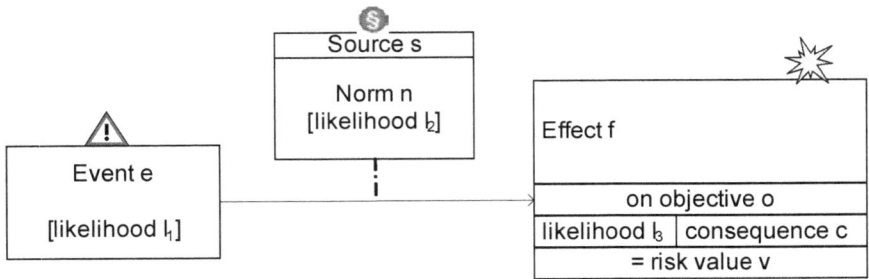

Fig. 1 – Modelling legal risk

An example of a simplified legal risk diagram regarding a contractual obligation to pay consequential damages is provided in Fig. 2 below. The diagram is meant to illustrate the following risk. In the unlikely event that a delivery is sufficiently delayed to result in loss of profit on the part of Buyer, Seller may decide to pay damages. The payment of damages is based on the contractual obligation to pay consequential damages, including loss of profit in cases of delay. The monetary consequences of the decision (a moderate consequence on the profits from this project) are a result of the identified factual event and the application of the legal norm to these facts. The likelihood of the decision depends on the likelihood of the initiating factual event, and the assessment of Seller's obligations in this event. The model in Fig. 2 is simplified in order to illustrate the main features of the modelling approach. In particular, it would be possible to decompose the initiating event by adding further initiating events that contribute to the delay and to add further consequential events and decisions.

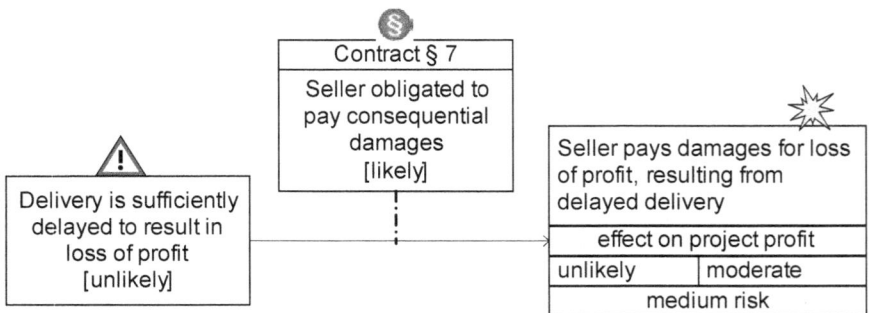

Fig. 2 – The risk of obligation to pay damages for delayed delivery

The above examples are insufficient to conclude whether this preliminary graphical modelling language as such is useful. However, the diagrams are only included here as *examples* of graphical models that could support a legal risk assessment. This is a tentative suggestion rather than a comprehensive solution to our problem.

This modelling approach is intended for the type of interdisciplinary legal risk assessment meeting described above. A previous (and more complex) version of the graphical language was tested in a full-scale industrial case study. Of course, the models imply a significant need for simplification, and the risk of over-simplification. However, this is a necessary consequence of introducing a model. If our limited brain resources could deal with all aspects of a complex reality, both today and in the future, then there would be no need for modelling. However, because we have to take bounded rationality[32] into account, some degree of selective simplification may in some situations be better communication rather than the full complexity of lengthy legalese documents. In any case, graphical models are not necessarily intended to be used instead of detailed legal analyses, but rather as an additional instrument to communicate a summarized result. If the output of a legal analysis is summarized in a concrete statement about risk and available options to manage such risk, then this output may be better understood and more easily used and implemented by non-lawyers. A suitable graphical legal risk management tool could therefore provide a simpler interface between the legal analyses and the risk analyses carried elsewhere in the organization. Graphical models alone will not solve the problem of delayed legal input, but if successful they may be amongst the measures that can partly solve some of the communication difficulties during legal risk identification and assessment. This again might contribute to an increased and earlier consultation of lawyers, as intended by Susskind.

---

[32] The concept of bounded rationality is used to question the assumption, made in traditional economics and other sciences, that humans can be reasonably described as "rational" entities (for example in rational choice theory). Instead, bounded rationality theory seeks to account for the fact that perfectly rational decisions are often not feasible in practice due to the finite computational resources available for making them. This has also consequences for the way risks can be analyzed and described. For example, a recent article describes the communications problems when discussing medical risk assessments, and discusses ways for simplified and still correct presentation of a medical doctor's risk estimates, see GERD GIGERENZER and ADRIAN EDWARDS, "Simple tools for understanding risks: from innumeracy to insight", *BMJ* 2003; 327:741-744, doi: 10.1136/bmj.327.7417.741.

C. RISK MANAGEMENT AND LEGAL INFORMATION SYSTEMS

Ideally, any support tool for legal risk management should be integrated or interoperable with a law department's information systems. Today, these include at least (1) legal information systems and (2) contract management systems.

First, law firms and law departments use a variety of legal information systems to retrieve legal information like statutory or case law, soft law (codes of conduct), contract templates and legal literature. Some systems already include a limited functionality for contract drafting, based on contract templates. Moreover, some of these systems already include modules which bare the title "legal risk management". The latter typically includes checklists or similar tools to support day-to-day legal work. One example of a risk assessment tool is a German tool on a set of CDs entitled "tool-box of international trade law", where the user of the "risk analysis tool" can retrieve information about particular legal questions relevant to international trade law, with respect to a number of jurisdictions.[33] This type of tool may thus be used to estimate the legal outcome of a standardized set of facts, which are relevant to international trade.   However, the tool only focuses on providing rather limited information and thus only covers a minor part of the overall risk management process, and does not offer any support for risk estimation and evaluation in general. Nevertheless, legal risk management tools could in the future be integrated or made interoperable with relevant legal information systems.

The second type of system, which could be a candidate environment for legal risk management tools, could be contract management systems. In general, contract management is the administration of an organisation's contracts. Contract management includes negotiating the terms and conditions in contracts and ensuring compliance with these, as well as documenting and agreeing to any changes that may arise during its implementation or execution. Today, contract management is in many organisations still carried out in manual processes without dedicated systems. However, e-mail negotiations and paper archiving routines often lead to poor availability of contracts in an organisation. Contract management software promises to solve this problem. Contract management software is intended to support contract creation, to ensure the availability of contracts and to support contract analysis. There are

---

[33] VERWEYEN, FOERSTER and TOUFAR, *Tool-Box des Internationalen Warenkaufs UN-Kaufrecht (CISG)* (2008).

different approaches to contract management, but most contract management systems today allow a selected number of users to upload and change contracts, which then are made available for other users in the company.[34] Currently, contract management systems seem to provide limited support for risk assessment. However, in the future, such functionality could and should be added to contract management systems. The contract management system could, for example, assist in assessing the risk in a particular contract text that was uploaded into the database. Moreover, once the risk is identified and assessed, the results of the risk assessment could be used as meta information about the contract, which is documented and available for future reporting and other uses. The identified risks may thus be monitored adequately. The identified risk may also be relevant for the analysis of other comparable contracts, where similar risks could be identified. Thus, it could become possible to consistently manage the risk present in a portfolio of contracts.

D. A CAUTIOUS APPROACH TOWARDS AUTOMATION

Lastly, it may be possible to cautiously introduce selected elements of automation into legal risk management systems. The need for caution is based on the fact that risk management, at least in the legal domain, needs to involve a considerable amount of human judgement, which is difficult to automate. Nevertheless, it might be possible to use automated systems to support human judgement and analysis. A cautious approach to automation could imply the use of text parsers, that is software for syntactic text analysis, e.g. to select rules that may be a source of legal risk. One option for automation could thus be that a tool extracts some of the conceptual notions[35] in legal texts, and makes the results available as a text paste option in a tool based on the above outlined graphical approach. Thus, the text "Seller obligated to pay consequential damages, including loss of profit" in Fig. 2 could be extracted from the contract document, identified as an obligation and suggested as a text paste option in the diagram. This could save some time and improve consistency. Moreover, the transparency could be improved if the legal source quoted in the diagram could be made directly available as a link to the full-text version of the legal document.

---

[34] A list of contract management software providers is available at the website of the International Association for Contract and Commercial Management, www.iaccm.org.

[35] C. BIAGIOLI , E. FRANCESCONI , A. PASSERINI , S. MONTEMAGNI , C. SORIA, "Automatic semantics extraction in law documents", *Proceedings of the 10th international conference on Artificial intelligence and law*, June 06-11, 2005, Bologna, Italy.

IV.Outlook

Although there are a number of potential benefits to be obtained through the introduction and use of methods and tools for legal risk management, we need to acknowledge the significant difficulties and obstacles.[36] For one, lawyers are not trained in risk management methods, and are used to a substantial methodological freedom for all tasks outside the interpretation of the law. Moreover, law is often open to interpretation and legal decisions are not always predictable from the outset, so most legal risk assessments need to deal with rather uncertain assessments. Legal risk assessments may, in addition, be rather time consuming and costly. Consider, for example, the possibilities of failure in a major commercial contract. The consistent analysis of all risks may be more costly than the potential improvement of the contract. Therefore, it may only be cost efficient to carry out a full-scale risk assessment for contracts that either have an exceptional value or that are sufficiently representative of other, similar contracts, so that the risk analysis results also are useful for those contracts that are not analyzed in detail. Last, but not least, clients may be less interested in paying expensive lawyers for a proactive legal risk assessment, compared to a situation in which a risk has already materialized and they necessarily have to face a major and costly legal problem. As a business model, legal risk assessment may therefore have some limitations for law firms.

These obstacles and limitations need to be taken into account in any development of legal risk management methods and tools. Nevertheless, there is sufficient potential in legal risk management to justify further research. The real benefit of new methods and tools for legal risk management can only be verified by defining a method for legal risk assessment, together with initial tool support, and testing these in a suitable case study.

V. Acknowledgements

The work presented in this paper was kindly financed by the Norwegian Research Council under the ENFORCE project grant.

---

[36] See also WAHLGREN, *Juridisk riskanalys: mot en säkrare juridisk metod* pp. 133-145.

Peeping HALs: Making Sense of Artificial Intelligence and Privacy

M. Ryan Calo
Center for Internet and Society, Stanford Law School

The field of artificial intelligence, broadly defined as the study and practice of designing intelligent agents,[1] is at least six decades into its existence as a formal discipline.[2] Sometimes called "computational" or "synthetic" intelligence, AI borrows from and informs a wide variety of subjects, including philosophy, psychology, linguistics, neuroscience, statistics, economics, and law.[3] Techniques of AI underpin all manner of industrial and consumer applications—from the complex neural nets used in data mining, down to the 'fuzzy logic' used by commercial washers and driers.

Insofar as "the issues of AI are directly related to [the] self-image of human beings",[4] and because the central projects and techniques of AI can often be articulated in lay language, few shy away from offering their insights and critiques.[5] This essay explores and updates a particular criticism—the long-standing claim that certain techniques and applications of AI violate human privacy—and discusses whether (U.S.) privacy law is adequately positioned to respond.

Historically, AI can be said to threaten privacy according to a specific pattern: AI substitutes for humans at various stages of observation or surveillance, allowing such activity to reach a previously impracticable scale. Whereas once telephonic surveillance required one listener per phone call, the development of voice recognition technology permits the

---

[1] S. RUSSELL and P. NOVIG, *Artificial Intelligence: A Modern Approach*, Saddle River, Pearson Education, Inc., 2003, pp. 1-2.

[2] The term "artificial intelligence" was coined by John McCarthy at the Dartmouth Conference in 1956. P. MCCURDOCK, *Machines Who Think*, Natick, AK Peters, Ltd., 2004, p. 529.

[3] *Id.*, pp. 5-16.

[4] H.R. EKBIA, *Artificial Dreams: The Quest for Non-Biological Intelligence*, New York, Cambridge University Press, New York, 2008, pp. 30-31. The author of this essay is no exception.

[5] *See, e.g.*, MCCURDOCK, *Machines Who Think*, p. 406 (discussing Edward Fredkin's concern that AI will hyper-concentrate power in the hands of one country or institution); B. JOY, "Why the Future Doesn't Need Us," *Wired Magazine*, Apr. 2000 (worrying aloud that AI will turn hostile toward humanity).

substitution of a computer capable of monitoring thousands of calls simultaneously.[6] Whereas once hundreds of intelligence analysts might be required to pour over field records in search of connections, AI knowledge management techniques automatically spot patterns and call them to the attention of agents.[7] These developments vastly amplifying the potential for data gathering and analysis, and hence underpin ubiquitous surveillance.[8]

Such advances in technology have played a key role in driving privacy law. The seminal 1890 article by Samuel Warren and Louis Brandeis, wherein the authors in may ways introduced a right to privacy protected by four causes of action, begins with a concern over "[r]ecent inventions and business methods" such as "instantaneous photography" that make possible previously unheard of behavior.[9] In the Fourth Amendment context, U.S. courts grapple with whether a given new technology permits humans to witness behavior in which, or occurring where, the individual has a reasonable expectation of privacy.[10] A state or federal regulator identify new information gathering practices—for instance, tracking online behavior for ad targeting—and hold it up against established fair information practice principles such as notice and control.[11]

A recent trend in AI complicates this dynamic. Increasingly, practitioners of AI and its subfield of robotics and human computer interaction are imbuing machines with 'social' characteristics.[12] These robots and computer interfaces contain key anthropomorphic signifiers such as eyes, expressive faces and gestures, and natural language capabilities designed to improve machine-human interaction. This set of

---

[6] J. WEIZENBAUM, *Computer Power and Human Reason: From Calculation to Judgment*, San Francisco, W.H. Freeman and Company, 1976, p. 272.

[7] T. ZARSKY, "Mine your Own Business!: Making the Case for the Implications of the Data Mining of Personal Information in The Forum of Public Opinion," *5 Yale J. of L. & Tech.* 4 (2004), p. 4.

[8] *Id.*

[9] S. WARREN AND L. BRANDEIS, "The Right to Privacy," *4 Harv. L. Rev.* 193 (1890).

[10] *See, e.g, Kyllo v. United States*, 533 U.S. 27, 29 (2001) (discussing thermo-imaging devices).

[11] FTC Press Release, "FTC Staff Proposes Online Behavioral Advertising Privacy Principles," Dec. 20, 2007, available online at http://www.ftc.gov/opa/2007/12/principles.shtm.

[12] T.M. HOLGRAVES ET AL, "Perceiving artificial social agents", *Computer in Human Behavior* 23 (2007) 2163 ("One of the major trends in human-computer interaction has been the development of more natural human-computer interfaces"); *id.* at 2171 ("There is no doubt that this trend will continue to increase.").

techniques builds on extensive research suggesting that humans are exquisitely attuned to their own species, and that we react to computers, robots, and other social media as though it were actually human—including through the subconscious alteration of our attitudes and behavior. Its effect is to introduce apparent agents into a variety of new contexts.[13]

Some applications of social AI follow the original pattern of amplifying human capacities. For instance, commercial and governmental entities have begun to leverage social machines and software to stand in for marketers, recruiters, and other organization representatives in gathering information and influencing consumers and citizens. Just a single AI program—for instance, the U.S. Army's virtual recruiter "SGT Star"—can engage with thousands of individuals simultaneously and record every interaction. Thus, social machines can stand in for a human as interviewer or interrogator, preserving the persuasive skills of humans but adding additional advantages such as massive scale, tirelessness, and an essentially limitless memory.[14]

Other consequences of social AI, however, fall outside the prevailing pattern. Rather than standing in for some specific human task such as listening, pattern-spotting, or questioning, a machine that presents as an independent agent can stand in for a human *as subject*. That is, a humanoid robot's mere presence will signal to individuals that they are not alone, even if the robot is neither collecting nor evaluating information on behalf of a human, which in turn can sharply alter attitudes and behavior. Relatedly, where a computer interface engages with a user socially—a direction the global leader in Internet search expressly contemplates within the next few years[15]—extensive social science

---

[13] B.J. FOGG, *Persuasive Technologies: Using Computers to Change What We Think and Do,* San Francisco, Morgan Kaufmann Publishers, 2003, p. 10 ("With the growth of embedded computers, computing applications are becoming commonplace in locations where human persuaders would not be welcome, such as bathrooms and bedrooms, or where humans cannot go (inside clothing, embedded in automotive systems, or implanted in a toothbrush)."). *See also* H.R. EKBIA, *Artificial Dreams*, p. 8 (discussing fact that "[c]omputers are everywhere."); J. KANG and D. CUFF, "Pervasive Computing: Embedding the Public Sphere," *62 Wash. & Lee L. Rev.* 93 (2005), p. 94 ("[T]he Internet will soon invade real space as networked computing elements become embedded into physical objects and environments.").

[14] B.J. FOGG, *Persuasive Technologies, o.c.*

[15] *See* http://www.techcrunch.com/2008/12/10/marissa-mayer-at-le-web-the-almost-complete-interview/ (interview with Marissa Mayer).

research shows that the individual will feel and react as though she is engaging with an actual person.

Although this set of applications does not augment the human capacity to observe in the tradition sense, it nevertheless threatens core privacy values. As detailed below, a key role of privacy is to preserve solitude, in the sense of a temporary respite from interference with respect to curiosity, development, and thought.[16] Yet it is clear that people react to social machines as though they were human beings, including with respect to the sense of being observed. If, as many predict, social machines become ubiquitous—turning up in cars, bedrooms, bathrooms,[17] even within cell phones and mirrors[18]—possibilities for solitude may shrink intolerably. We may even witness a sea change of attitudes away from the prevailing view of computers as passive data conduits, in turn chilling curiosity at the borderline and creating discomfort around widespread machine custodianship of personal information.

It is exactly here, where AI begins to substitute for the human not as a gatherer or organizer of information but directly as subject, that privacy protections begin to break down. This is partly because American privacy law and theory focuses on the flow of information, on quantifiable harms, and on the level of notice and consent. It is also a function of limited imagination around the role of objects in our social lives. This essay concludes with thoughts on where to look in American law for legal analogues to vindicate the core privacy values threatened by social AI.

I. Traditional intersection of AI and privacy

On the traditional view, technology threatens privacy by increasing the power or reach of human observation. As prominent American privacy scholar Michael Froomkin sums up the space: "Privacy-destroying technologies can be divided into two categories: those that facilitate the acquisition of raw data and those that allow one to process

---

[16] A. WESTIN, *Privacy and Freedom*, New York, Antheum 1970, p. 35.

[17] B.J. FOGG, *Persuasive Technologies*, p. 10.

[18] P.J. O'RORKE, "Future Shlock," *The Atlantic*, Dec. 2008 ("Various passages had caught my attention when I'd read it, and raised my blood pressure: 'Closets will help pick out the right dress for a party.' Imagine that: a talking mirror telling you, 'That makes your butt look big.'").

and collate that data in interesting ways".[19]   Speaking on the subject of privacy invasive technologies, Harvard Law School's Jonathan Zittrain identifies "three successive shifts in technology from the early 1970s: cheap processors, cheap networks, and cheap sensors".[20]   He continues that "[t]he third shift has, with the help of the first two, opened the doors to new and formidable privacy invasions".[21] The thought is that humans will use cheaper and better technology to collect and organise information to greater effect, sometimes necessitating additional protections.

An early example of this analysis in the context of AI is synthetic intelligence pioneer Joseph Weizenbaum's concern over the use of AI in data mining.[22] In 1976, Weizenbaum wrote a scathing critique of artificial intelligence along multiple lines. Weizenbaum had developed a program called ELIZA that was designed to mimic psychoanalysis by engaging in a credible dialogue with a human operator, in keeping with the "Rogerian technique of encouraging a patient to keep talking".[23] ELIZA asked its users questions based on their previous answer and, where it did not have a response, merely supplied filler such as "I see" or "interesting". Weizenbaum claimed that he was profoundly disturbed by the tendency of humans to react ELIZA as though it were a person, which prompted him to write a book about what computers should never be pressed to do.

In one powerful passage, Weizenbaum argues that the most obvious application of some artificial intelligence techniques is massive surveillance. Weizenbaum observes that, as of 1976, there were "three or four major projects in the United States devoted to enabling computers to understand human speech".[24] According to the "principle sponsor of this work, the Advanced Research Projects Agency ... of the United States Department of Defense", (now "DARPA") potential applications were uncontroversial and benign.   For instance, the Navy wanted voice

---

[19] M. FROOMKIN, "The Death of Privacy?," *52 Stan. L. Rev.* 1461, 1468 (2000). *But see id.*, pp. 1469-70 (acknowledging that "[f]or some, just knowing that their activities are being recorded may have a chilling effect on conduct, speech, and reading").

[20] J. ZITTRAIN, *The Future of the Internet: And How to Stop It*, New Haven, Yale University Press, 2008, 205.

[21] *Id.*

[22] "Data mining is correctly defined as the 'nontrivial process of identifying valid, novel, potentially useful and ultimately understandable patterns in data." T. ZARSKY, "Mine your Own Business!: Making the Case for the Implications of the Data Mining of Personal Information in The Forum of Public Opinion," *5 Yale J. of L. & Tech.* 4 (2004), p. 6.

[23] J. WEIZENBAUM, *Computer Power and Human Reason: From Calculation to Judgment*, San Francisco, W.H. Freeman and Company, 1976, p. 3.

[24] *Id.*, p. 270.

recognition technology in order to "control its ships, and the other services their weapons, by voice commands".[25] Weizenbaum rejects this explanation:

> *Granted that a speech-recognition machine is bound to be enormously expensive, and that only government and possibly a few very large corporations will therefore be able to afford it, what will they be used for? ...There is no question in my mind that there is no pressing human problem that will more easily be solved because such machines exist. But such listening machines, could they be made, will make monitoring of voice communications very much easier than it is now.*[26]

Today, many varieties of sophisticated voice recognition technology exist.[27] Weizenbaum was wrong about the range of applications to which voice recognition would eventually be put—such technology has been used in everything from computers for the blind, to voice dialing, to hands-free wheelchairs. He was correct, however, that voice recognition would make massive government surveillance practicable.

Another concern closely related to Weizenbaum's insight that computers endowed with AI can stand in for human surveillants is the notion that AI can bring certain patterns of activity to the attention of humans. Thus, techniques of artificial intelligence have been used to decide where to point cameras or to 'flag' events such as the same face appearing in multiple transit stations. Weizenbaum hints in 1976 at this functionality as well:

> *Perhaps the only reason that there is very little government surveillance in many countries of the world is that such surveillance takes so much manpower. Each conversation on a tapped phone must eventually be listened to by a human agent. But speech-recognizing machines could [recognise and] delete all "uninteresting" conversations and present transcriptions of only the remaining ones...*[28]

More recently, Israeli legal scholar Tal Zarsky discusses the power of AI to sift through and organise data in seconds that would take a human an eternity. Zarsky argues that "[m]ere surveillance ... is not grounds for concern, at least not on its own. The fact that there are an eye watching

---

[25] *Id.*, p. 271.

[26] *Id.*, p. 272.

[27] *See, e.g.*, Mass High Tech, "MIT adds robotics, voice control to wheelchair," Sept. 19, 2008, available online at http://www.masshightech.com/stories/2008/09/15/daily64-MIT-adds-robotics-voice-control-to-wheelchair.html (describing a voice-controlled wheelchair).

[28] J. WEIZENBAUM, *Computer Power and Human Reason*, p. 272.

and an ear listening is meaningless unless the collected information is *recorded and emphasised*".[29]   Zarsky goes on to provide a detailed description of "knowledge discovery in databases" (or "KDD"), in which "complex algorithms, artificial intelligence, neural networks and even genetic-based modeling ... can discover previously unknown facts and phenomenon about a database".[30] These techniques are indeed central to AI applications, in which the ability to search for the right answer↓particularly in a complex and even dynamic environment—is the key to performance.[31] After exploring the dangers of consumer and citizen data profiling, Zarsky concludes that greater public awareness of the AI techniques involved in data mining—well understood within, but not beyond, the field of computing↓will lead to more ethical deployment of KDD.

Thus, according to Weizenbaum, Zarsky, and others, AI plays a role in supporting human surveillance that might otherwise prove impossible. The issue is considered serious enough that a popular AI textbook has cited the potential to invade privacy as one of six principle ethical questions around AI.[32]

II. The role of social machines

A. ROBOTICS AND COMPUTER INTERFACES

A long-standing and accelerating goal of AI, especially within the subfields of robotics and human-computer interaction ("HCI"), has been to develop machines and programs that interact more naturally with humans. Due in part to increased worldwide demand for personal robotics (one research agency predicts that personal robotics will be a \$15 billion dollar industry by 2015),[33] roboticists have made close study of the human reaction to robots in the field. Some have reached the conclusion that humans are less likely to accept robots in certain capacities absent

---

[29] T. ZARSKY, "Mine your Own Business!," p. 4 (emphasis in original).

[30] Zarsky further observes that KDD can make predictions about the future. *Id.*, p. 8 ("After establishing the 'clustering,' both *descriptive* and *predictive* inquiries are possible.") (emphasis in original). Beyond the scope of this essay is whether these techniques create new categories of relevant, invasive personal information that was never disclosed (or perhaps known) to the data subject.

[31] H.R. EKBIA, *Artificial Dreams*, p. 44.

[32] S. RUSSELL and P. NOVIG, *Artificial Intelligence*, p. 960.

[33] ABA Research, "Personal Robots Are Here," New York, Dec. 28, 2007.

sufficient resemblance to humans and/or social complexity.[34] Thus, for instance, in developing the "Nursebot" Pearl for use in hospitals or elderly care facilities, researches at Carnegie Melon found that "if the Nursebot is too machine-like, her human clients ignore her, and won't exercise or take pills."[35] It was therefore necessary to make Nursebot appear more human and interact more naturally for it to be an effective tool in elderly care.

Other drivers behind socializing robots are the view that "to build systems that have human-level intelligence", it is necessary to "build robots that have not merely a physical body but in fact a humanoid form",[36] and the related hope that very complex behaviors can 'develop' over time through social interaction. Cynthia Breazeal, a pioneer in the emerging field of "social robotics" and the head of the influential MIT Media lab, has helped create a class of "Mobile/Dexterous/Social" robots capable of mimicking emotion and responding to social cues. In describing Kismet, among her first efforts in social robotics, Breazeal told the New York Times: "I hoped that if I built an expressive robot that responded to people, they might treat it in similar way to babies, and the robot would learn form that".[37] Her impressive work continues to advance in this direction.[38]

Software developers and computer engineers have similarly turned to more social interfaces. According to psychological science professor T.M. Holtgraves and colleagues, "[o]ne of the major trends in human-computer interaction ... has been the development of more natural human-

---

[34] *See* http://robotic.media.mit.edu/projects/robots/mds/social/social.html ("Given the richness and complexity of human life, it is widely recognized that personal robots must be able to adapt to and learn within the human environment from ordinary citizens over the long   term.");   *see*   *also* http://robotic.media.mit.edu/projects/robots/leonardo/socialcog/socialcog.html ("One way robots might develop socially adept responses that seem to reflect beliefs about the internal states of others is by attempting to simulate –in its own cognitive system – the behaviors of others.").

[35] P. MCCURDUCK, *Machines that Think*, p. 467. Conversely, the researchers worried that were Nursebot Pearl *too* humanlike, clients might form unnatural attachments to her. *Id.*

[36] H.R. EKBIA, *Artificial Dreams*, p. 259 (citing others).

[37] P. MCCURDUCK, *Machines that Think*, p. 454 (citing the New York Times).

[38] *See, e.g.,* C. BREAZEAL, J. GRAY and M. BERLIN, "An embodied cognition approach to mindreading skills for socially intelligent robots," *International Journal of Robotics Research*, 2008 (to appear); A.L. THOMAZ and C. BREAZEAL, "Teachable robots: Understanding human teaching behavior to build more effective robot learners." *Artificial Intelligence*, vol. 172(6-7), 2008, p. 716-37.

computer interfaces".[39] Moreover, "[w]ith the advent of the Internet, the appeal of even more natural, human-like interfaces has increased dramatically".[40]

As a consequence of such research, the number of applications that leverage social dimensions is growing. Companies and other institutions make use of virtual representatives, discussed in greater detail below, in order to handle customer service calls and even sales and recruitment.[41] We are also seeing the deployment of human-like robots into a variety of spaces, including the home for entertainment and service.[42]   Many computer systems, particularly those running on cell phones or in an environment that requires a 'hands free' user experience, have moved toward spoken language and other, more natural interfaces.[43] After some initial setbacks,[44] websites are becoming more interactive and personalised.

B. EFFECTS OF SOCIAL MACHINES ON HUMANS

It turns out that making robots and computers more social yields a profound effect on humans.   Consider social scientist Sherry Turkle's report after her encounter with the social robot Cog in the MIT Media Lab1990s:

> Trained to track the largest moving object in its field (because that will usually be a human being) Cog "noticed" me soon after I entered its room. Its head turned to follow me and I was embarrassed to note that this mad me happy. I found myself competing with another visitor for its attention. At one point, I felt sure that Cog's eyes had "caught my own."[45]

Studies across multiple disciplines have confirmed this human tendency to treat social objects as social, sometimes called the "ELIZA effect" in AI literature after Weizenbaum's program.[46] In their influential book *The Media Equation: How People Treat Computers, Television, and*

---

[39] T.M. HOLTGRAVES et al., "Perceiving artificial social agents," *Computers in Human Behavior*, 2007, No 23, pp. 2163-2174, at p. 2163.

[40] *Id.*

[41] I. KERR, "Bots, Babes," *o.c.*

[42] P. MCCURDUCK, *Machines that Think*, p. 467.

[43] *See* D. GARLAN et al., "Project Aura: Toward Distraction-Free Pervasive Computing," *IEEE Pervasive Computing*, vol. 01, no. 2, pp. 22-31, Apr-Jun, 2002.

[44] *See* http://en.wikipedia.org/wiki/Microsoft_Bob (describing Microsoft's unpopular virtual helper).

[45] *Id.*, p. 277.

[46] *Id.*, p. 8.

New Media Like Real People and Places, Byron Reeves and Clifford Nass detail their findings that humans treat computers as social actors.[47] Their method consists largely of reproducing experiments around known human behaviors toward other humans and substituting social computer for one set of people.[48] In this way, Reeves and Nass show that computers that evidence social characteristics have a similar, or, in some case, the exact same, effect on humans. Computers programmed to be polite, or to evidence certain personalities, have profound effects on test subjects.[49] Humans respond to flattery and criticism from computers,[50] and rate their experiences with computers more highly if the computer has a similar 'personality' (e.g., submissive) to their own.[51] The results applied to people of all ages and of diverse backgrounds, including those with a familiarity with technology.[52]

Further data around human-technology interaction suggests that the more human-like the medium, the greater the response. Canvassing the literature on human interaction with androids↓i.e., "artificial system[s] designed with the ultimate goal of being indistinguishable from humans in its external appearance and behavior"[53]↓informatics professors Karl MacDorman and Hiroshi Ishiguro conclude that "[h]umanlike appearance and behavior are required to elicit the sorts of responses that people typically direct toward one another",[54] and that "the more humanlike the robot, the more human-directed (largely subconscious) expectations are elicited".[55] In one cited study, test subjects exhibited greater unconscious eye contact behaviors (fixating on the right eye, typical of human-human interaction) when engaging with more humanoid robots.[56] In another,

---

[47] B. REEVES and C. NASS, *The Media Equation: How People Treat Computers, Television, and New Media Like Real People and Places*, New York, Cambridge University Press, 1996.

[48] *Id.*, p. 14.

[49] *Id*, p. 24.

[50] *Ibid.* (Chapters 2, 4).

[51] *Ibid.* (Chapter 8).

[52] *Id.*, p. 252.

[53] K. MACDORMAN and H. ISHIGURO , "The uncanny advantage of using androids in cognitive and social science research," *Interaction Studies* 7:3, 2006, pp. 298-99.

[54] *Id.*, p. 316

[55] *Id.*, p. 309. There is an apparent point of similarity, often referred to as the "uncanny valley," at which humans can become repulsed by an android. Many theories exist to explain this phenomenon, including that almost human androids create certain expectations that they necessarily violate (in that they are not perfect replicas). *Id.*, p. 299.

[56] *Id.*, p. 316.

Japanese subjects only averted their gaze (a sign of respect) when engaging with the most human-like machines.[57] MacDorman and Ishiguro further offer several anecdotal examples of disparate treatment of robots. For instance, visitors to Ishiguro's lab could be convinced to treat more mechanical robots roughly, but show respect toward Uando, a robot with an enhanced "aura of human presence," due to automated response such as "shifting posture, blinking, and breathing".[58] One visitor reportedly asked his wife's permission before touching a 'female' robot.[59]

Importantly, research also shows that this tendency to anthropomorphise social media can also recreate in humans the sense of being observed. Thus, Terry Burnham and Brian Hare of Harvard University subjected 96 volunteers to a game in which they anonymously donate money or withhold it. Where players were faced with a mere photo of Kismet↓the robot designed by Cynthia Breazeal to elicit a social reaction in humans↓they gave considerably more then those who were not.[60] In another experiment involving donation, subjects consistently donated more where the computer terminal they were using had eyespots on its screen.[61] In yet another study published in *Biology Letters*, UK psychologists found that the presence of a picture with eyes above a collection bin led people to pay for coffee on the honor system far more often then the presence of a picture of flowers.[62]

The standard explanation for this set of phenomena is that humans evolved at a time when representation was largely impossible, such that what appeared to be real was real in fact. As Reeves and Nass explain, "people are not evolved to twentieth-century technology. The human brain evolved in a world in which *only* humans exhibited rich social behaviors, and a world in which *all* perceived objects were real objects".[63] In evolutionary terms, we are not much further along than our oldest ancestors.

American cognitive science professor H.R. Ekbia puts it slightly differently: humans as highly social animals have developed an innate

---

[57] *Id.*

[58] *Id.*, pp. 313-14.

[59] *Id.*, p. 317.

[60] V. WOODS, "Pay Up, You Are Being Watched," *New Scientist*, Mar. 18, 2005 (reporting a 30% increase in giving when faced with Kismet).

[61] O. JOHNSON, "Feel the Eyes Upon You," *N.Y. Times*, Aug. 3, 2008.

[62] M. BATESON et al., "Cues of Being Watched Enhance Cooperation in a Real-World Setting," *Biology Letters*, 2(3), Sept. 22, 2006, pp. 412–14.

[63] B. REEVES and C. NASS, *The Media Equation*, p. 12 (emphasis in original).

ability to identify with other humans. This confers a tremendous survival advantage in that it tends to foster cooperation. The ability is often indiscriminate, however, with the result that humans often unconsciously attribute human emotions to objects or animals. Ekbia adds: "The AI community has, often inadvertently, taken advantage of this human tendency, turning what could be called innocent anthropomorphism to a professional and often unjustified, technoscientific one".[64] That is, Ekbia believes that practitioner of AI have sometimes relied on the ELIZA effect to gloss over the difficulty in programming truly fulsome intelligent or social interactions.

III. The privacy threats posed by social AI

A. OLD PARADIGM: AI AS ACTIVE GATHERERS OF INFORMATION

We have seen that social machines are on the rise and that humans treat social machines as though there were truly people. One application of this insight is to free computers from their historically hidden or passive role within surveillance and set machines to the active, interpersonal task of gathering of information. B.J. Fogg is a Stanford researcher who coined the term "captology"↓"an acronym based on the phrase computers as persuasive technologies".[65] In his 2003 book *Persuasive Technology: Using Computers to Change What We Think And Do*, Fogg details some of the techniques of captology, many of which consist of embedding physical, psychological, and social cues in computer interfaces for a variety of purposes. It turns out that one of the primary applications of persuasive technology has been information gathering.

Building on the work of Reeves, Nass, and others, Fogg directly compares mechanical persuaders to persuasive people. He explains certain advantages thoughtfully modeled computers will typically have. Computers can be more persistent than humans, in that humans tire and respond to social cues such as anger and shame.[66] Machines have no necessary form or clear identity, and can therefore facilitate anonymous persuasion. Computers can also "store, access, and manipulate huge volumes of data". They can leverage a variety of "modalities," beyond speech and body language. Computers can "scale," in the sense of

---

[64] H.R. EKBIA, *Artificial Dreams*, p. 310.

[65] B.J. FOGG, *Persuasive Technologies*, p. xxv.

[66] *Ibid.*

reaching millions of people at once. Similarly, computers can go where ordinary human strangers cannot↓reaching into the home, a bathroom, or even a person's clothing.

Fogg also details the dangers of persuasion by computer↓some of which overlap his advantages. He identifies six "unique ethical concerns related to persuasive technology".[67] First, he notes that a technology's novelty can mask its persuasive intent. Humans may not be 'on alert' to an agenda in a neat new gadget. Second, computers have a positive reputation as credible and unbiased; this reputation can be exploited to hide a persuasive intent. Third, unlike sales people, computers do not tire; they can reach thousands simultaneously and persistently. Computers also control all "interactive possibilities", i.e., the computer decides what happens next and what the user can see or do. Fifth, computers "can affect emotions but can't be affected by them".[68] Programmers can expect a social reaction from humans but can control the reaction of the persuasive technology that elicits it. Finally, computers are not "ethical agents", in the sense that they cannot take responsibility for an error[69]

The gist of captology, then, is that computers and robots can be pressed into the task of persuading humans to engage in or refrain from behaviors through both direct and subtle social methods. This tasks has so far mostly involved gathering information. Canadian legal scholar Ian Kerr has explored the use of virtual representatives and other online "bots" that leverage techniques of AI and human-computer interaction in order to establish trust with, gather information about, and ultimately influence consumers.[70] In an insightful 2004 law review article Kerr asks, "What if bots could be programmed to infiltrate people's homes and lives *en masse*, befriending children and teens, influencing lonely seniors, or harassing confused individuals until they finally agree to services that they otherwise would not have choose?"[71] The question proves a set up: Kerr observes that "[m]ost such tasks can be achieved with today's bot technologies".[72]

Kerr goes on to detail several "interactive agents" operating on the Web since 2000. One such agent is ELLEgirlBuddy, a text-based virtual representative for ELLEgirl.com that operates over instant messenger

---

[67] *Id.*, p. 213.
[68] *Id.*
[69] *Id.*, pp. 213-220.
[70] I. KERR, "Bots, Babes," *o.c.*
[71] *Id.*, p. 312.
[72] *Id.*

("IM"). As Kerr explains: "ELLEgirlBuddy is programmed to answer questions about her virtual persona's family, school life and her future aspirations, occasionally throwing in a suggestion or two about reading ELLEgirl magazine." Although she has no actually body, she sometimes writes about her body image problems. Although she is in actuality only a few years old, ELLEgirlBuddy purports to be sixteen and seeks to replicate the lingo of a teenager, complete with emoticons.[73]

Among ELLEgirlBuddy's most alarming functions is straightforward data collection. Every single response the bot receives or elicits is recorded↓in all, millions of conversations over IM. This information is used in turn to further deepen the bond↓and therefore trust –between the bot and its interlocutor.[74] (In social robotic parlance, ELLEgirlBuddy is an "expressive robot that respond[s] to people" and, when people treat it like the teen it purports to be, the robot learns form that.) Kerr points that the data has other, commercial value in that it could be used to target advertisements.[75]

The use of virtual personalities is not limited to the private sector. The U.S. Army has deployed an interactive virtual representative for its recruitment website.[76] The program, SGT Star,[77] appears as an avatar. He speaks out loud in addition to displaying text. He can act both funny and agitated, as when in response to a command to do pushups he yells: "Hey, I'm the sergeant, here, YOU drop down and give me twenty! I CAN'T HEAR YOU!!! COUNT 'EM!!!" He can also take a compliment; if you tell SGT Star that you like him, he responds: "Thanks, I try".

SGT Star purported function is to engage with users of the GoArmy website in order to answer questions and to provide other guidance such as the location of forms or local recruitment offices. Yet SGT Star also gathers information. As an initial matter, SGT Star prompts the user for his or her name before beginning the chat session. Moreover, the website invites users to sign in and provide more information (e.g., date of birth, address) for a more "personalised" SGT Star experience. SGT Star even invites users to "Tell A Friend" about him by submitting a name and email address, which will cause SGT Star to generate an email invitation

---

[73] Emoticons are faces drawn with text. ;o)

[74] I. KERR, "Bots, Babes," p. 316 ("In other words, these companies are constantly collecting incoming data from users and strong that information for the purposes of future interactions.")

[75] Id.

[76] See http://www.goarmy.com/ChatWithStar.do.

[77] The SGT stands for "strong, trained, and ready." Id.

to start a chat session with a third party.

According to the GoArmy privacy policy (in general a notoriously under-read document[78]), the Army records everything anyone says to SGT Star. The Army reserves the right to use all information gathered SGT Star for recruiting purposes, and to disclose such information as required by law.[79] The Army may therefore use chat transcripts in the aggregate to improve SGT Star's 'social skills', or to identify particularly promising candidates for eventual follow up by a human recruiter. It remains largely unclear, however, whether the Army might use a SGT Star chat transcript to reject a candidate↓for instance, by discovering the sexual orientation of a potential recruit on the basis of questions he asked about Army policy toward gays↓a question he might not ask of a human recruiter.[80]

In short, through a combination of powerful processing and sophisticated social mimicry, it appears possible for companies and other institutions to collect information from individuals beyond that which even a large human work force could accomplish. As in the context of data mining, a computer equipped with artificial intelligence is capable of engaging thousands of individuals simultaneously, twenty-four hours a day. But here the agent is able to leverage the power of computers to persuade via carefully orchestrated social tactics known to elicit responses in humans. In an age of national security and targeted advertising, citizen and consumer information is at an all time premium.[81] Techniques of AI and HCI create the opportunity for institutions to leverage the human tendency to anthropomorphise and other advantages computers hold over humans (ubiquity, diligence, trust, memory, etc.) to facilitate and otherwise impracticable depth and breadth of data collection.

B. NEW PARADIGM: SOCIAL AI AS SUBJECT

We have seen various applications of AI that threaten privacy by

---

[78] See, e.g., E. MORPHY, "Consumers Trust Brands, Not Policies," CIO Today, Jan. 29, 2004 (citing research at Michigan State Univeristy).

[79] If you ask SGT Star about privacy, he responds: "I keep a record of all the chats I have with GoArmy users. My conversations are reviewed to ensure all potential recruits are getting the information that they need. However, your information will not be shared with the public."

[80] The U.S. Army uses a "don't ask, don't tell" approach wherein gays may serve as long as they do not self-reveal their orientation. See 10 U.S.C. Sec. 654.

[81] See, e.g., A. MCCLURG, "A Thousand Words are Worth a Picture: A Privacy Tort Response to Consumer Data Profiling", 98 Nw. U. L. Rev. 63 (2003) (discussing institutional data demand and data mining trends).

substituting a machine or software function for a human task, thereby augmenting the human power to observe. Thus, AI can listen to phone conversations so that a human does not have to, comb through video or other data better and faster than a human, or be sent out to recruit or inquire on behalf of an organization using much of the social leverage of a real person, but with none of the limitations.   Yet given the power of social AI to signal the presence of a human, the distribution of social machines may have still deeper, if unintended, impacts on privacy.

As an initial matter, the appearance of social AI in historically private spaces may lessen the opportunity for solitude and free reflection. Many privacy theorists have expounded upon the importance of private space, wherein one can "be themselves" and even transgress otherwise oppressive social norms.   As Alan Westin famously writes in his 1970 treatise on privacy, *Privacy and Freedom*: "There have to moments 'off stage' when the individual can be 'himself'; tender, angry, irritable, lustful, or dream filled. ... To be always 'on' would destroy the human organism".[82] Westin further cites the "need of individuals for respite from the emotional stimulation of daily life. ... [T]he whirlpool of active life must lead to some quiet water, if only so that the appetite can be whetted for renewed social engagement."[83]   According to Westin, "[p]rivacy provides the change of pace that makes life worth savoring".[84] For Westin, privacy protects "minor non-compliance with social norms" that "society really expects many persons to break", and the important opportunity to "deviate temporarily from social etiquette".[85]

Many other scholars have explored the same line of thought.   In the words of political theorist Hannah Arendt, "[a] life spent entirely in public, in the presence of others, becomes ... shallow. ... A space apart from others has enabled people to develop artistic, political, and religious ideas that have had lasting influence and value when later introduced into the public sphere".[86] American law scholar Paul Schwartz argues that the belief that one is being constantly observed interferes with self-determination.[87] Julie Cohn argues similarly that "pervasive monitoring of every first move or false start will, at the margin, incline choices

---

[82] A. WESTIN, *Privacy and Freedom*, New York, Antheum 1970, p. 35.
[83] *Id.*
[84] *Id.*
[85] *Id.*
[86] D. SOLOVE, "A Taxonomy of Privacy," pp. 554-55.
[87] *Id.*, p. 494.b

toward the bland and the mainstream".[88]   According to prolific privacy scholar Daniel Solove, "[n]ot only can direct awareness of surveillance make a person feel extremely uncomfortable, but it can also alter her behavior.   Surveillance can lead to self-censorship and inhibition". Solove further notes that "[e]ven surveillance of legal activities can inhibit people from engaging in them".[89]

If, as many contend, safeguarding occasional solitude is a central goal of privacy law, social AI may bypass existing protections by introducing the appearance and feeling of a human in an unlimited array of contexts. Consider just a few examples: Japanese software company MetaboInfo makes a virtual wife that appears on your cell phone and reminds you of chores;[90] an exhibit of a future house by Disney showcases a mirror that sees you and suggests outfits;[91] the Figera vacuum approaches its owner and responds to voice commands;[92] experiments are being conducted around whether placing robots or voice-interface computers in cars can stop road rage; etc.[93] As captology expert BJ Fogg explains, "computing applications are becoming commonplace in locations where human persuaders would not be welcome, such as bathrooms and bedrooms, or where humans cannot go (inside clothing, embedded in automotive systems, or implanted in a toothbrush)".[94]

Social AI may also impact personal privacy in the aggregate, by creating unease around the massive computer custodianship of human data.   Hardly any aspect of human life today remains untouched by computers; this trend will only grow as computer become embedded into our streets, walls, and even our clothing.   Meanwhile, the public sense of computer intelligence and evaluative capabilities↓fueled by our tendency to anthropomorphise, by the rise in prominence of tech media coverage, and by claims of competitive practitioners↓continues to develop.   This synergy could, in theory, lead to widespread and intractable discomfort with computer information custodianship.

---

[88] *Id.*

[89] D. SOLOVE, "'I've Got Nothing To Hide' and Other Misunderstandings of Privacy," *44 San Diego L. Rev.* 745 (2007), p. 267.

[90] *See* http://www.metaboinfo.com/okusama/ (website in Japanese).

[91] P.J. O'RORKE, "Future Shlock," The Atlantic, Dec. 2008.

[92] *See* http://gizmodo.com/5105633/the-figura-vacuum-bot-allows-you-to-boss-it-around.

[93] T.E. GALOVSKI and E.B. BLANCHARD, "Road rage: A domain for psychological intervention?", *Aggression and Violent Behavior*, 2004, No 9, pp. 105—127.

[94] B.J. FOGG, *Pervasive Computing*, at p. 10.

Artificial intelligence has clearly seen its share of breakthroughs throughout its history, many of which have been widely reported by the media.[95] The field stands poised to make many more. In part by leveraging well-understood AI tactics and incredible but steady gains in computational power, projects such as the Defense Advanced Research Agency (DARPA)'s "Cognitive Agent that Learns and Organises" are making notable strides in advancing computer learning, and setting ambitious but attainable long-term goals.[96]

Indeed, computer and robotics insiders publicly predict that machines will be as or more intelligent than humans within a few decades. Jim Gray of Microsoft Research has speculated that computers will pass the famous Turing Test↓i.e., the test of machine intelligence devised by Alan Turing wherein a machine must fool a trained expert into believing it is human↓by the middle of this century.[97] A German software program competing in the International Turing Competition managed recently to fool three of twelve judges into believe it was a person.[98] Speaking as a keynote at a large technology conference, Justin Ratner, Intel's chief technology officer, observed in August 2008:

The industry has taken much greater strides than anyone ever imagined 40 years ago. There is speculation that we may be approaching an inflection point where the rate of technology advancements is accelerating at an

---

[95] *See, e.g.,*
http://www.sciencedaily.com/news/computers_math/artificial_intelligence/
(compiling artificial intelligence headlines); http://ai-depot.com/news/ (same);
http://www.aaai.org/AITopics/pmwiki/pmwiki.php/AITopics/AINews (same).

[96] R. BRACHMAN and Z. LENIOS, "DARPA's New Cognitive Systems Vision," *Computing Research News*, Vol. 14/No. 5, pp. 1, 8. (Nov. 2002):
A cognitive computer system should be able to learn from its experience, as well as by being advised. It should be able to explain what it was doing and why it was doing it, and to recover from mental blind alleys. It should be able to reflect on what goes wrong when an anomaly occurs, and anticipate such occurrences in the future. It should be able to reconfigure itself in response to environmental changes. And it should be able to be configured, maintained, and operated by non-experts.

[97] *Id.*, p. 501. *See also id.*, p. 460 (robotics pioneer Hans Moravec predicting strong AI by 2030).

[98] WILL PAVIA, "Machine takes on man at mass Turing Test," Times Online (Oct. 13, 2008),   available   online   at
http://technology.timesonline.co.uk/tol/news/tech_and_web/article4934858.ece.

exponential rate, and machines could even overtake humans in their ability to reason, in the not so distant future.[99]

According to a recent report, the manager of the Adaptive Systems group at Microsoft estimated that "about a quarter of all Microsoft research is focused on AI efforts".[100] Google founders Sergey Brin and Larry Page have repeatedly articulated their goal of creating "obviously artificial intelligence", in the sense of a truly "smart" program that "understands" user queries and the universe of potential results to the point that searches as well as a human with immediate access to most of the Internet.[101]

Clearly the impact of "strong" artificial intelligence↓in the John Searle sense of actual self-awareness↓would be profound across all sectors.[102] Predictions of strong AI have fallen flat before, however, and many within the field argue that humans may never recreate actual intelligence.[103] This particularly achievement is at a minimum decades away. A potentially more interesting question in the short run (i.e., the next five to ten years) is whether computers will reach a level of sophistication at which humans become unsure of the AI's intelligence and, consequently, *uncomfortable* with their extensive 'knowledge'.

Today, humans appear to trust computers and computer servers with their personal information. The prevailing view of computers remains the desktop↓a complex but lifeless automaton that manipulates data without

---

[99]   Intel News Release, Aug. 21, 2008, available online at http://www.intel.com/pressroom/archive/releases/20080821comp.htm?cid=rss-90004-c1-211570.

[100] J. GASKIN, "Whatever Happened to Artificial Intelligence?," *Network World*, Jul. 23, 2008 (emphasis added).

[101]   See   http://ignoranceisfutile.wordpress.com/2008/09/13/google-founders-artificial-intelligence-quotes-archive/ (collecting AI quotes from Google principals). Brin reportedly said the following in November of 2002: "Hal could... had a lot of information, could piece it together, could rationalise it. Now, hopefully, it would never... it would never have a bug like Hal did where he killed the occupants of the space ship. But that's what we're striving for, and I think we've made it a part of the way there." *Id.*

[102] *See* L. SLOCUM, "Legal Personhood for Artificial Intelligence," *70 N.C. L. Rev.* 1231 (1992) (discussing whether AI could serve as a trustee); *id.* (discussing John Searle). *See also* C. STONE, "Should Trees Have Standing? Toward Legal Rights for Natural Objects," *45 Cal. L. Rev.* 450, 453-57 (1972) (discussing whether AI could have standing).

[103] *See* S. RUSSELL and P. NORVIG, *Artificial Intelligence*, pp. 947-60 (canvassing the literature).

interest.[104] Thus, in seeking to allay fears over its practice of scanning web-based email messages in order to display contextual advertisements, the Internet giant Google is careful to represent that the scanning is conducted by a computer. "Google does NOT read your email… Gmail [or Google Mail] is a technology-based program, so advertising and related information are shown using a completely automated process".[105]

In the context of national security, American thought leaders debate whether machine shifting through public and private data can amount to a government invasion. Judge and scholar Richard Posner argues that "[m]achine collection and processing of data cannot, as such, invade privacy", such that computer data access or citizen surveillance does not in and of itself trigger a search or seizure for purpose of the Fourth Amendment. [106] Prosecutor turned legal scholar Orin Kerr also holds that no search occurs until "information from or about the data is exposed to human observation," not when it is simply "processed by a computer".[107]Law professor Larry Lessig also uses the example of a search by a government computer program that mindlessly borrows through citizen data (a so-called "worm") to test the parameters of search and seizure law in cyberspace.[108]

This image of a passive conduit may change, however, if and when computers reach a threshold of apparent intelligence wherein processing begins overly to resemble human judgment. Given a handful of factors↓namely, the human tendency to anthropomorphise discussed in detail above, the aggressive claims of AI practitioners and critics, the occasional hyperbole of the media, and the lack of any definitive test of intelligence↓humans could come to equate computer mentality with human mentality in the relatively near term. This in turn could lead to an uncomfortable reexamination of computers as passive custodians of consumer and citizen data.[109]

---

[104] It is precisely this human view of computers as unbiased, trustworthy data processors that creates the opportunity for persuasion present in captology. B.J. FOGG, *Persuasive Technologies.*

[105]*See* http://mail.google.com/support/bin/answer.py?answer=6599&topic=12787.

[106] R. POSNER, "Our Domestic Intelligence Crisis," *The Washington Post*, Dec. 21, 2005.

[107] O. KERR, "Searches and Seizures in a Digital World," *119 Harv. L. Rev.* 531, 551 (2005).

[108] L. LESSIG, *Code 2.0*, New York, Basic Books, 2006, pp. 20-23.

[109] Changes to user interfaces may have more immediate effects, however, in the realm of voice-driven search. In a recent interview, Google's vice president for search Marissa Mayer discussed the hope that, within a few years, users might be able to interact with Google   orally   by   "asking   questions   by   voice."   *See*

IV. The (in)adequacy of U.S. privacy law

American privacy law already contains the seeds of a solution to many of the emerging privacy harms identified in this essay. A notorious patchwork, American privacy law nevertheless requires notice about the collection, use, and disclosure of personal and other information[110] and is relatively steadfast in its protection against invasions into private space without adequate process.[111]

The privacy community has already begun to propose concrete solutions to perceived abuses of sophisticated and widespread data mining by government and industry. Andrew McClurg argues, for instance, for a resuscitation of the U.S. common law tort of appropriation (discussed by Warren and Brandeis in *The Right to Privacy*[112]) as a response to the creation and use of consumer profiles.[113] Appropriation refers to the use of another's identity↓generally, their name or "likeness"↓to one's own benefit without consent. Such a use can amount to an invasion of privacy under American common law.[114] McClurg argues convincingly that the digital profile that results from sophisticated data mining constitutes an "inner identity" that can trigger the tort.

American law professor Daniel Solove also urges a more comprehensive understanding of privacy law that encompasses the "Kafkaesque" nature of modern surveillance[115] and has shown how to arrive at an appropriate balance between security interests and privacy rights by meticulously cataloguing the harms of data mining. Digital rights groups such as the San Francisco based Electronic Frontier Foundation have brought suit against telephone providers and the

---

http://www.techcrunch.com/2008/12/10/marissa-mayer-at-le-web-the-almost-complete-interview/. Query whether individuals will search for the same things when it feels to the user that they are speaking with a person.

[110] *See, e.g.*, California Online Privacy Protection Act of 2003, Bus. & Prof. Code Sec. 22575-22579 (California statute requiring companies that collect personal information to link to a privacy policy). The FTC also holds companies to their claims about data and sets minimum thresholds of notice for material changes to policy. *See, e.g.*, *In the Matter of Gateway Learning Corp.*, FTC File No. 042-3047 (2004).

[111] D. SOLOVE, "A Taxonomy of Privacy," *154 U. Pa. L. Rev.* 477 (2006), p. 552 ("For hundreds of years, the law has strongly guarded the privacy of the home.").

[112] S. WARREN AND L. BRANDEIS, "The Right to Privacy," *4 Harv. L. Rev.* 193 (1890).

[113] A. MCCLURG, "A Thousand Words are Worth a Picture."

[114] *See* Restatement (Second) of Torts Sec. 652C (1977).

[115] D. SOLOVE, "'I've Got Nothing To Hide,'" p. 756.

government itself in an effort to understand and domesticate government data mining.[116]

Similarly, the use of social media to persuade consumers to give up information or to purchase particular products has a ready analog in tactics already being investigated by national and local consumer protection agencies. In the United States, Section 5 of the FTC Act prohibits "unfair or deceptive trade practices," broadly defined.[117] The Federal Trade Commission is charged with enacting and enforcing policy aimed at prohibiting unfair, deceptive, or anti-competitive practices within the industries in its jurisdiction. The agency has turned its attention in recent years to online data collection practices such as the traffic of users' surfing habits,[118] as well as the use of 'buzz' or subliminal marketing wherein products are promoted without notice that the speaker is affiliated with an advertising company. State attorneys general have also investigated online information gathering practices and, in cases, reached agreements with companies perceived to gather or use data too aggressively.[119] Ian Kerr explains that the use of AI bots particularly for marketing and consumer information gathering may violate similar Canadian consumer protection regulations.[120]

In other cases, however, the law may have no obvious starting point in addressing these emerging privacy harms. As discussed above, the effect of social media is often a direct but subconscious one. It is not that humans will use a technology to invade one another's privacy; rather, the object will be treated as itself human. The danger is that voice-driven, natural language interfaces will become the norm; that computers will increasingly be endowed with personalities; and that robots with

---

[116] See EFF Press Release, "EFF Sues NSA, President Bush, and Vice President Cheney to Stop Illegal Surveillance," Sept. 18, 2008, available online at http://www.eff.org/press/archives/2008/09/17-0.

[117] Federal Trade Commission Act, 15 U.S.C. Secs. 41-58, as amended.

[118] FTC Press Release, "FTC Staff Proposes Online Behavioral Advertising Privacy Principles," Dec. 20, 2007, available online at http://www.ftc.gov/opa/2007/12/principles.shtm.

[119] Online adverting company DoubleClick entered into a consent decree with a coalition of state attorneys general in 2001, agreeing not to combine certain categories of information following a merger with offline consumer profiler Abacus. See, e.g., Washington State Office of the Attorney General Press Release, "States Settle with DoubleClick," April 2001, available online at http://www.atg.wa.gov/pressrelease.aspx?&id=5848.

[120] I. KERR, "Bots, Babes," at p. 321 ("The fair information practices set out in Appendix 2 of the Canadian Code contain a number of requirements that are clearly not respected by ActiveBuddy and many other bot-based business models.").

anthropomorphic features will come to be voluntarily accepted as a daily part of life (as is increasingly the case in Japan). Simultaneously, but at an examined level, privacy will be eroded by the subconscious perception that we are always being watched and evaluated.

An extreme example with intentional and obvious chilling effects on speech, such as a holographic police officer that follows around each citizen, could in theory trigger the First Amendment of the U.S. Constitution.[121] But there may be no immediate legal solution to a diffuse introduction of social media into private space by natural means. Similarly, the discomfort we may begin to feel at AI custodianship of data may not be reducible to a legally cognizable injury. Although real anxiety could result, perhaps little more can be said about AI capable of extremely accurate judgments or vested with the appearance of common sense is that it is 'creepy'. American privacy law may be ill-suited to protect against such subtle and (for now) speculative harms.[122]

Solutions may ultimately come from outside of privacy law. It turns out that in other contexts, American law forces consideration of subjective interests such as fear or discomfort. Thus, for instance, in the (pun-ridden) case of *Stambovsky v. Ackely*, a New York appeals court recognised a buyer's right to rescind purchase of a home after he learned that it was haunted by a poltergeist.[123] It was no reply that poltergeists do not exist. The buyer could not be forced to live with a ghost merely because the existence of ghosts has not been established.[124] Sellers and brokers must also disclose other stigmas such the occurrence in a home of a multiple murder.[125] In the context of pollution, litigants have pursued a variety of harms bred of unrealised fears.[126] Accordingly, one can imagine

---

[121] *Cf. Laird v. Tatum*, 408 U.S. 1, 11 (1972) ("In recent years this Court has found in a number of cases that constitutional violations may arise from the deterrent, or 'chilling,' effect of governmental regulations that fall short of a direct prohibition against the exercise of First Amendment rights.").

[122] D. SOLOVE, "A Taxonomy of Privacy," p. 562-63 ("Too many courts and policymakers struggle even identifying the presence of privacy problems. . . . Unfortunately, due to conceptual confusion, courts and legislatures often fail to recognise privacy problems . . .").

[123] 169 A.D. 2d 254 (N.Y. Ct. App. 1991).

[124] In *Stambovsky*, the tongue-in-cheek court actually held the house to be haunted "as a matter of law." *Id.*

[125] *See Reed v. King*, 145 Cal. App. 3d 261 (1983) (holding that plaintiff stated a cause of action for defendant-broker's failure to disclose that house was site of multiple murder).

[126] *See, e.g., City of Santa Fe v. Komis*, 845 P.2d 753, 757 (N.M.1992) (awarding land owner damages due to fear of nuclear waste); *Lunda v. Matthews*, 613 P.2d 63, 67-68 (Or.Ct.App.1980) (allowing emotional distress damages for fear of air emissions from

a requirement that an entity disclose that it is using sophisticated AI and offer to store user information separately.

Another useful analog might be the requirement of warning labels for non-obvious product defects. The Food and Drug Administration and individual states often require harmful goods to contain warnings as to their contents, and the existence of a warning label can sometimes provide a meaningful defense against a civil action for product liability. Where a car comes equipped with an active AI passenger, for instance, its user manual could warn that humans react to social machines as though they were truly humans, and that constantly being in the presence of others can lead to discomfort.

Viable solutions are equally likely to come from outside the law, especially in the short term. They might include the inclusion of privacy in ethics discussions around social media, the participation of developers of AI in efforts to build privacy protections into emerging technology,[127] and sustained efforts at public education by industry and government.[128] In his aforementioned book on captology, Fogg creates a framework by which to assess the ethical implications of a given instance of persuasive technology. He concludes that:

> *Ultimately, education is the key to more ethical persuasive technologies. Designers and distributors who understand the ethical issues ... will be in a better position to cerate and sell ethical persuasive technology products. Technology users will be better positioned to recognise when computer products are applying unethical or questionably ethical tactics to persuade them.*[129]

Calling attention to and discussing these phenomena is a necessary first step to heading off or addressing a novel set of privacy threats.

---

cement plant); *Heddin v. Delhi Gas Pipeline Co.*, 522 S.W.2d 886, 888 (Tex.1975) (awarding damages to landowner due to fear that pipeline on adjoining land would explode); *Texas Elec. Serv. Co. v. Nelon*, 546 S.W.2d 864, 871 (Tex.Civ.App.1977) (allowing landowner to recover for fear of nuclear waste transported nearby).

[127] UK's Information Commissioner's Office has, for instance, commission the Enterprise Privacy Group to produce a new report on the impact on personal privacy of various activities across multiple industries. Applications of social AI should be included in such a report.

[128] *See also* T. ZARSKY, "Mine Your Own Business!," Sec. III (discussing the role of public education in addressing AI data mining techniques).

[129] B.J. FOGG, *Persuasive Technologies*, p. 235.

V. Conclusion

Our conception of what constitutes an invasion of personal privacy continues to evolve↓over time, dramatically. Consider the origin of the term "Peeping Tom.''Tom was an adolescent with the bad luck to be within the city limits of Coventry when Lady Godiva made her (in)famous naked ride to protest taxes. Unlike other young men, Tom openly gawked at Lady Godiva's naked form as she passed. Today, were a young man *not* to gawk at naked woman on a horse, we might be amazed. We would certainly give no credence to a complaint by or on behalf of the naked woman. (We would say that she willingly exposed herself in public where she has no expectation of privacy.) At the time of the legend, circa 1050, Tom was blinded for his impudence.[130]

Even as our privacy norms evolve, however, a set of basic biological facts remains constant: humans react to social media as though it were human[131] This disconnect between the state of evolution and the state of our technology continues to be exploited↓sometimes inadvertently↓by developers of certain types of AI in order to develop machine intelligence, foster machine acceptability, and improve user experiences. As a consequence, humans may face a meaningful reduction in their already waning privacy. Upon a thorough canvass of the literature, German privacy theorist Beate Rössler concludes that "a person's privacy can be defined, therefore, in these three ways: as illicit interference in one's actions, as illicit surveillance, as illicit intrusions in rooms or dwellings".[132] Particular techniques of artificial intelligence can be said to violate each of these definitions.

Clearly, artificial intelligence has led to important medical, commercial, and other benefits, and promises many more. And where AI merely supports a human practice↓as in the case of data mining or interviewing consumers↓the law seems well-equipped to provide a meaningful solution. All that may be needed is to expand the law through ordinary methods to encompass and limit the underlying offensive activity. In other cases the solution is not as simple. More subtle and comprehensive changes may be required to mitigate the impact of sophisticated social agents in our midst. Ultimately, however, it may be that "we won't know enough to regulate [AI] until we see what it actually looks like".[133]

---

[130] D. SOLOVE, "A Taxonomy of Privacy," p. 492.

[131] B. REEVES and C. NASS, *The Media Equation*.

[132] B. ROSSLER, *The Value of Privacy*, Cambridge, Polity Press, 2005, p. 9.

[133] J. MCCARTHY, "Problems and Projections in CS for the Next 49 Years," *Journal of the ACM*, 2003.

Property in Personal Data: a European Perspective on Instrumentalist Theory of Propertisation

Nadezda Purtova
Tilburg Institute for Law, Technology and Society, Tilburg University, The Netherlands

Since early 1970s the US scholars have been 'playing' with the idea to introduce property rights in personal data. Next to acknowledging already existing phenomenon of commodification of personal data, propertisation would potentially offer a solution to the data protection problem resulting from the Information Revolution. Introduction of property rights in personal data has been advocated from several perspectives. The focus of this paper is an instrumentalist theory of propertization of personal data developed by Lessig. The paper tests the viability of the theory in the context of the European legal system. For the purposes of the analysis, Lessig's propertization argument is scrutinized on its face and on substance. That is, the questions are answered whether propertization of personal data is a legal option for Europe, and if yes, whether the content of the proposed property rights is consistent with European legal system. The conclusion is reached that although propertization is possible both on the level of the EU and individual Member States, the idea is suspect in light of the European doctrine of unenforceability of waiver of fundamental rights, and incompatible with the rationale of European property tradition to protect transfer of the right rather than entitlement.

I. Background, research question, and structure of the paper

Since early 1970s the US scholars have been 'playing' with the idea to introduce property rights in personal data.[1] Next to acknowledging already existing phenomenon of commodification of personal data, propertisation would potentially offer a solution to the data protection problem resulting from the Information Revolution. Introduction of property rights in personal data has been advocated from several

---

[1] A. F. WESTIN, (1967). *Privacy and Freedom*. London, Sydney, Toronto, the Bodley Head. P. E. AGRE, M. ROTENBERG, eds. (1997). *Technology and Privacy : the New Landscape*. Cambridge, MIT Press.

perspectives: arguably it would help individuals reclaim lost control over their personal data, or acknowledge an inherent connection between an individual and data pertaining to him (natural rights theory).[2] Other commentators see benefits of propertization in a rhetorical value of property talks.[3] Some believe that only propertisation is able to overcome inherent limitations of the US legal and political system.[4] The most discussed approaches to information privacy as property have been taken from the perspective of economic analysis of law.[5] Of a special interest is a part of the economic argument, made among others by Lessig[6] who invokes property as a regulatory tool and an instrument to create a general, more effective system of data protection incorporating *inter alia* privacy enhancing technologies (PETs). This paper will refer to this argument as the instrumentalist theory of propertisation.

In brief, new developments in personal-data related practices both in Europe and the US have been generally attributed to several interconnected processes: emergence of the service economy, new marketing techniques, welfare state and recently, security concerns in the aftermath of 9/11 – all reinforced by technological developments.

In the circumstances of industrialization businesses were striving to wear off detrimental consequences of mass production for the salesperson-customer relationship and tune their products and services more in accordance with customers' preferences. Targeted marketing has emerged as a solution largely based on linking demographic information to consumer behaviour and as a result giving rise to the interest in bulk

---

[2] D. J. SOLOVE, (2001). "Privacy and Power: Computer Databases and Metaphors for Information Privacy." *Stan. L. R.* 53: 1393, p. 1446 (although he does not develop the natural law argument further); V. BERGELSON, (2003). "It's Personal, but Is It Mine? Toward Property Rights in Personal Information." *U.C. Davis L. Rev.* 37: 379, p. 430; M. J. RADIN, (1982). "Property and Personhood." *Stanford Law Review* 34(5): 957-1015, p. 959;

[3] "Property talk is just how we talk about matters of great importance. [...] "If you could get people (in America, at this point in history) to see certain resource as property, then you are 90 percent to your protective goal." (L. LESSIG, (2002). "Privacy as Property." *Social Research: An International Quarterly of Social Sciences* 69(1): 247 - 269).

[4] See J. LITMAN, (2000). "Information Privacy / Information Property." *Stan. L. R.* 52: 1283.

[5] Although this is a simplification, when applied to the argument for propertization, this article uses "utilitarian," "economic," and "instrumental" interchangeably.

[6] Cohen also speaks of law as only a mechanism to create incentives to build a general privacy infrastructure (see Cohen 2000, p. 1437-38). Cohen refers to Phil Agre who described 'technologies of identity' which made it possible to prevent collection of personal data (P. E. AGRE, M. ROTENBERG, eds. (1997). *Technology and Privacy : the New Landscape.* Cambridge, MIT Press).

quantities of those data to build a consumer profile. Simultaneously in public sector, state's functions expanded to the provision of welfare for the citizens on the grounds of family and employment status, health condition, etc. To exercise those obligations state, too, needed more personal information. The 9/11 events gave rise to major security concerns which were addressed by tremendous increase in surveillance practices and even more intensive (also secret) collection of information about (suspect groups of) individuals, data mining and profiling.

It became necessary for public agencies and private businesses alike to collect more information about individuals. These developments have resulted in both qualitative and quantitative growth of personal data collection which would not be possible without technology. Besides the fact that computers made processing of personal information faster, they also made storage of bulks of data and linking previously disintegrated records a reality and enabled data mining, profiling, and automated-processing based decision-making. Internet has provided a new and unique source of data. Along with the data routinely recorded as a result of every online transaction, the non-static nature of a web-page enables the data collectors to secretly track the way people browse the Internet (clickstream data). Internet made massive online social networking possible by means of which people knowingly disclose their personal information and (often unknowingly) make their data available for third parties commercial collection.[7]

Given profits personal information brings and costs its collection and processing require, marketers soon realized an opportunity to avoid the costs by buying the needed data from already existing databases of other enterprises.[8] A new branch of the information industry – the database builders - has emerged devoted to the collection of information, also via web-sites where people are offered to trade their personal data for goods, discounts, or services. A market of databases has emerged.[9] This process is also referred to as commodification of personal information.

Despite the fact that Europe faces similar challenges of the Information Revolution, including commodification of personal data,[10] so

---

[7] A. ACQUISTI, R. GROSS, (2005) "Information Revelation and Privacy in Online Social Networks (The Facebook case)." *ACM Workshop on Privacy in the Electronic Society (WPES)*.

[8] D.J. SOLOVE 2001, p. 1407.

[9] D.J. SOLOVE 2001, p. 1407.

[10] For an overview of personal data practices in the US see e.g. D.J. SOLOVE. In Europe - L. A. BYGRAVE, (2002). *Data Protection Law: Approaching Its Rationale, Logic and Limits,* Kluwer Law International. On surveillance, data mining, and profiling in the context of security in Europe and the US see P. DE HERT, R. BELLANOVA, (2008).

far only few European commentators have reflected on the possibility of propertisation.[11] This paper will try to fill in a small part of the gap and make some first tentative steps to answer the question whether the proposal to create a general system of data protection by introducing property rights is feasible in and/or compatible with the European legal system,[12] or, alternatively, if the instrumentalist theory of propertisation may be applied to Europe as well. The preliminary answer to this question is that it cannot.

With regard to the scope of the paper, three important remarks should be made. First, although "European" may have several alternative meanings, by European perspective on the idea of propertization this research means the one unique for the framework of the European Union which is also bound by the law of the Council of Europe. Given that the EU legal system represents a coherent legal order, defining Europe as EU offers a much better chance of developing a coherent approach to the idea of propertization. Second, present research limits itself to legal analysis and is not aimed at establishing or verifying any causal connections which are, in the author's opinion, a domain of the sociology of law. In other words, the paper will not examine whether the measures meant by propertization will achieve the results they are argued to be able to achieve, or whether they will be more effective than alternative legal tools. That is, it is out of the scope of this paper whether application of Lessig's proposal actually leaves Europe with a 'better' system of protection of personal data. The final remark is that the paper is only the first attempt to sketch the roadmap of analysis of Lessig's idea of propertization in the European context and is largely exploratory.

The argument against viability of Lessig's instrumentalist theory in Europe will be made in several steps. First, the paper will explain the very idea of Lessig's theory of propertisation of personal data as explained in the book *Code and Other Laws of Cyberspace*[13] with a special emphasis on the economic notion of property it operates with. The conclusion will be made that economic analysis of law in general and as utilised by Lessig seems to put an equation between economic and common law concepts of

---

Data protection from a Transatlantic Perspective: the EU and US move towards an International Data Protection Agreement? Brussels.

[11] see, e.g. J. E. J. PRINS, (2006). "Property and Privacy: European Perspectives and the Commodification of our Identity." *The Future of the Public Domain, Identifying the Commons in Information Law*, Kluwer Law International. 16: 223-257.

[12] By European legal system this paper will mean the legal system of the European Union.

[13] L. LESSIG, (1999). *Code and Other Laws of Cyberspace*. New York, Basic Books.

property. Finally, Lessig's theory will be considered on its face and substance, *i.e.* two questions will be answered: whether without regard to the content of the property rights, propertization in Europe is formally possible, and if yes, whether Lessig's scenario of propertization in its substance is compatible with the reality of the European legal system. The conclusion will be made that although propertization of personal data is a legal possibility, when executed in the European legal system it will not be able to fulfil the functions expected from it according to Lessig's theory.

II. Instrumentalist discourse on propertisation

Lessig's instrumentalist theory of propertisation is just one of at least three versions of the economic argument to introduce property rights in personal data.[14] The other two versions consider property as a tool enabling market exchange which, provided transaction costs are minimal, will achieve an optimal (i.e. efficient) level of privacy by balancing the value of personal information to a company against the value of the (non-disclosure of) information to the individual and the larger social value of data protection.[15] Instrumentalist theory stands out since it is not concerned with efficiency but merely uses the logic of the economic analysis to propose the creation of an overall system of data protection which would comprise law, technology and market tools. Their interaction can ensure a proper level of information privacy.

In Lessig's theory, property is an engine bringing the general system of data protection into action. Lessig builds an economic argument that property rules would permit each individual to decide what information to disclose and protect "both those who value their privacy more ... and those who value it less."[16] First, he argues pretty traditionally, information privacy is in essence control over personal information. Second, unlike in the real world, the architecture (or "code") of a cyberspace makes

---

[14] For a more detailed analysis of all three interpretations see N. PURTOVA, "Propertisation of Personal Data: Learning from American Discourse"_– coming in *SCRIPT-ed*.

[15] Solove brings as examples of such an approach J. HAGEL III & M. SINGER, *Net Worth: Sharing Markets When Consumers Make the Rules* 19-20 (1999) (advocating for an "infomediary" between consumers and vendors who would broker information to companies in exchange for money and goods to the consumer); P. FARHI, "Me Inc: Getting the Goods on Consumers", *Wash. Post*, Feb. 14 1999, at H1].

[16] L. LESSIG, (1999).

collection of information difficult to spot, and control over that information – unrealistic to exercise for lay people. Third, such an architecture is a result of human activity and, therefore, can be altered.[17] Fourth, the US information processing practices are based on self-regulation, *i.e.* there is no general legislation requiring businesses to alter this architecture and use privacy-friendly technologies. Nor is there motivation to account for interests of the individuals. In absence of property interests, the companies make use of personal data for free. However, if individuals had property rights in personal data, it would force businesses to negotiate with the individuals, account for their interests, and alter the architecture, i.e. invest into development of PETs. The individual privacy would be better secured, not only by law but by interaction of the latter, market mechanisms and technologies.[18]

Lessig's argument operates with the reading of the legal concept of property given by Calabresi and Melamed[19] and adopted by the literature on economic analysis of law. Property is defined as the opposite of the liability rule. Both are the means invoked to protect a certain entitlement. When the entitlement is protected by a property rule, it cannot be taken away except when sold by the holder voluntarily at the price set by the holder.[20] Whereas the property rule protects the entitlement, the liability rule allows and ensures that the transfer thereof is possible provided the holder of the entitlement is compensated for his loss against "an external, objective [i.e. set by a third party] standard of value."[21] Based on this understanding, because no other way to transfer the entitlement (in data) but via voluntary transaction with data subjects is allowed, Lessig's model works in theory and property in personal data motivates the information industries to enter negotiations with data subjects and, as a result, implement PETs.

The validity of Lessig's theory has been questioned on numerous grounds already in the US context. Among others, Litman doubts whether the understanding of property employed by the theory at hand corresponds to the actual law,[22] and how effective the whole enterprise to promote

---

[17] Point also made by Cohen in COHEN 2000, p. 1437.

[18] L. LESSIG, (1999).

[19] Point also made in G. CALABRESI, A. D. MELAMED, (1972). "Property rules, liability rules, and inalienability: one view of the cathedral." *Harv. L. Rev.* 85.

[20] *Ibid.*, p. 1105.

[21] *Ibid.* p. 1106, text in the square brackets added.

[22] Based on the definition of property given in the Restatement, Litman argues that "the raison d'être of property is alienability; the purpose of property laws is [not to prevent but to encourage and] … prescribe the conditions for transfer." Restatement of Property, §489

investments in PETs can be.[23] An extensive analyses of the validity of the theory in question under the US system goes beyond the scope of this paper. The following section attempts to 'test' Lessig's theory in European context.

III. Viability of the Instrumentalist theory in Europe

The analysis of the viability of Lessig's propertization argument in the European settings may be broken into two parts: one may consider Lessig's proposal on its face and on substance. The former approach leaves aside the content of the proposed property rights and merely focuses on propertization of personal data in Europe as a formal possibility. The question to be answered here is whether introduction of the property rights in personal data, whatever scope of those rights may be, is a legal option in the European Union. A mere lack of competence to create these new rights is sufficient to discredit Lessig's theory - as applied to Europe - on formal grounds. The latter - substantive - approach looks deeper into the argument and considers the actual content of the proposed rights in order to establish whether they are consistent with the European notion of property. The following analysis will proceed along these lines and consider the viability of Lessig's instrumentalist theory when applied to Europe "on its face" and "substance".

A. LESSIG'S INSTRUMENTALIST THEORY ON ITS FACE: IS PROPERTIZATION OF PERSONAL DATA A LEGAL OPTION IN EUROPE?

To establish if propertization of personal data may be a legal option in the system of the European Union, one may think of two possible ways in which propertization may happen. The decision to substitute the current system of data protection via regulation by property rights may be taken either on the level of the European Union or by the individual Member States. The question to be answered at this stage is the one of competence, *i.e.* if the EU and individual Member States have the legal power to make such a decision.

When examining the EU competence, let's rest our analysis on the

---

cmt. a (1944) referred to in J. LITMAN, (2000). "Information Privacy / Information Property." *Stan. L. R.* 52: 1283, p. 1295, text in the square brackets added.

[23] Litman labels Lessig's argument "a fairy-tale picture": industries do not respect information privacy because it is expensive to honour privacy preferences, not to express them. (Ibid. p. 1297).

assumption that regulation in the area of data protection lies within the scope of the EU powers. Without going into details of the basis of such regulation in the European Treaties, the existence of the Directive 95/46/EC of the European Parliament and of the Council of 24 October 1995 on the protection of individuals with regard to the processing of personal data and on the free movement of such data[24] is a good evidence of such a competence. However, the case of *propertization* of personal data requires additional consideration since it involves not only the area of data protection, but also the subject-matter area of property rights. Whether the EU has a competence to force Member States into propertization of personal information and to regulate (this sector of) property law is the question that needs to be answered.

The first step on the way to the answer is to acknowledge that introduction of property rights in personal data on the EU level would effectively mean harmonization of a (newly created) sector of property law. Propertization of personal data would not be the first area where the issue of the common European law of property is discussed. According to Van Erp, "several Directorates General are working on various projects concerning harmonization of property law."[25] A debate has been going on whether the structure of the Common Framework of Reference (CFR), a project meant "to restructure existing European private law and to be a "toolbox" for future European private law"[26] should cover assignment of claims, personal security rights, security rights in movables, related matters in property law. Although Art. 295 of the European Community Treaty[27] seems to ban the EU intervention in property law issues,[28] in practice the effect of this Article is more restricted than one would assume at first sight[29] and has been interpreted more likely "to address the

---

[24] Hereinafter referred to as EU Data Protection Directive.

[25] S. VAN ERP, (2006). "European and National Property Law: Osmosis or Growing Antagonism?" *Walter van Gerven Lectures*, Europe Law Publishing, p. 9.

[26] *Ibid.* pp. 10-11.

[27] Hereinafter referred to as EC Treaty.

[28] Art. 295 EC: "This Treaty shall in no way prejudice the rules in Member States governing the system of property ownership." For possible reasons of such treatment of property law see, e.g. D. CARUSO, (2004). "Private Law and Public takes in European Integration: the Case of Property." *European Law Journal* 10(6): 751-765. ("For the Union to signal that property rules will not be easily tinkered with is a highly symbolic gesture in the spirit of subsidiarity.").

[29] S. VAN ERP.

member states' competence in nationalization and privatization."[30] Moreover, some EU legislation in the area of property law has already been passed.[31]

Given that information industry and *de facto* market in personal data have already become a large part of the European economy and personal data long have been treated as a good, a possible legal ground for creating property rights in personal information on the EU level could be Art. 95 EC. To have Art. 95 EC as legal basis, the measure has to be necessary to attain the establishment and functioning of the internal market.[32] To qualify as such, according to Art. 14 EC, the measure should be aimed at establishing an area where free movement of goods, persons, services and capital is ensured. A top-down introduction of uniform property rights in personal data would certainly address the issue of free movement of the data within the EU without obstacles of different legal regimes.

The question to be answered next is whether the aim of ensuring free movement of personal data can be legally achieved by a measure of such level of detail as the one of establishing property rights. As the subsequent analysis will show, the provisions on powers of the EU may be interpreted in a way allowing even such an extensive intervention as top-down propertization. That can be decided based on the subsidiarity principle as laid down in Art. 5 EC, Art. 2 TEU and Protocol 30 to the EC Treaty on the application of the principles of subsidiarity and proportionality. Art. 5 EC reads that the Community shall take action in areas which do not fall within its exclusive competence, in accordance with the principle of subsidiarity, only if and in so far as the objectives of the proposed action cannot be sufficiently achieved by the Member States and can therefore, by reason of the scale or effect of the proposed action, be better achieved by the Community. The idea behind is that matters should be dealt with on the level closest to the ones affected.[33] However, as many commentators of the EU law point out, the very reason of existence of the European Union will "often demand Community action to ensure the uniformity of *general approach* which is of central importance to the realization of a

---

[30] M. J. MILO, (2006). "Property and Real Rights." *Elgar Encyclopedia of Comparative Law*. J. M. Smith, Edward Elgar: 587-602, p. 588.

[31] for more detail see *Ibid.* and S. VAN ERP.

[32] ECJ 5 October 2000, Case C-376/98 *Federal Republic of Germany v. European Parliament and Council of the European Union* (so-called '*Tobacco case*').

[33] P. CRAIG, G. DE BURCA, (2008). *EU Law: Text, Cases and Materials*, Oxford University Press, p. 104.

common market."[34] The subsidiarity principle, however, may have an effect on the form of the Community action for propertization which may be through framework directives or guidelines rather than regulations.

The remaining question of competence is whether the individual Member States may take an action independent on the EU and introduce property rights in personal data. Such an action would not be a complete novelty since, as Milo rightly points out, property law has traditionally been "national law par excellence,"[35] since the national rules of private international law mainly rely on the principle of *lex rei sitae*,[36] *i.e.* the law applicable to an object in an international property law case is derived from the jurisdiction where the object is situated."[37] However, in light of the fact that the EU has already taken action in the field of data protection in the form of the EU Data Protection Directive, the Member States will not be able to unilaterally introduce property rights in personal data the scope of which would substantially differ from the general approach to treating personal data adopted in the Directive. Any propertization on the level of the individual Member States will have to be in line with the Directive. Even more, the Directive has been adopted with a view to leave a margin for the Member States to adopt actions which would respect the national legal systems, yet achieve the goals established in the Directive. Provided property rights introduced do not contradict those guidelines, a Member State which decided in favour of propertization may serve as a laboratory to test the workability of the idea.

The above analysis shows that the idea to introduce property rights in personal data may be a legal option in the EU, both on the level of the Union and individual member states, although only the former may introduce propertization altering the current general approach to data protection. The conclusion that follows is that Lessig's proposal understood on its face withstood the test. The focus of the next section is on whether it withstands the examination on its substance.

B. LESSIG'S INSTRUMENTALIST THEORY ON ITS SUBSTANCE: PROPERTIZATION AS AN ENGINE OF THE GENERAL SYSTEM OF DATA PROTECTION?

The purpose of the following analysis is to demonstrate that although Lessig's theory withstands scrutiny on its face, it is not viable when it

---

[34] *Ibid.*; see also A. ESTELLA, (2002). *The EU Principle of Subsidiarity and its Critique*, Oxford University Press, p. 113-114.

[35] M. J. MILO, p. 587.

[36] Emphasis added – N.P.

[37] M. J. MILO, p. 587.

comes to the actual substance of the argument. To examine the value of Lessig's theory for Europe on its substance, one has to consider the actual content of the rights labelled by the theory at hand "property rights." As it has been explained earlier in this paper, Lessig's argument operates with the definition of property given by Calabresi and Melamed[38] by opposing it to the liability rule. When the entitlement is protected by a property rule, it cannot be taken away except when sold by the holder voluntarily at the price set by the holder.[39] Therefore, property rule protects the entitlement, whereas the liability rule allows and ensures that the transfer thereof is possible provided the holder of the entitlement is compensated for his loss against "an external, objective standard of value."[40] Because no other way to transfer the entitlement (in data) but via voluntary transaction with data subjects is allowed, property rule motivates industries to respect privacy choices of the individuals and invest in PETS thereby bringing the general data protection system into action. Thus, there are two elements of the proposed property rights essential to Lessig's argument: in their core Lessig's property rights are there to protect entitlement rather than transfer, but simultaneously, leave a right holder an option to waive the entitlement for established price in the process of voluntarily transaction. The subsequent two parts of the paper will examine each element against the background of the EU legal system. In general, in this section the point will be made that in the context of the European legal system, first, the right to waive entitlement to data protection although not prohibited, is not protected against state intervention. Second, the proposed scope of rights does not fit into the European understanding of property, namely, that traditionally property law has been securing commerce, *i.e.* transfer, rather than preservation of the entitlement.

1. Lessig's approach versus the doctrine of waiver of fundamental rights

The first European-centered criticism of Lessig's approach rests on the assumption that, legally speaking, data protection is an element of the fundamental right to privacy as secured by Art. 8 of the Convention for the Protection of Human Rights and Fundamental Freedoms[41] and

---

[38] G. CALABRESI, A. D. MELAMED.

[39] *Ibid.*, p. 1105.

[40] *Ibid.* p. 1106, text in the square brackets added.

[41] Hereinafter referred to as ECHR.

therefore enjoys full protection of a fundamental right.[42] As a part of such protection, it is an established position of jurisprudence (*Mellacher* case)[43] and the literature that the ECHR does not protect a right to obtain remuneration for the waiver or sacrifice of a fundamental right, as an individual cannot claim a violation when the state prevents him, e.g. via regulation, from waiving a fundamental right.[44]

An alternative view is represented by, *e.g.* Paul De Hert and Serge Gutwirth.[45] They consider the categories of privacy and data protection against a background of a democratic constitutional state and as a result define them as two too distinct tools of state power control to be considered as one fundamental right. [46] Cuijpers argues that data protection is not a fundamental right. Therefore, freedom of contract has precedence over the rules of the 1995 EU Directive on processing of personal data, and the right to data protection may be waived or contracted around.[47]

There has been no authoritative pronouncement by the European Court of Human Rights or any other authority directly deciding in favour or against classifying data protection (both in public *and* private sector) as a fundamental right. The jurisprudence of the European Court of Human Rights is clear on including data protection into the scope of Art. 8 ECHR protection of private life when public authorities are involved. The Court's interpretation of Art. 8 ECHR right to respect of private life is said to correspond "with that of the Council of Europe's Convention of 28 January 1981 for the Protection of Individuals with regard to Automatic Processing of Personal Data, which came into force on 1 October 1985 and whose purpose is "to secure ... for every individual ... respect for his rights and fundamental freedoms, and in particular his right to privacy

---

[42] The relationship between privacy and data protection is a too complicated issue to be fully discussed within the limited scope of this paper.

[43] *Mellacher v. Austria* (1989) 12 E.H.R.R. 391.

[44] O. DE SCHUTTER, (2000). "Waiver of Rights and State Paternalism under the European Convention on Human Rights." *N. Ir. Legal Q.* 51: 487, p. 506.

[45] P. DE HERT, S. GUTWIRTH, (2003). "Making sense of privacy and data protection: a prospective overview in the light of the future of identity, location-based services and virtual residence in the Institute for Prospective technological studies". *Security and Privacy for the citizen in the post-September 11 digital age: a Prospective overview*, European Parliament Committee on Citizens Freedoms and Rights, Justice and Home Affairs (LIBE).

[46] DE HERT AND GUTWIRTH, p. 134.

[47] C. M. K. C. CUIJPERS, (2007). "A private law approach to privacy; mandatory law obliged?" *SCRIPT-ed* 4(4): 304-318.

with regard to automatic processing of personal data relating to him" (Article 1), such personal data being defined in Article 2 as "any information relating to an identified or identifiable individual".[48] ... Art. 8 is applicable "where it is systematically collected and stored in files held by the *authorities*""[49] [emphasis added]. However, there is no similar ruling concerning ill data processing practices in private sector.[50] This partially can be explained by the nature of the European Convention as an international treaty creating obligations for its signatories, i.e. states. To rule finally on the applicability of Art. 8 to the private sector data processing, two issues of a more ground nature have to be decided first: whether Art. 8 of the Convention creates positive obligations for the contracting parties, and if it has horizontal effect.[51] Although of a principal importance, this discussion is too big and does not fit into the limited scope of this contribution. However, if, as the author believes, the fundamental right to privacy comprises data protection *also* in dealings of private parties, transactions in which individuals waive their entitlement in personal data in return for remuneration or services are not enforceable on the level on the ECHR and therefore are not guaranteed against ban by the individual Member States. Although that does not exclude the possibility of waiver, it has to be taken into account.

Another important remark that can be made at this point is that unenforceability of waiver is only a policy choice enshrined in the current jurisprudence of the European Court of Human Rights in Strasbourg. As any policy decision, it can be changed following numerous proposals to drop the idea of paternalistic state and let people trade their rights and thus take more charge. However, this change has not been made yet, unenforceability of waiver is the law of the day and has to be taken into account.

2. Lessig's approach versus European property law principles

The last, and probably most decisive piece of criticism of the value of

---

[48] see *Amann v. Switzerland* [GC], No.27798/95, 16 Feb. 2000.

[49] *Rotaru v. Romania*, No. 28341/95, 4 May 2000.

[50] Although there is a series of ECHR cases dealing with data protection on business premises, intervening actors are still public authorities (e.g. *Copland v. UK*, no. 62617/00, 7 Apr. 2007: public school authorities monitoring applicant's e-mail and phone calls).

[51] For a more detailed discussion on the horizontal effect of the ECHR see, e.g. D. GOMIEN, D. HARRIS, L. ZWAAK, (1996). *Law and Practice of the European convention on human rights.* Strasbourg, Council of Europe Publishing.

Lessig's theory for Europe which this paper advances is that property rights defended by Lessig do not fit into the European framework of property law. The following analysis will demonstrate how.

To say that a certain understanding of property does not fit into the European idea thereof is a rather bold statement. Indeed, it would imply existence of a uniform approach to the concept of property throughout Europe. However, there is no such uniform approach to property. Each Member State determines the scope and regime of property rights independently. Besides purely national differences in defining and treating property, there is another major obstacle on the way to uniformity, *i.e.* common law-civil law divide. This allows different theories of property rights flourish simultaneously and take place in the property discourse which otherwise would be occupied by a statutory or case-law definition.

To reflect on the multiplicity of different types of property (also varying from one national legal system to another), Harris in his book *Property and Justice* develops a spectrum of the ownership interests ranging from a 'mere property' to 'full-blooded ownership.'[52] In case of a mere property, "the idea of property comprises the notion that something that pertains to a person is, maybe within drastic limits, his to use as he pleases and therefore his to permit others to use gratuitously or for exchanged favours. ... It embraces some open-ended set of use-privileges and some open-ended set of powers of control over uses made by others."[53] That has been also referred to as *erga omnes* effect or trespassory rule. An example of such a mere property right according to Harris' classification may be a right of a tenant with regard to the leased apartment. Although he cannot alienate the object of the right, he still may exclude even his landlord, the 'owner,' from entering the flat. This understanding is more characteristic of common law systems. At the upper end of the ownership stands so-called 'full-blooded ownership,' a relationship between a person and a resource when the person is free to do what he pleases with his own, "whether by way of use, abuse, or transfer"[54] To describe this type of the ownership interest, scholars refer to Blackstone and his Commentaries where he expresses the idea of the full alienability.

Despite such a wide range of different understandings of property rights, as it has been shown earlier in this paper, efforts to overcome differences and develop a pan-European property law (although only in

---

[52] J. W. HARRIS, (1996). *Property and Justice*. Oxford [etc.], Clarendon Press, p. 27.
[53] *Ibid.*, p.28.
[54] *Ibid*, p.29.

some sectors) have already been taken. Behind those efforts lies impressive work of comparative legal scholars who, after analysis of the property laws in the European national legal systems have arrived at the conclusion that "it will certainly be possible to find common thought patterns"[55]. The analysis of this paper rests in particular on the work of professor Van Erp and his lecture *European and National Property Law: Osmosis or Growing Antagonism?*.[56] He explains that such drastic differences between property rules of national legal systems are often a result of historical developments, the needs of legal practice, case law and academic legal analysis.[57] However, Van Erp continues, the differences are lying on the surface, on the level of technical rules, whereas more core norms and rationales – leading principles and ground rules – are shared and those are those core norms and rationales that have to be considered.[58] To evaluate how Lessig's property rights fit into the European legal context, let us examine them against those leading principles and ground rules.

In Van Erp's classification, leading principles of property law are "the filters through which a legal relationship must pass, before it can be characterized as a property right"[59] and not a personal (e.g. contractual) right. The leading principles are *numerus clausus* (content and number of property rights is limited, since property rights are the rights against the world with *erga omnes* effect) and *transparency* (given that they are against the world, others must be able to know about those property rights, when possession of an object is not decisive – by means of registration).[60] Transparency principle promises to be difficult but possible to respect in case of propertization of personal data. Since the possession of data is not obvious, some kind of registry of property rights in personal data similar to the ones applied in the area of intellectual property may be created. Lessig's property rules also seem to meet the *numerus clausus* and *erga omnes* classifications, since the entitlement protected by those property rules is against the world. However, so do the liability rules – the opposite of property rules in Melamed and Calabresi's (and Lessig's) classification.

However, the main obstacle for implementing Lessig's theory in

---

[55] S. VAN ERP, (2006). "European and National Property Law: Osmosis or Growing Antagonism?", p. 13.

[56] *Ibid.*

[57] *Ibid.*

[58] *Ibid.*

[59] *Ibid.*

[60] *Ibid.* pp. 14-15.

Europe on its substance lies in the ground rules of property. According to Van Erp, they describe the consequences of the establishment of a property right and "focus on how property rights relate among themselves."[61] These rules are: the *nemo dat* (or *nemo plus*) rule, according to which one cannot give away more than one has; the *prior tempore rule*, according to which the oldest property right has priority over a younger property right over one object; limited rights have priority over fuller rights, and protection rules such as the right to (re)claim the object of the property right.[62] However, behind these principles and rules lie certain policy choices, in particular, the protection of commerce above protection of the original owner.[63] For instance, although according to *nemo dat* rule, one cannot give away rights which he did not have, it is counterbalanced by rules on third party protection. As Van Erp explains, a third party who acquired a right and paid for it in good faith, is often protected against the original owner, who claims his right of ownership.[64] Protection of a transfer seems to have priority over the entitlement in the European system of property law. Such rationale is not compatible with the principle division drawn by Melamed and Calabresi between property rules and liability rules based on the fact that the latter protected the transfer, whereas the former protected the entitlement.

The above analysis makes it legitimate to conclude that content-wise Lessig's instrumentalist theory does not fit into the European legal context because the scope of rights in personal data it advocates for is not what is meant by property in Europe. In case property rights in personal data are introduced in Europe, they will not be able to play the role of that engine which brings into action Lessig's general system of data protection comprising law, market, and technology. Ironically, what does approximate the function of such an engine is already existing system of data protection via regulation. If we recall the two core elements of Lessig's property rights, they are there to protect entitlement rather than transfer, and simultaneously, leave a right holder an option to waive the entitlement. The question of waiver being considered earlier, this is the general system of protection of human rights and of data protection in

---

[61] *Ibid.* p. 16.

[62] *Ibid.* pp. 16-17.

[63] *Ibid.* p. 17; see also on the principle of predictability and protection of commerce M. J. MILO, p. 587.

[64] S. VAN ERP, (2006). "European and National Property Law: Osmosis or Growing Antagonism?", p. 16.

particular that secures the entitlement and prevents illegitimate transfer.[65]

IV. Conclusions

The ambition behind this paper was to test the viability of Lessig's instrumentalist theory of propertization in the context of the European legal system. For the purposes of the analysis, Lessig's propertization argument was considered from two angles: on its face and on substance. The content of the proposed property rights left aside, it was established that propertization of personal data in Europe is a formal legal possibility, both on the level of the European Union and individual Member States. Although, only the former may introduce propertization altering the current general approach to data protection. The substantive analysis of Lessig's argument looked deeper into the actual content of the proposed rights. It was established that although propertization of personal data in the EU is a legal option, it is suspect since it implies the possibility of waiver of the right to data protection, whereas such waiver is not enforceable in the system of ECHR against state intervention. The last, and probably most decisive piece of criticism of the value of Lessig's theory for Europe was that property rights defended by Lessig do not fit into the European framework of property law. Despite all differences between technical rules of the national property law systems, characteristic of the European approach to property is that protection of a transfer seems to have priority over the entitlement in the European system of property law. Such rationale is not compatible with the principle division drawn by Melamed and Calabresi between property rules and liability rules based on the fact that the latter protected the transfer, whereas the former protected the entitlement. Therefore, content-wise Lessig's instrumentalist theory does not fit into the European legal context because the scope of rights in personal data it advocates for is not what is meant by property in Europe. In case property rights in personal data are introduced in Europe, they will not be able to play the role necessary for Lessig's general system of data protection to function.

---

[65] "Illegitimate" since prohibition of transfer of personal data in the information society is impossible.

The Myth of Odin's Eye: Privacy vs. Knowledge

Paolo Guarda
University of Trento, Department of Legal Sciences, Italy

The digital world quite often presents conflicting relations. We have already got used to argue about privacy vs. security, privacy vs. intellectual property and so on. There is another dichotomy that needs to be taken into account: privacy vs. knowledge. In the information society, but actually all the time in human history, knowledge represents a sort of treasure that gives a great power to the owner. Whether we are dealing with the fruition of intellectual works protected by property rules (i.e. IP law) or we are describing Open Access, and apparently free of charge, models, there is always a price we are paying. Thus, the paper is aimed to answer this specific question: what are we willing to give up in order to have access to knowledge? Or rather: are we really aware of the cost of our access to knowledge, particularly in the digital context and despite the outward gratuitousness of the provided service? Starting from an interesting similitude with a Nordic legend, the following pages will analyze the issues related to the use of Digital Rights Management systems, suited to incorporate intellectual property rules, with respect to the several dimensions of privacy; then, the problematic aspects of Open Access will be taken into account, with particular attention devoted to their impact on users' privacy. In the end, pulling the strings of the matter together, the paper will provide some final remarks on the relationship between privacy and knowledge in the digital context.

I. Introduction

Knowledge has always represented a sort of human unrealizable dream and omniscience. The complete and unlimited knowledge is considered by most of the cultures as a divine characteristic. To know means to have the power: in human history – and in recent philosophical reflections – it is a full stop!

But what are we willing to give to get access to knowledge? Myths and stories on knowledge research tell of long trips and of supreme sacrifices.

In the portrayals of Odin, the father of the gods in the Scandinavian tradition, he is often represented with a single eye[1]. One of the several changing Nordic legends tells that, in order to satisfy his thirst for knowledge, the god sacrificed his eye to Mimir, the Mimirsbrønd's keeper, the magic fountain of wisdom placed on Yggrdrasil's roots.[2] Since then, the divine eye is situated in the icy water of the fountain, as the price paid to acquire the eyes of the sage and to discern the essence of things, behind the appearance.

This is the price paid by Odin. But what are we willing to pay? Or rather: are we really aware of the cost of our access to knowledge, particularly in the digital context and despite the outward gratuitousness of the provided service? I will try to give an answer to these questions in the following pages.

In the first part I will focus on the issues linked to the utilization of Digital Rights Management systems (DRM), suited to regulate the fruition of intellectual works protected by intellectual property rules, with specific reference to users' privacy in its different dimensions; then, always from a privacy oriented point of view, I will outline the problematic aspects that open access to knowledge presents; I will analyze a paradigmatic example of free of charge service that poses monstrous risks from the point of view of users profiling activity. At the end, in order to pull the strings of the matter together and to take back the cues offered by Odin's saga, I will develop some final reflections on the relationship between privacy and knowledge in the digital context.

II. Intellectual property, Digital Rights Management (DRM) and Privacy

The advent of digital technologies gave rise to two phenomena: on the one hand, we register a heightening of the rigid and concentrated control (i.e. the DRM systems), based on commercial rules; on the other hand, we have the coming of new ways to fruitions focused on open access rules.

I will concentrate on the hidden "price" that the user pays to get access to digital intellectual works, whether in the platforms that incorporate values and rules of the intellectual property, or in the architectures inspired by openness (I will analyse this issue in the next

---

[1] For closer examination on Nordic saga, see V. GRØNBECH, *Miti e leggende del nord*, Torino, Einaudi, 1996 (Italian translation of the Danish edition *Nordiska Mita og Sagn*, Copenhagen, 1965).

[2] See *Völuspá* (*Prophecy of the Völva*), the first and the most famous of *Edda poems.*

paragraph).

From a purely technological point of view, the information production model based on the information closure and its rigid and concentrated control is implemented through DRM systems.[3] This term singles out the most advanced anti-access and anti-copy protection system on the market. The heart of every DRM is constituted by two modules. On the one hand, the so called "content-module", that contains the digitalized data (text or audio files) "secured" through a cryptography process and ready to be distributed; before it happens, the name of the author, the copyright owner, the creation date, the title, the format, the dimension, and other technical information in order to identify the file (*i.e.* the ISBN) are incorporated into the content. On the other hand, the "licensing-module" generates the digital license that guarantees to the final user the access to the contents in the light of the usage rights of business rules. These determine the "what", that means the precise piece of content to be used, and the "when", that means to link particular features to every right: the type of user authorized to assert the "right", the extension of every right (duration or numbers of permitted utilizations), and the price in order to assert the right.

Let's see an example so as to understand how this mechanism works.[4] Suppose I wish to get access to the new publications of an on-line law journal. I registered myself giving my profile details to the portal that contains the journal: my data are saved in a database assigned to store information regarding the users' identity inside the licensing-module. At the same moment, the system generates the usage rules that sets the type of utilization, the cost, and the specific category of authorized users; then it puts all this information into the licensing-module. Whenever I desire to read the latest publication, the DocuReader device contacts the content-module and a decrypted copy is sent to my computer. Now I am able to display what I was looking for, but every future access attempts will be

---

[3] In-depth analysis, see R. CASO, *Digital Rights Management. Il commercio delle informazioni digitali tra contratto e diritto d'autore*, Padova, Cedam, 2004 (digital reprint, Trento, 2006, available at the Web-site: <http://eprints.biblio.unitn.it/archive/00001336/>); A. PALMIERI, "DRM e disciplina europea della protezione dei dati personali", in R. CASO (eds), *Digital rights management: problemi teorici e prospettive applicative: Proceedings of the Conference Trento Faculty of Law 21-22 March 2007*, Trento, Alcione, 2007, pp. 197 ff..

[4] The example, modified in the lights of the considerations I am developing, is partially taken from P. GANLEY, "Access to the Individual: Digital Rights Management Systems and the Intersection of Informational and Decisional Privacy Interests", *International Journal of Law and Information Technology*, 2002, p. 241.

denied. In order to get other accesses, I will have to take out a subscription that will enable me to get more displays, or greater usage margins. This is a simple example of how a DRM system works.

The DRM system also presents functionalities that have a direct impact on user privacy.[5] It contains at least one of the following basic functions:[6] a) content access control; b) content usage control; c) content identification, content owners, and general condition of usage; and, d) authentication of identification data.

Moreover, for its own particular peculiarities, a DRM system is able to monitor the content fruition and, in case it has been set in that way, it can "sanction" the behaviours that are not compliant with its rules, for instance disconnecting the access.

Looking through what a DRM can do, a privacy scholar immediately thinks of "profiling".[7] Personal data of Internet users, consumers of intellectual works, and, more generally, their commercial interests symbolise a real treasure for people working on the Net. The possibility of monitoring the user activities does not only represent the way to control-manage his digital content fruition in order to impose – and when it is supposed to be necessary to sanction – the behaviours allowed according to the license that regulates the usage rights; but it becomes also a way to commodify the profile itself: this profile can be used by the profiler to adopt a more effective marketing strategy (maybe through some advertising banners answering user interests) or becomes itself an exchanging good, when the information is sold to a third party.

This kind of considerations makes us easily understand the real impact that these technologies have with respect to users' privacy. Now I need to clarify what I mean by the term "privacy". When you deal with the description of this concept, even more if you place yourself by the point of view of the relation between law and technology, you tell how from a privacy intended as the "right to be let alone", originating from the

---

[5] In the digital age law, privacy and copyright often know clashing points. See, for example, the case *Peppermint* annotated in R. CASO, "Il conflitto tra copyright e privacy nelle reti peer to peer: in margine al caso Peppermint. Profili di diritto comparator", *Dir. dell'Internet*, 2007, p. 471 (available at the Web-site: <http://www.jus.unitn.it/users/caso/DRM /Libro/peppermint/home.asp>).

[6] See R. CASO, *Digital Rights Management*, o.c., p. 100.

[7] On the profiling activity, see B. CUSTER, *The Power of Knowledge. Ethical, Legal, and Technological Aspects of Data Mining and Group Profiling Epidemiology*, Nijmegen, The Netherlands, 2004.

paper of great-renown of Warren and Brandeis[8], we arrived to a meaning much more linked to the idea of control of personal data, thanks to digital technologies diffusion. And actually, when we say "privacy" referring to the provisions that regulate it, we immediately hasten to remember that we are talking of personal data, of data control, of information to data subject, etc.[9]

But now I would like to quote a more extensive concept of privacy. This kind of description of the concept allows us to better understand the real importance of privacy in the Net, its actual role, in a context in which more and more information, and the commodification of it, comes into the limelight. People's personalities are clustered in small pieces that are personal data. These pieces, once you have reassembled them, sketch out the profile of a person in the digital context, his virtual identity. The control on these pieces of identity has more dangerous repercussions than we can imagine if we take into account a narrow interpretation of privacy, since it involves the life fundamental aspects of the person to whom the data are related.

After all these expectations, I will describe which these theories I was referring to are. The consumption of intellectual works, intended as the fruition of work of the intellects and of other information, is directly linked to three fundamental dimensions of the concept of privacy: "spatial", "informational", and "decisional."[10]

The first dimension, the "spatial" one, concerns the physical space, and in particular the size of the area in which the solitude of a person is protected from external invasion: this kind of privacy corresponds to a particular idea that sociologists connect to the relation between the private and the public space. The dimension I am talking about is related to freedom from external nuances or, more generally, from every kind of

---

[8] D. WARREN, L. D. BRANDEIS, "The Right to Privacy", *Harvard L. Rev.*, 1890, vol. 4, p. 193.

[9] For closer examination on privacy regulation, see *ex plurimis* L. A. BYGRAVE, *Data Protection Law. Approaching Its Rationale, Logic and Limits*, The Hague – London - New York, 2002; P. GUARDA, "Data Protection, Information Privacy, and Security Measures: an Essay on the European and the Italian Legal Frameworks", *Ciberspazio e dir.*, 2008, p. 65.

[10] See J. KANG, "Information Privacy in Cyberspace Transactions", *Stan. L. Rev.*, 1998, vol. 50, p. 1193, at 1202-1205; P. GANLEY, "Access to the Individual", *o.c.*, at 251 ff.. Professor Caso draws from an American commentator a double dimensions of the concept of privacy (informational and spatial): R. CASO, *Digital Rights Management, o.c.*, p. 103 ff.; J. COHEN, "DRM and Privacy", *Berkeley Tech. L.J.*, 2003, vol. 18, p. 575. More generally, on the implications of DRM systems with respect to privacy and freedom of speech, see I. KERR, J. BAILEY, "The Implications of Digital Rights Management for Privacy and Freedom of Expression", *Info., Comm. & Ethics in Society*, 2004, vol. 2, p. 87.

source of disturbances coming from the outside. In the matter I am dealing with now, spatial privacy involves those spaces in which a person is at liberty to behave in such a way that would be considered aberrant by the point of view of the dominant social norms or, more plainly, not normally used in public.

The second dimension, "informational" privacy, regards the flow of personal information. More accurately, it relates to the individual control with respect to processing of his personal data. Therefore, it is directly linked to that conceptualization of privacy focused on the control and the regulation of personal data treatment. From the point of view that focuses on the impact of DRM systems, processed data are information regarding the intellectual consumption, acquired by means of the functionalities we saw typifying the technological protection measures.

The third, and certainly most important, dimension of privacy is the "decisional" one: it concerns the choice, the freedom that must be recognized to every person in order to be able to take a decision without any kind of external conditioning. I wish to focus my attention on this dimension.

The "decisional" privacy involves the essence itself of human being. The free will, the freedom of self-determination, ultimately the freedom to be a man. There is not law, if there is not free will, if there is not the possibility to choose, even if to be wrong. Therefore, the violation of this dimension straightforwardly affects the "capacity" to be a man. The monitoring activity, the awareness of being spied on, the consciousness that the context around us is unceasingly changing in the light of the profile that other people are designing to us, modify person's behaviour. The famous Panopticon of Bentham was based on this idea:[11] the radiocentric form of the building and the appropriate architectural and technological contrivances, that enabled a single warden to watch all the prisoners at every moment, without the possibility for these to establish if they were actually controlled or not (this point reminds us dreadfully the monitoring on the Net), gave the inmates the sentiment of an invisible omniscience, influencing their behaviour and persuading them to not violate the rules.

Therefore, the perception of being watched influences, and will influence, our intellectual consumption, in such a way that we probably are not yet able to clearly determine.

---

[11] J. BENTHAM, *The Panopticon Writings*, edited by M. BOZOVIC, London, Verso, 1995. Bentham himself described the Panopticon as "a new mode of obtaining power of mind over mind, in a quantity hitherto without example".

Let's go back to the example I was using to better understand the potential consequences of DRM systems with respect to privacy.

Before the published content in the on-line law journal has been encrypted, a metadata, called "Digital Object Identifier" (DOI), is inserted into every section of all the articles. The granularity level of this DOI (every article, every section, or every paragraph), that are unique for every type of content, is decided by the editor. The outcome of this process is the following: all crypted data in the content-module are directly linked to some "pieces" of identifier metadata, that will always remain in the content when this is subsequently distributed. Then, every time I wish to modify the content of the document I have asked to the system (for instance to open, display, print a specific section of the publication), the "ContentControl" application sends an information package to the licensing-module, inclusive of the DOI and of the details of the action carried on; the package will be stored in the "logging program". Simply accessing to the licensing-module, the editor can compile aggregate statistics of the utilization of the contents or display the profile of a specific user combining the information stored in the logging program with data saved in the database suited to collate users personal information.

III. "Free of charge" on-line information access services and privacy

I will deal in this section with the other moon's face: the Open Access world or, more in general, the open – and seemingly free of charge – access to the fruition of on-line information.[12] I will hold the "Google" search engine as a paradigmatic example, also in its versions of "Google Scholar" and "Google Book Search."[13] I made this choice since it represents a model, among the most invasive ones in the Net, of personal data gathering and of users profiling. Obviously, many of the issues I am going to describe can be met in other portals that provide access to scientific knowledge, especially when they are provided by an

---

[12] For a closer examination on Open Access issues, see R. CASO, *Ricerca scientifica pubblica, trasferimento tecnologico e proprietà intellettuale*, Bologna, Il Mulino, 2005, p. 312; ID., "Proprietà intellettuale, tecnologie digitali ed accesso alla conoscenza scientifica: Digital Rights Management vs. Open Access", available at the Web-site: <http://eprints.biblio.unitn.it/archive/00001407/>.

[13] I took as a point of reference of this part: O. TENE, "What Google Knows: Privacy and Internet Search Engines", (October 2007), available on the Web-site: <http://ssrn.com>.

authentication system.

From a purely economic point of view, this scenario could seem as an ideal world, that is, the world of the free of charge and completely open access to knowledge; unfortunately, it is actually hiding a dark side. Notwithstanding the outward idyll, also in this context we are paying, often completely unawares, a very expensive price.

Google is one of the most evident examples of personal data collection and, more generally, of information related to users. Every day millions of people use this search engine, giving to it information regarding their interests, needs, desires, fears, etc..

I want to begin with a starting remark: Google is recording every query and is connecting them to a given Internet Protocol address (IP). This sentence probably frightens, astounds, immediately makes us calling to mind all the queries we have done, fearful of "what did we ask to Google?".

Let's proceed in order. From this point of view, privacy concerns personal data, the information that European Directive 95/46/EC ("on the protection of individuals with regard to the processing of personal data and on the free movement of such data") at article 2, lett. a, defines as relating to "an identified or identifiable natural person ('data subject'); an identifiable person is one who can be identified, directly or indirectly, in particular by reference to an identification number or to one or more factors specific to his physical, physiological, mental, economic, cultural or social identity". Hence, in reverse order, information that cannot be connected with a specific person is not a privacy issue. Then, the question lies in the possibility to establish this connection.

In the following part I will explain how the log files relating to our queries can be associated to our person (*rectius*, identity).

First of all, it happens through the IP collection. These are numbers that identify unequivocally the devices connected to a single network; IPs can be statics, that means fixed, or dynamics, that means assigned each time by the Internet Service Provider (ISP) to his subscribers depending on necessity. The IP address, which can be banally considered the equivalent of a street address or of a telephone number, is regarded as a personal data according to art. 2 Directive 95/46/EC (and art. 4, Italian Data Protection Code).[14] Even if Google is not able to match the IP address linked to the log file that contains the queries, to a certain user, the

---

[14] See Opinion of Article 29 Data Protection Working Party 2/2002 on the use of unique identifiers in telecommunication terminal equipments: the example of IPv6, available at the Web site: <www.ec.europe.eu>.

fact that the ISP has this kind of data and that the public authority could force him to communicate data relating to the subscribers makes the log files close to personal data.

In second place, to overtake the difficulty of profiling users caused by dynamic IP addresses, an open access service portal can use "cookies": these mark the user browser (the application used for surfing in the Net) with some "unique identifying numbers"[15]. Actually these files, that are supposed to facilitate users in remembering their login data and queries at every connection to the same Web page, permit the search engine to recognize the user as a "recurrent visitor" of the site and to collate the history list of his queries, even if the user connects to the Net using different IPs.[16]

Cookies in themselves cannot be considered personal data, since they identify a particular browser (*rectius*, a computer), rather than a user. The cookie can be imagined as a sort of label, as "7583co39481e24", without any visible repercussion on privacy, but as it were stick on a personal data box of an anonymous person. If you could match a given cookie, linked to a log file, with the queries on the search engine, to a specific person, then again you would relapse into the personal data uncomfortable – at least for the profilers – hat. But also this obstacle can be bypassed: let's see how. As everybody knows, in addition to the search engine, Google provides several additional services (from the e-mail account to the investment portfolio) that are subject to registration through credentials, as the real name or the e-mail address (the most obvious example is Gmail). At this point, Bob's your uncle: the user logs into the Internet, loads the search engine portal, in the meanwhile he introduces a query. Google uses the same cookie to identify the list of queries and the e-mail account: the cookie anonymity is once and for all lost, the missing name on the users' interests log files box has now a name and a surname!

In the end, a final possibility to collate personal data is left over: this time the only guilty party is the user himself, apart from every kind of tactics he could adopt to reduce the use and the identification of his cookies. We all have tried in our life to look for our name on Google or, in

---

[15] In-depth analysis, see J.J. THILL, "The Cookie Monster: From Sesame Street to Your Hard Drive", *S.C. L. Rev.*, 2001, vol. 52, p. 921.

[16] Google has lately announced the intention to reduce the cookies retention period, initially stated until 2008, to "only" two years starting from the latest user search in its search engine: see "Cookies Expiring Sooner to Improbe Privacy", Official Google Blog, 16 July 2007, available at the Web site: <http://googleblog.blogspot.com/2007/07/cookies-expiring-sooner-to-improve.html>. If we think that we all use it almost every day, we immediately realize that this undertaking has very little impact on privacy.

our specific case, to search for our essays on a scientific database, maybe repeatedly in the same year.[17] These queries are called "ego searches" or "vanity searches". They allow the profiler to link the information relating to users interests to a certain identity.

Now let's put another question to ourselves: where do the log files containing all these information on our queries go to?

In the Google privacy policy we find innocently stated: "We use cookies to improve the quality of our service by storing user preferences and tracking user trends, such as how people search. Most browsers are initially set up to accept cookies, but you can reset your browser to refuse all cookies or to indicate when a cookie is being sent. However, some Google features and services may not function properly if your cookies are disabled."[18] Thus, the declaimed reason lies in the wish to improve the quality of the service! What a pity if we understand that in the meanwhile Google is starting the most extended and unprecedented in human history "Database of Intentions": "the aggregate results of every search ever entered, every result list ever tendered, and every path taken as a result."[19] Incentives to maintain this huge amount of information are represented by: the relatively low gathering and maintaining costs, the lack of a unique and clear regulation on this issues (this even more in the US legal system), and the very remunerative potential utilization of information.

The Database of Intentions symbolizes also a very valuable good, a sort of goldmine if we take into account the economic value of information contained, that are a great temptation for many people: national security agencies, hackers, identity thieves, etc.. Just now, the search engine provider is not allowed (or should not be allowed) to sell personal data to third persons. Hereafter it does not mean that it is not going to be allowed in the future; they exchange user data with subsidiary companies or other trusted business partners, in order to process this information and to provide services.[20]

---

[17] See C. SOGHOIAN, "The Problem of Anonymous Vanity Searches", Winter 2007, available on the Web-site: <http//ssrn.com>.

[18] See "Google Privacy Policy", available on the Web-site: < http://www.google.com/intl/en/privacypolicy.html>.

[19] Term taken by J. BATTELLE, "The Database of Intentions", *John Battelle's Searchblog*, 13 November 2003, available at the Web site: <http://batellemedia.com>; see also ID., *The Search: How Google and its Rivals Rewrote the Rules of Business and Transformed our Culture*, Boston, MA - London, Nicholas Brearley Publishing, 2005.

[20] Again in the Google Privacy Police we read: "We offer some of our services in connection with other web sites. Personal information that you provide to those sites may be sent to Google in order to deliver the service. We process such information in

However that may be, there is always a third party with respect to data processing that could try to obtain personal data communication from the search engines, through a completely lawful procedure. I am referring to public authorities that could be interested in using log files for national security purposes. Especially after the tragic event of September 11th, a progressive trend is modifying the way in which citizens consider the State and its tasks, and is gaining force, remarking the traditional role of public security guardian. At the beginning the State remained in the background in Internet regulation, but now it is more and more starting again to play a protagonist role, making strategic alliances with ISPs: these persons are in possession of very precious information for prevention and contrasting activities against criminality. Then, we talk about "Invisible Handshake."[21]

I took into account the Google example, but the same considerations could be developed for the scientific specialized portals that offer services of the same kind. Actually most of them require a prior necessary authentication in exchange for the download of full text materials proposed by the Web site (otherwise you are allowed to get only the abstract of the paper: see, as example, the Social Science Research Network (http://ssrn.com).

IV. Conclusion: toward the overcoming of privacy vs. knowledge conflict

At the end of the way I lead, let's pull together the strings of what I said, trying to unveil, if it is not already clear, what the Odin saga has to do with our issue.

Whether we are dealing with fruition of scientific knowledge under the proprietary schemes transposed in the digital context by DRM systems, or with free access to contents following the trend that brings to Open Access, we are losing (exchanging, if we were aware of that) our identity, our profile, our data in return for intellectual works we wish to enjoy. As it happened for Odin, we are handing over an eye, that means a very important part of our body, to Mimir, that is the holders of the knowledge we are so fervently seeking. Remaining on the same

---

accordance with this Policy. The affiliated sites may have different privacy practices and we encourage you to read their privacy policies".
[21] See M.D. BIRNHACK, N. ELKIN-KOREN, "The Invisible Handshake: The Reemergence of the State in the Digital Environment", *Va. J. L.* Draft, 2003, vol. 3., available at Web-site: <http://ssrn.com>.

mythological example, other interesting – and at the same time appalling – similitudes occur to us. To drink by the magic fountain a gulp of knowledge we hand over an eye, and with that we are giving to other persons the possibility to see inside us through the given eye, to know what we think, what we desire, briefly speaking to appropriate our most hidden, and simultaneously most precious, part: our thoughts.

Privacy is not only characterized by the tridimensional concept I described before (spatial, informational, and decisional). It represents also a cultural phenomenon: everybody must be fully aware of the risks connected to an unlawful data processing and becoming themselves the first "security measures", proper to avoid illegal utilization of data. Until Internet users understand the risks connected to the processing of their personal data and the real cost they pay to get access to the several services offered by the Net, they will always be dreadfully exposed to the monitoring of all those who, on the contrary, commodified exactly this awareness.

Furthermore, we may have to say: scientific knowledge vs. privacy. And actually this conflict is manifest enough, I hope even more. But, if you really want to solve the contrast, you have to get over the traditional way to conceive the opposite poles.

Privacy does not consist only in making some rules, some restrictions, after all some obstacles to data circulation; it must be declined in the correct management of the flows of data that marks out the information age in a decisive way. Knowledge, on the other hand, knows the already famous phenomenon of dematerialization that changes books, poems, music, and drawings, into files expressed in binary code. Maybe it does not anymore make sense to conceive both terms of our subject in a physical way, carrying on a contrast that does not exist anymore in the digital context. It would be better to start reasoning on the fact that they can be considered as they are in the digital world, which is information, and thus reconsidering rules, technologies, and customs in the light of this new uniforming category that moves our attention to the management aspect of the exchanging flows, rather than to their inherent diversity.

Genetic Enhancement and Autonomy

Wojciech Załuski

Department of Law of the Jagiellonian University, Krakow, Poland

The paper examines 'the argument from autonomy' against genetic enhancement, i.e., against enhancing an embryo's nature through genetic engineering. The argument says the genetic enhancement is inadmissible because it violates human autonomy. The core part of the paper aims at clarifying the very notion of autonomy. The clarification proceeds in two stages. First, a distinction is made between personal and moral autonomy. Second, the concept of presuppositions of moral autonomy is introduced. It is argued that one can distinguish two conceptions of moral autonomy depending on whether one assumes that the contingency of birth is a presupposition of moral autonomy or not. In the final part of the paper, relations between the two conceptions of moral autonomy and two types of genetic enhancement ('directed' and 'all-purpose') are analyzed. It is argued, inter alia, that (a) if one assumes the conception of moral autonomy according to which the contingency of birth is a presupposition of moral autonomy, one is led to accept the conclusion that all the types of genetic enhancement violate moral autonomy; (b) if one assumes the conception of moral autonomy according to which the contingency of birth is not a presupposition of moral autonomy, one is led to accept the conclusion that directed genetic enhancement violates personal autonomy but does not have to violate moral autonomy, and that all-purpose genetic enhancement does not violate either personal or moral autonomy.

I. The problem of the admissibility of genetic enhancement

The present paper deals with an oft-raised argument against the admissibility of enhancing an embryo's nature through genetic engineering (hereafter: genetic enhancement), namely, the argument from autonomy. The argument asserts that genetic enhancement is not admissible because it violates human autonomy (i.e., the autonomy of a person who is to grow up from the embryo subjected to genetic engineering). Clearly, in order to appraise this argument, one must have a clear understanding of the notion of autonomy. Accordingly, a large part of this paper is devoted to clarifying this notoriously unclear notion. The clarification proceeds in two stages. First, a distinction is made between personal and moral autonomy. Second, the concept of presuppositions of moral autonomy is introduced. It is argued that one can distinguish two conceptions of moral autonomy depending on whether one assumes that the contingency of birth is a presupposition of moral autonomy or not. In the final part of the paper, relations between the two conceptions of moral autonomy and two types of genetic enhancement ('directed' and 'all-purpose') are examined.

II. Autonomy

A. TWO CONCEPTS OF AUTONOMY

As it seems, there are two concepts of autonomy – personal and moral. As we shall see, personal autonomy has two varieties, and moral autonomy has three varieties.

1. Personal autonomy

Personal autonomy can be defined as the agent's freedom at the level of choosing her desires (preferences, goals). The somewhat vague phrase 'having freedom at the level of choosing one's desires' can be explicated in the following way: 'having the second-order capacity to distance oneself from one's first-order, i.e., action-guiding desires, to evaluate them in a critical way by considering reasons for their acceptance and for the acceptance of alternative desires, and to change them if they do not pass the critical scrutiny'. The concept of personal autonomy has two varieties – material and formal. The formal variety does not forestall what desires (preferences, goals, etc.) an agent should choose (whether they be moral or amoral, whether they are to satisfy some ideal of human excellence or not, whether they are to be loyalty, commitment, obedience to a group or rather some kind of substantive independence, whether they can be self-destructive or not). The only thing it requires is that an agent should be able to critically evaluate her first-order desires, and, should these desires not pass the critical evaluation, to change them. Accordingly, on this variant, a personally autonomous agent can be just as well a self-sufficient individualist insensitive to the needs of others as an altruist treating others' needs as one's own needs – just as well a villain as a saint, etc. By contrast, the material variety requires that an agent should choose a specific type of desires (moral, realizing some ideal of human excellence, prudent, or rational, etc.).[1]

Three further remarks on the formal variety of the concept of personal autonomy are in order here. First, personal autonomy does not operate in an all-or-nothing fashion; rather, an agent may be personally autonomous to a higher or lesser degree. As it seems, though, no human being can be called an agent (i.e., the true author of her own actions) if she loses completely her personal autonomy. This is so because the agent's first-order, i.e. action-guiding desires can be really called hers only if she really wants to have these desires, i.e., if she has second-order desires to have and to realize her first-order desires. Accordingly, some level of personal autonomy is indispensable to human agency (though, as it must be admitted, it is difficult to determine what level exactly constitutes the threshold between agency and the lack of agency). As we shall see presently, the fact that in order to be called 'an agent' a subject must exhibit some level of personal autonomy is relevant to the question about the relations between personal autonomy and moral autonomy. Second, personal autonomy is a value – a desirable feature of human being. One can argue for this claim indirectly: personal autonomy is a value, as it is a necessary condition of human agency, or directly: personal autonomy is a value because the very capacity not to yield unreflectively to one's first-order desires is valuable in itself. Third, personal autonomy should be distinguished from freedom at the level of realizing one's desires, i.e., from freedom understood as the lack of obstacles in realizing one's desires. It is worth noting that an agent may be personally autonomous and free (in the sense 'encountering no obstacles in realizing her desires'), personally autonomous and non-free, personally non-autonomous and free, and personally non-autonomous and non-free.

Let me now turn to the second concept of autonomy – moral autonomy.

2. Moral autonomy

Moral autonomy can be defined as the agent's capacity to reflectively choose moral principles which are to govern her actions and/or

---

[1] Defining autonomy as a second-order capacity, i.e., as a capacity to distance oneself from one's first order, i.e., action-guiding desires, is widespread in the relevant literature. Also my distinction between formal and material autonomy is not new. See, for instance, G. DWORKIN, *The Theory and Practice of Autonomy* (6th edn, 2001) [Dworkin writes about formal and substantive autonomy], H. G. FRANKFURT, 'Freedom of the Will and a Concept of a Person', *Journal of Philosophy*, 1971, No 68, p. 5-25.

reflectively affirm moral principles which she already accepts (and which she may have originally accepted on unreflective grounds), i.e., as the capacity for normative self-government. I shall call this understanding of moral autonomy 'the strong variety of moral autonomy' (to be distinguished from its two other varieties discussed below). This variety has a formal and material variant. The material variant specifies what moral principles an agent should reflectively choose and affirm if she is to be called 'morally autonomous', while the formal variant requires only that the agent should reflectively choose moral principles which are to govern her actions and/or reflectively affirm moral principles she already accepts.

Moral autonomy can be understood also in a weaker way – as the capacity to understand moral principles as a specific kind of reasons for action (i.e., as different from conventional rules) requiring obedience in an especially categorical way. I call this understanding of moral autonomy 'the weak variety of moral autonomy'. What this variety implies is that an agent understands moral principles *qua* moral principles. In other words, it implies that an agent can discern the specificity of moral principles which consists in that they (as opposed to conventional rules) constitute particularly strong reasons for action, i.e., reasons overriding other reasons for action. It does not imply that the agent has the capacity to reflectively choose moral principles and/or reflectively affirm principles which she already accepts. Of note is the fact that this variety of moral autonomy constitutes a cognitive element of the moral sense and thereby a condition of moral accountability (the second element of the moral sense is motivational – it is a tendency of the agent to comply with moral principles). Accordingly, an agent who commits a crime can be held morally accountable for her deed only if she exhibits a cognitive element of the moral sense (clearly, by definition, such an agent has a defective motivational element of the moral sense). Similarly to the strong variety of moral autonomy, one can also distinguish a material and formal variant of the weak variety of moral autonomy.

Apart from the strong and weak variety of moral autonomy, one should also mention about what can be called 'Kantian moral autonomy' or 'the strongest variety of moral autonomy'. Kantian moral autonomy can be defined as the agent's capacity to reflectively choose moral principles which are to govern her actions and/or reflectively affirm moral principles which she already accepts, and – additionally – to be motivated by these moral principles alone, without interference of any empirical causes. Analogously to the weak and strong variety of moral autonomy, Kantian moral autonomy can also be divided into a formal and material variant. As can be readily seen, the formal variant of Kantian moral autonomy implies the formal variant of the strong variety of moral autonomy (which, in turn, implies the formal variant of the weak variety of moral autonomy).

The results of the analyses conducted in sections 1 and 2 can be schematically summarized in the following way:

Personal autonomy

I. Formal variety (second-order capacity to choose one's first-order desires; it is not specified which desires should be chosen).

II. Material variety (second-order capacity to choose one's first-order desires; it is specified which desires should be chosen).

Moral autonomy

I. Weak variety

1. Formal variant (understanding moral principles *qua* moral principles; moral principles are not specified).

2. Material variant (understanding moral principles *qua* moral principles; moral principles are specified).

II. Strong variety

1. Formal variant (capacity to reflectively choose moral principles which are to govern one's actions and/or reflectively affirm moral principles which one already accepts; it is not specified which moral principles should be chosen).

2. Material variant (capacity to reflectively choose moral principles which are to govern one's actions and/or reflectively affirm moral principles which one already accepts; it is specified which moral principles should be chosen).

III. Strongest variety (Kantian moral autonomy)

1. Formal variant (capacity to reflectively choose moral principles which are to govern one's actions and/or reflectively affirm moral principles which one already accepts, and to be motivated by these moral principles alone, without interference of any empirical causes; it is not specified which moral principles should be chosen).

2. Material variant (capacity to reflectively choose moral principles which are to govern one's actions and/or reflectively affirm moral principles which one already accepts, and to be motivated by these moral principles alone, without interference of any empirical causes; it is specified which moral principles should be chosen).

In the remainder of this paper, by personal autonomy I shall mean 'the formal variety of personal autonomy', and by moral autonomy I shall mean 'the formal variant of the strong variety of moral autonomy'. The narrowing down of my considerations to the two varieties of autonomy is due to the fact these two varieties seem to be the best explications of the concepts of personal and moral autonomy. The material variety of personal autonomy seems to be too strong: the requirement that an autonomous agent ought to choose a concrete type of firs-order desires does not harmonize well with the notion of personal autonomy as it is usually used in the philosophical discourse. Besides, the material variety of personal autonomy becomes hard to distinguish from moral autonomy. As for moral autonomy, its weak variety seems to be too thin – moral autonomy seems to require something more than just the capacity to understand moral principles *qua* moral principles, while its strongest variety seems to be too thick – moral autonomy does not have to require that the agent should have the capacity to be motivated by moral considerations alone. However, I want to emphasize that, in my view, all the above varieties of autonomy are legitimate explications of the notion of autonomy. The formal variety of personal autonomy and the formal variant of the strong variety of moral autonomy seem to be just the best explications from among a number of legitimate explications, i.e., they seem to be explications that capture best the specificity of the concept of autonomy as it is used in the philosophical discourse.

Before I turn to the problem of the presuppositions of moral autonomy, I shall devote some attention to the problem of the relationships between these two concepts. Two different views of these relationships emerge. The first view states that they are entirely independent in the sense that an agent can be morally autonomous without being personally autonomous. This view leads to a rather counterintuitive conclusion that an agent's being entirely incapable of freely shaping and/or changing her first-order desires does not exclude her capacity to reflectively choose and/or reflectively affirm moral principles. According to the second view, the two concepts are partially dependent in the sense that an agent must be at least to some extent personally autonomous in order to be morally autonomous (to the same extent to which human agency presupposes personal autonomy, because moral autonomy presupposes human agency). This second view seems to be more plausible, because the capacity to reflectively choose and/or affirm moral principles seems to require some level of the capacity to distance oneself from one's first-order desires.

B. PRESUPPOSITIONS OF AUTONOMY

What has been said so far – that there are two main concepts of autonomy, and that moral autonomy presupposes human agency ('being a true author of one's actions'), which, in turn, presupposes some level of personal autonomy – seems to be rather uncontroversial. What is controversial is whether moral autonomy has any other presuppositions and whether personal autonomy has any presuppositions at all. Before tackling these questions, let me clarify the concept of a presupposition of autonomy (used so far intuitively). Presuppositions of autonomy are conditions that must be satisfied in order to make sense of the concept of autonomy. They are therefore conditions which have to be met if one wants to speak of true rather than apparent autonomy. Accordingly, if a presupposition of a given concept of autonomy is not satisfied, the concept, so to say, falls apart: an agent who chooses her desires in a free way is only apparently personally autonomous, and an agent who chooses and/or affirms moral principles which are to govern her actions is only apparently morally autonomous. In short and less metaphorically, the notion of a presupposition can be equated with the notion of a necessary condition. This account of the notion of presupposition is general – it refers also to presuppositions of other notions than autonomy – for instance, to the notion of human agency, which strictly connected with the notion of autonomy. In the following two sections I shall argue that personal autonomy does not have any presuppositions, that it is not entirely clear whether human agency has two presuppositions (personal autonomy, free will) or three presuppositions (personal autonomy, free will, the contingency of birth), and – consequently – that it is not clear whether moral autonomy (which presupposes human agency) has two presuppositions or three presuppositions.

1. Free will

Free will can be defined as the capacity to choose alternative actions in a given situation: an agent who has chosen an action at a given time has free will if she could have chosen some other action at that time. The question arises whether free will can be regarded a presupposition of personal or moral autonomy.

Personal autonomy requires that an agent have a second-order capacity to critically evaluate and to change her first-order desires. Now, there seems to be no connection between thus understood personal autonomy and free will. There seems to be no contradiction in assuming that an agent has the above mentioned second-order capacity and does not have free-will, i.e., that she has the second-order capacity but all her thoughts, desires, actions are inevitable consequences of preceding events. In short, an agent can have the second-order capacity and simultaneously be deprived of free will. However, one may plausibly argue that even though free will is not a presupposition of personal autonomy, it is a presupposition of human agency. This is so because if an agent is deprived of free will, i.e., if her actions are just links in causal chains, then she can hardly be called 'an agent' – a *true* author of her actions. Accordingly, it seems plausible to maintain that human agency has (at least) two presuppositions – not only some level of personal autonomy but also free will. However, one could criticize this account of the relations between personal autonomy, free will and human agency by pointing out that free will *is* personal autonomy.[2] This explication of free will, though, seems to forfeit what seems to be an essential part of free will – the capacity to choose various options in a given situation, or, put alternatively, not being determined to choose a given option in a given situation. Accordingly, free will should be regarded as a presupposition of human agency, not as the presupposition of personal autonomy. Personal autonomy and free will should therefore be regarded as two *different* presuppositions of human agency.

Let me now turn to the question of whether free will is a presupposition of moral autonomy. Moral autonomy requires that an agent reflectively choose and/or affirm moral principles which are to govern her actions. Since the requirement that agent should reflectively choose and/or affirm moral principles implies that an agent should assume moral accountability for not complying with these principles, it can be said that moral autonomy implies moral accountability. And it can be plausibly argued that moral accountability for not complying with moral principles is justified only if the agent is not causally determined to act in a given way, i.e., if she has free will. Moral autonomy, therefore, presupposes free will. Clearly, one may argue for this just by pointing out that it is a direct consequence of the above account of the relations between personal autonomy, free will and human agency: given that some level of personal autonomy and free will are presuppositions of human agency, and that moral autonomy seems unthinkable without human agency, then moral autonomy presupposes free will (and some level of personal autonomy).

---

[2] Such explication of the notion of free will was put forward by Harry G. Frankfurt; see H. FRANKFURT, 'Freedom of the Will and a Concept of a Person' above note 1.

2. The contingency of birth

As we shall see, the question of whether the contingency of birth is a presupposition of human agency and thereby of moral autonomy is much more intricate than the question of whether free will constitutes such a presupposition. The claim that the contingency of birth is crucial for moral autonomy was put forward by Jürgen Habermas.[3] Habermas argues that our ethical self-knowledge as a species is grounded in the fact that our genetic constitution does not depend on the will of other persons, i.e., is contingent. What Habermas means by that is that a person cannot consider herself to be a real author of her actions and – more generally – of her life if she knows that other people decided about her genetic constitution. Accordingly, a person whose birth was not contingent cannot be expected to be able to take full responsibility for her actions, and thereby cannot be morally autonomous. Habermas's argument can therefore be plausibly construed as saying that the contingency of human birth is a presupposition of human agency. This argument is very profound – it seems to capture something really important about the nature of human agency and autonomy. However, it is not easy to articulate what exactly it captures and how it should be ultimately assessed. I shall start my analysis of Habermas's argument from a remark that if this argument is correct, it is not as self-evidently correct as the argument that some level of personal autonomy and free will are presuppositions of human agency. While it is (at least, in my view) self-evident that the possession of the second-order capacity to distance oneself from one's first-order desires (personal autonomy) and the capacity to have a real choice between various first-order desires (free will) are presuppositions of human agency, there seems to be nothing self-evident in the claim that human agency requires that a subject's genetic constitution should not have been designed by some other person. One might say that if a subject is personally autonomous and has free will, there seems to be nothing more needed to call her 'an agent'. Accordingly, it seems that the lack of contingency of birth does not by itself undermine human agency; it undermines it only in so far as it decreases personal autonomy beneath the 'threshold level' between agency and the lack of agency and/or violates her free will. Therefore, on this interpretation of human agency, contingency of birth is not a

---

[3] See J. HABERMAS, *Die Zukunft der menschlichen Natur. Auf dem Weg zu einer liberalen Eugenik* (2001). Habermas mentions that similar claim was made earlier by Hannah Arendt who (in *The Human Condition*) introduced the notion of natality as a pre-condition of human ability to initiate action.

presupposition of human agency. Is therefore Habermas's claim that contingency of birth is a presupposition of human agency untenable? The matters are not so simple. There seem to be two main ways of defending this claim – one may call them 'philosophical' and 'psychological'. The philosophical way consists in pointing out that if we *really deeply* understand the concept of human agency as the concept of *true authorship* of one's actions, we cannot fail to notice that this concept requires the contingency of birth; absent the contingency of birth, our authorship is not 'true', for the simple reason that we were designed not just by chance (which, on this argument, is a condition of our being true authors of our actions) but by some other person's conscious will. This way of defending Habermas's argument, however, encounters serious difficulties. First, one repeat the above made remark that the conception of human agency as based on personal autonomy and free will is sufficiently profound, so that there is no need to make it still 'more profound' by positing a somewhat obscure condition of the contingency of birth. Second, one may point out that, contrary to what Habermas seems to assume, the contingency of birth is an all-or-nothing notion. It is true that either a birth is contingent or not. However, it is also true that there is a fundamental difference between a negligent and substantial intervention in the embryo's genotype. On Habermas's view both types of intervention seem to undermine human agency to the same degree, while on the view that the contingency of birth is not a presupposition of human agency, they undermine human agency in varying degrees – depending on how they affect the presuppositions of human agency (personal autonomy and free will). The latter view seems more plausible. What's more, the view that the contingency of birth is a presupposition of human agency gives rise to a counterintuitive conclusion that an elimination of an embryo's genetic defects (i.e., negative genetic engineering) with a view to enabling the child's normal functioning as a human being undermines her agency (whereas, in fact, it would be right to say that it enables her agency). This counterintuitive conclusion can be avoided if we reject the claim that the contingency of birth is a presupposition of human agency. The psychological way of defending Habermas's argument, in turn, consists in asserting that a person who is aware that her birth was not contingent, i.e., that her genetic constitution was consciously shaped by other people, is unlikely to feel herself to be a true agent and thereby is unlikely to be able to reflectively choose and/or affirm moral principles which are to govern her actions, and, consequently, to accept moral accountability for compliance with these principles. One can respond to this argument by saying that this feeling of the lack of agency which an agent is likely to experience if she knows that her birth was not contingent can be eliminated by rationally arguing to her that the necessary and sufficient conditions of agency are personal autonomy and free will (or, if possible, by not revealing to her the information about the non-contingency of her birth). However, one could strengthen the psychological argument by claiming that such rational argumentation is not sufficient to eliminate this feeling, as this feeling is overwhelming, not open to rational argumentation about the bases of agency. Whether this feeling can be of such kind is an empirical question. In my view, it is rather implausible to maintain that it can. But even if it could, what would it show? Clearly, it would not show that contingency of birth is a presupposition of human agency. It would only show that a person who knows that her birth was not contingent is likely to experience a difficulty with feeling herself the true author of her actions and thereby with taking full responsibility for her actions. But, let me repeat the point already made, by virtue of this fact the contingency of birth would not become a presupposition of human agency.

To sum up, the foregoing considerations seem to support the claim that contingency of birth is not a presupposition of human agency and thereby of moral autonomy. It is difficult, though, to provide a conclusive argument for this claim. Especially, it will be difficult to convince someone who just posits that the *profound* conception of human agency implies the contingency of birth. Therefore, given that it is not entirely clear what the presuppositions of human agency and thereby of moral autonomy are, one should distinguish two competing conceptions of moral autonomy (the arrows on the figures point to presuppositions of a given concept):

I.   *Moral autonomy*

                                              ↓

                                        Human agency

Personal autonomy   Free will

II.   *Moral autonomy*

                                              ↓

                                        Human agency

Personal autonomy   Free will   Contingency of birth

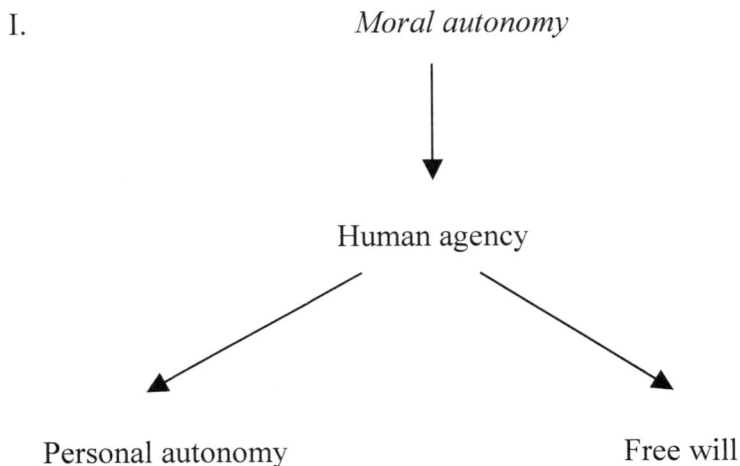

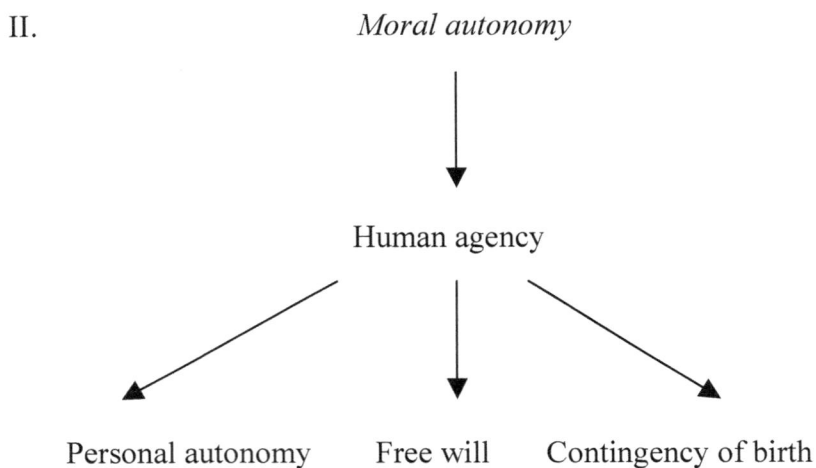

III. Genetic enhancement

Before passing to the problem of whether genetic enhancement violates human autonomy, it is necessary to distinguish two markedly different types of genetic enhancement (the distinction to be presented is widespread in the relevant literature[4]). The first type, which I call

---

[4] For a discussion of various aspects of genetic enhancement see, e.g., J. HARRIS, *Enhancing Evolution. The Ethical Case for Making Better People* (2007); M. J. SANDEL,

'directed genetic enhancement', consists in that a decision-maker (e.g., parents) has an embryo's genotype modified in such a way that the embryo's development is strongly determined to proceed in a certain definite direction (i.e., a child is strongly determined to choose a given way of life wished by the decision-maker). The second type, which I call 'all-purpose genetic enhancement', consists in that a decision-maker (e.g., parents) has an embryo's genotype modified in a way that increases the embryo's overall capacities and powers to effectively pursue various life careers but does not determine the choice of any of those careers. Three additional remarks regarding the notion of genetic enhancement seem to be in order. First, when I speak of genetic enhancement and its influence on human autonomy, I mean a situation in which some decision-maker decides to enhance the nature of an embryo through genetic engineering, not just eliminate its defects that would preclude the embryo's normal functioning as a human being; I mean, then, positive, not negative, genetic engineering. Incidentally, it is worth noticing that negative genetic engineering does not seem to pose serious problems in the context of autonomy (unless, as mentioned, one assumes that contingency of birth is a presupposition of human agency): it enables a child's proper functioning of human beings, and therefore it enables her/his autonomy. Second, since the decision-maker may be – but does not have to be – the child's parents (the decision-maker may be, e.g., the state), the situation may take place both in the context of 'liberal eugenics' and in the context of 'authoritarian (state) eugenics'; the crucial point is only that some decision-maker decides to improve the other human being's – an embryo's – nature through genetic engineering. Third, an essentially different situation arises when a decision-maker uses genetic engineering to improve her own nature. In this situation genetic enhancement does not seem to pose any obvious threat to autonomy. It may be an expression of one's personal autonomy or not, depending on whether a subject has freely chosen her first-order desire to undergo a genetic improvement or not. And, depending on concrete effects of this improvement, it may diminish, increase, or leave intact her personal and moral autonomy.

IV. Does genetic enhancement violate human autonomy?

The answer to the question of genetic enhancement violates autonomy

---

The Case against Perfection. Ethics in the Age of Genetic Engineering (2007); P. VEZZONI, *Il futuro e il passato dell'uomo. Considerazioni sull'evoluzione umana* (2006).

will depend on which conception of moral autonomy one accepts.

If one accepts the conception I of moral autonomy, then the answer will comprise the following theses:

(1) Directed genetic enhancement diminishes personal autonomy. This is so because by determining an agent through genetic engineering to choose a concrete life career or at least to be capable of choosing from a smaller set of life careers than she would have been without the genetic intervention, one undermines the effectiveness of her second-order capacity to freely choose her goals. However, directed genetic enhancement does not have to affect moral autonomy. As argued, moral autonomy is only partially dependent on personal autonomy. Accordingly, the violation of personal autonomy will also be a violation of moral autonomy only if the violation of personal autonomy is so substantial as to make personal autonomy fall beneath 'the threshold level' between agency and the lack of agency.

(2) All-purpose genetic enhancement does not diminish personal autonomy and does not affect in any way moral autonomy. *Au contraire*: all-purpose genetic enhancement increases a subject's personal autonomy, as it widens the range of goals from among which she can choose those goals she wishes to be *hers*.

If one accepts the conception II of moral autonomy, then the answer to the question of whether genetic enhancement violates autonomy will be composed of the following theses:

(1) Directed genetic enhancement diminishes personal autonomy (for the same reasons as it does on the grounds of the conception I of moral autonomy). Directed genetic enhancement violates moral autonomy, as it violates one of the presuppositions of human agency (and thereby of moral autonomy), namely, the contingency of birth.

(2) All-purpose genetic enhancement does not diminish personal autonomy but it violates moral autonomy (because it violates one of the presuppositions of moral autonomy, namely, the contingency of birth).

It should also be noted that irrespective of which conception of autonomy we accept, the following thesis holds: no type of genetic enhancement threatens the first presupposition of human agency – free will, since if one believes that humans possess free will, one will continue to do so, even if one knows that they are 'designed', not contingently born.

Clearly, for anyone for whom autonomy is an important value and who accepts the conception II of moral autonomy, the conflict between moral autonomy and genetic enhancement will be a strong argument against the admissibility of the genetic enhancement of embryos.

However, as I have argued, the conception II of moral autonomy seems to be less plausible than the conception I. The preceding remark, though, does not imply that, if we accept the conception II or moral autonomy, genetic enhancement of embryos becomes admissible, because, apart from the argument from autonomy, one may advance many other arguments against genetic enhancement, not discussed in the paper.

The future of the trade in information and a world history of the legal types of contracts giving access to information

Jon Bing
Norwegian Research Center for Computers and Law, Oslo, Norway

I. Introduction: The trade in Information

It is unusual to be invited to speculate over the possible development of the law. My own interest in information systems and intellectual property law has been a basis for an interest in considering the legal framework for a trade in "information" or "knowledge". These terms are not in this paper used in a technical sense – for instance qualifying the difference between "information" (semantics), "data" (syntactic) and "signs" (atomic), perhaps with "knowledge" as a pragmatic fourth member. I will use the terms in an informal way, hoping the context will be sufficient for the reader to understand the meaning. In this way, "information" will include many different aspects: The advice of a lawyer or a consulting engineer to a client will be an example of "information", as will the reports of a news service, a science fiction novel or a rock opera.

When considering the future, it is often useful to look back and consider the development up to the present – it is like an archer drawing the string of his bow back in order to give the arrow impetus to plunge forwards to the target.

II. A brief history of the trade in information: From the beginning to the present

The *first* example of trade in information might have happened in the Stone Age. One hunter approaches another and offers advice: he knows where there is a valley in which fat bison graze. He is willing to reveal the location of this valley for a fee, for instance a royalty of one bison ham for each animal actually killed by the other.

This might be the first example of a consultancy contract. It has one important condition – the existence of a spoken language which makes it possible for the consultant to peddle his advice to the hunter. And it has two critical limitations – the unity of time and place. The transaction has to take place with both persons present at the same time and at the same location; they have to be within earshot of each other.

The payment has to be agreed before the information actually is exchanged. The "administration of rights" is limited to choosing *not* to communicate if the terms are not satisfactory. After the communication, there is no practical way to control the use of the knowledge as such apart from brute force (for instance banging the hunter in the head with a club if the royalty is not paid as agreed), and there is the risk of the hunter communicating the information to a third party without informing the original consultant or including him or her in the transaction.

This may be an example of the first trades in information, but it is still very popular. Not only are there still consultants around, but employment contracts are generally based on the presumption that the employee can contribute through his or her experience, knowledge or insight to the business of the employer. It is the knowledge of the employee that most often is the reason for hiring or contracting a person rather than this person's strong arms or beautiful face.

The *second* example presumes that writing has been invented, that is a system of written signs which can communicate information. This occurred approximately two thousand years BC, almost simultaneously in Sumer and Egypt – probably somewhat later in the Indus valley. In Sumer, the information was represented by cuneiform characters made by pressing a wooden triangular tool in a wet clay tablet. Luckily some of these tablets were fired, and have therefore been preserved. In Egypt, hieroglyphs were carved in stone or painted on walls. Writing originally was motivated for accounting purposes. The cities developing in the Middle East required a trade in agricultural products with the surrounding districts, and the writing was necessary to keep track of purchases and payments. But the writing made it possible to record more interesting information, like the *Epic of Gilgamesh*. The story is probably the first example of fiction, not claiming to be a myth or legend of the past or gods. It is a variant of the Perseus myth: The King of Babylon determines by oracle that his grandson Gilgamesh will kill him, and throws him out of a high tower. An eagle breaks his fall, and the infant is found and raised by a gardener. The epic was retrieved in 1853 when excavating the library of the last great Assyrian king, Ashurbanipal (1200 BC).

Writing made it possible to imprint signs on physical objects – like clay tablets, rolls of papyri, books of vellum or paper. The object was subject to trade like any other objects – it could be purchased or sold, if there was a market for such objects, the imprinted signs being a property of the object like an elaborate carving or a polished surface. The fact that the value was related to the information communicated by the text rather than the function of the object was not very important in a legal perspective. The object was a *unicum.*

The writing broke the unity of time and place. The information could be communicated over time (as our own reading of the tablets with the story of Gilgamesh demonstrates). A favorite example of mine[1] is what happened when the Caliph of Bagdad, Nasir, decided to ask Djengis Khan for assistance against his enemy, Shah Mohammed. Making sure the written request does not fall into the hands of the Shah, the Caliph has the head of one of his slaves shaved, then tattoos the message on the scalp, and waits for the hair to grow out and cover the text. Then he sends the slave through the enemy lines until he finds the Khan, who shaves the head of the slave once more to read the request. The Khan refuses to help the Caliph, and that is the end of the story – which does not tell us what happened to the slave after his career as a data carrier was brought to an end.

In this context, the law of the sales of goods sufficed. The "administration of rights" was limited to the control of the physical carrier. No further elaboration was necessary.

But this was changed, of course, when Gutenberg invented the printing process in 1448.[2] Prior to his invention, it has been estimated that there were 30 000 volumes of books in Europe. Fifty years later – approximately 1500 – there were three hundred printing shops in Venice alone, and the number of books had increased to 15 million![3] The impact on society was major, but we look towards the impact on law.

It is rather obvious that the old form of "rights management" no longer was sufficient. Printers were in competition. A printer could identify an interesting text in Greek or Latin; have it translated into Italian and experience great demand, selling a large number of copies. However, the printer next door thought it unreasonable that only his neighbor should enjoy success, so copied the text and sold his own reproductions – to a lower price, because he did not have to pay a translator. To regulate the

---

[1] Tor Åge Bringsværd: *Gobi: Min prins,* Gyldendal, Oslo 1994:208.

[2] Printing from moveable type was actually invented in Korea prior to Gutenberg, the oldest printed book being the *Buljo Jikji.*(1372). But the invention of printing in Korea did not have the socio-political consequences that Gutenberg's invention had in Europe.

[3] Sources give rather different figures, though the relative relation remains the same. The text is based on HELMER DAHL. *Teknikk, kultur, samfunn,* Ingeniørforlaget, Oslo 1982:33.

market, the Venetian republic resorted to the traditional solution of the middle ages: The republic awarded a "patent", that means an exclusive right to a printer to reproduce a certain text or book. Originally this was a right awarded to the printer, but occasionally the privilege was given also to the author. One of the early examples was Ludevico Ariosto, the author of one of the more famous novels of the Italian renaissance, *Orlando furioso,* which first appeared in 1515. This tells about Roland, one the paladins of Charlemagne and misfortune in losing his wits, which he luckily can retrieve by travelling to the Moon.[4]

The Venetian solution was exported, for instance to England where the Stationary Guild, organising the printers, kept a record of which of its members had been granted an exclusive right to reproduce which texts. This record was known as a register of "copy rights".

This is indeed a sketchy indication of one of the origins of the modern copyright. But it may suffice to demonstrate how it was developed in order to meet the challenge of the developement of information technology. Before the printing press, possession was sufficient to govern the rights to the text in a book. But this was not sufficient for the printer – and the notion of an "intellectual right" was born, a right to reproduce the text residing in the text as an abstract object, today we call this a "work".[5]

This system of rights management has been carried onwards to modern times. According to the conventional publisher's contract, the author authorises the reproduction of an edition (the number of copies being specified). The printer confirms this with a receipt from the printing, and the publisher furnishes an annual statement of how many copies have been sold. Typically the author has a right to inspect the warehouse to ascertain the number of copies in store. In such a way, the author is supervising that his or her right to payment in the form of royalty (a fraction of the price paid for a copy by the end user) is fulfilled.

Similar schemes were developed and implemented for other types of physical objects carrying information – like phonograms, videos *etc*. They all were based on control of the objects, the stock. But there were alternative schemes for rights management developed – for instance – for the public performance of music or dramatic works, the broadcasting of

---

[4] In the wall of Albergo del Sol (which may be the oldest hostel in the world) at Piazza della colonna in front of the Pantheon in Rome, there is a plaque stating that Ludevico Ariosto stayed there in March through April 1513.

[5] There is another important basis, clearly stated by the decision of the French parliament of 15 March 1586 to award the rights of the French poet and scientist Marc-Antoine Muret to his heirs, each person being the owner of what he or she had created as God governs what he has created.

works *etc*. In most cases this was based on contractual agreements between the producer (theatre) or broadcaster, which was possible in practice because there were rather few of them. This was not possible for public performance of music, and for the administration of the rights of authors (the composer, the writer of lyrics *etc*), a system of collective societies developed, each authorised by the individual copyright holder to represent them, and with reciprocal international agreements to represent the portfolio of rights held by sister organisations.

Until the 20th century information could only be traded in these two categories – either as a service or employment contract with the person who had the information (experience, skill or whatever) in his or her head, or by purchasing a physical object in which the information was recorded in a certain script. Certainly there may be examples that do not fit into the very general categories characterised above, but they will just be details in the general design. There is no claim made that this grossly simplified outline is appropriate for any purpose, it is just drawn to emphasise the typical characteristics of the development in the trade in information.

III. The invisible copies

The third category of trade was made possible by information technology. Today we are comfortable in selling the *representation* – the signs, the characters – separately from a physical medium, and certainly without involving an individual's real time services. This is what we do when we download a file, send an email, and browse the Internet *etc*. It is part of our daily routines. But when it first emerged, it was perceived as something new – at least by those who were able to cast the technological development in legal terms, like Michael Keplinger[6] in his paper "The Case of the invisible copies".[7] It is mainly related to computers and the fact that any representation of information may be computerised: Text in the form of codes identifying the sign of a script represented, sound in the form of sampling the frequencies at very short intervals and representing the frequency as a number, and pictures by resolving an image into tiny squares (pixels) and entering codes for the blend of colours (red, blue, green) and gray scale for each pixel.

This make it possible to trade in information without there being (1)

---

[6] Mr Keplinger is currently Deputy Director General of the World Intellectual Property Organization (WIPO) in the Copyright and Related Rights and Enforcement Sector.

[7] *Revue International de Droit d'Auteur*, October 1970

human beings communicating within the unity of time and space, or (2)) without any physical object changing hands. This is a new way of trading information. This simple observation has several consequences.

One is that the other two categories of trade are associated with major changes in the history of man. The spoken language is by many seen as the characteristic setting man apart from animals. And the written language is closely related to the development of the cities in the Middle East, which at least formed the foundation of the European culture.

Second is that the traditional schemes for the administration of rights fail. There is no "consultant" to make communication of information conditional to a fee, as in our Stone Age example. And there is no physical object which can be controlled to ensure payment of royalty or similar remuneration for making the object available (like selling a painting).

Some has in this failure of the traditional schemes for the administration of rights seen the failure of copyright as such – that is the failure of the original Venetian strategy of a right in an abstract object, the copyrighted "work".

Obviously this is too facile. In the information society, there is an even greater importance than before placed on the need to exchange information, and to take sufficient payment for information. Information technology makes information more important. Therefore there is a need for a legal regime for govern the trade in information. Indeed, we are in a situation not too unlike the aftermath of the Gutenberg invention. The old ways for the administration of rights to information fail due to the novel reproduction technology. There is a need to govern the market in order for it to develop and give society the advantages promised by the technology. Therefore there has to be found an alternative to the traditional way for the administration of the rights.

IV. Digital Rights Management

There has been suggested that the answer to the challenge of the computerised systems is Digital Rights Management (DRM), and the WIPO Copyright Treaty of 1996 Art 11 introduces an obligation to members to "provide adequate legal protection and effective legal remedies against the circumvention of effective technological measures that are used by authors in connection with the exercise of their rights".

But the technical solutions for DRM have been rather primitive. They have mainly taken the form of access control (also conditional access control deployed for cable or satellite television), perhaps best known as the encryption schemes protecting movies on a DVD. [8] Or the solution has been a copy control, made controversial by the inclusion of compact disk carrying music, and to a large extent abandoned by phonogram producers as a protection strategy. In my opinion, these attempts of introducing DRM systems have been too crude to be general, and have therefore generated bad-will with the policy backfiring into the more general legal development. However, it would be wrong to interpret this as a general failure of DRM. It should rather be interpreted that DRM has to meet certain requirements in order to win user acceptance, and obviously will have to be more sophisticated than what is exemplified above.

An example may be a scenario developed by Giovanni Sartor and myself.[9] There is no need to repeat the scenario in all its details, but the three basic elements can be emphasised:

First, the work to be purchased has to be *identified*. The purchaser may know something about the work, typically author, performing artists, title or even a digital object identifier (DOI)[10] or similar identifier. For music, the purchaser may not know much at all, but sampling the music, an electronic fingerprint can be formed and used as a key to access one of the several existing public available databases, identifying not only the work, but also the exact session from which this performance of the work has been recorded. In this way, the purchaser has many ways to identify the work he or she wants to have made available.

Second, the DRM will be flexible, and will interact with software for the management of licenses residing on the end user's computer or digital device. This implies that the end user may purchase a license tailor-made to the desired use. If the work is a song, the licence will determine whether the song should be available for one time performance, or for a longer period, or even permanent, whether the licence should permit reproduction or only access, for private or public performance, *etc.* Such

---

[8] The Norwegian prosecution of "DVD-Jon", a teenager who posted a descrambling program for circumventing the access control of DVDs, has become well known. DVD-Jon was aquitted. The decision is available in English translation at several websites, see for instance http://www.ictlex.net/?p=61 (the translation is by the author).

[9] The scenario is presented in several versions, but is generally known as the "Lovely Rita Scenario", after the song "Lovely Rita Meter Maid" by Lennon and McCartney, which is the subject for trade in the example, see for instance JON BING and GIOVANNI SARTOR "Lovely Rita: A Scenario" in Jon Bing and Giovanni Sartor (eds) *The Law of Electronic Agents*, CompLex 4/03, Norwegian Research Center for Computers and Law, Oslo 2003:11-21.

[10] Cf http://www.doi.org/.

diversity obviously presumes the presence of an infrastructure not yet available. But it would make it possible for the end user to purchase a licence designed for the user he or she want to make of the work, and it will relate to the payment. This in contrast to the "one seize suits all"- DRM solutions we have seen up till now.

Third, the complexity indicated above has to be set off by smarter consumer technology. This would make it extremely simple to purchase works on the net. In the scenario, it is suggested that the solution is developed using autonomous intelligent electronic agents – computer programs that have sufficient knowledge based technology components to make them able to negotiate on behalf of the end user. The agents of the end user would negotiate with agents of the right holders, offers would be compared and the agents would try to make the best bargain, guided by instructions given by the end user.

Therefore, behind the scenes there would be a greater complexity than today. There would be a large choice of different licences interacting with monitoring software on the device of the end user. There would be negotiations by electronic agents, perhaps hundreds of parallel negotiations going on before the "best buy" would be qualified. But in front of the stage would be the simple world of the end user – the consumer listen to a tune, perhaps on an old-fashioned radio broadcast and pushes the button "purchase". His or her agent flings itself into cyberspace, carrying with it the pre-instructions of its owner, identifying the tune, accessing possible alternative sources, negotiating price and licensing terms with the agents representing the right holders, initiating payment from the end user's account at the same time as the music file is made available to the end user for the device or devices the end user will prefer for accessing the file and enjoying the music. And the music will be available for the end user before the music has been played to its end by the broadcast. A purchase made simple by complex technology.

Regrettably the payment scheme necessary for such a scenario is not fully developed. But the ease of purchase will – it is suggested – ensure trade, and the variety of licenses will ensure freedom of choice.

Of course the payment will be one of the crucial elements. iPod has demonstrated that the end user is willing to pay if the purchase scheme is simple and user friendly, and also the price not unreasonable. In the future market there will be a large variety of pricing schemes in parallel. The pricing will vary between phonogram producers (the "big four" dominating the current international stage), YouTube videos uploaded by individuals, advertisements, academics posting their own papers, self-promotion of different kinds, *etc.* A similar variety will be in the licensing terms, and the terms will be enforced by programs residing within the device of the end user (or, if this is a "thin" device, as possibly will become more common, the programs will govern the end user access point to the net).

The simple or brute solutions of the past have proved too brittle to be sustained over time. They will possibly be replaced by a variety of technically more complex solutions, ensuring free consumer choice. This profusion of possibilities may at first glance be mistaken for a confusion – but there is an important difference been confusion and profusion. Information of different kinds – text, images and sound – will be available by many very different services, and also there will be many solutions. But they will have one thing in common – they are easy to use, otherwise they will not will end user acceptance.

And for the consumer, it all will be perceived as simple and easy. The end user may not understand the complexity behind the scenes – in the same way that a person in front of a television screen hardly understands the technology bringing him or her the high definition movie that he or she is enjoying. That does not overly bother the consumer, for the end user it is simple – a touch to a button on the remote control. Like the "one-click purchase" of amazon.com tomorrow's information services for the consumer will be models of simplicity – on the surface.

V. A final word

It may be fitting to end this little essay on the future of the trade in information by an example of a work of fiction, which in our future may be subject to such trade. It also may offer some comfort to those who feel that the issues are too many and too complex really to grasp, and feel overwhelmed by the policy issues brought to us on the foaming crests of the waves of the onrushing future. It an aphorism by the Norwegian author Gene Dalby:[11]

"He, who holds his head above the waters,

sees only the tip of the iceberg."

---

[11] From his collection *Den tatoverte tungen (The tattooed tongu)*, Aschehoug, Oslo 1986. Translation by the author.

The Legal Status of Software Interoperability Information: A Law & Economics Analysis of Application Programming Interfaces and Communication Protocols

Federico Morando

IEL - International Programme in Institutions, Economics and Law, Carlo Alberto, Torino/ NEXA Center for Internet & Society, Politecnico di Torino (DAUIN)

This paper shows that interoperability specifications are not protected by copyright. The paper also demonstrates that existing doubts and uncertainty concerning the legal status of software interoperability information are typically related to a poor understanding of the technical nature of software interfaces. To remedy to such a misunderstanding, the paper focuses on the distinction between interface specifications and implementations and stresses the difference between the steps needed to access the ideas and principles constituting an interfaces specification and the ones needed to re-implement a functionally equivalent interface through new software code.

Leaving interoperability specifications outside the domain of copyright protection (and outside intellectual property in general) is not only coherent with general copyright law principles, as the idea/expression dichotomy; it is also likely not to generate any significant market failures and to increase competitive pressure on software market leaders.

The results of the paper are specifically discussed with respect to the legal systems of the EU and of the US. The analysis is also likely to apply (with minor adaptations) to any copyright system compliant with the Berne Convention, since it is mainly based on general copyright law principles, technical arguments and economic reasoning. At the normative level, the paper does not recommend major modifications to the existing model of legal protection of software (and software interfaces), as long as it is interpreted and enforced according to the descriptive part of the work. However, it suggests that policymakers could reduce the fear of legal actions, other forms of legal uncertainty and several residual doubts by explicitly stating that interface specifications are unprotectable and freely appropriable.

I. Introduction

In the field of software, the term interoperability describes the capability of different programs to exchange data, to read and write the same file formats, and to require services from one another.[1] Loosely speaking, interoperability is a synonym of compatibility. Software interoperability is at the core of several recent antitrust cases and policy debates. In the field of competition policy, the European Microsoft case (Microsoft IV),[2] concerning the disclosure of information necessary to achieve interoperability among client and server computers, is worth mentioning. Similarly popularized by mass media is the discussion concerning interoperability between digital rights management (DRM) technologies, leading to the adoption of specific regulations in France[3] and fostering much debate in other countries.[4]

The interest concerning interoperability information comes from the fact that controlling interfaces among different pieces of software (and/or hardware) is strategically crucial. This strategic relevance originates from technological and economic phenomena, in particular from the modular nature of software programs and various kinds of network effects. In the US v. Microsoft (*Microsoft III*),[5] the US Department of Justice (DoJ) summarized this point in a very effective way, quoting a Microsoft

---

1 The Digital Millennium Copyright Act 1998 (or "DMCA"), s.1201 (f) (4), defines interoperability as "the ability of computer programs to exchange information, and of such programs mutually to use the information, which has been exchanged". This definition has been taken, almost word by word, from the one provided by Recitals 10-12 of the Council Directive 91/250/EEC of 14 May 1991 on the legal protection of computer programs (hereinafter, Software Directive).

2 With Microsoft IV I refer to the Case COMP/C-3/37.792 Microsoft, that led to the Commission Decision of 24.03.2004 relating to a proceeding under Article 82 of the EC Treaty. The European Court of First Instance delivered its judgement on Microsoft's Appeal on the 17th of September 2007, substantially confirming the approach of the Commission. I refer to this ruling as Microsoft CFI.

3 Chapitre IV (Mesures techniques de protection et d'information) of the LOI n° 2006-961 du 1er août 2006 relative au droit d'auteur et aux droits voisins dans la société de l'information (modifying the French code de la propriété intellectuelle).

4 In Italy, for instance, see the proposal of reform of the Author's Right Law (Legge 22 aprile 1941, n. 633).

5 With Microsoft III or Microsoft US case I refer to the famous US antitrust case, which risked leading to the dismembering of Microsoft, following J. Jackson's ruling 87 F.Supp.2d 30 (D.D.C., 2000). In appeal, the case was vacated and remanded, with ruling 253 F.3d 34 (C.A.D.C., 2001). The case has been ended by the Consent Decree ratified by J. Kollar-Kotelly, with ruling 231 F.Supp.2d 144 (D.D.C., 2002). With J. Jackson's findings of fact I refer to ruling 84 F.Supp.2d (D.D.C., 1999).

executive's statement: "to control the APIs is to control the industry".[6] I will come back on the definition of APIs (Application Programming Interfaces) and other kinds of interoperability information (see § II); the point of the DoJ, however, is clear: being able to decide which programs are compatible with a crucial platform such as Windows, and to what extent, gives the possibility of dominating the entire software industry. Moreover, it can be argued that "owning" interoperability information is a way of controlling even more than the software industry, since this control could lead to significant influence in several other fields, from information and communication technology in general, to the whole content industry.[7]

Nevertheless, antitrust authorities and legislators have usually adopted an agnostic attitude with respect to the actual legal status of information needed in order to achieve interoperability. An example of this agnostic attitude is the recent Decision of the EU Commission in the Microsoft (IV) case.[8] In that Decision, the Commission imposed on Microsoft the disclosure of "interoperability information", but also stated that "[t]o the extent that any of this interface information migh*t be protected by intellectual property in the European Economic Area, Microsoft would be entitled to reasonable remuneration"*,[9] without providing any guidance concerning the cases in which such a protection may indeed exist.[10] This agnostic attitude is even more evident in the Court of First Instance's ruling:

> *"Although the parties devoted lengthy argument, both in their written pleadings and at the hearing, to the question of the intellectual property rights which cover Microsoft's communication protocols or the*

---

[6] United States v. Microsoft, 65 F.Supp.2d (1999) 1, at p.15. Also quoted in : T. A. PIRAINO, Jr., Identifying Monopolists' Illegal Conduct Under the Sherman Act, *75 New York University Law Review*, 809 (2000), pp. 888—889; P. J. WEISER, "The Internet, Innovation, and Intellectual Property Policy", *103 Columbia Law Review*, 534--613 (2003).

[7] See, among many, BRIAN FITZGERALD. "Intellectual Property Rights in Digital Architecture (Including Software): The Question of Digital Diversity", *23 European Intellectual Property Review*, 121--127 (2001).

[8] See supra note 2.

[9] Press Release IP/04/382, Brussels, 24 March 2004 (emphasis added).

[10] Of course, this attitude of the Commission is perfectly consistent with the competences of the European Union, which leave to Member States the bulk of the intellectual property related legislation.

*specifications of those protocols, the Court considers that there is no need
to decide that question in order to resolve the present case.*"[11]

The Consent Decree which brought to an end (at least for the
moment) the main chapter of the US Microsoft antitrust saga (*Microsoft
III*)[12] adopted wording that is similar to that of the Commission.[13]

Overall, despite the relevance of interoperability information in case
law and policy debates and the richness of the literature about the legal
protection of software,[14] only a relatively small portion of this literature
explicitly deals with the specific problem of the legal status of software
interfaces.[15] In 1989 Cornish[16] observed that, at the time, there was "still
considerable misunderstanding about interfaces and access protocols, and
therefore about how they should be characterised in relation to copyright
concepts". Unfortunately, misunderstanding remains widespread today
and no clear-cut solution concerning the legal status of these pieces of
code seems to have been reached: according to Välimäki,[17] "[i]t hasn't
been, and still isn't, so clear that some form of intellectual property can
really cover interoperability information". Rotenberg[18] even argues that
"interfaces are neither completely private, nor completely public property,

---

[11] *Microsoft CFI* (see *supra* note 2), § 283 and 313.

[12] *United States District Court for the District of Columbia, Civil Action No. 98-1233
(Ckk), State of New York, et Al. v. Microsoft Corporation*, publ. as 231 F.Supp.2d 144
(D.D.C., 2002) (hereafter, *Consent Decree*). The measures adopted with the *Consent
Decree* will stay in place only for 5 years, unless the Court will find "*willful and
systematic violations*" of the terms of the agreement.

[13] See sections III.D and III.I of the *Consent Decree* (see supra note 12).

[14] Some of the authors having written about this topic include Gordon, Landes, Posner,
Gemignani, Ginsburg, Menell, Reichman, P. Samuelson and Liebowitz, just to quote a few
of them.

[15] Among the ones explicitly dealing with interfaces, interconnections, interoperability and
APIs, see GIOVANNI GUGLIELMETTI, *L'invenzione di software -- brevetto e diritto d'autore*,
(Giuffrè first ed, Milano. 1996); N. T. NIKOLINAKOS, "The New Legal Framework for
Digital Gateways – the Complementary Nature of Competition Law and Sector-specific
Regulation", 9 *European Competition Law Review*, 408--414 (2000); C. R. McMANIS,
"Taking Trips on the Information Superhighway: International Intellectual Property
Protection and Emerging Computer Technology", *41 Villanova Law Review*, 207 (1996).

[16] W. R. CORNISH, "Inter-operable Systems and Copyright", *11 European Intellectual
Property Review*, 391--393 (1989).

[17] MIKKO VÄLIMÄKI, 'Software Interoperability and Intellectual Property Policy in Europe',
3 European Review of Political Technologies, 1--11 (2005). See also MIKKO VÄLIMÄKI &
VILLE OKSANEN, "Patents on Compatibility Standards and Open Source – Do Patent Law
Exceptions and Royalty-Free Requirements Make Sense?", *2 SCRIPT-ed*, (2005).

[18] BORIS ROTENBERG, *The Legal Regulation of Software Interoperability in the EU*, NYU
School of Law, Jean Monnet Working Paper 07/05 (2005).

but something in between." Even one of the most specific articles about this topic[19] offers a detailed survey of US case law, and then concludes that "the extent of copyright protection afforded to APIs varies considerably depending on the specifics of the underlying computer program and the nature and function of the APIs with respect to that program".[20]

Making some clarity about the legal status of interoperability information – or, at least, understanding the reasons of the apparent lack of clarity in this field – is thus the main purpose of the paper at hand.

A. PLAN OF THE PAPER

The present article proceeds in several sections. Part II offers an introduction to some relevant technical problems and proposes some definitions concerning the basic and fundamental technical "objects" discussed in the paper (APIs, communication protocols and similar interfaces). Since achieving interoperability with software, established in the market, is frequently one, if not the main, goal of a decompilation project, this section will also explicitly address the problem of reverse engineering. Part III defines the fundamental distinction between specification and implementation of interfaces. Summarizing, an interface specification is essentially a set of technical requirements that must be respected in order to achieve interoperability, while an implementation is the actual software code that is written respecting the rules spelled out in the specification. The goal of parts IV and V is to survey the status quo concerning the legal protection of interoperability information, with a particular attention to the US and the EU legal systems. Part VI draws some preliminary conclusions and offers some comments about the insights that emerge from the survey of US case law, to be confronted with the European situation. In part VII, I will provide some economic comments about the legal findings of the paper. Part VIII explores the risk that contractual agreements may disrupt the careful balance of interests described in the previous parts of the paper. Issues related to the limited, but significant, application of patent law to software products are also briefly discussed. Finally, part IX offers some conclusions.

---

[19] EFTHIMIOS PARASIDIS, "A Sum Greater than Its Parts? Copyright Protection for Application Program Interfaces", *14 Texas Intellectual Property Law Journal*, 59 (2005).
[20] Id., p. 89.

II. Interoperability information: technical definitions and law & economics simplifications

Application programming interfaces (APIs) and communications protocols (CPs) are pieces of software designed to allow interoperability between different computer programs at computer or network level. In other words, APIs and CPs provide (different kinds of) "compatibility" between software programs, thus allowing different programs to communicate between them. Technically, an API is the interface that a computer program provides in order to allow requests for services to be made of it by other pieces of software (including the exchange or sharing of data). A CP is the set of standard rules for data exchanging (including signaling, authentication and error detection) over a communications channel. More concretely, APIs are functions including complex sets of arguments: depending on the arguments used, running an API will make a certain piece of software return some specific information and/or behave in a certain way.

In this paper, I will stress that APIs and similar interfaces[21] are actually composed by two different aspects (or logical layers, if one prefers). At the lowest possible level of abstraction there is an API *implementation*, which is the source and object code actually working in a PC. At a higher level of abstraction there is an API *specification*, which is a "generalization" of the specification, stating only the necessary conditions to achieve interoperability. Drawing a clearer dividing line between implementations and specifications will be one of the main goals of the paper (see, in particular, § *III.* API specification *versus* implementation).

A. ACCESS TO INTEROPERABILITY INFORMATION

Interoperability information may or may not be readily available: gaining access to this information is a necessary step (both conceptually and practically) in order to make any use of it. Even if this paper is focused on the use and legal status of interoperability information, it is useful to provide some hints concerning this (preliminary, but essential) access phase.

In some cases, the original interoperability specification may be easily available. It actually happens quite frequently that needed API

---

[21] Using the term APIs, I will frequently (and implicitly) include similar software objects, as CPs.

specifications are effortlessly and freely accessible, because software developers, wanting to foster the creation of interoperable programs, willingly provide them. In these cases, the access phase is not a problem: interoperability specifications, indeed, are very frequently available during the introductory phase of a new software technology. In this phase it is normal to perform true "evangelization efforts" to spread knowledge of the new technology, as much as possible, amongst independent developers, in order to reach a critical mass of complementary products and to attract consumers' attention.[22]

In some other cases, the original implementation may also be available (with or without a separate description of the abstract specification), with full comments (indirectly describing the specification). This is the case when the original source code (of the software with which one may want to achieve interoperability) is accessible (to everyone – as in the case of open source projects – or to the developer of complementary products, maybe as an effect of specific agreements). I will come back about the definition of source and object code. For the moment, notice that the source code of a piece of software is the program as developers wrote it: it is, somehow, the blueprint of the software project and other developers may fully read and understand it, especially if it is accompanied by the comments of the original programmers (which are normally interposed between the lines of actual code). If the commented source code of an implementation is available, the API specification may not be explicitly available, but its re-creation is, in principle, relatively easy (even if it may be costly and time consuming). According to some commentators, the availability of the source code of the original implementation is actually the best possible case for developers wanting to achieve interoperability.[23]

Finally, only the object (also called compiled, or binary) code may be available. Notice that even skilled human beings (e.g. talented professional developers) may be somehow able to read object code, but are essentially unable to understand more than a few lines of compiled code. Moreover, object code does not normally contain all the useful comments that may facilitate the human understanding of the piece of software. Indeed, it is not by chance that the "normal" case – when dealing with interoperability in law courts – is the one in which only the

---

[22] See also JAAP H. SPOOR, Copyright Protection and Reverse Engineering of Software: Implementation and Effects of the EC Directive, *19 U. Dayton L. Rev.*, 1063 (1994), 1079.
[23] See, among others, A. JOHNSON-LAIRD, "Software Reverse Engineering in the Real World", *19 University of Dayton Law Review*, 843 (1994).

object code of the original software is available and direct access to interoperability information is impossible (or economically unfeasible, because of strategic behaviour of the holder).

Thus, in the cases of the third group, when only the object code is available, software reverse engineering is the normal approach to try to reconstruct an approximation of the original implementation, which will be used in turn to understand the requirement of the original interoperability specification. Indeed, reverse engineering "represents a remedy of last resort for obtaining information not otherwise available."[24]

1. Software reverse engineering (decompilation)

Software reverse engineering, also called *decompilat*ion, is a labour intensive, difficult and time-consuming process. To decompile a program means (loosely speaking, from the technical point of view) to translate it from the object (binary) code directly "understandable" (executable) only by a computer into a (relatively) "higher level" programming language, directly understandable by trained human beings. Languages are defined "high-level" or "low-level" depending on their "level of abstraction" from machine language. Simplifying, very high level programming languages (like the famous BASIC) are more similar to normal human language (with a strict syntax), while very low level programming languages tend to decompose anything in the single steps that a computer will perform to actually execute the program. We may imagine executable object code as the programming language with the lowest level of abstraction. When the level of abstraction is too low, human beings are incapable of keeping track of the overall logic of the operations performed by the computer, so that they are unable of understanding it. Of course, an overall understanding of a computer program is necessary in order to make another piece of software capable of interoperating with it. Hence, programmers wanting to achieve interoperability with an existing piece of software need to decompile it (unless source code or interoperability specifications are already available).

Case law and a rich literature[25] can be used to describe legal issues

---

[24] JOHNSON-LAIRD, *Software Reverse Engineering*. The work of Johnson-Laird is one of the most authoritative papers in this field, quoted also in the Sony v. Connectix ruling (203 F.3d 596 at 599).

[25] *See*, also for more references: JOHNSON-LAIRD, *Software Reverse Engineering*, ; PAMULE SAMUELSON & S. SCOTCHMER, 'The Law and Economics of Reverse Engineering', *111 Yale Law Journal*, 1575--1663 (2002); JOHN ABBOT, Reverse Engineering of

concerning software reverse engineering (decompilation) used to acquire interoperability. Here, I can just mention that, to understand potential copyright problems arising from decompilation, it is important to know that "intermediary copies of the original software must be made"[26] in order to decompile it. In other words, in order to increase the degree of abstraction, going from the available object code to an approximated reconstruction of source code, it is necessary to write down several intermediate steps. At the same time, in order to increase the degree of abstraction, the developers performing reverse engineering intensively use their own know-how and write down from scratch new comments, names of variables and other elements which may be useful in order to make sense of the overall program. This is why a common feature of scholarly works authored by technologists is to describe decompilation "as a process of painstakingly attempting to understand the ideas embodied in the object code of a computer program."[27]

In this paper, I assume that decompilation is lawful, at least if performed for the purpose of achieving interoperability. On the one hand, there are elements to say that this assumption is reasonable – as a first approximation – both in the US[28] and in the EU[29] (see below). On the other hand, this assumption could be discussed and qualified further: given the focus of the paper at hand, I cannot but remand to the articles mentioned in present section. For my purposes, I will take the conclusions of Samuelson and Scotchmer (2002)[30] as a starting point:[31]

Software: Copyright and Interoperability, 14 J.L. & Inf. Sci., 7 (2003). See also, in Italian, GIOVANNI GUGLIELMETTI, "Analisi e decompilazione dei programmi", in *La legge sul software*, 152--201 (Luigi Carlo Ubertazzi ed., 1994).

[26] SAMUELSON & SCOTCHMER, *The L&E of Reverse Engineering*, p. 1608–1613.

[27] JOHNSON-LAIRD, *Software Reverse Engineering*. See also ABBOT, Reverse Engineering and additional references in SAMUELSON & SCOTCHMER, *The L&E of Reverse Engineering*

[28] See the Atari (975 F.2d 832) or Sega (977 F.2d 1510) cases, with a broad application of fair use, but consider also the limitations imposed by the DMCA. See also SAMUELSON & SCOTCHMER, *The L&E of Reverse Engineering*.

[29] See, in particular, ESTELLE DERCLAYE, Software Copyright Protection: Can Europe Learn from American Case Law? -- Part 1, 22 *European Intellectual Property Review*, 7-16 (2000); ESTELLE DERCLAYE, Software Copyright Protection: Can Europe Learn from American Case Law? -- Part 2, 22 *European Intellectual Property Review*, 56-68 (2000); GUGLIELMETTI, *in* Analisi e decompilazione, and GUGLIELMETTI, *L'invenzione di software (1st ed.)*, .

[30] SAMUELSON & SCOTCHMER, *The L&E of Reverse Engineering*.

[31] This conclusion seems to be shared by the majority of the law&economics literature focused on reverse engineering, frequently mentioning also the technical findings of JOHNSON-LAIRD, *Software Reverse Engineering*. For additional comments and a synthetic

The first [conclusion] is that reverse engineering has generally been a competitively healthy way for second comers to get access to and discern the know-how embedded in an innovator's product. If reverse engineering is costly and takes time, as is usually the case, innovators will generally be protected long enough to recoup R&D expenses. [...] Second, we have found it useful to distinguish between the act of reverse engineering, which is generally performed to obtain know-how about another's product, and what a reverse engineer does with the know-how thereby obtained (e.g., designing a competing or complementary product). The act of reverse engineering has rarely, if ever, market-destructive effects and has the benefit of transferring knowledge. Harmful effects are far more likely to result from post-reverse-engineering activities (e.g., making a competing product with know-how from an innovator's product). Because of this, it may be more sensible to regulate post-reverse-engineering activities than to regulate reverse engineering as such.[32]

As I already hinted, similar conclusions seem to be essentially shared, as the goal of decompilation is to achieve interoperability, also by the European legislators and by American Courts. In fact, the first paragraph of article 6 of the *Software Directive* explicitly addresses software reverse engineering ("decompilation"), authorizing reproductions of copyrighted programs "where reproduction of the code and translation of its form [...] are indispensable to obtain the information necessary to achieve the interoperability of an independently cre*ated* computer program with other programs" (emphasis added). Similarly, in the US, in the widely quoted case Sega v. Accolade[33] the Court "conclude[d] that where disassembly[34] is the only way to gain access to the ideas and functional elements embodied in a copyrighted computer program and where there is a legitimate reason for seeking such access, disassembly is a fair use of the copyrighted work, as a matter of law. *Our conclusion does not, of course, insulate Accolade from a claim of copyright infringement with res*p*ect to its finished products*" (emphasis added).

As a conclusion of this long parenthesis about reverse engineering, it looks meaningful to concentrate our attention on the issue concerning the

---

survey of the debate about the social desirability of rules allowing reverse engineering, see also ABBOT, *Reverse Engineering*, 18—20.

[32] SAMUELSON & SCOTCHMER, *The L&E of Reverse Engineering* 1608—1613.

[33] Sega v. Accolade, 977 F.2d 1510.

[34] Disassembly and decompilation are frequently used as synonyms (in non-technical statements). Disassembly is – so to speak – the first step in decompilation: the binary code is translated in the sequence of commands that are used to instruct the processor of a given computer. Additional steps are needed to arrive to an approximation of the original source code.

use of interoperability information (collected through reverse engineering or otherwise): in other words, we are back to the question concerning if and when APIs should be protected (and – in particular – to what extent). To discuss this issue, a fundamental prerequisite is a precise understanding of the difference between an API specification and its implementation.

III. API specification *versus* implementation

In general, a specification is an accurate description of a set of requirements, to be satisfied by a certain product (or service).[35] An implementation (of a given specification) is a product respecting the criteria stated in the specification.[36]

The specification/implementation distinction is strictly related to the traditional distinction between form (expression) and content (ideas), which is at the core of copyright law.[37] Nevertheless – as the idea/expression dichotomy – also the specification/implementation distinction may be quite tricky.[38] A problem concerns the protection of the so called "internal form" or "internal expression" of a work. Or – stating the problem in a different way – the issue of non-literal copying, that is reproducing a (potentially) copyright-protected part of the structure of a work.[39] More generally, the distinction between ideas and expressions is a blurred one and – I concede – also theoretically questionable.[40] Indeed, we cannot "express" ideas without recurring to some kind of "expression:" So where is the boundary between abstract ideas and external form of expression? No clear-cut or easy answers may be provided. Yet, despite these difficulties, the idea/expression dichotomy is a pillar of intellectual property, and not only a theoretical one: courts recur to this distinction in

---

[35] See also *Microsoft CFI*, § 198—199 and the *Commission's Microsoft Decision*, § 24 (and § 570).

[36] JOHNSON-LAIRD, *Software Reverse Engineering*, 856.

[37] This principle has strong common law bases. *See* Baker v. Selden, 101 U.S. 99, 25 L.Ed. 841 (1879). It has also been incorporated in Section 102(b) of the US Copyright Act. The same principle has been codified in civil law countries, for instance in the European *Software Directive* at article 1.

[38] As the 2nd Circuit Court of Appeals puts it in Computer Associates Intern., Inc. v. Altai, Inc. (982 F.2d 693): "Drawing the line between idea and expression is a tricky business."

[39] There are countless works addressing this issue. A critical survey is provided by EDWARD SAMUELS, "The Idea-Expression Dichotomy in Copyright Law", 56 *Tennessee Law Review*, 321 (1989).

[40] For a strong critique of (certain uses of) the dichotomy, *see* Id., 355—371.

dealing with cutting-edge issues, like the protection of TV format or fictional characters.

Let me come back to the specificities of interfaces. On the one hand, an API specification may be seen as a collection of ideas, describing formulas, methods of operation and other non-copyrightable matters. At the same time, it is usually expressed and embodied in a manual or other document: this is clearly a copyrighted work, as any physics or mathematics book. On the other hand, an API implementation is the source/object code actually able to communicate with other software respecting the principles described in the API specification. This is another copyrightable work, both in its source-code and object-code (compiled) version.[41] Remember also that any piece of software is protected by copyright, but this protection does not extend to single words, mathematical functions or technically determined solutions.[42] Consider also, as pointed out by many authors,[43] that two programmers implementing the same specifications will not write the same source code and will generate programs with different performances. Even if copyright can surely be used to protect a specific interface (or protocol) implementation, it is not clear if copyright can be used to create a broader monopoly, *de facto* encompassing any use of an interface specification. In other words, it is quite uncontested that copyright can be effectively used to protect an implementation, but the protection of a specification seems to be nearer to the domain of patent law (if any protection, at all, may exist).

The reason for which I stress this specification/implementation dichotomy is that I argue that it is possible to find a way to reconcile several theoretical points of view and the large majority of case law, by stressing the distinction between API specifications and API implementations. Here it is important to notice that through the paper I will normally use the term *specification* as a kind of shorthand notation for the *ideas, methods and technical principles embodied in the specification*. Hence, the word specification will refer to these non-protectable technical requirements. I will call "specification document"

---

[41] See article 10(1) TRIPs. See also Apple v. Franklin, 714 F.2d 1240, 3d Cir. (1983).

[42] This should be the case at the international level, applying – for instance – article 2 ("Scope of Copyright Protection") of the Wipo Copyright Treaty of December 20, 1996: "Copyright protection extends to expressions and not to ideas, procedures, methods of operation or mathematical concepts as such." Where "as such" means that the expression of these ideas may be protected, but not the idea itself, nor the expression in such as a way that also the idea is monopolized.

[43] E.g. ROTENBERG, *Regulation of Software Interoperability*.

any kind of description of this specification. In fact, there can be an implementation/specification dichotomy only as long as the "specification" we are talking about is formed by non-protectable technical principles. On the contrary, any "specification document" is copyright protected as a technical manual. The protection of such a manual may be "thin" (as would be the case for a geographic map or other functional creations), because the freedom of expression of the author is constrained by the necessity of respecting technical principles (and the same can be said about part of the internal structure of the work). However, one may be sure that literal copying of more than a few lines of the manual (for instance, photocopying it) will result in copyright infringement.

To provide an example of the usefulness of the specification/implementation dichotomy, I will use it to rephrase the conclusions of an article by Parasidis,[44] surveying US case law concerning APIs. He argues that "the extent of copyright protection afforded to APIs varies considerably depending on the specifics of the underlying computer program and the nature and function of the APIs with respect to that program." But, one aware of the specification/implementation dichotomy may simply say that it is not possible to speak about the legal protection of APIs in general, because we need to distinguish between specifications and implementations. The author also states: "[t]o the extent APIs are not dictated by industry standards, efficiency or the need for a program to interact with a central host computer, they are likely to be afforded protection under the copyright laws. Similarly, copyright protection for APIs is warranted in circumstances where the APIs manifest original expression is not integral to the structure and organization of a software program." Alternatively, we may say that ideas and technical procedures described by API specifications are not granted protection, generally, while implementations are copyrighted, if they respect the general requirements or copyright law. "On the other hand, copyright laws do not protect instances where the structure of a program's APIs is dictated by external factors or where the structure of the APIs merges with the underlying function of the program itself. Likewise, to the extent that copying of APIs is necessary for purposes of compatibility, a claim for copyright infringement is not likely to be upheld." Once again, elements dictated by API specifications are not protected by copyright, because they expression ultimately merges with their functional purpose. Finally, Parasidis argues that "[i]n situations where copying of APIs may be the

---

[44] PARASIDIS, *Copyright Protection for APIs.*

basis for a claim of copyright infringement, the fair use doctrine may be utilized as a defense. For these cases, a thorough examination of the nature of the APIs, in relation to the underlying computer program, must be the focus of the analysis of the statutory factors which form the basis of the fair use defense." That is to say, literal copying dictated by an existing or reconstructed interoperability specification is not likely to be considered an infringement. Even if a court decided that we are dealing with copying of protected expression, at least a fair use defence would likely be available, if a certain amount of "copying" has been dictated by the respect of a common specification (and not by straightforward appropriation of an existing implementation). But – regarding the latter point – see below the discussion concerning the usefulness of the fair use doctrine in dealing with software interfaces.

In a few lines, I will go on to provide some real world examples, taken from case law, in order to better clarify how the dichotomy applies in practice.

A.   DECISIONS   OF   THE   EUROPEAN   COMMISSION   ADOPTING   THE SPECIFICATION/IMPLEMENTATION DICHOTOMY

The European Commission has (quite) explicitly adopted the distinction between interface specifications and implementations (even if the Commission is not competent in IP law issues, so that it did not draw all the intellectual property related consequences of this distinction). In its Decision in the Microsoft (IV) Case, the Commission described interoperability policies of software vendors as follows:

"Software vendors frequently agree to establish open interoperability standards. In this context, they usually agree on interface specifications (that is to say, specifications needed to implement compatible interfaces). Thereafter, different competing implementations compatible with the specification can be created. Such implementations may vary widely in terms of performance, security, etc. They will in principle always differ as regards their source code".[45]

The Commission went on to stress the importance of the distinction between interface specifications and implementation. In particular, the Commission quoted computer scientists highlighting that "a specification does not have to be concerned with details that are relevant to the implementation". Hence, it may be highly more abstract and can ignore several problems requiring paramount attention during the actual

---

[45] Recital 34 of the *Commission Decision.* See also recital 35.

implementation phase.[46] That means that it is possible to "provide interface specifications without giving access to all implementation details" and, the Commission observed, "it is common practice in the industry to do so."[47]

Coherently with the approach proposed in this paper and with previous quotations, in its disclosure order issued within the Microsoft Decision, the Commission ordered Microsoft to release an interoperability specification ("interface documentation") and not the associated implementation ("Windows source code").[48] Using the wording of my paper, Microsoft's competitors are supposed to write down new implementations ("their own specification-compliant interfaces"), not to copy Microsoft's implementations, nor to violate the copyright on the specification documents provided by Microsoft ("the specifications should also not be reproduced, adapted, arranged or altered"). So the Commission[49] recognizes both that specific implementations are protected by copyright and that a given specification document may also be protected. In any case, since the Commission is not competent in the field of Intellectual property rights, which are left to the competence of national legislators, the EU authority is prudent and specifies that limitations to the full enforcement of Microsoft's Intellectual property rights could possibly be necessary to end Microsoft's abuses.

B. IMPLEMENTATION V. SPECIFICATION: SOME MORE HINTS FROM US CASE LAW

US case law provides several insights, which are coherent with the specification/implementation dichotomy that I proposed as a general category to systematize the various positions concerning the protectability of software interfaces. In the following paragraphs, I will describe in some detail a technologically simple case, because this application will make clear that transposing the dichotomy in actual decisions is possible and coherent with the present findings of the courts.

The case E.F. Johnson Co. v. Uniden Corp.[50] concerned an innovative mobile radio communication system ("logic trunked radio" or LTR system). The defendant entered into the market for compatible radios and repeaters, realizing a piece of software which had to be compatible with

---

[46] Ibid. at recital 570.

[47] Ibid. at recital 571.

[48] Press Release IP/04/382, Brussels, 24 March 2004.

[49] Notice that the approach of the Commission has been fully upheld in the recent ruling of the Court of First Instance (*Microsoft CFI*), ending the European Microsoft case.

[50] 623 F. Supp. 1485 (D. Minn. 1985).

the one managing plaintiff's devices. Analysing the radios of the defendant, the plaintiff's engineers found (as the court confirmed) several suspect analogies (including likely copied portions of code).[51] Hence, one could be tempted to list this case among the ones "indicating that copyright protection for APIs is warranted". However – keeping in mind the previously discussed dichotomy – it will be easy to understand that it is actually a case which is perfectly coherent with the protection of API implementations against literal copying, while allowing almost complete freedom to reproduce elements dictated by API specifications.

As an example of a typical (even thought quite minimal) interoperability requirement, I quote a part of the court's findings:

> *"Due to the fact that Uniden designed its radio to be compatible with EFJ's LTR system, both parties acknowledge that some similarities in software design were inevitable. The Court finds that in order to make its radios compatible with LTR repeaters Uniden was required to copy the 'Barker code' found in the copyrighted EFJ program. A 'Barker code' is a pattern of ones and zeroes alternated in a prepatterned sequence. Both the sending and receiving units must identify the Barker code in order for communication to be established. The EFJ Barker code is numerically depicted as 1011000. In order to make its radios compatible, Uniden was required to and did copy this aspect of the EFJ program."*

Therefore, as it frequently happens, an interoperability specification dictated the reproduction of some apparently arbitrary expressions (the "Barker code") in any compliant implementation. To deal with this problem, the Court summarized, in this way, the test created by the Third and Ninth Circuits[52] to analyze copyright infringement in the field of software:

> *"If other programs can be written or created which perform the same function as the copyrighted program, then that program is an expression of the idea and hence copyrightable. If a specific program, even if previously copyrighted, is the only and essential means of accomplishing a given task, their later use by another does not amount to infringement."*[53]

---

[51] Software code was embodied in physical devices, but this is not relevant (as the parts conceded and the Court correctly recognized).

[52] See Apple Computer v. Franklin, 714 F.2d at 1251 and Apple Computer v. Formula, 725 F.2d at 525.

[53] It should be said that the Johnson v. Uniden court seems to interpret the "only and essential means" requirement not in absolute terms, but at a given level of efficiency.

[To the same effect, the Court also quoted the CONTU[54] final report]: "In the computer context [...] when specific instructions, even though previously copyrighted, are the only and essential means of accomplishing a given task, their later use by another will not amount to an infringement."[55]

That having said, however, the Court specified also that some specific parts of the expression, like the already mentioned "Barker word", were "of necessity identical in both codes" (in order to achieve interoperability), but other parts of the software needed not to be identical (and hence could not be legitimately reproduced). In particular, the Court found some identical mistakes in the two software and this was considered a very reliable proof of literal copying, which was surely technically unnecessary (and actually technically detrimental).[56] The courts clearly summarized its conclusion saying that "[d]efendant has reproduced the expression, not merely the idea of plaintiff's copyrighted program." *A contrario*, reproducing ideas, and not expression, would be legitimate and also reproducing expression would be allowed, in cases in which this is "the only and essential means" of creating a compatible product (see § IV.A for more details).

1. How to distinguish between copying ideas and expressions?

The aforementioned case also offer some hints about practical rules used to distinguish between the copying of ideas and Expression. In particular, EFJ v. Uniden makes evident that a typical way of detecting the copying of the expression is simply to find similar bugs in two pieces of software. In general, finding statistically unlikely similarities, in cases in which the same technical problem had several different solutions (without one being more efficient or appropriate than the others), provides a relevant evidence of copying of protected expression. The favour that the so-called "clean room" process of software reverse engineering finds in front of US courts confirms that American judges share the previous reasoning. In the aforementioned clean room process, two separate teams of engineers perform the reverse engineering work frequently needed to

---

[54] The National Commission on New Technological Uses of Copyrighted Works (CONTU) had been established by the US Congress to survey issues concerning the application of copyright to new technologies.
[55] 623 F. Supp. 1485 at 1502, quoting National Commission on New Technological Uses of Copyrighted Works, Final Report 20 (1979) (*CONTU Report*).
[56] 623 F. Supp. 1485 at 1496.

access interoperability information and the reimplementation work needed to create a new specification-compliant interface.

IV. Investigating the legal status of interoperability information: US case law and doctrines

The literature suggests that US case law concerning both reverse engineering and interoperability issues is far richer and more consistent than that established from EU Cases.[57] That is coherent with the fact that the United States saw the fastest development of the software industry and represented for years (and possibly still today) the biggest market for software goods. Fortunately, E. Derclaye showed[58] that there are fundamental similarities between the statutory texts concerning software protection on both sides of the Atlantic Ocean, which are fundamentally "reflect[ing] the same policies". Thus, US case law is "readily applicable" in the EU on several points, including "the general idea/expression principle".

A. THE PROTECTION AGAINST COPYING OF NON-LITERAL ELEMENTS

The starting point to understand copyright protection of interfaces is a deeper understanding of the copyright protection of software against non-literal reproductions. To analyze this issue, I will start discussing the "look and feel" test of the Whelan case and the three-step test of Computer Associates v. Altai.

1. The Whelan or "look and feel" test

In *Whelan*,[59] the defendant had allegedly copied the non-literal structure of a dental lab management program and the idea/expression distinction test proposed by the Third Circuit was the following:

> "*the purpose or function of a utilitarian work would be the works idea, and everything that is not necessary to that purpose or function would be part of the expression of the idea [...] Where there are various means of*

---

[57] See – in particular – DERCLAYE, *Software Copyright Protection -- Part 1.*
[58] See Id. and DERCLAYE, *Software Copyright Protection -- Part 2.*
[59] 797 F.2d 1222.

achieving the desired purpose, then the particular means chosen is not necessary to the purpose; hence there is expression not idea."[60]

This test is (appropriately) based on the idea/expression dichotomy, but it risks being overbroadly interpreted, as happened in the Whelan case itself. Indeed, in that case the Court concluded that the idea of the plaintiff's program was *"the efficient management of a dental laboratory"*, invariably deciding that any kind of similarities with other software programs were copying of "the program's expression". Even if this same test may be interpreted in a more strict way, it definitely leaves an excessive scope to the discretion of the court, increasing legal uncertainty. Moreover, protecting everything but "the idea" behind a program (in the sense of its purpose) would imply a broadness of copyright protection that would be similar to the one offered by patents. Since software (at least in the US) may enjoy patent protection, but only if it is able to integrate restrictive conditions, it would be very problematic to offer an almost equivalent protection via copyright, because this would create incoherence in the intellectual property law system, at a systematic level.[61] Even offering a monopoly on a single means of achieving a desired purpose only when other means are available, as suggested by the Court in *Whelan*, would transform software copyright into something equivalent of an automatically granted and almost everlasting patent (with the only qualification that an alternative means to achieve the same end must exist).

2. Adoption of the "three-step test" of Computer Associates v. Altai

Due to the aforementioned reasons amongst others, the *Whelan* test has, nowadays, been supplanted by the so-called *Altai*[62] or three-step test.[63] The Second Circuit developed the three-step analysis in *Computer Associates v. Altai*,[64] based on the abstractions test, originally developed in the '30ies by Judge Learned Hand in dealing with similarities between plots and other "structural" elements of traditional literary works (plays,

---

[60] 797 F.2d 1222 at 1236.

[61] See GIOVANNI GUGLIELMETTI, *L'invenzione di software -- brevetto e diritto d'autore*, (Giuffrè second ed, Milano. 1997), 263—267, but also 243—247 (arguing that, for reasons of systematic coherence with patent law, copyright cannot have the same scope of patent protection and, *a fortiori*, cannot have a broader scope).

[62] 1992 WL 139364 (2nd Cir.(N.Y.)).

[63] See, among others, DERCLAYE, "Software Copyright Protection -- Part 2".

[64] *Computer Associates v. Altai*, 982 F.2d 693.

in particular):

> *"In ascertaining substantial similarity under this approach, a court would first break down the allegedly infringed program into its constituent structural parts. Then, by examining each of these parts for such things as incorporated ideas, expression that is necessarily incidental to those ideas, and elements that are taken from the public domain, a court would then be able to sift out all non-protectable material. Left with a kernel, or possible kernels, of creative expression after following this process of elimination, the court's last step would be to compare this material with the structure of an allegedly infringing program. The result of this comparison will determine whether the protectable elements of the programs at issue are substantially similar so as to warrant a finding of infringement."*[65]

The fist step of the test, called "abstraction", requires a court to "dissect the allegedly copied program's structure and isolate each level of abstraction contained within it." The two extreme levels are represented by the actual program code (at the minimum level of abstraction) and by "an articulation of the programs ultimate function" at the highest level of abstraction.[66] The second step is that of "filtration", which "entails examining the structural components at each level of abstraction to determine whether their particular inclusion at that level was 'idea' or was dictated by considerations of efficiency."[67] In other words, at this stage the merger doctrine is applied, along with *scenes à faire* doctrine (see below). Only in the last step, "comparison", is the issue of substantial similarity addressed, in an examination of the parts that survived the filtration step, to determine "whether the defendant copied any aspect of this protected expression, as well as an assessment of the copied portion's relative importance with respect to plaintiff's overall program."[68]

B. MERGER DOCTRINE

According (to remain in the field of software) to Baystate v. Bentley (1996)[69] under the merger doctrine, protection is denied to expression that is inseparable from the ideas. Similarly, when there are "only a few means

---

[65] Id., 706.

[66] 1992 WL 139364 at 13.

[67] 1992 WL 139364 at 14.

[68] 1992 WL 139364 at 19.

[69] Baystate v. Bentley, 946 F.Supp. 1079 (U. S. District Court, D. Massachusetts. Baystate Technologies, Inc., Plaintiff, v. Bentley Systems, Inc., Defendant. Civil Action No. 96-40196-NMG. Dec. 6, 1996).

of expressing an idea", copyright protection is denied to these expressive means. In other words, "[t]he doctrine's underlying principle is that '[w]hen there is essentially only one way to express an idea, the idea and its expression are inseparable and copyright is no bar to copying that expression.'"[70] Also notice that part of the literature[71] criticized the merger doctrine as an excessively restrictive reading of the broader idea/expression dichotomy. For instance, Karjala[72] stressed that this doctrine should not be reversed and used to say that anything that may be expressed in more than one way deserves copyright protection.

If a philosophical parenthesis is allowed, not applying the merger doctrine would violate the "Lockean Proviso" – frequently recalled by Nozick and other libertarians –, concerning property (obtained by labour) on scarce resources: the property of one should leave "enough and as good" for others.[73] Hence, a given expression of an idea can be protected, but not to such an extent that protecting it significantly increases the cost of expression of other people.

C. *SCENES A FAIRE* DOCTRINE

The doctrine of *scenes à faire* – or 'scenes that must be done' – is based on principles which are similar to the ones underlying the merger doctrine, but it is more generous in taking into account external constraints, which are not necessarily immutable over time:

> "*In the computer-software context, the doctrine means that the elements of a program dictated by practical realities – e.g., by hardware standards and mechanical specifications, software standards and compatibility requirements, computer manufacturer design standards, target industry practices, and standard computer programming practices – may not obtain protection.*"[74]

---

[70] Altai, 982 F.2d 693 at 707-708 (internal quotations omitted).

[71] *See*, in particular, DENNIS S. KARJALA, "Copyright Protection of Computer Documents, Reverse Engineering, and Professor Miller", *19 University of Dayton Law Review*, 975 (1994).

[72] Id., 987-989. See also SHUBHA GHOSH, "Legal Code and the Need for a Broader Functionality Doctrine in Copyright", *50 Journal of the Copyright Society of the U.S.A.*, 71 (2003), 101—106.

[73] ROBERT NOZICK, *Anarchy, State, and Utopia*, Basic Books (1974); JOHN LOCKE, *Second Treatise of Government* (1690).

[74] Lexmark v. SCC (387 F.3d 522) at 535—536. Internal citations omitted. Other relevant cases mentioning the doctrine include Chamberlain Group, Inc. v. Skylink Techs., Inc., 381 F.3d 1178 (Fed. Cir. 2004), cert. denied, 544 U.S. 923 (2005); Sony, 464 U.S. 417; Computer Assocs. v. Altai, Inc., 982 F.2d 693 (2d Cir. 1992); Sega, 977 F.2d 1510.

It must be noted that the *scenes à faire* doctrine, according to some commentators, "lends itself to abuse".[75] Indeed, one has to be very careful not to read this doctrine in such a way as to penalize successful firms just because of their success. The problem is that, if an undertaking created a *de facto* standard and if the author owned some intellectual property rights to it, it would not be fair to tell him or her that this creation is no longer protected, precisely because it was so successful. Indeed, I share the scepticism of part of the literature about the opportunity of embracing such a doctrine, in particular because its effect could be reached through other doctrines and/or general principles. First of all, whenever the control over a *de facto* standard is also coupled with a dominant position in a "relevant market" (having the competition policy meaning of the expression), the exercise of intellectual property may entail "special responsibilities" under antitrust law. Moreover, and more generally, I submit that it is possible to deal with the need of accessing compatibility requirements and similar technical issues by just using merger doctrine (or directly adopting the idea/expression dichotomy).

D. FAIR USE

Fair use is a well-known US common law doctrine, also incorporated into the Copyright Act of 1976. It shields from copyright infringement and allows reproducing copyrighted materials by virtually any means, as long as the use of such materials is deemed "fair" and related to some purposes, as "criticism, comment, news reporting, teaching […], scholarship, or research" (but this listing is non-inclusive). According to 17 U.S.C. § 107, four non-exclusive factors should be considered in determining whether a particular use is a fair one: (1) the purpose and character of the use (including whether commercial or for non-profit or educational purposes); (2) the nature of the copyrighted work; (3) the amount and substantiality of the portion used (in relation to the copyrighted work as a whole); (4) the effect of the use upon the potential market for or value of the copyrighted work.

An application of the fair use doctrine will be needed, in order to deal with software interfaces, only as long as the interface under examination is protected *and* the use that is being made of this interface potentially infringes copyright (unless a fair use is found). Hence, in cases in which the idea/expression dichotomy tells us that a certain element is on the "idea side of the divide", it is not necessary to recur to fair use.

---

[75] See for instance TITUS, *Reverse Engineer Software: Is Japan Next?*.

Additionally, even if a given implementation is protected by copyright, one may read it (assuming one has access to the source code) and write down a specification, which may be abstract enough not to be considered a derivative work of the existing specification. In this case, once again, we do not need to resort to fair use. However, when one needs to perform several copies of the distributed object code of a piece of software in order to decompile and understand it (i.e. to perform reverse engineering), then a copyright object is copied and – without fair use (or an *ad hoc* exception) – the analyzer may be in trouble.

1. Risks in applying fair use to determine the legal status of interoperability information

Notice that fair use is so flexible that it may be prohibitively difficult to apply in a predictable way. Hence, it may lead to such a degree of uncertainty that – at the end of the day – recurring too frequently to fair use, which is essentially an *ex post* analysis that is very sensitive to the smallest details of each case, may ultimately harming the status of the doctrine itself. And, since I think that it is healthy for the copyright system to keep fair use as a "doctrine of last resort" – giving the possibility to avoid economically paradoxical effects of formal copyright rules – I suggest avoiding fair use where alternative tools are available.[76] Luckily, following the approach proposed in this paper, fair use is not a central doctrine in determining the legal status of software interoperability information.

Another significant problem of fair use (if used as a general tool to deal with API issues) is that applying the traditional tests (economically analyzed, for instance, by W. J. Gordon)[77] one could mistakenly end up saying that copying is allowed to the benefit of the producers of complementary products, but not of the producers of competing products.[78] That may happen, in particular, if we do not carefully avoid blurring the distinction between the direct product of decompilation and the use of the information obtained. In fact, I submit that fair use analysis

---

[76] See THOMAS F. COTTER, "Fair Use And Copyright Overenforcement", *93 Iowa Law Review*, 1271 (2008), 1312.

[77] WENDY J. GORDON, "Fair use as market failure: A structural and economic analysis of the Betamax case and its predecessors", *82 Columbia Law Review*, 1600 (1982). For references, see COTTER, *Fair Use And Copyright Overenforcement*.

[78] This result is also similar to the solution proposed by WEISER, *The Internet, Innovation, and IP Policy*.

should concern (only, or – at least – primarily) the activity of accessing the original API implementation, fairly copied, as a step in reconstructing a proxy of the original specification. Notice that this access phase does not typically involve any direct commercial use of its product. Instead, the reconstructed code is used "privately" and for purposes which are of study (and possibly of criticism and/or teaching). Indeed, the final product of the access phase may not be the proxy of the original source code, but a technical manual describing it: a reconstructed interface specification document. Then, we may shift to the reimplementation phase, where a completely new software code is written from scratch, but respecting the indications of the "manual", which may mandate – if technically needed – the reproduction of some lines of code or specific expressions. I will come back on these issues in § VI.

V. Investigating the legal status of interoperability information: the European setting

In 1989, W. R. Cornish[79] stressed that the legal status of interoperability information was a relevant issue that deserved a clear solution in the *Software Directive*, which was being discussed at the time. In particular, he appreciated what the Commission already stressed in the draft directive at article 1(3): "protection ... shall apply to the expression in any form of a computer program but shall not extend to the ideas, principles, logic, algorithms or programming languages underlying the program."[80] Unfortunately, that "unambiguous statement [was] at once clouded by a further sentence", specifying that "[w]here the *specification of interfaces* constitutes ideas and principles which underlie the program, those ideas and principles are not copyrightable subject matter". The problem was that, according to Cornish, "*[s]pecification of interfaces, as distinct from their implementation in code*, necessarily constitutes 'ideas and principles'." Instead, the wording of the Commission introduced the suggestion that this may not always be the case, creating "a puzzle which [could] only be resolved by courts in expensive litigation."[81] Despite the fact that the final wording of the Software Directive was different from the one commented by Cornish, we may say that he was right, indeed, since the puzzle he refers to is still to be solved.

---

[79] CORNISH, *Inter-operable Systems*, in particular at 392.
[80] See Id., 391.
[81] *Ibidem*. Emphasis added.

In fact, as I already showed, there is a way to reconcile the opinion of Cornish and the aforementioned wording of the Commission. Abstract interface specifications are always unprotected ideas, principles and methods, as Cornish argued. However, a given specification document may contain protected expression and it is normally protected by copyright, at least against straightforward literal reproduction, as the Commission implied. In any case, the final version of the *Software Directive* eliminates the specific ambiguous wording criticized by Cornish. In fact, article 1 ("Object of protection") recites at par. 2:

> *"Protection in accordance with this Directive shall apply to the expression in any form of a computer program. Ideas and principles which underlie any element of a computer program, including those which underlie its interfaces, are not protected by copyright under this Directive."*

Notice that the Directive speaks about "interfaces" in general, not "interface specifications", hence it is possible to read it as suggested by Cornish and as recommended in the paper at hand: implementations are protected, but not specifications (with or without accepting the additional qualification I proposed concerning abstract interface specifications and specification documents). Moreover, point 13 of the *Software Directive*'s Preamble also clarifies that this principle is a general one of copyright law, and it is stated just "for the avoidance of doubt". In other words, the Preamble recognizes the idea/expression dichotomy as an undisputed fundamental principle of copyright law also in the Europe Union.

However, ambiguity is probably increased in the final text of the Directive. Indeed, that text is perfectly compatible with the thesis of this paper, but it is also vague enough to be compatible with other readings. In particular, the word "specification" completely disappeared from the approved Directive, so that it is still technically possible to argue that there are cases in which interface specifications are somehow copyright protected (possibly also abstract interface specifications). It is probably legitimate to suspect that the exercise of political balancing performed by the Commission required some ambiguity to remain, and prevented the introduction of a clearer statement saying that "the expression of interface implementations may be protected by copyright, according to the general principles of copyright law, but ideas, principles and methods underlying interface specifications cannot be protected, so that the realization of an original interoperable interface implementation shall always be allowed." In any case, and despite the absence of such a clear statement, I argue that the *Software Directive* has to be read in this way and, to show that, I will start from the analysis of its article 6.

The first paragraph of article 6 of the *Software Directive* addresses software reverse engineering ("decompilation"), authorizing reproductions and translations of copyrighted programs, where "indispensable to obtain the information necessary to achieve the interoperability of an independently created computer program with other programs". The same article also provides several conditions to be met, in order to enjoy the decompilation "privilege": (1) the initial copy of the program to decompile must be legally owned by the reverse engineer; (2) the information necessary to achieve interoperability must not be already "readily available"; and (3) reverse engineering is "confined to the parts of the original program which are necessary to achieve interoperability".

Also the second paragraph of article 6 is interesting (and complex) to analyze. It states that:

> *"[t]he provisions of paragraph 1 shall not permit the information obtained through its application: (a) to be used for goals other than to achieve the interoperability of the independently created computer program; (b) to be given to others, except when necessary for the interoperability of the independently created computer program; or (c) to be used for the development, production or marketing of a computer program substantially similar in its expression, or for any other act which infringes copyright."*

In particular, and despite its incoherence with general copyright principles, this paragraph seems to imply that "raw information" and more abstract ideas and methods (like API specifications!) are forced to remain "confidential" if obtained thanks to the decompilation exception of article 6. Notice that this would impose disadvantage for decentralized and collaborative models of development, like the open source one.[82] Yet, I will not discuss further this specific issue here: for the moment, I will simply interpret article 6.2 following Samuelson and Scotchmer:[83]

> *"[t]he EU rule essentially requires each firm that wants to reverse-engineer to bear the full expense of decompiling the program on its own. This preserves the lead time of the firm whose program has been decompiled, but leads to more socially wasteful costs unless the software developer licenses interface information to foreclose the decompilation effort."*

---

[82] Open source projects, because of their inherent tendency to spread information, may present higher risks of potentially harmful distribution of (copyright protected) intermediate copies.

[83] SAMUELSON & SCOTCHMER, *The L&E of Reverse Engineering*.

I think that the limits imposed on the disclosure of the "raw information" obtained through decompilation are likely economically unnecessary and inappropriate. In any case, they do not change the legal status of software interoperability information, but just the regime under which this information may circulate, when it has been achieved through reverse engineering.

Finally, paragraph three (6.3) states that:

> *"In accordance with the provisions of the Berne Convention for the protection of Literary and Artistic Works, the provisions of this Article may not be interpreted in such a way as to allow its application to be used in a manner which unreasonably prejudices the right holder's legitimate interests or conflicts with a normal exploitation of the computer program."*

This is clearly a common principle to almost any jurisdiction. US courts interpreted similar principles as allowing not only "vertical (or direct) interoperability" (that is, interoperability with complementary goods, like another application for a given operating system), but also "horizontal (indirect) interoperability".[84] A similar interpretation would be confirmed by the Preamble of the Directive, where recital 21 clearly talks about "reproduction of the code and translation of its form [...] indispensable to obtain the necessary information to achieve the interoperability of an independently created program *with other programs*" [plural] and *not just with the decompiled program*.[85] A similar reading is also backed by the general interpretation of the Directive, proposed by the Commission (and confirmed by the Court of First Instance) in the recent Microsoft Case.[86]

Overall, I share the view of part of the literature,[87] according to which the European legal setting is fairly clear. Carefully considering article 6, one has to conclude that "Copyright [...] can't prohibit in any way independent implementations of the specifications themselves."[88] In fact, from a systematic reading of the Directive it is undisputable that the discussed article would be meaningless if it was not legitimate to use (in independently recreated implementations) the information obtained from

---

[84] In the US, see *Sony v. Connectix*, 203 F.3d 596, concerning a case in which "horizontal interoperability" allowed to play the same applications (games) on a different hardware.

[85] *Contra*, see, in particular, R. J. HART, "Interoperability Information and the Microsoft Decision", *28 European Intellectual Property Review*, 361--365 (2006).

[86] See *Microsoft CFI*, § 118 ff..

[87] See, in particular, VÄLIMÄKI, *Software Interoperability and IP*.

[88] Id., 4.

decompilation. So, the absence of a specific exception to *use* interoperability information could be read in two ways. Either there is an implicit (but quite obviously existent) exception allowing to do so (despite the existence of copyright protection on interface specifications). Or – much more likely – the legislator considered as obvious the fact that these pieces of information (or ideas/methods) where not protected at all. I favour the second explanation, also because copyright exception and limitation are typically expressly stated in civil law countries, and not doing so would have been at least imprudent at the European level.[89] In any case, we must conclude that using the interoperability information, obtained following the procedure detailed in art. 6, is legitimate in Europe.

A. ACCORDING TO THE COMMISSION, SEVERAL APIS ARE NOT INNOVATIVE IN THEMSELVES

When technologists try to explain intuitively the role of APIs, they frequently analogize these pieces of software to the *"gear teeth, levers, pulleys, and belts that physical machines use to interoperate"*.[90] Analogies could be misleading, but let me continue with this one: gear teeth, levers, and so on may be innovative in themselves, but it is much more frequent to find innovative machines, which are connected to other machines using fairly obvious re-implementations of more or less typical gear teeth, levers, etc. Apparently, according to the Commission (as I will try to show in the following paragraphs), the same thing is frequently true for APIs.

Taking into account the advice of the Microsoft Monitoring Trustee (established after the Commission's Decision of March 2004[91]) and of the Commission's technical advisors, TAEUS, Competition Commissioner Neelie Kroes stated[92] that: *"The Commission's current view is that there is no significant innovation in these protocols"* [meaning Microsoft client/server communication protocols]. I suggest that here "innovation", "novelty" and similar concepts are used in their patent law sense: these protocols are actually new – or, at least, not fully copied – and (at least in part) original (in the copyright law sense of the word, i.e. independently written without copying). However, these protocols are the typical

---

[89] See, for instance, ANNE LEPAGE, "Overview of Exceptions and Limitations to Copyright in the Digital Environment", *January - March UNESCO e-Copyright Bulletin*, 1--19 (2003), § *Closed systems of exceptions* (pp. 6 ff.).

[90] SAMUELSON, et al., *A Manifesto*.

[91] Commission Decision of 24 March 2004, Case T-201/04 (see also IP/04/38 and MEMO/04/70).

[92] Official press release IP/07/269 of 01/03/2007.

software object: there is nothing dramatically new in them, and ten developers would likely adopt ten similar (and still different and technically incompatible) solutions in devising both their specification and implementation.

To conclude, and assuming that the technical arguments quoted by the Commission are correct, there is no reason to concede intellectual property rights to Microsoft API specifications, which are just particular versions of other specifications, likely realized with the main goal (or – at least – the main effect) of being specific for Windows and allowing Microsoft to decide which software developer should gain full interoperability and which others should be "left a little bit behind". At the same time, Microsoft's implementations of these (more or less standard and only slightly modified) specifications are likely to be original code, protected by copyright and by trade secret law. And, obviously, intellectual property law is not preventing Microsoft from making a strategic use of trade secret (even if this may be an interesting issue for competition law).

VI. Vertical and horizontal access; transformative and substitutive uses

Both in discussing the appropriate interpretation of interoperability in the *Software Directive* and in analysing the US fair uses doctrine, I already incidentally touched upon a question: should we distinguish (for the purpose of determining the legal status of software interoperability information) between completely transformative and alternative uses on the one hand and uses which are transformative, but lead also to the creation of substitutive products on the other hand? In other words, should we distinguish between uses that need the original product as an inspiration to understand technical principles, methods and ideas, but then use these ideas to create a complementary product and other uses which directly lead to the discovery of the same ideas and principles, but then indirectly show the way to the creation of a piece of software which is competing with the decompiled one?

If we do not decompose the analysis in an access phase and a re-implementation phase, in the field of APIs the transformative v. substitutive uses distinction becomes a distinction between vertical and horizontal interoperability. The likely effect – again, if we do not decompose the access/re-implementation phases – is that we may end up, as some authors,[93] recommending to treat in different ways the same kind of reimplementation, depending on the competitive relationship between the original developer and the decompiler/re-implementer.

According to Weiser, in particular, there is a "critical distinction" between "horizontal and vertical access".[94] To be sure, I will not try to deny that it is generally true in economic terms, since horizontal access is equivalent to direct competition between two agents, while vertical access is equivalent to complementarity and no (or – at most – merely potential) competition. However, if we decompose the access and the reimplementation phases, we discover that the access phase starts from a protected API implementation and creates a new work, that is an API specification, and this is always a highly transformative use. To obtain access to the ideas and principles needed to write a meaningful API specification document, unfortunately, formal copyright infringements are performed and unauthorized derivative works are created. Hence, a copyright exception is needed. That said, the "final good" of the access phase (i.e. a specification document) is surely a new, original and highly transformative product. What is more, when we speak about the reimplementation phase, the wording "transformative uses" may be even misleading: non-infringing re-implementations of APIs are completely new immaterial goods.

The main argument of those who criticize the decompilation exception is an economic one and concerns the last step of the fair use test (or the last paragraph of article 6 of the Software Directive). According to this argument, decompilation to achieve horizontal interoperability should be forbidden, since this kind of decompilation results in the creation of a product competing with the decompiled work, hence "conflicting" with the right holder's ability to exploit his/her work and recoup his/her investments. Of course, it is true that decompilation may be a preliminary step to compete with an incumbent, but notice that it is not so obvious that avoiding this kind of competition is a rightholder's "legitimate interest". To illustrate this, think about a visually impaired person needing a Braille version of a book in order to read it. Using a PC and some other device to obtain the Braille copy of the book may very likely constitute a fair use in the USA and would likely deserve a specific copyright exception in civil law countries: such an exception would certainly respect the conditions imposed by the Berne Convention. That is true, in particular, if the

---

[93] See, in particular, WEISER, *The Internet, Innovation, and IP Policy.*

[94] See also K. W. DAM, "Some Economic Considerations in the Intellectual Property Protection of Software", *24 The Journal of Legal Studies,* 321--377 (1995).

visually-impaired person also bought an original copy of the book and if he acts according to several additional restrictions, including the fact that this Braille copy may not be reproduced or sold without the right-owner's permission. But what is relevant here is that the blind person of this example, having read the Braille version of the book, is not restricted in any way (whit respect to what would happen with an ordinary reader) in the uses that he/she can do of the ideas and methods learned reading the book. And this freedom is not altered by the fact that he/she needed to take advantage of a fair use or other copyright exception in order to access these ideas. Now, imagine that this person decided to write a ferocious and well-founded critique of the book, with the effect of almost annihilating its sales. Logically speaking, the critique may be a consequence of the possibility of reading the book, and this possibility has been granted through a fair use. Nevertheless, this market destructive "indirect effect" of the fair use allowing the person to read the book in the first place would likely not be taken into account by a judge evaluating the fairness of realizing the Braille version of the book.

VII. Elimination of free riding vs. the creation of economic monopoly

It is now time to compare the legal and technical findings of the paper with a sketched economic model of the legal protection of software works. The main idea of this part of the paper is that (1) copyright seems to be flexible enough to generate software innovation, in particular if it is seen as a tool devised (a) to impede free riding on up-front sunk costs of first comers, but (b) with correctives devised in such a way as not to multiply the sunk costs of late comers (in other words, copyright should not allow the first comer to force followers to have higher sunk cost than those he had to pay). Putting it in a different way, the first comer should have a fair chance of recovering its sunk costs of expression, but no or very limited possibilities of making a strategic use of copyright to increase the cost of expression of the followers. In this setting, (2) the traditional "idea/expression dichotomy" is especially useful in addressing interoperability problems, (a) provided that one re-declines this idea in software markets under a "specification/implementation dichotomy": (b) merger, scenes a faire and fair use doctrines may provide additional tools to fine-tune copyright (under the approach of point 1-b).

I will start from the idea that the typical condition for an efficient market to work is not that producers are able to appropriate the entire social benefit generated by their activity. Of course, such a condition has an interesting property: it ensures that – in a static setting – each and every socially profitable investment is performed. However, it does not consider the huge transaction costs generated by a capillary system of exclusive powers, able to extract the entire surplus generated by a given innovation. What is sufficient to have an efficient market is that investors are able to recoup their costs (taking into account risk), as long as consumers appreciate their products. Obviously, in a market in which there are investments and fixed costs, this condition cannot be respected by the equality among price and marginal costs. Instead, it is verified when gross profits are equal to sunk costs.

As long as reverse engineering is not prohibitively difficult and/or hindered by the law, coupling copyright (preventing literal copying and other form of parasitism) and trade secret (giving limited but significant protection to some categories of innovations) could create a structure of incentives working as a quasi-liability system in the field of software interfaces.[95] This system avoids two polar and opposite risks of a patent-like systems. On the one hand, rightholders cannot block subsequent innovation for strategic reasons and self-help remains an available solution also in cases in which transaction costs (frequently increased by strategic behaviour and/or asymmetries of information) would have prevented the working of a market. On the other hand, significant incremental innovation, which would not qualify for patent protection, is still protected against easy and cheap appropriation from third parties. A quotation from Prof. Reichman's seminal 1994 article may be useful in clarifying the role of trade secret as a stimulus for innovation:

> *Legal theorists have particularly underestimated the important role of trade secret laws [...] in mediating between formal intellectual property regimes and free competition. These laws [...] do require would-be competitors to extract an innovator's undisclosed know-how by proper methods of reverse engineering. [...] Second comers who cannot extract valuable undisclosed information by proper means or independently reach similar solutions must acquire the unpatented know-how through licensing agreements with innovators. Either way, these legal requirements normally provide those who develop unpatented, noncopyrightable innovation with a period of natural lead time in which to recover their*

---

[95] *See* J. H. REICHMAN, "Legal Hybrids Between the Patent and Copyright Paradigms", *94 Columbia Law Review*, 2432 (1994).

investments while establishing their reputations as producers of quality goods.[96]

In fact, I have to stress that Prof. Reichman does not believe (or, at least, did not in 1994) that trade secret is likely to work as described above in the field of software. Indeed, in this and in similar fields, Prof. Reichman thought that innovation is too "near to the surface" of products and risks being easily appropriated, so that the protection offered by secret would be insufficient. Hence, he proposed that the law should reinforce the natural lead-time of innovators, exposed to an excessively cheap reverse engineering.[97] That having been said, and despite the fact that this influential article provided an impressive theoretical analysis, I suggest that it was slightly less well-grounded in terms of empirical and technical evidence. Indeed, there are no elements to think that reverse engineering in the field of software is so cheap that it is likely to create market failures. Moreover, the law already reinforced significantly trade secret in the software field, limiting decompilation in various ways. Hence, I submit that "technology copyright" does create the kind of quasi-liability rule that Prof. Reichman described as competitively healthy.

I acknowledge that adopting the interpretation of APIs' legal protection proposed in this paper may seem to largely disregard incentives to realize interfaces. Yet, I already mentioned that, because of the cost of reverse engineering software, there is actually a quite broad scope for the licensing of API specification documents (typically under non-disclosure agreements). The kind of incentive to create that comes from the possibility of licensing specification documents is something similar to a liability rule. In other words, licensing API specifications is equivalent to "selling" (substitutes of) the reverse engineering activity needed to discover interfaces. Moreover, even assuming that reverse engineering would be so simple as to destroy direct incentives to innovate (which is an absurd assumption at present), alternative sources of incentives to the realization of good interfaces abound. Actually, the majority of advanced two-sided models concerning software platforms (i.e., the kind of programs that typically expose more interfaces) suggest that controllers try to subsidize developers of complementary software;[98] this implies that there is actually a strong incentive, in order to maximize the value of a

---

[96] Id., 2438—2439. See also 2440—2441.

[97] Id., 2442.

[98] *See* J. C. Rochet & J. Tirole, "Two-Sided Markets: A Progress Report", *37 RAND Journal of Economics*, 645--667 (2006) (or J. C. Rochet & J. Tirole, *Two-Sided Markets: An Overview*, IDEI Toulouse working paper (March, 2004)).

platform, to develop and give away for free high quality interfaces. Obviously, problems remain about competing software (i.e. horizontally interoperable software), but here an empirical example may be useful. After all, several open source software are perceived as being of very high quality – in some cases even better than their commercial counterparts – but this does not allow commercial firms to develop their one competing software at no cost (unless they distribute themselves as open source under the GPL or similar licenses). Why so, if knowing the source code of a competitor is enough to free ride on it? Probably simply because that is not enough at all, and well-written and developed software does make the difference, even when the ideas behind it are free to be taken.

Overall, the problem is mainly to choose what kind of costs one wants to pay in order to spur investments. For instance, the actual working of "technology copyright" prevents "incremental innovators" from taking someone else's software as a basis for writing new software and developers are continuously forced to "reinvent the wheel" (and/or to generate waste through reverse engineering).[99] Nevertheless, it is precisely in responding to these kinds of difficulties that copyright proved its flexibility. Indeed, a nice feature of the copyright paradigm is that it allows developers to easily (and cheaply) contract around potential market failures. In particular, the open source (and free software) movement – as Determann[100] already recognized – can be seen (also) as a response to the costs generated by copyright:[101] instead of going on reinventing the wheel every time, some developers decided to use copyright law to create a pool of code that they can freely build upon, as long as they keep contributing to the common.

VIII. Further dimensions

In this section, I touch on several points, which should be considered in order to provide more robustness to my tentative conclusion that copyright – coupled with trade secret and in an environment where reverse engineering is legitimate – may provide a (relatively) optimal tool of protection for software interfaces. In section A, I analyze the possibility

---

[99] See RICHARD R. NELSON, "Intellectual Property Protection for Cumulative Systems Technology", *94 Columbia Law Review*, 2674 (1994), 2676; MARK A. LEMLEY & DAVID W. O'BRIEN, "Encouraging Software Reuse", *49 Stanford Law Review*, 255--304 (1997).

[100] Id..

[101] See also STEPHEN M. MAURER & SUZANNE SCOTCHMER, *Open Source Software: The New Intellectual Property Paradigm*, NBER Working Paper No. 12148 (March, 2006), 4.

that contractual arrangement could empty of any meaning the careful balancing exercise performed in interpreting copyright law. Section B will discuss another important source of risk menacing to disrupt the aforementioned balance of interests: patent law, as currently applied to software.

A. CONTRACTUAL ARRANGEMENTS

The general finding of this paper about the appropriateness of protecting software interfaces through copyright and trade secret would have little or no empirical relevance if it were possible for copyright holders to use standard software licenses "contracting out" the possibility of accessing or using interoperability information. Indeed – in order to obtain access to interoperability specifications – one should usually become a licensee of the original software and accept the associated licenses. Hence, the licensor may impose on the licensee standard licenses (in particular "shrink wrap" and "click wrap" licenses),[102] which could be used to contractually limit the freedom to reverse engineer, replicate interface specifications and so on. Fortunately, there are several "interne antibody" of intellectual property law which may prevent some contractual limitations from being legally bounding. I will concentrate on copyright misuse[103] (or equivalent civil law approaches, if existent at all)[104] and preemption.

The basic idea behind copyright misuse can be understood in analogy with the following example: if you are a lock producer, your could make keys to open your locks containing your three-dimensional trademark (in the sense, that the trademark is part of the design of a "compatible" key for your lock). However, using trademark law to prevent independent technicians from copying your keys for end-users would risk being considered as a trademark-misuse (because you use your trademark to have a patent-like monopoly on the production of certain objects). In the same way, I suggest that there should be a finding of copyright-misuse if

---

[102] *See* CHARLES R. MCMANIS, "The Privatization (or "Shrink-Wrapping") of American Copyright Law", *87 California Law Review*, 173--190 (1999).

[103] *See* K. JUDGE, "Rethinking Copyright Misuse", *57 Stanford Law Review*, 901--952 (2004). *See also*, for a much more synthetic review of the doctrine, JACQUELINE LIPTON, "The Law of Unintended Consequences: The Digital Millennium Copyright Act and Interoperability", *62 Washington and Lee Law Review*, 487 (2005), 540—543.

[104] The possibility of finding, in civil law, a doctrine reproducing the effect of the common law (actually US) doctrine of copyright misuse is likely very low. Fortunately, the *Software Directive* explicitly preempts contracts forbidding reverse engineering.

you devised a copyrightable lockout code (like a "poem" used as "compatibility password") and then tried to use copyright law to prevent someone from realising a compatible program reproducing your lockout code.[105] Indeed, in the Atari case[106] the court of appeals recognized that several other courts had previously discussed a defense of copyright misuse, in analogy to the well-established patent misuse defense, and even mentioned that "[a]lthough it has yet to apply the copyright misuse defense, the United States Supreme Court has given at least tacit approval of the defense". However, the court concluded that "[i]n absence of any statutory entitlement to copyright misuse defense, defense is solely equitable doctrine".

In the European Union, article 9 of the *Software Directive* explicitly forbids any contractual limitation to software reverse engineering for interoperability purposes, so that "[a]ny contractual provisions contrary to article 6 [...] shall be null and void." In the US, the situation is far from clear. Prof. McManis,[107] for instance, is (moderately) favourable to a reading of US law accommodating for a Copyright pre-emption of anti-reverse-engineering clauses. McManis analogizes click-wrap and shrink-wrap licenses to an *ad hoc* level of protection for a given work, which is not create by state law, but which is almost equivalent to it, so that "§ 301(a) itself might preempt any effort to provide contractual protection against reverse engineering of a publicly distributed computer program, where the program would fail to achieve federal copyright protection against such reverse engineering because of the fair use provisions of § 107." The analogy between shrink- and click-wrap licenses and state law is discussed also by other authors, with similar conclusions.[108] Moreover, not only copyright, but also patent law could prevent some anti-reverse engineering provisions.[109]

B. MAY PATENT LAW (AS CURRENTLY APPLIED TO SOFTWARE) LIMIT INTEROPERABILITY?

The bulk of this paper focuses on copyright/author's rights, since this

---

[105] See Lexmark International, Inc. v. Static Control Components, Inc., 387 F.3d 522.

[106] Atari Games Corp. v. Nintendo of America Inc., 975 F.2d 832.

[107] MCMANIS, *IP Protection and Reverse Engineering.*

[108] *See* OTTOLIA & WIELSCH, *Legal Aspects of Modularization and Digitalization*, text accompanying f.n. 286—292.

[109] See Bonito Boats, Inc. v. Thunder Craft Boats, 489 U.S. 141 (1989), also quoted by MCMANIS, *IP Protection and Reverse Engineering*; SAMUELSON & SCOTCHMER, *The L&E of Reverse Engineering* and others.

is the main tool used to protect software innovation and because case law concerning interoperability focused on copyright violations. Indeed, the great majority of so-called "software patents" concern "software implemented inventions" and are actually not developed by software houses; instead, they apply to the software/hardware interaction or to software embedded in specific devices.[110] Nevertheless, the role of patents in protecting innovation achieved through software is growing and it is appropriate to analyse the possibility that patent law – as applied to software – may hinder interoperability.

In the US, the answer is probably yes, at least potentially. In fact, at least for "pure software patents"[111] interoperability itself (or a procedure needed to achieve it) may be the object of a patent. The only qualification to this is that, as shown by the evaluation of Microsoft protocols performed by the European Commission and already discussed, not many communication protocols and APIs are likely to be innovative enough to involve an inventive step. Moreover – in several cases – it should be possible to "invent around the patent", at least if the claim has been kept appropriately narrow. At the same time, it is quite clear that – in this context – there may be significant inefficiencies, if low quality patents are granted in the field of software.[112] One of the most crucial problems in this field concerns how "abstract" patent claims are allowed to be. This issue is considered in particular by Bessen and Meurer 2008.[113] As the authors put it, "The distinguishing feature of an abstract patent claim is not that it covers a broad range of technologies, although that is often the case, but rather that it claims technologies unknown to the inventor."[114] In the field of software interfaces, I argue that granting patents covering any technique of implementation of a given specification – including techniques of implementation that the patent holder never thought about –

---

[110] According to some estimates, the software industry is granted only 5% of all software patents. *See* JAMES BESSEN & ROBERT M. HUNT, "An Empirical Look at Software Patents", *16 Journal of Economics and Management Strategy*, 157--189 (2007).

[111] Shemtov suggests that even decompilation could be hindered by pure software patents. See NOAM SHEMTOV, *Rethinking Entitlements in the Context of Decompilation of Computer Programs: A Market-Based Perspective*, Working paper presented at the 3 rd Annual Workshop on the Law and Economics of Intellectual Property and Information Technology, 5-6 July 2007, Queen Mary, University of London (July, 2007).

[112] ROBERTO DI COSMO, *Legal Tools to Protect Software: Choosing the Right One*, 4 UPGRADE, (2003).

[113] *See* JAMES BESSEN & MICHAEL J. MEURER, *Patent Failure*, (James Bessen ed., Princeton Univ. Press. 2008), ch. 9.

[114] Id., § IX.B.2.

could frequently border on the field of abstract patents. However, I do not think that this issue could be tackled at such an abstract level and – depending on the kind of technical problems that a specification addresses – it is reasonable to argue that software patents, at least in the US, may cover the entire specification (so that any implementation would be infringing).[115]

Even though the previous description concerned the US in particular, also in Europe, and despite significant existing limitations to the patentability of software "as such", it is not so easy to rule out the possibility that patents may significantly hinder interoperability. For instance, Välimäki[116] suggests that: "European copyright laws have a well-established principle that a single right owner cannot control interoperability information through copyright. Unfortunately patent law does not know such exception." In fact, I share these doubts, however I do not completely agree with the likelihood of major problems hindering interoperability, because of the absence of pure software patents in Europe, so that it is difficult to imagine a patent covering (and hence impeding) software interoperability. Here, it may be appropriate to distinguish between vertical and horizontal interoperability. In fact, where pure software patents are not admitted (and hence software 'per se' is not patentable), it is difficult to envisage how a software patent could limit vertical interoperability. In these cases, indeed, interoperability would normally not require the new software to implement the patented technology. However – in the case of horizontal interoperability, including cases in which it is important to read a common file format – it may be the case that there are problems in re-implementing the necessary features of a protected software, without violating a patent on a software related invention. Finally, notice that the debated on the recently rejected proposal of European Directive on software-implemented inventions did not help in significantly clarifying these doubts.[117]

---

[115] The US PTO does not require source code, nor detailed flowcharts, to be attached to applications concerning software. Hence, it is possible that a patent concerning interoperability would resemble much more an interoperability specification, than its implementation.

[116] See VÄLIMÄKI, *Software Interoperability and IP*, and VÄLIMÄKI & OKSANEN, *Patents on Compatibility Standards and Open Source*.

[117] See MICHAEL CHAPIN, "Sharing the Interoperability Ball on the Software Patent Playground", *14 Boston University Journal of Science and Technology Law*, 220 (2008), 235.

IX. Conclusions

The definition of the legal status of APIs and CPs comes from a balancing exercise concerning incentives to innovate – on one side – and constraints to subsequent derivative and complementary innovation – on the other. Despite the possibility of addressing some of these problems *ex post*, using competition policy, it is important to address this trade-off also in the initial stage consisting in the definition of intellectual property rights.[118] In this setting, the analysis performed in this paper allows for the drawing of some conclusions concerning the optimal scope of intellectual property protection of interoperability information.

First of all, it looks clear that APIs and CPs implementations are protected by copyright, as any other piece of software. This is economically sound: copyright protects first comers against complete free riding on their investments in writing source code.[119] However, this protection is relatively thin: it covers literal copying and mechanical modifications/translations, but it does not extend to ideas and methods. This is why I argue that abstract interface specifications are not copyright protected, no more than the contents of a math book, even if the book itself – as an interface specification document/manual – is protected against copying.

Moreover, the value of interface specifications is frequently related more to their strategic value than to their technical innovativeness. This is probably why, in practice, patent law does not seem to represent a major obstacle to software interoperability. And that is even truer in Europe, where the law prevents the patenting of software "as such" and hence makes it quite difficult to claim patent protection for software tools that are aimed at allowing the exchange of data between pieces of software, without any direct industrial application. That said, a patent-like protection for software interfaces could potentially disrupt the careful balancing between incentives to innovate and possibility of creating

---

[118] In fact, as is has been made clear in the Magill and IMS-Health antitrust European cases, poorly defined intellectual property rights are likely to push competition policy in the direction of an excess of intervention or of the definition of blurred rules. See also DREXL, *IMS Health and Trinko.*

[119] There are some decisions, like the Lexmark (387 F.3d 522) one, arguing that some pieces of software are not protected at all because of a broad interpretation of merger and '*scenes a faire*' doctrines: I think that this approach – even if yielding reasonable results in this case – is likely to set weak precedents and unclear legal standards.

interoperable products as I described in this paper. Hence, legislators are advised to maintain copyright and trade secret as the main tools used to protect software innovation, thus avoiding recurring to patent in a significant way.

The crucial points of the paper are the constant reference to the specification/implementation dichotomy and the clear distinction between an access (to interoperability information) phase and a reimplementation phase. I already discussed at large the consequences of the first distinction. But also the second distinction is critical, as only the access phase needs – in order to be insulated from copyright liability – to enjoy a precise copyright exception (statutorily provided or coming from fair use analysis), which is typically conditional on the absence of a significant negative impact of this access to the market for (or value of) the original program. In that way, one can avoid the necessity of recurring to fair use or other "rules of reasons", which could be tempting for economists, but which could lead to excessive legal uncertainty. Instead, the interpretation of copyright that I propose, not discriminating between horizontal and vertical access, is not only coherent with both the prevalent US case law and the EU legislation (as interpreted by the Commission), but it is also compatible with a sketched economic model of software markets. In such a model, copyright is an appropriate tool to impede free riding on up-front sunk costs of first comers, but it also embeds appropriate correctives, devised in such a way not to increase development costs of late comers.

In March 1993, Prof. Miller argued[120] that – more than fourteen years after their deliberation – CONTU's recommendations were still essentially correct and that the copyright regime was flexible enough to deal with computer programs.[121] Indeed, it seems to me that it is still meaningful to ask oneself if there's "anything new since CONTU". In the meantime, a network of judicial decisions (in particular in the US) and scholarly articles adapted traditional copyright law to software. Already at the time of Miller's article, it was evident that copyright's flexibility and usefulness had played a significant role in allowing the development of the software industry. Today, there are even more reasons to think so, including the development of the open source model of software development.

Overall, copyright and trade secret (as long as reverse engineering is allowed) provide a pro-competitive environment for software innovation, being able to accommodate both the traditional model of software

---

[120] MILLER, *Is Anything New Since CONTU?*.
[121] Id., 980-981 and 1073.

development and the new open source model. Legislators and scholars should be aware of that and should become aware of the reasons for which the current system is actually working. These reasons rely on copyright and on the circumscribed, but significant, possibility of free riding on technical ideas that it entails (positive externalities or technological spillovers, if you like). For the same reasons, policymakers should also avoid to disrupt the current system, as may happen by offering excessive protection to ideas and algorithms (including interface specifications) through software patents or through an excessive expansion of copyright toward the protection of ideas.

All that said, I think that the conclusions of this paper should derive more immediately from a well-designed copyright law: a clear-cut statement that interface specifications needed to achieve interoperability are never protected by copyright would be very useful in order to eliminate residual legal uncertainty in software markets.

Let Them Be Peers: The Future of P2P Systems and Their Impact on Contemporary Legal Networks

Ugo Pagallo
Faculty of Law, University of Turin

I. Introduction

The subject of this paper – "the future of P2P systems and their impact on contemporary legal networks" – requires three preliminary elucidations.

First, it does not rely on any prophetic powers or divinatory commitments; rather, the aim is to draw attention to some major issues concerning today's P2P systems. By highlighting these problems, the idea is to specify possible developments and changes induced by technology.

Secondly, I look at file sharing application-systems and not at social networking on the Web 2.0. Peer production, among other things, has created and continues to raise new interesting cases in contemporary legal networks. Here, I only consider peer interaction mediated by P2P systems because this strict limitation allows me to focus on more precise targets.

Finally, the study of the impact of P2P systems on contemporary legal networks is not blind to the reciprocal interaction between technology and the law. On the contrary, I will stress how legislators and courts often shape (or try to influence) the evolution of technology. All in all, P2P systems are excellent examples for such a bidirectional connection between technical evolution and social environment.

Following these premises, this paper is presented in four parts.

The first part on "P2P and legal systems" is divided in three sections. In section A, I illustrate the way in which technology has changed contemporary legal systems in complex and often unpredictable manners, and how legislators (and courts) have responded to such transformations. In the case of P2P systems, the price of success has been high: a determined and even aggressive protection of copyright holders against "peer-to-peer" file sharing application-systems that make it easy for the Internet users to obtain items for free.

In section B, I examine this new crusade by looking at some well-known cases like *Napster*, *Grokster*, and *Elektra v. Baker* from 2008. The trend is such that some politicians in Washington (D.C.) like the Government Reform Committee Chairman, Henry Waxman (D-CA), Rep. Tom Davis (R-VA), and Rep. Paul Hodes (R-NH), have even argued the technology used in P2P systems represents a serious problem for national security!

In section C, I notice however that things are recently changing, at least, in Europe. In fact, P2P systems do not only concern matters of copyright, but of privacy as well. Copyright protection is not reason enough to carry out extremely invasive monitoring techniques. The European Court of Justice's decision in *Promusicae v. Telefónica de España* (C-275/06) shows that "a fair balance [has] to be struck between the various fundamental rights protected by the Community legal order."

Hence, by adopting this latter perspective, it is possible to address both threats and opportunities of P2P systems in a well-balanced way, so that today's issues and persisting problems help casting light on tomorrow's developments.

In part III, I explain why I disagree with scholars who claim that hubs or Super-peers are unessential to P2P systems inasmuch as these systems would be only distributed networks, that is systems where "authoritative nodes" may exist but are not necessary as in the Internet.

In part IV, I deepen some technical solutions which have been proposed and discussed by both legal experts and computer scholars, in order to cope with some of the most relevant issues on the political agenda.

The conclusion is that time has come to leave behind some exaggerations in the current debate: P2P systems are not a menace or risk that should simply be banned or shut down, and they are not the key to a new egalitarian paradigm that has to be encouraged as such. Rather, by analyzing the future of these systems it is important to insist on the mutual interaction through which technology is reshaping both legal concepts and their environmental framework, while political decisions influence or attempt to determine the development of technology. Following this fruitful third way, the aim is to show why it is so important to let peers be and evolve.

II. P2P and legal systems

A. THE PRICE OF SUCCESS

The ICT revolution has changed contemporary legal networks in, at least, three different ways.

First, technology has deeply transformed the approach of experts to legal information as it occurs, say, with documental legal informatics, e.g., information retrieval and legal databases.[1] Furthermore, computer science sheds new light on such traditional areas as jurisprudence and legislation insofar as electronic maps of their topological structure can be made, according to specific laws of informational distribution.[2]

Secondly, technology has induced new kinds of lawsuits, or has radically modified old forms. On one side, it is enough to mention some new types of offences such as computer crimes; on the other side, technology has also changed traditional rights such as privacy (1890) and copyright (1710), both turned most of the times into a matter of access, control, and protection over information in digital environments.[3]

Finally, technology has blurred conventional national boundaries as information on the Internet tends to have an ubiquitous nature that transcends traditional legal borders and questions the notion of the law as made up of commands enforced through physical sanctions. Spamming, for instance, is a good example: It is *par excellence* transnational and does not seem to diminish despite severe criminal laws (as the *CAN-SPAM Act* approved by the U.S. Congress in 2003).

This undeniable impact of the ICT revolution has however led to some misunderstandings: One misconstruction concerns the idea that technology is something neutral, another is that legislators (and courts) cannot influence the development of technology. As far as the first error is concerned, technology would only be a means for whatever end, regardless of good or evil; in the second case, technology would be too

---

[1] A good introduction in G. SARTOR, *Corso d'informatica giuridica*, vol. I: *L'informatica giuridica e le tecnologie dell'informazione*, Torino, Giappichelli, 2008.

[2] Cf. U. PAGALLO, "'Small world' Paradigm and Empirical Research in Legal Ontologies: a Topological Approach", in *The Multilanguage Complexity of European Law: Methodologies in Comparison*, edited by G. Ajani, G. Peruginelli, G. Sartor, and D. Tiscornia, European Press Academic Publishing, Florence 2007, pp. 195-210.

[3] Further details in U. PAGALLO, *La tutela della privacy negli Stati Uniti d'America e in Europa: modelli giuridici a confronto*, Milano, Giuffrè, 2008.

swift and powerful to be effectively limited by the slow pace of law-making and jurisprudence.

Yet, this picture is incomplete since it omits to stress how deeply technology modifies the ways in which scholars address most of their legal issues and, vice versa, how legal systems influence the architecture of digital environments. This is precisely what happens with copyright: Law-makers react both to changes and challenges brought on by technological evolution as they mould or try to shape such a development via the law and its applications. So, the more relevant a technology is in terms of innovation speed, transformation, and social impact, the more it is likely policy-makers and courts will intervene.

This straight correlation is just the legal price of technological success and it is confirmed by several cases involving privacy, computer crimes, and of course, P2P systems-related copyright issues.

Here, a brief account of this trend over the last ten years suffices: In 1998, the U.S. Congress approved the *Digital Millennium Copyright Act* (DMCA) and the so-called *Sonny Bono Act*; three years later, the European Parliament and the Council adopted the first EU directive on "copyright and related rights in the information society." Then, the U.S. Congress passed the *Consumer Broadband and Digital Television Promotion Act* in 2002, the *Family Entertainment Copyright Act* in 2005, and the *Net Neutrality Bill* in 2006. Meanwhile, the IPRED saga developed in Europe: the first directive on the enforced intellectual propriety rights is from 2004 (n. 48), and on April 25th, 2007, the European Parliament supported a new version (IPRED-2).

In a nutshell, this legal outline confirms the twofold process mentioned above: As technological progress reshapes key assumptions in legal arguments, legislators react to this by favouring certain technical and political choices over others. While technology transfigures the essence of traditional copyright issues – since there is no longer any theoretical difference between original and copy – law-makers have generally overreacted to this revolution. It seems that the second comma of art. 27 of the Universal Declaration of Human Rights – i.e., "the right to the protection of the moral and material interests resulting from any scientific, literary or artistic production of which he is the author" – simply prevails over the first one, stating "the right freely to participate in the cultural life of the community, to enjoy the arts and to share in scientific advancement and its benefits."

In order to explain this trend, let me go back to the realm of P2P systems: Indeed, these file sharing application-techniques were developed from the late 1960s onwards, but they became extremely popular only in the late 1990s, *et pour cause*, with the legal misadventures of Napster. Again, we witness the legal price of technological success.

B. COPYRIGHT CRUSADERS

The first important decision on copyright and P2P systems came in July 2000, when the U.S. District Judge Marilyn Patel granted the *Recording Industry Association of America* (RIAA)'s request to stop making copyrighted recordings available for download through Napster services. Although the San Mateo company did not store any information, such as the recordings on its own computers, it was declared illegal to provide the information of where the songs were available on the computers of the community logged on. In other words, it was not considered enough to claim that the DMCA grants immunity to ISP providers for what their customers do. As a matter of law, this kind of protection would not include "contributory infringers" as the District Court of Appeals confirmed in its own decision on Napster, in February 2001.

(Later on, I insist on how this wave of mandatory assessments suggested the next generation of P2P systems to adopt a more massively distributed way of spreading and exchanging information on the Internet. In fact, Napster's centralized architecture meant that operators of the central server used to index each peer's files and, hence, they could have intervened to stop copyright infringements pursuant art. 512 of the DMCA. For the moment, it is sufficient to stress the relevance of these first verdicts on Napster, insomuch as they confirm the abovementioned twofold process: Technological progress reshapes some key legal issues of contemporary networks while law-makers and courts react to this evolution by favoring certain choices over others.)

Four years later, in 2005, it was the turn of the U.S. Supreme Court in *MGM v. Grokster* to present P2P systems as Steamcast or Grokster, as a kind of technology that promotes the "ease of infringing on copyrights," so that its producers "can be sued for inducing copyright infringement committed by their users." Notwithstanding this unanimous holding by the Court, the legal consequences on further developments of P2P technology remained however unclear. Indeed, the Supreme Court justices were divided between the need to protect every technology "capable of substantial non infringing uses" as they declared in *Sony v. Universal City Studios* from 1984, and the necessity to provide remedies against new ways of copyright infringement.

So far, in the U.S., the problem remains to determine whether the software creates "shared files folders" making the very information protected by copyright "available for distribution" and hence illegally shared via those "files folders." In *Elektra v. Baker*, for example, a judge from the Manhattan federal court, Kenneth Karas, rejected the RIAA's "making available"-theory in January 2008, even if he admitted the sufficiency of the allegations of "downloading" and "distributing," thereby giving the RIAA an opportunity to reformulate its pleadings. Whereas Karas' idea is to grasp the whole issue with the legal hypothesis of "offering to distribute for purposes of redistribution," it seems more fruitful to note how the suit in *Elektra v. Baker* was based on a report of an Internet investigator who claimed to have detected the "shared files folders" which I presented above.

In fact, there is a second major legal issue, besides copyright, that involves P2P systems and their technological evolution: that is privacy. As it occurred with another highly controversial decision in the U.S. opposing an American ISP, Verizon, and the RIAA again, scholars have pointed out "how the privacy of Internet users participating in P2P file-sharing practices is threatened under certain interpretations of the Digital Millennium Copyright Act (DMCA) in the United States [as] a new form of 'panoptic surveillance' that can be carried out by organizations such as the RIAA."[4]

The thesis was confirmed in 2007, when the *Motion Picture Association of America* (MPAA) required (lawfully, according to federal judge Florence-Marie Cooper) the IP addresses of those connecting to TorrentSpy files via their service in the U.S. The MPAA had in fact filed a lawsuit against the popular P2P system, alleging that the company violated copyright law by helping sharers find pirated movies.[5] The dispute then overheated when TorrentSpy accused the MPAA of hiring a hacker (by the way an ex TorrentSpy employee) in order to pilfer the company's trade secrets. Judge Cooper's interpretation, however, did not favour the European company: in the name of the *Wiretap Act*, the word "intercept" would only mean that someone must intentionally intercept e-mails and not just acquire them from an electronic storage. Therefore, since TorrentySpy used to store e-mails on its server before they were copied and forwarded to the hacker's e-mail account, the result was that no interception would have occurred! Forced to enable server logging

---

[4] The thesis in F. S. GRODZINSKI, H. T. TAVANI, "P2P Networks and the Verizon v. RIAA case: Implications for personal privacy and intellectual property", *Ethics and Information Technology*, 7, 4, pp. 243-250.

[5] Cf. U. PAGALLO, *La tutela della privacy, o. c.*, pp. 230-231.

against its own privacy policy, it is not a surprise that TorrentSpy, whose servers are physically located in the Netherlands, announced its decision to stop doing business in the U.S. on August 27th, 2007.

C. PRIVACY CONCERNS AND FUNDAMENTAL RIGHTS

Legal troubles of P2P systems with both copyright and privacy issues illustrate some peculiarities of the U.S. legal system as well as some key differences between U.S.- and EU-law. If a property standpoint prevails in the former legal system, privacy is widely considered as a fundamental right in the latter, proclaimed both by the European Convention from 1950 and the EU Charter of Nice in 2000, let aside the specific constitutional traditions of Member States. In order to understand this hiatus and, thus, the different ways in which legal frameworks affect the evolution of technology, it suffices to recall two cases recently discussed in Europe.[6]

The first one took place in Italy in 2006, when a German music company, Peppermint, commissioned the Swiss firm Logistep to raise the IP addresses of people making available copyrighted works by means of P2P systems on the Internet. On the basis of the claim that Peppermint would have been the only right holder, the plaintiff required a section of the Tribunal in Rome to obtain both the "real addresses" and names of 3000 suspected illegal file sharers from the involved ISPs. At first, judges granted the request so that three thousands letters were sent by a lawyer from Bozen to the indicted P2P users, asking them for EUR 330 in order to settle the case and avoid any further inquiry. (In this way, Peppermint would have received cash worth almost ten times its own annual revenues...) Later on, in April 2008, the Bar Association of Paris interdicted a lawyer who sent similar letters to French P2P users. However, even the Tribunal in Rome changed idea: In fact, on June 16th, 2007, it declared that spying citizens on the Web in order to guarantee the protection of alleged copyrights holders pursuant articles 13, 23, and 37 of the Italian "code of privacy" (ICP) as well as articles 2 and 15 of the Italian Constitution, was illegal. Neither articles 8 and 9 from D-2004/48/EC, nor the exceptions from articles 3.2 and 13 D-1995/46/EC, could eventually legitimate such a violation of P2P users' privacy.

Yet, there is another important ruling that confirms the relevance of data protection laws in deciding lawsuits against P2P file sharing systems. The case is *Promusicae v. Telefónica de España*, decided by the European Court of Justice on January 29th, 2008. According to the judges in

---

[6] More details in U. PAGALLO, *La tutela della privacy, o.c.*, pp. 232-234.

Luxembourg, the EU law does *not* require Member States to lay down "an *obligation to communicate personal data* in order to ensure effective protection of copyright in the context of civil proceedings." In addition, the Court warned that, when transposing directives into national legal systems, Member States must "take care to rely on an interpretation of them which allows a fair balance to be struck between the various fundamental rights protected by the Community legal order."[7]

The ECJ decision, however, is problematic for the following reasons.

First, it does not mean that a national provision is incompatible with EU law because it obliges ISPs to disclose the identities of their subscribers for alleged violations of copyright law.

Secondly, the final output of such a "fair balance to be struck between the various fundamental rights," protected by any western-like legal order, is far from clear.

Even so, the ruling has the merit of highlighting that P2P systems do not only involve private claims on copyright infringements, but also privacy concerns about data protection in digital environments. Whereas legal scholars in the U.S. still discuss the possibility to ascertain whether P2Ps are a technology capable of substantial non infringing uses, it is clear that, at least in Europe, such a copyright protection must go along with the fair respect of P2P users' personal data. Although these systems have become infamous as file sharing applications that make it particularly easy for users to access copy(right)-protected files for free, the problems arisen cannot be resolved simply by banning this technology from campuses, schools, military areas, and the like. Indeed, you need not be an advocate of this technology or of Yochai Benkler's ideas on "peer production" to recognize that people are creating, via P2P systems, brand new ways of producing and distributing goods via networks that are of cooperative nature and that are highly decentralized;[8] that is, networks that have been embraced even by colossuses like IBM. So, it is time to show why it is important to let them be peers.

III. Theoretical perspectives: a topological approach

The new generation of strongly decentralized and encrypted P2P architecture that provides plausible anonymity for its members, is actually

---

[7] E.C.J., Case C-275/06, *Promusicae v. Telefónica de España*, 2008/C 64/12, § 70.

[8] On the very notion of "peer production" see Y. BENKLER, *The Wealth of Networks. How Social Production Transforms Markets and Freedom*. New Haven, CT., Yale University Press, 2005.

producing new problems and original forms of uncertainty, compared to those deriving from the first generation of weakly decentralized systems in which the origin and destination of information could be traced with relative ease. However, the sophisticated post-Napster generation – from Gnutella's unstructured P2P system to KaZaA's decentralized one – should not be criminalized. Despite numerous problems like security and privacy, copyright and connectivity issues, and the free riding phenomenon, P2P systems offer means for optimizing the distribution of information in complex social networks and they have surpassed the Web as the single most bandwidth-consuming application in many parts of the Internet today.

Thus, it is not hard to understand why it is crucial to address the topic of the future of P2P systems: It involves tomorrow's Internet as well as some of the main issues of contemporary legal networks. Let me start here with some theoretical remarks.

First of all, the horizontal architecture of P2P systems has created wider opportunities, both in scope and quantity, for the production and distribution of information on the Internet. Furthermore, scientific papers have shown the existence of spontaneous clustering of users, according to content which is distributed in P2P networks such as Gnutella or KaZaA. These "small world" properties have been detected via different methods as the "data sharing graphs",[9] or the "affinity networks".[10] The typical high clustering coefficients go along with short diameter networks thanks to the performance of hubs, as in other complex networks like the Internet, the Web, telephone graph calls, scientific quotations as well as the structure of both the U.S. Congress and the Swedish Parliament. Indeed, many complex networks present these very features of "small worlds" – high clustering, short diameter, and presence of hubs – because the distribution of information is spontaneously optimized in this way by complex systems.[11]

This effect of "rich gets richer" has suggested some scholars to claim that hubs or Super-peers are actually unessential as proper P2P systems would be only distributed networks, that is systems in which

---

[9] As in A. IAMNITCHI et al., "Small-world file-sharing communities" in the 23rd Conference of the IEEE Communications Society. Hong Kong, InfoCom, 2004.

[10] As in G. RUFFO, R. SCHIFANELLA, "A Peer-to-Peer Recommended System Based on Spontaneous Affinities", in Technical Report RT 96/06, Dept. of Computer Science, University of Turin, 2006.

[11] Cf. U. PAGALLO, Teoria giuridica della complessità. Dalla polis primitiva di Platone ai mondi piccoli dell'informatica: un approccio evolutivo, Torino, Giappichelli, 2006.

"authoritative nodes" may exist but are not necessary as it occurs with the Internet.[12]

However, the assumption rests upon utopian visions of pure egalitarian relationships, missing the crucial connection that emerges from a topological viewpoint: The "long tail" of information with the "rich gets richer"-effect – characterized by few nodes with very high values, and by most nodes with small degree – has to be seen in light of the clustering coefficients of the network. If these coefficients are low, we have a simple random network, i.e., a kind of network that illustrates some of the main criticism to current globalisation for hubs would have an anti-democratic nature as it was stressed by Barabási.[13] But, if these coefficients are high, local gathering of the nodes suggests that hubs which reduce the diameter of the network are indeed useful and justifiable. After all, what P2P systems obtain spontaneously on the Internet, is precisely what contemporary globalisation lacks: self organized-based clusters of users evolve together with hubs that shorten the diameter of the network.[14]

Besides, it is a matter of fact that most P2P systems *still* present hubs: Namely users who share a large amount of items, thereby playing a main role in providing connectivity. Such a "small world" feature of the system is in fact rather crucial as it has been exploited to obtain both new recommendation systems on the Web and new methods for attacking, say, copyright infringements. In the first case, by exploiting the high clustering coefficients of the network – its "affinity circles" along with its transitive properties – it becomes feasible to recommend information without requiring personal data as hubs can be seen as vectors for developing all the opportunities offered by this technology.[15] In the second case, hubs may be conceived, on the contrary, as targets in order to break these systems and, therefore, the relative emerging communities of digital

---

[12] This is the thesis of M. BAUWENS, *P2P and Human Evolution. Placing Peer to Peer Theory in an Integral Framework.* On line at http://integralvisioning.org/article.php?story=p2ptheory1 (the paper is from 2005; last checked on Nov. 26, 2008)

[13] The classical text is of course A.-L. BARABÁSI, *Linked. The New Science of Networks.* Cambridge, Mass., Perseus, 2003.

[14] Cf. U. PAGALLO, "'Small World' Paradigm in Social Sciences: Problems and Perspectives", in *Glocalisation: Bridging the Global Nature of Information and Communication Technology and the Local Nature of Human Beings*, edited by T. Ward Bynum, S. Rogerson, and K. Murata, e-SCM Research Center and University of Meiji, Tokyo, 2007, pp. 456-465.

[15] As shown by G. RUFFO, R. SCHIFANELLA, "Efficient Profit Sharing in Fair Peer-to-Peer Market Places", *Journal of Network and System Management*, 15(3), pp. 355-382.

affinity.[16]

The panoply of possible applications, pro or contra privacy, pro or contra copyright, does not imply, of course, that technology should be considered once again as "neutral," i.e., a means to obtain whatsoever end. Rather, it is crucial to insist on the mutual interaction through which technology reshapes both legal concepts and their own environmental framework, while political decisions influence or attempt to determine possible developments of technology. After some theoretical remarks on new feasible horizons of P2P networks, it is now necessary to look at their future through some more technical lenses.

IV. A fair balance for new developments

In the summer of 2008, Andrea Glorioso, Giancarlo Ruffo, and I were working on a chapter for a Springer book on P2P systems, analyzing the topic of their "social impact." In fact, while hundreds or even thousands of papers and dozens of meetings focus on technical developments of those systems, they rarely couple their research with the societal boundaries which limit or restrict the universe of possible extensions for such an evolution. What about the consequences of the Grokster case in light of that "fair balance" to be struck between fundamental rights, according to the ECJ ruling in *Promusicae v. Telefónica*?

Let me sum up some of our conclusions in the forthcoming chapter by considering new ways of sharing and distributing information in digital environments. I take into account three of these.

First, it is well-known how users, within P2P systems, turn out to be "servents," i.e., both clients and servers, or "prosumers," namely producers and consumers at the same time. Hence, boundaries between owners and providers, distributors and consumers, are becoming increasingly blurred as owners do not always coincide with providers. Therefore, technical solutions for the next generation of P2P systems will not only need to cope with dependable and scalable models, but also with plain revenues for owners and ways for sharing profits with providers or mediators such as banks, credit card companies, brokers, or certification authorities.

Second, the structured vs. unstructured P2P systems-debate should be

---

[16] As discussed in U. PAGALLO, G. RUFFO, "On the Growth of Collaborative and Competitive Networks: Opportunities and New Challenges", in *Ethicomp Working Conference 2007*, edited by S. Rogerson e H. Yang, Yunnan University, 2007, pp. 92-97.

reformulated in legal terms: At an overlay level, indeed, structured models seem preferable in order to prevent legal claims as liability for actions committed by users of these systems. Further, compared to centralized systems, such structured overlays do not seem to present single points of failure or problems of efficiency as the flooding search method adopted by Gnutella. Besides, they do not push legal responsibility over few super-peers as it occurs with KaZaA.

Third, privacy must be accounted for as well: Both anonymity and confidentiality in P2P interaction should be addressed at the lowest level of the technological platform since using the overlay network makes it possible to easily identify users inserting or storing information in the system. Authentication protocols as well as identification policies should provide for use of pseudonyms, OpenID, and ways of ciphering content. In this way it is safer to prevent not only unauthorized access to the information stored at the overlay level, but also legal liability of the content provider whom does not happen to be the source or the owner of that very information.

Of course, anonymity and confidentiality techniques, along with ways of encrypted communication, can be used by criminal organizations as well: All in all, it is still a debatable question whether OpenID solutions represent the ultimate way to solve these issues. In any case, it is certain that, among other things, 'al Qaeda has been using encryption since 1993, that is in their first and partially failed attack on the Twin Towers.[17]

Again, this does not mean technologies as P2Ps are something "neutral." On the contrary, it must be stressed how developments of such techniques are transforming key concepts of current legal and political debate – as it clearly occurs with notions of copyright, privacy, security, and the like – while law-makers, courts, and scholars attempt to tell fair and lawful practices from unlawful activities.[18]

Indeed, societal constraints determine the horizon of possible technological improvements which influence, at the same time, the evolution of contemporary legal networks. What is at stake, in both cases, is the way information is created, distributed, and shared in digital environments, according to that "fair balance" that must be struck

---

[17] Cf. A. ETZIONI, *How Patriotic Is the Patriot Act? Freedom versus Security in the Age of Terrorism*, New York-London, Routledge, 2004, p. 35.

[18] See again U. PAGALLO, *La tutela della privacy, o.c.*, pp. 10-12; and my paper "Ethics Among Peers: From Napster to Peppermint, and Beyond", in the *5th itAIS Conference on "Challenges and Changes: People, Organizations, Institutions and IT"* organized by the Italian Association for Information Systems in Paris, France, on Dec. 13-14, 2008, at http://eventseer.net/e/7947/ and to be published by Springer, 2009

between fundamental rights. From a technical viewpoint, it is essential to cope with issues of connectivity, availability of resources, and system performances in order to optimize flow of information within a given system. Hence, in the legal field, scholars should take into account the ways in which copyright has changed in a world of servents and/or prosumers, privacy has been deeply modified by new techniques of data protection and aggression in the informational age, security is challenged by new powerful tools of encryption and anonymity, up to the general remarks I did introducing part II.

Such a bidirectional connection between technology and the law, in which one affects or feedbacks the other in a continuous cycle, brings us back to some popular exaggerations in current debate. In the introduction, I recalled some politicians in Washington, who claim the only way to solve P2P problems would be to simply ban them or shut them down; in part III, on the contrary, I mentioned scholars who interpret these systems as a sort of new paradigm which should be encouraged as such. The need to tell fair from unlawful outcomes is a good way to leave behind such overstatements: It is time to draw some conclusions.

V. A normative conclusion

Throughout these pages, I have pointed out that debate on P2P systems can be summarized in two extreme positions. Some scholars, like Michael Bauwens, claim that P2P technology represents the key of a new paradigm insofar as sharing of information via strongly decentralized or distributed forms of coordination among geographically dispersed actors would be the paramount example of a deep social transformation that should be further encouraged.[19] Others, on the contrary, as Andrew Keen, stress risks and threats of new technologies and how they undermine vital elements of our societies for "digital piracy, enabled by Silicon Valley hardware and justified by Silicon Valley intellectual property communists [sic!] such as Larry Lessig, is draining revenue from established artists, movie studios, newspapers, record labels, and song writers."[20]

However, it is not so difficult to show limits and faults of both viewpoints.

On the side of the new paradigm-advocates, it is enough to mention

---

[19] See again M. BAUWENS, *P2P and Human Evolution, supra* note 12.

[20] A. KEEN, *The Cult of the Amateur. How Today's Internet is Killing Our Culture*, New York, Doubleday, 2007, quoted by D. TAPSCOTT, A. D. WILLIAMS, *Wikinomics. How Mass Collaboration Changes Everything*, London, Portfolio (Penguin), 2008, p. 273.

some of the serious problems afflicting P2P technology as security and privacy threats, copyright claims, issues of connectivity, availability of resources, and, to be pessimistic in some cases, even the collapse of the system.

On the side of P2P censors and opponents, vice versa, it should be stressed both the vitality and strength of these file sharing application systems that, optimizing how information is distributed and shared by their peer users, have created wider opportunities in digital environments.

In any case, it is not a simple matter of equalizing the exaggerations of both sides: On the contrary, my thesis is that most of the challenging issues come from the latter side for a couple of reasons.

The first point is cynical: Most of the times, critics and detractors of P2P systems are not simply scholars but powerful politicians and lobbyists, who have played a major role in passing the increasing amount of law as those illustrated in parts I and II.

The second reason is theoretical: ideas sponsored by advocates of the new paradigm can be fairly confuted by experience, but the reverse is not true in case of a ban. Actually, interventions for reducing potential risks of P2P systems would be carried out until the thesis is finally proven to be false. Nevertheless, full validation of that thesis, i.e., P2P systems are too risky so they should be banned, cannot be satisfied due to the early imposition of that ban![21]

So, how can we prevent such a deadlock? How can we convince P2P detractors that the main task is not to shut them down but, rather, to further develop them?

One way is to remind policy-makers of the real essence of an open society, say, in the wake of Karl Popper, Friedrich Hayek, or according to supporters of contemporary digital openness as Lawrence Lessig.[22] Still another possibility is to insist on the strict link P2P technology has with open source approaches, peer production, and collaborative models, which are transforming today's economy and social relationships.[23] In this latter case, it is not hazardous to predict how prohibitionist legislations will only have a short breath, while in the former case it is likely that the next

---

[21] See U. PAGALLO, "Something Beyond Technology: Some Remarks on Ignorance and Its Role in Evolution", in *Living, Working and Learning Beyond Technology*, edited by T. W. Bynum, M. C. Calzarossa, I. De Lotto e S. Rogerson, Tipografia Commerciale, Mantua, 2008, pp. 623-631.

[22] Cf. L. LESSIG, *The Future of Ideas. The Fate of the Commons in a Connected World* [2001], New York, Vintage Books, 2002.

[23] An overview in Ch. ANDERSON, *The Long Tail. Why the Future of Business Is Selling Less of More*, New York, Hyperion, 2008.

crucial legal issue would be freedom of research.

(In fact, another way to grasp the point is to reconsider it via an evolutionary approach. That means, in informational terms, that any attempt to adapt to the environment has to reduce its complexity, e.g., the aim of P2P systems to avoid the noise while optimizing the distribution and sharing of information on the Internet. But, in doing so, it is still an open question whether such informational reduction enriches the complexity of the whole or, rather, diminishes it. For example, it is obvious that P2P opponents think these systems fall within the latter case as it is confirmed by hypotheses of copyright infringement and threats to creativity and innovation which deserve to be shut down. Yet, there is a lot of evidence that shows how P2P systems do improve the informational complexity of the whole: let aside means of distribution and sharing, think of all the old songs people discover on the Web that even their copyright holders had forgotten in their catalogues! Therefore, what is required in order to cope with the undeniable problems of P2Ps is not to shut them down. Rather, further research is needed: Q.E.D.)

So, the future of P2P systems can be summarized in three final remarks.

First, it is quite likely that the single most bandwidth-consuming application of the Internet will be increasingly improved by experts, trying to resolve issues like availability of resources, connectivity, the free riding phenomenon, and the overall system performance. From this viewpoint, you need not follow Friedrich Hayek's thesis on the complexity of *cosmos* and how spontaneous orders overrule human plans (*taxis*) to foresee the shortcomings of attempts to stop both the economical and sociological trends mentioned above.

Second, the future of P2P systems has to be considered in connection with the necessary restraints imposed by a (wise) set of legal rules as discussed in this paper. While changing the very way in which scholars debate on some crucial topics as copyright, privacy, or security, the evolution of P2P systems is entwined with new forms of intending what is right (to information) in digital environments. Once again, against the short-minded motives of P2P opponents, it is more a matter of research and scientific evidence than of ideology.

Third, this evolution highlights the mutual feedback between technology and the law, i.e., the thread of Ariadne in this paper and object of a conclusive remark. The state-of-the-art in today's research is not able to predetermine, with any likelihood, the mutual conditioning of P2P systems and the key legal issues dealing with them. However, from the normative viewpoint, what we ignore today also teaches us how to construct the work of tomorrow. Despite threats and risks of P2P systems, significant evidence suggests that this technology enriches human interaction by opening ways of sound collaboration, creative relationships, and participation "in the cultural life of the community." In the name of the Universal Declaration of Human Rights, we should therefore let them be peers.

Digital libraries and Silent works

María J. Iglesias
Centre de Recherche Informatique et Droit, Facultés Universitaires Notre-Dame de la Paix, Namur, Belgium

The natural destiny of a work is the public. Most intellectual creations, at least those which have been published, embody a discourse to be transmitted to the public. But there are some situations where copyrighted works are, because of the very copyright, obliged to remain in silence. Sometimes it is impossible to identify the rightholder or, if identifiable, it is impossible to locate her. Without the possibility of gaining her permission, the so-called *orphan works* can be neither reproduced nor communicated to the public. Therefore the access to these works is severely restricted. But this is not the sole situation in which Copyright Law forces the works into captivity. Such a silence occurs again in relation to *out of print works*, to those works that are out of the market. These creations, sterile from a commercial point of view, also become sterile from the cultural one. Captivity may appear again in the case of other situations of abandonment, for example when rightholders do not reply to the request of potential users or when they have not published their works.

Our society is moving towards a knowledge society, towards a society where information is conceived as the main tool to create wealth. Production and access to knowledge then become an issue of public interest. In order to enhance the knowledge-based economy, the European Commission has adopted the Lisbon strategy and, as a tool to implement some of its goals, the Digital Libraries Initiative (DLI). The DLI aims to make the European cultural heritage easier and more interesting to use online for work, leisure and/or study. Among the legal challenges identified by the DLI is that connected to the use of two kinds of silent works: orphan and out of print works. More recently, the Green Paper also refers to the problem of orphan works. Silent works are clearly on the Copyright Agenda.

Needless to say that Digital libraries have a key role in preserving the voice of copyrighted works and giving access to a very relevant part of our cultural patrimony. In the cases mentioned above, the *copyrights* impose a mandatory silence justified on exclusive rights, on the autonomy of will. But this silence cuts short preservation and access to DL projects and increases the risk of a black cultural hole, without providing any benefit to the rightholders or society.

At the European and national levels, policymakers are discussing *ad hoc* solutions to some silent work situations. This paper will examine the main proposals. It will also report on other mechanisms which, even if not intended to solve the silent works problem, may in practice reduce its consequences.

The problem of silent works is, without a doubt, a problem of market failure having the perverse effect of the underutilisation (even the no-utilisation at all) of copyrighted work. Any solution to alleviate it requires, once again, a reflection exercise on the rationalities of the copyright system and on the best way of configuring exclusive rights. Most of the proposals dealing with the silent works problem neither offer an inclusive solution nor facilitate the running of DL projects. This paper proposes some basis for an inclusive system that might permit the rescue of silent works by digital libraries.

I. Introduction

The natural destiny of a work is the public. Most intellectual creations, at least those that have been published, embody a discourse to be transmitted to the public. But there are some situations where copyrighted works are, because of *copyright*, obliged to remain in silence. The most obvious situation is that of orphan works, which occurs when it is impossible to identify or locate the rightholder. Without the possibility of getting her permission, these works can be neither reproduced nor communicated to the public. Therefore, their role in the public sphere is drastically damaged. Such a silence surfaces again in relation to out of print works, to those works that are out of the market. It might be said that an out of print work is an abandoned work.[1] Unlike orphan works, the

---

* This article has been prepared as a result of two contributions made by the author for two international conferences. The first: the "COMMUNIA conference on Public Domain in the Digital Age", organised by the COMMUNIA project (The European thematic network on the digital public domain: http://communia-project.eu) and celebrated in Louvain-la-Neuve, on the 30th June and the 1st July 2008. The second one: ""The future of..." Conference on Law & Technology" (http://www.one-lex.eu/futureof/), organized by the InfoSoc Working Group in conjunction with the Law department of the European University Institute, and hosted in Florence, on the 28th and 29th October 2008. I would like to thank the organisers and especially the public in both Conferences for their comments on the two presentations. They have been taken into account for the preparation

rightholders are known and even locatable, but they do not show any immediate interest in exploiting their works. Since the copyright on these works persists, and will persist for the life of the author plus 70 years[2], digital libraries cannot digitise or make the works available to the public. Therefore a sterile work from a commercial perspective also becomes a sterile work from a cultural one. Captivity may appear again in the case of other abandonment situations, for example when rightholders do not reply to the request of potential users. According to the applicable legislation, the rightholder has the right not to answer. Her silence is equivalent then to a negative response. Silent works may also refer to unpublished items, to works which, in some cases, may not have even been intended to be a *work* and contribute to the public sphere. Such is the case of personal letters and diaries. Unpublished material may have an inestimable value for future generations. All these situations become more complicated when dealing with works of multiple authorship: when authors, artists and other copyright holders retain their diverse bundle of rights over a single work. The silence or unjustified negative of one of them may cause the total silence of the copyright work.

Although the practical importance of the problem has not yet been assessed[3], it could be said that the existence of silent works more than an exceptional situation is the general rule. The estimations contained in the Gowers Review point to this conclusion. Here, it is suggested that 40 per cent of all printed works are orphan works and that only 2 per cent of all works protected by copyright are commercially available.[4] On the other hand, in the Report on Distance Learning, the US Copyright Office acknowledges that, in addition to the difficulties relating to the location of copyrightholders, the main difficulties in obtaining permission for the use

---

of this paper which, however, is still a *work in progress*. Further comments and suggestions will be extremely welcome (maria-jose.iglesias@fundp.ac.be).

[1] Vid. D. KHONG, "Orphan Works, Abandonware and the Missing Market for Copyright Goods", *International Journal of Law and Information Technology*, 2007, vol. 15, n. 1, p. 57-58.

[2] Art. 1, Directive 2006/116/EC of the European Parliament and of the Council of 12 December 2006 on the term of protection of copyright and certain related rights (codified version), OJ L 372, 27.12.2006, p. 12–18.

[3] S. V. GOMPEL, "Unlocking the potential of pre-existing content: how to address the issue of orphan works in Europe", Draft: July 2007 (article published in *International Review of Intellectual property and Competition Law*, 2007, n. 6 p. 669-702), p. 7, accessible on http://www.ivir.nl/publicaties/vangompel/IIC_2007_6_orphan_works.pdf; and Copyright Office, *Report on Orphan works*, 2006, p. 92.

[4] A. GOWERS, *The Gowers Review of Intellectual Property*, December 2006, p. 69-70. Accessible on http://www.hm-treasury.gov.uk/media/6/E/pbr06_gowers_report_755.pdf.

of copyrighted material in distance learning activities are long delays in response time, or no response at all, and unreasonable prices, terms and conditions.[5] Similar concerns have been reported by the Registers of Copyright on its Report on Orphan Works.[6] Therefore, most of the informational resources with the potential to model and influence our future society will be formed either by in-market goods-works or by public domain items. The so called silent works are thus restrained from feeding the public sphere.

The silent works problem is not new. Orphan and out of print works have always existed. Nevertheless some phenomena have contributed to make the problem more acute and to gain the attention of users and policymakers. On the one hand, the development of Information and Communication Technologies (ICTs) has facilitated new means of creation[7] and dissemination. Moreover, new ICTs offer valuable tools for facilitating the preservation of copyrighted works and even the very existence of digital library projects. On the other hand, the intangibility and ephemeral nature of new digital copyrighted works, the lack of information on ownership of the works circulating on the net –and also on other media- and the utilisation of technological measures to restrict access, may represent a risk for the proliferation of future silent situations, in particular concerning digital goods. The expansion of copyright protection and terms has also contributed to this silence. Changes to Copyright Law during recent years have resulted in an over protection of copyright works or subject matter. More and more works are copyright protected, while less and less works are passing to the public domain.[8]

In most of the situations mentioned above the will of the right holder is unknown. The only certain information is that she has abandoned her

---

[5] Copyright Office, *Report on Copyright and Digital Distance Education*, 1999, p. 17 y p. 79 et seq. Vid also Appendix B: I. HINDS, *Marketplace for licensing in digital distance education*, p. 249-326.

[6]   Copyright   Office,   *Report   on   Orphan   works*,   2006, http://www.copyright.gov/orphan/orphan-report-full.pdf.

[7] J. COHEN, "Copyright, Commodification, and Culture: Locating the Public Domain", L. GUIBAULT AND B. HUGENHOLTZ (eds.), *The future of the public domain*, 2006, p. 121-166; and URS GASSER & SILKE ERNST, "From Shakespeare to DJ Danger Mouse: A Quick Look at Copyright and User Creativity in the Digital Age", *Berkman Center Research Publication*,   2006,   accessible   on http://papers.ssrn.com/sol3/papers.cfm?abstract_id=909223#.

[8] Copyright Office, *Report on Orphan works*, supra note 6, p. 23 and ss.; B. HUGENHOLTZ, M.M.M. VAN EECOUD, S.J. VAN GOMPEL ET AL., *The Recasting of Copyright & Related Rights for the Knowledge Economy*, 2006, p. 162 et ss.; and S. V. GOMPEL, "Unlocking the potential of pre-existing…", supra note 3, p. 4-7.

work and that she seems not to have any immediate interest in its exploitation. This inactivity does not make any difference to the copyright status. Without clear authorisation, and always beyond the uses tolerated by copyright limitations, it is not permitted to make any use of the work. Nevertheless, Copyright has a social function. Leaving aside the rationalities for the moral rights, exploitation rights function as an incentive for creation or innovation. But this creation incentive serves an ultimate goal: to promote the progress of science and useful arts[9] and then to feed the public cultural sphere to be enjoyed by the public. It is extremely important to retain this perspective and not to impede the analysis of copyright justification in the incentive or productive intermediate goal. The subordination of private interests to the public interest justifies the establishment of limits[10] and limitation to copyright, and might support the configuration of new limits or limitations if this is demanded by the public interest. The inactivity, the passive abandonment of her rights by the copyrightholder neither justifies the privilege of being conferred with exclusive rights nor helps to achieve the very ultimate goal of copyright. Also and more importantly, the existence of silent, captive works, does not provide any benefit to the author, or to society. On the contrary, it generates a very significant imbalance where empty rights are protected and access to culture is unreasonably damaged. These empty rights lead to an underutilisation of copyrighted works[11] with perverse effects on creativity and, more importantly, on the access to culture and knowledge. The existing legal framework is thus restricting, in an (apparently) unjustified way, the access to knowledge. It seems quite reasonable to question whether this effect is in line with the public interest rationalities of Copyright Law. If exploitation rights do not grant any incentive to create and, on the contrary, their sole result is to impede the access and re-utilisation of copyrighted work by citizens and potential creators, does it not make sense to think of the possibility of introducing new limits or limitations to the exploitation rights? Changes which have occurred in society during recent years may help us to lay the foundations for an affirmative answer.

---

[9] Article I, Section 8, Clause 8, US Constitution.

[10] Hence the idea-expression dichotomy, and the delimitation of the subject matter and protection terms.

[11] Vid, B. HUGENHOLTZ, M.M.M. VAN EECHOUD, S.J. VAN GOMPEL ET AL., *The Recasting of Copyright & Related Rights for the Knowledge Economy*, 2006, p. 178; as concerns orphan works.

Our society is moving towards a knowledge society. Knowledge becomes the primary resource instead of capital and labour. Production of (that is creation) as well as access to knowledge thus become an issue of public interest. If, during the last 15 years, policymakers have understandably concentrated their efforts on granting a strong legal protection for creation, now the pendulum swings to the other side. The question of access to and use of information is firmly on the Copyright agenda, it is considered as a key for the advancement of Knowledge society. The main challenge is to conciliate the protection of knowledge with the facilitation of access.

In 2000, the *Lisbon Agenda* gave a boost to the European policy for the Information Society. It aimed to make Europe the most dynamic and competitive knowledge-based economy in the world by 2010.[12] A key element for the implementation of the Lisbon goals is the *i2010 programme* that defines the European Policy for the Information Society. As one of the flagships of the i2010 programme[13] the European Commission (hereafter EC) launched in 2005 the *Digital Libraries Initiative* (hereinafter the DLI), aiming to make the European cultural heritage easier and more interesting to use online for work, leisure and/or study and therefore to promote the knowledge society.[14] The DLI pays special attention to some kinds of silent works: orphan and out of print works. Main achievements of the DLI are that, on the one hand, it has stimulated a very productive dialogue among different stakeholders[15] and, on the other, without any Directive or Regulation, it has provoked a very positive reaction in almost all European countries that are in fact discussing how to deal with digital libraries and copyright. Orphan works have also been a point for discussion in the Green Paper on Copyright in the Knowledge Economy.[16] With the Green Paper, the European

---

[12] *Presidency Conclusions*, Lisbon European Council, 23 and 24 March 2000; accessible on http://consilium.europa.eu/ueDocs/cms_Data/docs/pressData/en/ec/00100-r1.en0.htm.

[13] http://ec.europa.eu/information_society/eeurope/i2010/index_en.htm.

[14] http://ec.europa.eu/information_society/activities/digital_libraries/index_en.htm.

[15] As a result, several reports prepared by the Copyright Subgroup of the High Level Group on Digital Libraries and the *Memorandum of Understanding* on orphan works have been issued (vid. infra).

[16] Green Paper on Copyright in the Knowledge Economy, COM/2008/0466 final, http://eurlex.europa.eu/LexUriServ/LexUriServ.do?uri=CELEX:52008DC0466:EN:HTML The Green paper (p. 12) poses the following questions concerning the orphan woks: Is a further Community statutory instrument required to deal with the problem of orphan works, which goes beyond the Commission Recommendation 2006/585/EC of 24 August 2006? If so, should this be done by amending the 2001 Directive on Copyright in the information society or through a stand-alone instrument? How should the cross-border

Commission intends to "foster a debate on how knowledge for research, science and education can best be disseminated in the online environment [...] aim[ing] to set out a number of issues connected with the role of copyright in the "knowledge economy"". It also considers the issue of digital libraries and copyright.[17]

The European Digital Libraries Initiative reveals the potential of libraries to facilitate the access to knowledge and to advance the Knowledge society. This function responds to the historical role of traditional archives, libraries or museums: to preserve and facilitate the access to our cultural patrimony by the general public. In the pre-Internet era traditional libraries, museums or archives took care of the preservation of silent works and facilitated, as permitted by the existing technologies, the public access and consultation of these works. In such an environment, libraries peacefully coexisted with the publishers and operated in conjunction with the editorial market: they served a very specific public, without competing with the business sector.[18] In the Internet era, libraries are also called to play a key role in the preservation and making available of silent works. What is more, ICTs give libraries the technical means to better comply with this very important task. Thanks to new technologies, libraries can carry out large scale digitisation projects to facilitate the preservation and access to information and resources which later on could be used by citizens, researchers and, also, the business sector.[19] Silent works represent a huge amount of the existing copyrighted works that should not be excluded from digitisation projects. If the market does not offer minimum access to captive works, libraries, by means of their digitisation projects, would seem to be the natural actor to do so. However, as pointed out in the previous paragraphs, the *copyright* cuts

---

aspects of the orphan works issue be tackled to ensure EU-wide recognition of the solutions adopted in different Member States?

[17] In relation to the DLI and the European Copyright legal framework see M. IGLESIAS & L. VILCHES, "Les bibliothèques numériques et le droit d'auteur en Europe: qu'en est-il ?", *Cahiers de Propriété Intellectuelle*, 2007, vol. 19, n. 3, p. 937-987; and M. IGLESIAS, "Digital Libraries: any step forward?", *Auteurs & Media*, 2008, vol. 5, in print.

[18] R. CASAS, "Derecho de autor y bibliotecas: historia de una larga amistad", Seminario Internacional sobre Derecho de Autor y Acceso a la Cultura, organized by IFRRO and CEDRO, on the 28th October 2005, accessible on http://www.cedro.org/Files/RamonCasas.pdf.

[19] For a general overview on the cultural and economic opportunities from digitisation projects see the *Communication from the Commission to the European Parliament, the Council, the European Economic and Social Committee and the Committee of the Regions - i2010: digital libraries*, COM/2005/0465 final, http://eur-lex.europa.eu/LexUriServ/LexUriServ.do?uri=CELEX:52005DC0465:EN:HTML

short the DL projects. Copyright dictates the content of digital library projects and increases the risk of a black cultural hole.[20] Preservation and access to culture is then left entirely to the market. The potential negative effects on creativity (much less raw material to build ideas upon) and on the dissemination of cultural material are clear. Copyright Law, instead of acting as an incentive to create, is acting (at least as far as silent works are concerned) as a barrier to the creative and knowledge economy.[21]

II. Silent works on the Copyright Agenda

Some countries have implemented or are already discussing partial solutions to combat some of these silent situations. The following paragraphs will report on the main solutions foreseen to deal with the problem. They will firstly focus on specific silent works situations, concerning either orphan or out of print works. They will then report on other horizontal mechanisms, which even if they are not intended to solve the silent works problem, may alleviate it.

A first group of solutions focuses on the orphan works problem. In Europe, the work done by the EC and the High Level Group on Digital Libraries[22] in the framework on the Digital Libraries Initiative is remarkable. The EC, in its *Recommendation on the digitisation and online accessibility of cultural material and digital preservation,*[23] advices the Member states to create mechanisms to facilitate the use of orphan works and to promote the availability of lists of orphan works and works in the

---

[20] O. NIIRANEN, "Online access to the World's Libraries: Legal risk analysis of book scanning and indexing projects in Europe and their implications for the freedom of information", *Computer law review international*, 2006, n. 3, p. 70.

[21] At this point, it is important to recall that some economists have already questioned if private property, if exclusive rights, always lead to creation and innovation. In a very interesting article SALZBERGER concludes that, in some (if not all) cases improving access (i.e. by means of including some flexibilities in copyright Law), also operates as an incentive to creation, by stimulating new forms of creativity. Vid. "Economic analysis of the public domain", in L. GUIBAULT AND B. HUGENHOLTZ (eds.), *The future of the public domain*, 2006, p. 27-57.

[22] The main mission of the High Level Expert Group on Digital Libraries (hereinafter HLG) is to advise the EC on how to best address the organisational, legal and technical challenges at European level and to contribute to a shared strategic vision for European digital libraries; (see Commission Decision of 27 February 2006 setting up a High Level Expert Group on Digital Libraries, OJ L 63, p. 25 et seq, 4.3.2006).

[23] *Recommendation on the digitisation and online accessibility of cultural material and digital preservation*, OJ L 236, 31.8.2006, p. 28-30.

public domain.[24] The reaction of the Member states has been quite positive. From a reading of the national reports on the implementation of the Recommendation[25], it can be concluded that most Member states have created committees or working groups focusing on workable solutions. Some of them have even drafted regulatory measures (vid. infra). Neither the European Commission nor the High Level Group declares in favour of or against any regulatory/self-regulatory measure to facilitate the use of orphan works. The Copyright Subgroup of the High Level Group (hereinafter the Copyright Subgroup) recommends that national solutions work under the mutual recognition principle in order to facilitate the cross-border effect of European digital libraries.[26] This group of experts has also agreed on some core principles for orphan works mechanisms. According to the Copyright Subgroup, the national solutions should cover all kinds of orphan works, require a diligent (and documented) search prior to use, include provisions for withdrawal and remuneration if the rightholder reappears and offer special treatment to cultural, not-profit establishments.[27]Very importantly, as an spin-off of the Group of Experts, a working group has been created formed by representatives of copyrightholders and cultural institutions. This Group has agreed on a Memorandum of understanding on Diligent Search Guidelines for Orphan Works.[28] The Memorandum contains a common definition of orphan

---

[24] Point 6 b) of the Recommendation.

[25] Available on http://ec.europa.eu/information_society/activities/digital_libraries/experts/mseg/reports/index_en.htm. Vid also the *Communication from the Commission to the Council, the European Parliament, the European Economic and Social Committee and the Committee of the Regions - Europe's cultural heritage at the click of a mouse - Progress on the digitisation and online accessibility of cultural material and digital preservation across the EU* COM/2008/0513 final, 11.8.2008, COM (2008) 513 final and the *Commission Staff Working Document accompanying the Communication EU,* SEC(2008) 2372.

[26] Copyright Subgroup, *Final Report on Digital Preservation, Orphan Works and Out of Print works,*   2008,   p.   14   et   seq., http://ec.europa.eu/information_society/activities/digital_libraries/experts/hleg/index_en.htm.

[27] Copyright Subgroup, *Final Report,* supra note 27, p. 10 et seq. Notice that in previous reports the Copyright Subgroup advices the national solutions to recognise that clearance of rights, in particular in large collections, may not always be possible at the level of each unique item. Vid. its *Interim Report on digital preservation, orphan works and out-of-print works,* de 2006, and its *Report on Digital Preservation, Orphan Works and Out-of-Print Works,   Selected   Implementation   Issues*;   both   published   on http://ec.europa.eu/information_society/activities/digital_libraries/experts/hleg/meetings/index_en.htm.

[28]http://ec.europa.eu/information_society/activities/digital_libraries/doc/hleg/orphan/mou.pdf.The Memorandum has been signed by 27 organisations.

works and some sectorial guidelines[29] defining what may constitute a diligent research. The guidelines include a list of resources available for the search. In addition to this, the Copyright Subgroup recommends the creation of national databases of orphan works as well as clearing rights procedures and right clearance centres. To ensure the interoperability of the national initiatives and to facilitate their coordination and a common access point, the Copyright Subgroup has published a Set of Key Principles for a Right Clearance centre and Databases for orphan works.[30] The main purpose of the orphan works databases is to facilitate the rightholders' identification and to avoid duplication efforts. Right Clearance centres might act as portals and common access points for the clearance of rights if there is any mechanism provided on a contractual or regulatory basis.[31]

Following the recommendation of the European Commission some European countries are discussing regulatory measures to solve the problem of orphan works. According to the national reports on the implementation of the Recommendation on Digital Libraries, Denmark, Germany and Hungary are adapting their legislation to facilitate the use of orphan works.[32] In France, the *Conseil supérieur de la propriété littéraire et artistique* has appointed a special commission to explore the appropriate measures for encouraging the digitisation and accessibility of

---

[29] See the Joint Report on Sector-specific guidelines on diligence search criteria for orphan works
(http://ec.europa.eu/information_society/activities/digital_libraries/doc/hleg/orphan/guideli nes.pdf) and its Appendix containing sector reports and specific guidelines for the audiovisual sector, the visual/photography sector, the music/sound sector and the text sector;
(http://ec.europa.eu/information_society/activities/digital_libraries/doc/hleg/orphan/appen dix.pdf).

[30] See Copyright Subgroup, *Final Report*, supra note 26, Annex 6, *Recommended Key Principles for rights clearance centres and databases for orphan works*. Vid also the Annex 5 on the ARROW project, for preparing a European database of orphan works.

[31] For a more detailed overview on the work done by the Copyright Subgroup, vid. M. IGLESIAS, "Digital Libraries: any step…", supra note 17; and M. RICOLFI, "Copyright Policy for digital libraries in the context of the i2010 strategy", *paper* delivered at the International Conference on Public Domain in the Digital Age (COMMUNIA Project), Louvain-La-Neuve, 30.06.2008-01.07.2008, p. 5-7; accessible on http://communia-project.eu/communiafiles/conf2008p_Copyright_Policy_for_digital_libraries_in_the_conte xt_of_the_i2010_strategy.pdf.

[32] *Communication on Europe's cultural heritage at the click of a mouse and accompanying documents* (vid. supra note 25).

orphan and out of print works.[33] In April 2008, the Commission published its *Avis* on how to deal with the orphan works problem.[34] First, it proposes to incorporate in the *Code de la Propriété Intellectuelle* an orphan work definition that is limited to published works. Second, after having assessed the impact of the orphan work situation in different sectors, the Commission recommends the implementation of different solutions depending on the kind of work. So, for print and visual works it has proposed the modification of the *Code de la Propriété Intellectuelle* to introduce a mandatory collective management system. For music, cinema and other audiovisual works it has preferred not to adopt any modification and to continue with the collective agreements that may be concluded by *l'Institute National de l'Audiovisuel* and the representatives of rightholders.[35] According to the proposal drafted for print and visual works, an entitled collecting society might grant authorisation to use orphan works. To benefit from the system the user must perform a serious and proven search. The legislation will not establish any specific criteria, but according to the proposal, search guidelines shall be fixed by a Commission bringing together representatives of the rightholders, the user and the public administration. The Opinion also recommends the implementation of a preventive policy for orphan works in order to improve the identification of rightholders by facilitating the development and access to information.[36]

---

[33] See *Lettre de mission du président du Conseil de la propriété littéraire et artistique du 2 août 2007,* accessible on http://www.cspla.culture.gouv.fr/CONTENU/lmoeuvres07.pdf.

[34] *Avis de la commission spécialisée du CSPLA sur les oeuvres orphelines,* (http://www.cspla.culture.gouv.fr/CONTENU/avisoo08.pdf). Vid. also the *Rapport de la Commission sur les oeuvres orphelines published* on March 2008: http://www.cspla.culture.gouv.fr/CONTENU/rapoeuvor08.pdf.

[35] See art. L49, *Loi n°86-1067 du 30 septembre 1986 relative à la liberté de communication.*

[36] For more details on the proposed solution, see the *Rapport de la Commission sur les oeuvres orphelines published* supra note 34. Notice, however, that some of the points of the report have not been incorporated in the *Avis.* Thus, the Rapport states that licences must be issued for a period of time. It also specifies that the amount to be paid will be agreed by the collecting society and the users. If the rightholders surface, they will be entitled to collect the remuneration before the collecting society. Her surface will not cause the termination of the licence, the user may continue on the exploitation until the expiration of the licence. Vid, the *Rapport de la Commission sur les oeuvres orphelines published,* p. 19-20.
On the other hand, it is worth mentioning that art. 122-9 of the French Law allows the judge to adopt appropriate measures when there is an abuse of the way rightholders representatives are exercising their rights. The Commission has also proposed some modifications in order to apply this article to orphan works situations.

The discussion on Orphan works also takes place outside Europe. In 2005 the US Copyright Office launched a request for comments on the issue of orphan works,[37] which was followed by a Report on orphan works.[38] The report recommends introducing in the *Copyright Act* a limitation on remedies.[39] In line with this recommendation two bills were introduced in 2008.[40] Both proposals are based on a limitation of remedies: the use of an orphan work is still an infringement but if the rightholder brings a legal action against the user, monetary and injunctive relief may be limited. To benefit from the system the user must prove that before using the work she performed and documented a reasonably diligent search to locate the copyright owner and that she provided attribution to the rightholder if known. Additionally, the user must include with the infringing work a symbol, in a manner prescribed by the Register of Copyrights, to give notice that the work has been used under the new orphan works provision. According to the bill entered into the House of Representatives, the user must also file a notice of use with the Register of Copyrights.[41] The proposals do not specify the requirements for searches. They only require the infringer to make a diligent attempt to locate the copyrightholder. The bills specifically clarify that the absence of identifying information in a particular copy is not sufficient to meet the conditions mentioned above. Furthermore, both proposals state that the Register of Copyrights shall maintain and make available to the public best practices for conducting the search. If all of these conditions are fulfilled, the monetary relief must be limited to reasonable compensation. Furthermore, non-profit educational institutions, libraries, archives or public broadcast entities may be exempted from paying reasonable compensation, if they stop the use after receiving a claim notice issued by the rightholder and prove that the infringement was performed without any purpose of direct or indirect commercial advantage and with educational, religious or charitable purposes. The injunctive relief may also be limited in the case of derivate works: it may not restrain the

---

[37] *Notice of Inquiry, Library of Congress - Copyright Office, Federal Register*, January 26, 2005, vol. 70, n. 16, Notices Notices, p. 3739.

[38] Copyright Office, *Report on Orphan works*.

[39] Copyright Office, *Report on Orphan works*, supra note 6, p. 92 and ss.

[40] The *Orphan Works Act of 2008* —A bill to provide a limitation on judicial remedies in copyright cases involving orphan works—, introduced in the House of Representatives on the 4th April 2008, [H.R.5889]. And the *Shawn Bentley Orphan Works Act of 2008* — A bill to provide a limitation on judicial remedies in copyright cases involving orphan works —, introduced in the Senate on the 28th April 2008, [S.2913.IS].

[41] As proposed by art. 514(b)(1)(A)(ii), *Orphan Works act of 2008*.

infringer's continued preparation or use of the work if she pays a negotiated and reasonable compensation and acknowledges the rightholders. In any case, the application of limitations of remedies is subject to an important additional requirement: the user cannot apply for the limitation if after receiving a notice of claim she fails to negotiate reasonable compensation with the copyrightholder or fails to render payment of such reasonable compensation in a reasonable time frame. The US proposals are also applicable to unpublished works. They follow, once again, the recommendations of the Report, where it is considered that, due to the difficulty in determining if a work is published or unpublished and the fact that many orphan works are unpublished, the system should also be applicable to unpublished works.[42] This option may be quite difficult to implement in *Droit d'auteur systems* where moral rights have a fundamental role. However, some continental copyright laws traditionally contain provisions that authorise the post-mortem divulgation of a work if rightholders unreasonably oppose to it.[43] [44]

A very different system is already in force in Canada.[45] According to the Canadian *Copyright Law*, the Copyright Board may deliver a non

---

[42] See Copyright Office, *Report on Orphan Works*, supra note 7, pp. 100-102.

[43] Vid. art. 40 Spanish Copyright Law or art. 122-9 French Law (supra note 36). In any case, beyond the problems raised by moral rights, the digitisation and making available of unpublished works might be in conflict with Privacy Law.

[44] For a critical analysis of the US proposals vid. J. C. GINSBURG, "Recent Developments in Us Copyright Law: Part I - "Orphan" Works", in *Revue Internationale du Droit d'Auteur*, October 2008, p. 99-197. In the US the legal doctrine on orphan works is more prolific than in Europe. See, for example: J. BRITO & B. DOOLING, "An Orphan Works Affirmative Defense to Copyright Infringement Actions", *Michigan Telecommunications and Technology Law Review*, 2005, p. 75-113; Duke Law School, *Center for the study of the public domain, Orphan Works, Analysis and Proposal*, 2005, http://www.law.duke.edu/cspd/pdf/cspdproposal.pdf; D. K. HENNING, "Copyright's Deus Ex Machina: Reverse Registration as Economic Fostering of Orphan Works", 2008, ExpressO, accessible on http://works.bepress.com/darrin_henning/1O; HUANG, "U.S. Copyright office orphan works inquiry: finding homes for the orphans", *Berkeley Technology Law Journal*, 2006, vol. 21, n.1, p. 265-288D. B. SHERMAN, "Cost and Resource Allocation Under the Orphan Works Act of 2006", *Virginia Journal of Law and Technology*, 2007, vol. 12, n. 4, p. 1-36; C. THOMPSON, "Orphan Works, U.S. Copyright Law, and International Treaties: Reconciling differences to create a brighter future for orphans everywhere", *Arizona Journal of International and Comparative Law*, 2006, p. 787-852; S. VALKONEN & L. J. WHITE, "An Economic Model for the Incentive/Access Paradigm of Copyright Propertization: an Argument in Support of the Proposed New §514 to the Copyright Act", *NYU, Law and Economics Research Paper*, 2006, n. 06-15, accessible on http://ssrn.com/abstract=895554.

[45] Art. 77 *Copyright Act*. More information on http://www.cb-cda.gc.ca/unlocatable/index-e.html.

exclusive licence to a user who has not been able to locate the copyrightholder after having made reasonable attempts. The system is applied only as regards published works. The remuneration, if any, is fixed as the other conditions by the Copyright Board. If the rightholders appears, she may collect the royalties not later than five years after the expiration of the license.[46]

Leaving aside some exceptions, (i.e. the Canadian Law),[47] few laws foresee specific provisions allowing the use of orphan works. Hence, the private sector has developed mechanisms to facilitate the use of orphan works. Such solutions mainly consist of safe harbour provisions or risk management policies. Thus, a group or scientific publishers have adopted an orphan works policy that allows the use of orphan works which they may own. According to the safe harbour provisions incorporated in their policy, in the event that a copyright owner is identified, the user must pay a reasonable royalty and must ensure that there is no further re-use or re-utilization of the work. When the user fulfils these conditions, the publishers agree to waive their rights to bringing an action against her.[48] Another example is the one provided by the SOFAM —la *Societé belge d'auteurs dans le domaine des Arts Visuels*. It offers the so called "convention de porte fort": a user signing this convention must pay remuneration to the SOFAM for the use of an orphan work. If the rightholder surfaces she may contact the SOFAM in order to collect the remuneration.[49] Last but not least, some, but not many, cultural institutions operate under a risk management policy. They assess the potential risk and, in some cases, decide just to confront it and make the use.[50]

---

[46] For more information on the regulatory solutions to orphan works see, Copyright Subgroup, *Final Report*, supra note 27, p. 11 et seq.; B. HUGENHOLTZ, M.M.M. VAN EECHOUD, S.J. VAN GOMPEL ET AL., *The Recasting of Copyright...*, supra note 12, p. 178 et seq.

[47] Non voluntary licences for orphan works also exist in South Korea, Japan and India. Vid Copyright Subgroup, *Final Report*, supra note 26, p. 12.; y S. V. GOMPEL, "Unlocking the potential of pre-existing...", supra note 3, p. 19.

[48] Safe Harbour Provisions for the Use of Orphan Works for Scientific, Technical and Medical   Literature,   An   STM/ALPSP/PSP   Position   Paper, http://www.alpsp.org/ForceDownload.asp?id=579.

[49] More information on http://www.sofam.be/mainfr.php?ID=104&titel=Conventions+de+porte-fort.

[50] An example may be consulted in the National Portrait Gallery case study: http://ec.europa.eu/information_society/activities/digital_libraries/doc/seminar_14_septem ber_2007/npg_perspective.pdf.

The second Group of *ad hoc* solutions concerns the out of print situations. It has also been a point of discussion under the Digital Libraries Initiative. As in the case of orphan works, the European Commission has decided not to implement specific European legislation on the matter, but to issue some recommendations to the Member States.[51] The Copyright Subgroup has in fact developed a very pragmatic solution that might be adapted and implemented by the Member states. This solution is intended to facilitate the conclusion of contractual agreements authorising the use of out of print works. The key elements of this solution are: a) a model license for the reproduction and making available of out of print works though closed networks, b) a second more open licence allowing online access to out of print books, and c), as in the case of orphan works, a set of principles to enhance the creation of national databases and rights clearance centres and procedures.[52]

The system proposed has valuable aspects. It intends to eliminate some transaction costs by facilitating, through the standardisation of contractual agreements, the conclusion of contracts between rightholders and libraries.[53] Its main purpose is to bring out of print works to light while guaranteeing a payment to rightholders. Furthermore, model licences may be used by rightholders to check the commercial possibilities of the work in the market.[54] The publication of the second model agreement intended for on line access must also be seen as an encouraging step forward.[55] Another positive aspect of the licences is that they have been drafted to be used when contracting on a national, European or multinational level. Last but not least, they foresee that a digitised version must be accessible to visually impaired persons. Having said this, it is worth noting that the position of the library —which takes the initiative and invests the money— is however weaker. When carefully reading the

---

[51] See point 6.b) *Recommendation on the digitisation and online accessibility of cultural material and digital preservation.*

[52] Copyright Subgroup, *Final Report*, supra note 26, pp. 17-30 and their following annexes: III (*Model agreement for a licence on digitisation of out of print works*), IV (*Model agreement for a licence on digitisation of out of print works with option for online accessibility*) y VII (*i2010 Digital libraries copyright subgroup's Recommenced key principles for rights clearance centres and databases for out-of-print works*). For a more in depth analysis of the work done by the Copyright Subgroup in relation to out of print works see M. IGLESIAS, "Digital Libraries: any step...", supra note 17; and M. RICOLFI, "Copyright Policy for digital...", supra note 31, p. 7-8.

[53] M. RICOLFI, "Copyright Policy for digital...", supra note 31, p. 8.

[54] Copyright Subgroup, *Final Report*, p. 22 and 24.

[55] For an assessment of the previous Copyright Subgroup proposals see vid. M. IGLESIAS & L. VILCHES, "Les bibliothèques numériques ...", supra note 17, p. 937-987.

licences, one can easily conclude that they do not offer a privileged status to *libraries*. They are just contractual templates for a very specific market: that referring to the exploitation of out of print works. They are not very far from a standard copyright contract and it is questionable as to whether the model licences will facilitate the digitisation and making available of the out of print works by (non profit) digital libraries. The fact that the licensor may at any time withdraw the licence could entail a lack of security for libraries. Moreover, since they are based on a voluntary basis, rightholders could, without giving any reason, deny authorisation[56] or even ask for a very costly remuneration. Therefore, many out of print works could still remain silent.

No specific solutions have been foreseen in relation to the lack of response situations. The main argument used to skirt the issue is the right to ignore permission requests. However, one exception is the mandatory licences in favour of developing countries contained in the Appendix to the Berne Convention. It presents a subsidiary system which authorises the adoption of compulsory licences when the rightholder has not proceeded with a specific exploitation. To benefit from these licences the user must comply with some information duties. The rightholder is given a period of time to decide whether to proceed or not to the exploitation of the work.[57]

In addition to these *ad hoc* solutions, some transversal mechanisms should be taken into account which, even if they were not intentionally designed to solve the silent works problem, they may, in practice, reduce its consequences. The most relevant example is, without a doubt, that of extended collective licences, often used in Nordic Countries to facilitate certain uses of copyrighted work. According to this system, an organisation representing a substantial number of rightholders may grant a licence to use the work in specific sectors.[58] Because of its extended

---

[56] Copyright Subgroup, *Final Report*, supra note 26, p. 21.

[57] Vid. *Berne Convention for the Protection of Literary and Artistic Works*, Appendix: Special provisions regarding developing countries. In relation to the Appendix to the Berne Convention see H. DESBOIS, "La conférence diplomatique de révision des conventions de Berne et de Genève", *Revue Internationale du Droit d'Auteur*, n. 68, 1971 ; H. DESBOIS/ A. FRANÇON/ A. KEREVER, *Les conventions internationales du droit d'auteur et des droits voisins,* 1976 ; R. FERNAY, "Paris 1971, ou les aventures d'un "package deal"", *Revue Internationale du Droit d'Auteur*, n. 70, 1971 ; S. RICKETSON, "Chapter 14: Developing countries", in *International copyright and neighbouring rights: the Berne convention and beyond*, (vol. 2), 2.ª ed., 2006.

[58] For example, in Denmark, extended collective licences are used, among others, in the following cases: reproductions for educational uses, reproductions for transmission by email of digitised copies of library material to library users or other libraries, or

effect, the licence also covers the works of those rightholders who are not members of the society. It may be said, in fact, that the system is very similar to mandatory collective management. The big difference is that rightholders can opt out of participating in the system. In Denmark, some modifications to the copyright law have been proposed in order to allow the application of extended collective licences to the use of orphan and out of print works. The new provisions allow the parties concerned to use extended collective licences in areas —outside the specific sectors where the system is already in use— to be decided by the contracting parties. Such licences might extend their effects to all the works of the same kind already managed by the entity. However, the rightholders may opt out and not participate in the system. Those entities opting for concluding agreements under the new provisions should ask for the authorisation of the Minister of Culture.[59]

Beyond the solutions found in positive law, some scholars have presented theoretical proposals that are for more fundamental reforms in Copyright Law. These proposals mainly deal with the (*ideal*) copyright term, the re-introduction of formalities in Copyright Law or the reformulation of copyright limitations granting a wider use of copyrighted work.[60] Even if they are not intended to solve the "silent works" problem, these proposals could actually facilitate the use of orphan and out of print works. Any of these systems would require a structural reform of national but also European and International Copyright Law, but... is this conceivable in the near future?

---

reproductions of radio or television programmes for the use of persons with visual or auditory impairments. H. VON HIELMCRONE, "Orphan works. The Danish solution: Extended collective licensing", *EBLIDA News*, 2008, n.6, p. 1-2.

[59] Cfr. Danish report on the implementation of the Recommendation on the digitisation and online accessibility of cultural material and digital preservation., p.2; accessible on http://ec.europa.eu/information_society/activities/digital_libraries/experts/mseg/reports/ind ex_en.htm. Vid also the EC Communication COM (2008) 513 final and accompanying working document, p. 15; supra note 25; and H. VON HIELMCRONE, "Orphan works", supra note 58, pp 1-2.

[60] Vid. i.e. W. LANDES AND R. POSNER, "Indefinitely Renewable Copyright", (August 1, 2002), *154 U Chicago Law & Economics, Olin Working Paper*, accessible on http://ssrn.com/abstract=319321, and "Chapter 8: The Optimal Duration of Copyrights and Trademarks", in *The Economic Structure of Intellectual Property Law*, (2003), pp. 210-253; L. LESSIG, *Free culture*, (2003); D. KHONG, "Orphan Works, Abandonware...", supra note 1; C. SPRIGMAN, "Reform(aliz)ing Copyright", *Stanford Law Review*, 2004; M. RICOLFI, "Copyright Policy for digital...", supra note 31.

III. A proposal to rescue silent works

Except for the provisions contained in the Appendix to the Berne Convention and the amendments to the Danish Copyright Law, all of the above mentioned systems are focused on a very specific silent situation: so, for orphan works, the US and the French or the Canadian non voluntary licences; for out of print works, the model licences proposed by the Copyright Subgroup. Moreover, the French proposal only applies to print and visual orphan works. This solution does not cover, as suggested by the Copyright Subgroup, all kinds of copyrighted work. Neither the French proposal nor the Canadian regime authorises the use of unpublished works. Despite the fact that most policymakers are working on different solutions for various kinds of silent Works[61], it may be concluded that all silent works situations respond to a very similar failure of the Copyright system[62], unable to react to a market failure which provokes the underutilisation or even the no-utilisation at all of copyrighted works. Therefore, it might be advisable, instead of promoting various legal regimes for each silent situation, to conceive of a system, or at least of a set of common principles, to deal with these situations. Orphan works are in fact a clear case of out of print works and both of them are, as well as those cases concerning the lack of responses, examples of abandoned works.

The social function of copyright has led the policymaker to recognise, as mentioned at the beginning of this paper, some copyright limits and limitations. Most countries have included in their Copyright laws limitations in favour of libraries.[63] Nevertheless these limitations have not

---

[61] Although this is not always the case: the new Danish provisions may be applied to all kinds of silent works.

[62] M. IGLESIAS & L. VILCHES, "Les bibliothèques numériques ...", supra note 17, p. 971; y D. KHONG, "Orphan Works, Abandonware...", supra note 1, p. 79. As concerns oprhan works see S. V. GOMPEL, "Unlocking the potential of pre-existing...", supra note 3, p. 669-702), p. 8.

[63] For more information on copyright limitations in favour of libraries around the world, see the Study on Copyright Limitations and Exceptions for Libraries and Archives prepared by K. CREWS for the WIPO, accessible on http://www.wipo.int/meetings/en/doc_details.jsp?doc_id=109192. The Study analyses the Copyright legislation in 149 countries and concludes that only 21 do not state limitations in favour of libraries. For more information on these topic see the following publications and cited bibliography: L. GUIBAULT, "Evaluation of the directive 2001/29/EC in the digital information society", *paper* delivered at International Conference on Public

been drafted taking into account the opportunities and challenges posed by the new information and communication technologies. In Europe, the adoption of *Directive 2001/29/EC of the European Parliament and of the Council of 22 May 2001 on the harmonisation of certain aspects of copyright and related rights in the information society* (hereinafter Directive 2001/29)[64] might have been a good opportunity to update the library limitations to the new environment. But the European policy maker adopted a very cautious approach, waiting for the development of new business models that might guarantee a certain leeway for libraries uses.[65] Yet the truth is that these business models have not been developed in an efficient way. The existence of a considerable number of orphan and out of print works and the (failed) projects of users willing to exploit and give access to these works, reveals the shortcomings of the market. Furthermore, the social function of copyright might justify the introduction of new limitations that facilitate the use of these abandoned works, taking into account the inactivity of the rightholders. These limitations might be applied when the rightholders have passively abandoned their prerogatives.

Copyright limitations, as in general all legal institutions, should respond to the needs and expectations of society. The definition and scope of copyright limitations may vary in the course of time according to the interests and values of a given society, without diluting the content and substance of exploitation rights.[66] And here, the specific need to advance the Knowledge society and the role that libraries may play to this end should be considered. Like traditional libraries, digital libraries have a key role in the preservation, access and dissemination of knowledge. Large scale digitisation (and making available) projects represent a key step towards improving the access and use of information which, notwithstanding the cultural and social benefits they bring, also generate

---

Domain in the Digital Age (COMMUNIA Project), Louvain-La-Neuve, Belgium, 30.06.2008-01.07.2008, accessible on http://communia-project.eu/communiafiles/conf2008p_Copyright_Policy_for_digital_libraries_in_the_context_o f_the_i2010_strategy.pdf; M. IGLESIAS & L. VILCHES, "Les bibliothèques numériques ...", supra note 17, p. 949-971; M. IGLESIAS, "Digital Libraries: any step...", supra note 17.

[64] *Directive 2001/29/EC of the European Parliament and of the Council of 22 May 2001 on the harmonisation of certain aspects of copyright and related rights in the information society*, OJ L 167 de 22.06.2001

[65] And this is, in fact, the starting point for some of the questions raised by the Green Paper (supra note 16); see questions 6 et seq. and their introduction.

[66] Vid, in relation to the configuration of the right to property, its social function and the limitations to its exercise, the *Decision n. 37/1987, 26 March, Spanish Constitutional Court.*

an important added value for the economic and business sector.[67] Without underestimating the public interest underlying the commercial uses of orphan or out of print works[68], the public interest of projects that intend to integrate those works in digital libraries is of vital importance for the creation of (cultural, scientific, economic and social) wealth. Hence, this paper, besides being for an inclusive solution covering all kinds of orphan works, focuses on and advocates a solution referring to certain projects with a public interest objective, to large scale digitisation projects that do not pursue a commercial advantage.

In the following paragraphs, the basis for an inclusive solution which might be applied to all kinds of silent works will be presented. Starting from the assumption that the silent works problem is clearly a problem of market failure, the policymaker should firstly privilege market oriented solutions intended to reduce transaction costs. She should encourage the various stakeholders to promote the conclusion of agreements on abandoned works. This may be done, for example, by promoting the adoption and dissemination of contractual templates such as the ones drafted by the Copyright Subgroup. Furthermore, policymakers should promote the running of private or public silent work databases.

But without a doubt policymaker action must not stop here. Since all the operators on the market are unlikely to adhere to the self regulation initiatives, and since the self regulation initiatives might not be operative as regards all silent works (notably orphan works), copyright laws should state a limitation to be applied only when rightholders are not exploiting their works or do not show any intention of doing so in the near future. Mandatory provisions of a subsidiary nature already exist in Copyright legal texts. Hence the compulsory licensing scheme for developing countries contained in the Appendix to the Berne Convention. A similar option is envisaged in the UK *Copyright, Designs and Patents Act,* for

---

[67] Vid. the *Communication from the Commission to the European Parliament, the Council, the European Economic and Social Committee and the Committee of the Regions - i2010 : digital libraries, COM/2005/0465 final,* COM/2005/0465 final.

[68] From this paragraph it must not be concluded that the use of silent works (especially orphan works) in commercial projects must not deserve singular attention and specific treatment in copyright law. Nevertheless, the characteristics of these commercial and for profit uses call for different logic and requirements. Most of the systems mentioned throughout this paper cover commercial and non commercial uses. Focusing for example on US proposals, their limitations on remedies, which may be very effective for single or commercial uses, do not seem to be very operative for large scale digitisation projects. Even if both proposals envisage special provisions for non-commercial uses (notably the elimination of the monetary relief), the risk for large scale digitisation projects continue to be quite high.

example as regards the provisions dealing with some copyright limitations or "permitted acts" —that will not apply when there is a licensing scheme available—[69], or the combination of voluntary schemes with mandatory licences also contained in the UK law.[70] A comparable approach is the one adopted by section 53a of the German Copyright Act. Section 53a explicitly deals with limitations in favour of libraries. It authorises the reproduction and transmission in other electronic form of single articles published in newspapers and journals as well as small sections of published works, if this is done in the form of graphic files and for the purpose of illustration for teaching or scientific research, and as far as it is justified for non-commercial purposes. These electronic reproductions and transmission are permitted only if access to the work is not possible for members of the public on a contractual basis and under reasonable conditions from the place and at the time of their choice. That is, so far the rightholder has not run a licensing scheme for the making available of her works. In any case, according to section 53.a, the rightholder will receive remuneration. It can be claimed only through a collecting society.[71]

There are several policy options for implementing the proposed solutions. The policymaker might opt for granting an extended effect to collective licensing agreements reached by the organisations representing the interests of rightholders to the works of those rightholders who are not members of the organisation. The main difference with the extended collective licences system is that here, more than an opt-out clause based on subjective grounds - the will of the rightholder, it would include an opt-out clause based on objective parameters: the actual exploitation or the immediate intention to exploit the work in the near term. Another possibility is to impose the mandatory collective management for silent works. A third option could be to establish a system of non-voluntary licences. And as regards this third option, the use of individual compulsory licences should be disregarded[72] in favour of blank

---

[69] D. KHONG, "Orphan Works, Abandonware...", supra note 1, p. 79.

[70] Cfr. sections 116 et seq., *Copyright, Designs and Patent Act 1988*.

[71] On the German solution vid: H. MUELLER, "The legal problems of document supply by libraries: an international perspective", in *Interlending and Document Supply*, vol. 36, n. 2, 2008, p. 68-73.

[72] By means of compulsory licences, an "obligation to contract" is imposed, but some of the conditions of the licence and, eventually, the remuneration, may be freely negotiated between the parties. The legal literature considers that the main difference between the legal and compulsory licences is the way in which the remuneration is established: by negotiation in the case of compulsory licences, by following the criteria established in the law in the case of legal licences. Vid. R. FERNAY, "Grandeur, misère et contradictions du

compulsory licences or of legal or statutory licences managed by the public administration or by an independent authority.[73] The imposition of a system of compulsory licences on an individual basis or for single works might not be very appropriate for large scale digitisation projects, taking into account the administrative burdens for both the institutions issuing the licences and the users.[74]

Nevertheless a solution consisting of legal or statutory licences would not be compatible with the European Copyright legal framework. Article 5 Directive 2001/29/CE contains an exhaustive list of limitations that Member states may provide for in their national laws. Member states may not contain in their national laws limitations not listed in art. 5. The sole limitation authorising the making available of copyrighted work by digital libraries is art. 5.3.n) [75]; but due to its restrictive requirements, the provision will be of little utility for DL projects.[76] Furthermore, Recital 40 Directive 2001/29 states that "Member States may provide for an exception or limitation for the benefit of certain non-profit making establishments, such as publicly accessible libraries and equivalent institutions, as well as archives. However, this should be limited to certain special cases covered by the reproduction right. *Such an exception or limitation should not cover uses made in the context of on-line delivery of protected works* or other subject-matter. [...] Therefore, specific contracts or licences should be promoted which, without creating imbalances, favour such establishments and the disseminative purposes they serve" (emphasis added). Limitations authorising the electronic delivery of

---

droit d'auteur", *Revue Internationale du Droit d'Auteur*, n. 109, 1981. p. 162; A. STROWEL, *Droit d'auteur et copyright*, 1993, p. 631. Also: L. GUIBAULT, *Licenses and Copyright Exemptions*, 2000, contribution to the meeting, organised by the Legal Advisory Board. European Commission, DGIS May 2000; S. DUSOLLIER, *Droit d'auteur et protection des oeuvres dans l'univers numérique: droits et exceptions à la lumière des dispositifs de verrouillage des Ouvres*, 2005, p. 424.

[73] By means of statutory licences, the legislator authorises the use establishing the remuneration —or the criteria to take into account for its determination— or entrusting it to a third party.

[74] I.e. the Canadian system requires an ex ante verification that may rest effectiveness to the system.

[75] It concerns «the use by communication or making available, for the purpose of research or private study, to individual members of the public by dedicated terminals on the premises of establishments referred to in paragraph 2(c) of works and other subject-matter not subject to purchase or licensing terms which are contained in their collections».

[76] L. GUIBAULT, "Evaluation of the directive 2001/29/EC...", supra note 63, p. 8.; M. IGLESIAS & L. VILCHES, "Les bibliothèques numériques ...", supra note 17, p. 956-958 y p. 986 ; M. IGLESIAS, "Digital Libraries: any step...", supra note 17.

copyrighted work are clearly forbidden –except when they refer to the specific uses authorised by art. 5.3.a) which permits certain uses with teaching or scientific purposes.[77] At this point, it is important to remember that the notion of "limitations and exceptions" used in the Directive only seems to refer to free exceptions and statutory or legal licences. Apparently, the Directive does not affect non voluntary systems of collective management (i.e. mandatory collective management or extended collective licences).[78] Recital 18 explicitly states that the Directive «is without prejudice to the arrangements in the Member States concerning the management of rights such as extended collective licences».[79] So, the mandatory system of a subsidiary nature proposed in the previous paragraphs could not be adopted under a free exception or a statutory licence, without modifying Directive 2001/29 and even the International Copyright provisions. However, the system would be in compliance with European and International Law if it was adopted under a mandatory collective management or an extended collective licence.

On the other hand, the specific characteristics of national institutions and legal systems should be taken into account when assessing which policy option better suits a specific country. The implementation of a sui generis system of extended collective licences will depend on the existence of representative organisations and whether these organisations are issuing collective licenses for large scale digitisation projects. If this is not the case, the mandatory collective management for silent works seems to be more suitable. If there are no collecting societies for all kind of works, then it makes sense to appoint one (or several) organisation(s) to issue the licences.

---

[77] Art. 5.3 states that "Member States may provide for exceptions or limitations to the rights provided for in Articles 2 and 3 in the following cases: a) use for the sole purpose of illustration for teaching or scientific research, as long as the source, including the author's name, is indicated, unless this turns out to be impossible and to the extent justified by the non-commercial purpose to be achieved".

[78] If the Directive deals or not with the compulsory licences is more controversial.

[79] The wording of Recital 18 and, in particular, the explicit mention of the extended collective licences were introduced into the Common Position of the Council at the request of Sweden. This was its sine qua non condition to accept the new limitation for the purpose of teaching. Cfr. Recital 18, Common Position (EC) No 48/2000 of 28 September 2000 adopted by the Council, acting in accordance with the procedure referred to in Article 251 of the Treaty establishing the European Community, with a view to adopting a Directive of the European Parliament and of the Council on the harmonisation of certain aspects of copyright and related rights in the information society, OJ C 344, de 01.12.2000, p. 1-22) and Council Document 9734/99, p. 6, note 31.

In any case, the policymaker should define the content and the elements of such a system. The very first point would be to define its scope, that is, to give a definition of silent works. This definition might refer to those copyrighted works which have not actually been exploited and whose rightholders do not show any intention to exploit them. Another relevant point is to identify what kind of projects should be considered as having an objective of public interest. This leads us to define the beneficiaries of the system, namely publicly accessible non for profit libraries, museums or archives. These entities should carry out large scale projects to digitise their collections and make them available on the Internet. These projects must not be for direct or indirect economic or commercial advantage. Remuneration might be asked by the library if it is of limited significance and just to cover the cost of digitisation and, if need be, the remuneration due to the rightholders (vid infra). The system should authorise the making available of silent works and the necessary reproductions. It means that it would authorise the electronic delivery of documents, always under the strict conditions explained below. Firstly, access to these works might be strictly limited to the users registered with the library. In contrast to the US proposals, the system should specify the obligation to pay fair remuneration and the circumstances under which fair remuneration should be paid. The configuration of the remuneration might be based on an ex ante system (the remuneration is fixed a priori), an ex-post system (based, for example, on the "hits on the work") or a combination of both (i.e. an initial flat rate plus a specific quantity for the actual use of the work). The rightholders could claim the remuneration before the intermediary organisation (i.e. the organisation representing the interests of the righolders, or, dealing with statutory licences, the competent authorities in charge of the licences). They could also claim their right to request the user to stop the use. On the other hand, a list of positive actions to make it easier to find the copyright holder or to give her the opportunity to enquire as to what their intentions as concerns the exploitation of the work are. Thus, the system should include strict information duties to be taken into account before proceeding to the use or before issuing the licence. Information duties might be on the shoulders of the intermediary organisation, of the users or be shared between both of them. It will depend on the specific role played by each of them in the implementation law. In any case, obligation duties might be inspired by the Guidelines for the diligent search contained in the *Memorandum of Understanding,* or even by the information duties established in the Appendix to the Berne Convention. Moreover the users or the intermediary organisation should file a notice of use (with the purpose of informing the rightholders about the exploitation of the work). It might be published in a register, managed by a private or public institution (i.e. in the database of silent works, mentioned above in relation to policy options). Provisions intended to impede unjustified harm on moral rights should be foreseen; they must require the mandatory attribution to the author and the source, if possible. When dealing with unpublished works, it seems appropriate to limit the authorised use to works whose authors have deceased and /or to authorise their use only in relation to the utilisations with a clear scientific interest. Finally, the system should make mandatory specific requirements to avoid the uncontrolled dissemination of the work by, for example, imposing the mandatory adoption of technical protection measures. Thus, it might not be possible to make copies of the works made available by digital libraries nor to further disseminate them to non authorised users. Technological protection measures should make it possible to track the use of the works (without, of course, invading the privacy of the users), and even to impose temporary restrictions on the use. A system such as the one proposed seems, in fact, to suggest the application of the functional equivalent theory in relation to what the lending right represents in the off line environment. Maybe it is time to again resume the discussion on digital lending.

IV. Conclusion

Digital libraries have a key role in advancing the knowledge society. New technologies offer them the means to rescue the voice of captive or silent works, of works whose rightholders do not show any interest in proceeding with exploitation and which, because of the specific configuration of exclusive copyrights, are obliged to remain silent. The European Commission and some European states have embarked on the search for solutions to facilitate the use of these works. In such a venture, most of them have decided to implement singular solutions depending on the kinds of silent works —ad hoc solutions for orphan works, ad hoc solutions for out of print works. In this paper, it is considered that this is not the most suitable approach. Hence, this paper presents the basis and some policy options for an inclusive system to be applied to facilitate the use of all kinds of silent works in large scale digitisation projects with the clear objective of serving the public interest.

Index of authors

In the same series

Legal Information and Communication Technologies

the following volumes are available:

Vol. 6. C. Biagioli, *Modelli Funzionali delle Leggi. Verso testi legislativi autoesplicativi*

Vol. 5 G. Peruginelli, M. Ragona (Eds.), *Law via the Internet. Free Access, Quality of Information, Effectiveness of Rights*

Vol. 4 P. Casanovas, P. Noriega, D. Bourcier, F. Galindo (Eds.), *Trends in Legal Knowledge, the Semantic Web and the Regulation of Electronic Social Systems*

Vol. 3 E. Francesconi, *Technologies for European Integration. Standards-based Interoperability of Legal Information Systems*

Vol. 2 G. Ajani, G. Peruginelli, G. Sartor, D. Tiscornia (Eds.) *The Multilanguage Complexity of European Law: Methodologies in Comparison*

Vol. 1 C. Biagioli, E. Francesconi, G. Sartor (Eds.), *Proceedings of the V Legislative XML Workshop*

European Press Academic Publishing – EPAP
http://www.e-p-a-p.com
http://www.europeanpress.eu
http://www.europeanpress.it
orders@e-p-a-p.com